Emergency Management: The American Experience 1900-2010

Second Edition

Emergency Management: The American Experience 1900-2010

Second Edition

Claire B. Rubin, Editor

CRC Press
Taylor & Francis Group
Boca Raton London New York

CRC Press is an imprint of the
Taylor & Francis Group, an **informa** business

CRC Press
Taylor & Francis Group
6000 Broken Sound Parkway NW, Suite 300
Boca Raton, FL 33487-2742

© 2012 by Taylor & Francis Group, LLC
CRC Press is an imprint of Taylor & Francis Group, an Informa business

International Standard Book Number: 978-1-4665-1753-0 (Paperback)

Library of Congress Cataloging-in-Publication Data

Emergency management : the American experience, 1900-2010 / editor, Claire B. Rubin. -- 2nd ed.
        p. cm.
    Includes bibliographical references and index.
    ISBN 978-1-4665-1753-0 (pbk. : alk. paper)
    1. Emergency management--United States. 2. Natural disasters--United States. 3. Hazard mitigation--United States. I. Rubin, Claire B.

    HV551.3.E46 2012
    363.340973'0904--dc23   2012007899

Visit the Taylor & Francis Web site at
http://www.taylorandfrancis.com

and the CRC Press Web site at
http://www.crcpress.com

Table of Contents

Preface

I am pleased to offer this new edition of *Emergency Management: The American Experience,* the history of emergency management at the national level in the United States. It follows in the tradition of the earlier edition, which documented how, since the beginning of the last century, the federal government has become increasingly involved in all phases of emergency management. This book continues to examine the major disaster events that we term "focusing events" and were, in essence, drivers of significant changes in the federal role and responsibilities in emergency management.

The first edition was initiated in 2004, when the Public Entity Risk Institute (PERI) provided me with grant support to edit a book that would discuss the emergence and growth of the emergency management profession in the United States. The result, which documents how the profession has gained the knowledge and experience needed to improve future understanding and enhance capabilities, was *Emergency Management: The American Experience, 1900–2005,* published in 2007. A special thanks is due to PERI for supporting this new edition, which began in early 2011. Even though they were in the midst of a major reorganization in August 2011, the PERI board members graciously agreed to continue support to get this book completed.

This edition, *Emergency Management: The American Experience, 1900–2010,* builds on the original theoretical framework and chronological approach, but improves on it by adding fresh information on older events as well as a new chapter on one major recent event. Most of the chapters dealing with events prior to 2005 have undergone minor revisions, while the chapter on Hurricane Katrina reflects a freshly revised perspective. The new chapter that was added documents the unusual characteristics of the disaster response to the BP oil spill in 2010. Finally, what was the last chapter in the previous edition has been divided into two chapters for this book: one chapter provides an overview of the events described and analyzed, and the second offers a discussion of the public administration concepts that constitute the larger context for this consideration of emergency management in the United States for more than a century.

As is true of most books, this one is the result of countless hours of effort by many people. I had thought that this edition would be much easier to prepare than the earlier one, but I learned otherwise during the preparation and review processes, which covered all of 2011.

I was once again able to recruit eight highly respected subject matter specialists to write chapters. These practitioners and scholars were chosen for their long experience in the field of emergency management and for the quality of their own research activities. Almost all of these authors had participated in the earlier edition, and I am grateful to them all for their diligent work during the current review and revision processes. One unexpected changed should be noted, however: in the earlier edition of this book, Prof. Robert Ward of Louisiana State University was the lead author of Chapter 9, the content of which is now contained in the revised Chapters 9 and 10. Tragically, Bob died of cancer in February 2011. His passing is a loss not only for those of us who knew and worked with him, but also for the community of scholars involved in the study of emergency management.

I extend my thanks as well to the nine members of the Advisory Committee, all of whom are also subject matter experts with a great deal of experience. These practitioners and researchers graciously reviewed the entire manuscript for accuracy and relevance, offering corrections and suggestions that were invaluable. Those who participated in this essential task were Lloyd Bokman, formerly of the Ohio Emergency Management Agency and owner of CEDAR Global— Community Emergency Disaster Awareness and Resilience; Lucien G. Canton, CEM, LLC, principal, Lucien G. Canton, CEM, LLC, and former director of emergency services for the city and county of San Francisco; Jude Colle, independent consultant, formerly with the Homeland Security Institute; William R. Cumming, ESQ, former staff attorney, Office of the General Counsel, Federal Emergency Management Agency, and president, Vacation Lane Group., Inc.; Larry Larson, executive director, Association of State Floodplain Managers; Francis McCarthy, analyst in emergency management policy, Congressional Research Service; Irmak Renda-Tanali, associate professor, Homeland Security Management and Emergency Management Studies Program, and director, Graduate School of Management and Technology, University of Maryland University College; Kathleen Tierney, director, Natural Hazards Center, University of Colorado at Boulder; and William L. Waugh Jr., professor, Andrew Young School of Policy Studies, Georgia State University.

I am truly grateful to Jane Cotnoir, the book editor, who worked diligently to ensure the highest standard of writing and fact checking for all the chapters. She brought years of experience in emergency management and other professional publications to the effort. Her patience and humor helped me get through the difficult review processes.

Thanks also to Gratzer Graphics LLC for the layout and graphics work. A final thanks to Jessica Hubbard, who kept the key players coordinated and the project on track, first when she worked at PERI and then when she worked for my company, Claire B. Rubin & Associates, when we assumed responsibility for this book and for the PERI bookstore operation in fall of 2011.

Claire B. Rubin, Editor
Arlington, Virginia
January 2012

Chapter 1

Introduction:
110 Years of Disaster Response and Emergency Management in the United States

Claire B. Rubin

"Experience is good—it allows you to recognize a mistake when you make it again." —Anonymous

In the four years that have gone by since the first edition of this book was published in 2007, we have seen a remarkable series of disasters—major to catastrophic in their impacts—not only in the United States but throughout the world. In the United States we experienced a record-setting man-made disaster, the BP oil spill (2010). Internationally, the floods in Pakistan (2010); the earthquakes in Haiti (2010), Chile (2010), and New Zealand (2010 and 2011); and, most recently, the earthquake and related disasters in Japan (2011) were quite extraordinary and, in many regards, overwhelming.

We now have some perspective on the first decade of the twenty-first century. In the past ten years, the United States experienced three major-to-catastrophic disasters,[1] providing milestone events for each of the three categories usually used to characterize disasters in this country:

- On September 11, 2001, three terrorist attacks constituted the greatest *intentional, man-made* disaster that has ever occurred on the U.S. mainland; these events are usually referred to in shorthand as 9/11.

- In September 2005, three *natural disasters*—Hurricanes Katrina, Rita, and Wilma—caused the greatest destruction seen to date in the United States in terms of area affected and impacts on people and property on the Gulf Coast; however, the Galveston Hurricane of 1900 still holds the record for the greatest number of deaths.

- In April 2010, the explosion of the BP *Deepwater Horizon* oil rig and resultant oil spill caused the largest *man-made, unintentional event* ever to occur in the United States, with the majority of damage affecting Louisiana and the Gulf Coast.

These events made it a historic decade for disasters. Collectively, they demonstrated some unusually destructive characteristics; attracted significant international attention; and laid bare many deficiencies in the plans, systems, and processes used for all phases of emergency management at all levels of government.

It is instructive to review how much has changed since 2005. The 2005 hurricanes did for natural disaster response what the terrorist attacks on 9/11 did for counterterrorism. Both glaringly displayed the weaknesses and failures of certain emergency management systems, processes, and leadership. The emergency response to Hurricane Katrina, which was so inadequate that government officials at all levels were humiliated at home and abroad, prompted the deepest and most sustained examination of U.S. emergency management functions and systems ever conducted. The passage of the Post-Katrina Emergency Management Reform Act in 2006 and the speed with which major changes were enacted at the national level reflect the urgency with which concerns were addressed.

Presenting an overview of more than a century of major disasters and governmental responses in the United States, this book covers select natural and human-induced events, including earthquakes, hurricanes, droughts, floods, a pandemic, and explosions. Some of these disasters, such as the 1906 San Francisco Earthquake, the 9/11 attacks, and Hurricane Katrina, have become part of our cultural history; others may be less well known. All offer lessons for those in the field of emergency management.

This overview is accompanied by an examination of the practice and philosophy of emergency management as it has evolved over the past century. Written by experts in the field, each chapter examines a specific period of time, focusing on the development of policies and organizations that deal with disasters at the national level. Through a discussion of the major disasters in the United States, the book poses answers to several pertinent questions, including

- Why did the federal government get involved in emergency management?

- Why and how has the federal government's role changed?

- What role should the federal government play in major disasters and catastrophes?[2]

This is not a traditional history book. None of the authors is a historian; in fact, all are longtime, experienced subject-matter experts and professional researchers—some academic and some privately employed. Since most of the disasters occurred before the authors were born, reliance on secondary sources was a given. Moreover, information on topics that are of interest today—such as details about the recovery process or considerations about community resilience—was not available or of concern to earlier researchers and so could not be presented here.

Additionally, this book has a specific focus: the response phase of emergency management. The authors have selected detailed descriptions and case studies of historic disaster events because such events contribute to the book's basic intention: to illuminate changes in public policies, administration, and organizations in response to major disasters and to identify the implications of those changes for emergency management today. Going beyond a summary of existing literature and case examples, the authors provide context, perspective, and meaning to the historic "focusing events" and the major programs, policies, and philosophies that resulted. In their analysis of key issues, problems, needs, and unrealized expectations, they discuss both successes and failures. The essential facts and issues are presented not only to help us better understand their impact but also to provide the basic platform for making changes in emergency management in the days, years, and decades to come.

The Evolution of Federal Emergency Management

For most of the past century, the federal government's role in emergency management has been expanding. With virtually every new presidential administration, the organizational forms and functions of emergency management have evolved. Changes have occurred not only within federal management systems and services, but also among state and local governments. In many instances, federal programs, policies, and grant requirements have driven changes in state and local emergency management organizations and efforts—with both positive and negative effects.

In recent years, Americans have come to regard emergency management as the quintessential public service, and they, as well as state and local government officials, expect the federal government to play a greater role in responding to a disaster than it ever has before. Unfortunately, many of the public's expectations are simply unrealistic. Consequently, government at all levels has fallen short of meeting the expectations not only of those affected by the catastrophic hurricanes in 2005 and the BP oil spill in 2010, but also of the many concerned citizens and public officials throughout the United States. (Moreover, as Rutherford H. Platt notes in *Disasters and Democracy,* the process of federalizing disasters has changed the public's perspective from compassion to entitlement.[3] One wonders at what point compassionate measures enacted by the federal government on behalf of citizens and localities harmed by disasters became an entitlement for state and local governments and victims.)

After 9/11, given the huge infusion of attention to and funding for emergency management in the context of homeland security, some practitioners and researchers lauded the progress that had been made in the field. However, many experts in the natural hazards and disaster response community did not share this optimism. They were seriously concerned about the extent to which the national focus on countering terrorism incidents was eroding the degree of attention, level of expertise, and retention of scientific and operations knowledge about natural hazards and disasters. The events of 2005 and in 2010 revealed that those with reservations about emergency management capabilities and capacity in the United States had good reasons for concern. For example, the 9/11 event called into question the adequacy of the National Response Plan, and the BP oil spill drove a reexamination of the National Contingency Plan.

The major disaster events of the past ten years have cast doubt on the adequacy of the current emergency management system and given greater urgency and prominence to the ongoing debate about fundamental emergency management principles and practices. Among the issues raised are those dealing with the responsibilities of each level of government for appropriate functions of emergency management and the notable lack of smooth and effective interrelationships among all levels of government and all sectors of society after a disaster strikes. Other issues and concerns relate to the organizational and logistical problems inherent in responding to a catastrophic disaster, as well as to the quantity and quality of personnel and resources needed to address such an event.

Disasters as Focusing Events

Over the decades, disaster researchers have identified some major disasters as pivotal events in the evolution of U.S. emergency management. Like many of the disasters that had preceded them, several of those in the years 2000–2010 revealed gaps in the emergency management system and focused attention on the need for improvement. In this book, the authors have identified some of these focusing events.

The hypothesis of this book is that changes in emergency management policies, processes, and authority are event driven. Therefore, major focusing events provide an opportunity to explore their effects on emergency management principles and practices. Focusing events have some, but not necessarily all, of the following characteristics:[4]

- **Magnitude.** Focusing events often affect a large geographic area or a large number of people. Natural disasters, such as catastrophic earthquakes, hurricanes, and tsunamis, tend to affect a broader area than do human-made disasters or terrorist events, but a successful terrorist attack may affect a greater number of people. Hurricane Katrina became a focusing event in terms of the extent of the damages, the number of homes destroyed or damaged, and the number of vulnerable people who were displaced or lost their lives.

- **High visibility.** An obvious example of high visibility is the 9/11 targeting of the World Trade Center in the heart of New York City's financial district and of the Pentagon, headquarters of the U.S. Department of Defense and a symbol of U.S. power, in Arlington, Virginia, just across the Potomac River from Washington, D.C.

- **Unusual location.** Some locations are less prepared than others for high-impact events, resulting in a greater likelihood of poorly managed, ad hoc response and recovery. Tropical Storm Agnes in 1972, for example, was a focusing event in large part because of the flooding that resulted in Pennsylvania, a landlocked state.

- **High impact.** If the duration and impact of the event are widespread and damaging to physical, economic, environmental, social, and political structures, the disaster is more likely to become a focusing event. Hurricane Katrina is an example of a high-impact event, particularly for the city of New Orleans.

- **A unique threat agent.** The use of an unusual threat agent—for example, commercial aircraft or common materials—to inflict devastation increases the likelihood that an incident will become a focusing event. Similarly, the low-probability but high-impact BP oil spill, which stemmed from a commercial deepwater drilling operation that exploded, gave way to a major oil leak in which thousands of barrels of oil contaminated the Gulf Coast and its wildlife, businesses, and residents.

- **Surprise.** Surprise was a major factor in the 9/11 attacks in which terrorists used commercial airliners as weapons of mass destruction; in the context of emergency management, *surprise* is often defined as unprecedented.[5]

- **Eligibility for disaster declaration.** A disaster declaration, which relies on the federal government's threshold for determining which events warrant federal assistance, is used as a measure of the magnitude and impact of a disaster event.

It is important to note that there is great disparity among authorities regarding the "worst" disasters in history—in part because of the lack of quantitative criteria for what makes one disaster worse than another (in terms of, for example, lives lost, damage inflicted, area affected) as well as because of discrepancies in the reports regarding the number of lives lost or the severity of damage. The disasters discussed in this book are cited primarily because of their significance,

In 2005, Hurricane Katrina devastated much of the Gulf Coast, drawing attention to gaps in the emergency management system. Shown here is destruction to New Orleans's Lower Ninth Ward. Photo courtesy of the Federal Emergency Management Agency/Andrea Booher.

their impact on the national emergency management system, and their lasting impression on the nation.

Although disaster researchers continue to lead the way in analyzing significant historical events, a few nonfiction writers have ably brought major disasters to life. *Isaac's Storm: A Man, a Time, and the Deadliest Hurricane in History*, Erik Larson's account of the 1900 Galveston Hurricane, and John Barry's *Rising Tide: The Great Mississippi Flood of 1927 and How It Changed America* are but two examples of popular books that not only capture the attention of a general readership but also offer important insights into disaster response and recovery.[6] In addition, the body of scholarship developed by disaster researchers, often academics, during the past several decades offers keen insight into the impact of disasters and depicts the reactive nature of emergency management.[7] Another contribution to the knowledge base about disasters is the Time Line Charts of key disaster events,[8] which offer a conceptual model for selective focusing events and identify subsequent developments and changes that have typically followed them.[9]

The Impact of Disasters on Emergency Management

As can be seen from time line charts covering the past several decades of disaster history in the United States, certain focusing events have driven changes in laws, regulations, plans, systems, and practice.[10] In fact, virtually all major federal laws, executive directives, programs, policies, organizational changes, and response systems have resulted from major and catastrophic disasters. Some of these changes, such as the reorganization and creation of new federal agencies that occurred following 9/11, have been instituted immediately, but many others have taken decades to implement.

A surprising number of misperceptions persist about the advent of emergency management. For example, many people believe that emergency management did not develop until the 1950s, arising in conjunction with civil defense programs. But in fact, emergency management as a profession has evolved gradually over the past century or more. For many decades, emergency management functions were performed primarily at the local level. The main national organization involved in providing humanitarian assistance to disaster victims prior to 1950 was the American Red Cross. It is true that some federal government and military agencies have been involved with disaster responses for more than a century; for example, the National Weather Service responded to the 1900 hurricane in Galveston, Texas, and the U.S. Army Corps of Engineers was active in the response efforts during the Great Mississippi Flood of 1927. However, federal government involvement by and large continued to be ad hoc and reactive until the latter half of the twentieth century.[11]

The descriptive accounts of some of the major disasters that occurred in the early 1900s reveal several chronic issues that plagued response efforts, including

- Centralized versus decentralized decision making by the federal government and/or military agencies

- The equitable distribution of relief to victims

- Confusion about the role of the American Red Cross vis-à-vis federal agencies

- Ad hoc disaster response and assistance plans

- Domination of powerful local business interests and civic leaders over local elected officials with respect to local mitigation and recovery efforts

- Variations in the capacity, capability, and public will of state governments regarding assisting communities affected by a disaster and serving as intermediaries between the federal and local governments.

Lamentably, many of these obstacles to disaster preparation, mitigation, response, and recovery still exist in the field of emergency management today.

Since the 1950s, organizational and intergovernmental arrangements related to emergency preparation and response have been shaped in large measure by federal requirements and funding. As more funding for researchers has become available, research and practice have contributed to the body of knowledge, creation of theory, and professionalism in emergency management. The National Science

Foundation deserves credit for being an important source of funding support for research and for fostering young researchers in the hazards and disasters fields.

In addition, a series of major disasters in the 1960s and 1970s led to the involvement of the executive branch on an ongoing basis and to the creation of the Federal Emergency Management Agency (FEMA). Many people make the mistake of equating federal emergency management with FEMA, but FEMA had many predecessors before it took the lead responsibility for emergency management in April 1979, and it will likely have numerous successors. Moreover, FEMA is just one agency involved in emergency management; several other federal departments and agencies (including the U.S. Army Corps of Engineers, the U.S. Department of Housing and Urban Development, the Department of Agriculture, the Federal Highway Administration, the U.S. Environmental Protection Agency, and the National Oceanic and Atmospheric Administration, which includes the National Weather Service) have also played critical roles in emergency management preparedness, mitigation, response, and recovery activities.[12]

About This Book

For this new edition, all the existing chapters have been revised to include additional information about past events and to provide some refinements and insights gained during the past four years. Virtually all the authors who participated in the first edition have contributed to this second edition.* We have also added one new chapter to deal with the BP oil spill.

The discussion in this book begins in 1900—a convenient, although perhaps somewhat arbitrary, starting point. Of course, many communities in the United States experienced major emergencies and natural disasters prior to 1900, and several organizations were in place to offer assistance. The American Red Cross, the U.S. Army, the National Weather Service, and the two component services of what is now the U.S. Coast Guard were all formed well before 1900. But disaster response and relief were not coordinated by any one government agency. In fact, well into the twentieth century, most of the response efforts made by federal government or military agencies were not part of a national policy, program, or system of emergency management.

In the next two chapters, David Butler explores disasters as focusing events from 1900 to 1950, when the first major federal legislation addressing disaster response was passed. Chapter 2 focuses on several catastrophic events that occurred early in this period: the Galveston Hurricane of 1900, the 1906 San Francisco and 1933 Long Beach earthquakes, and the 1918–1919 flu pandemic. Using these well-known, dramatic disasters, Butler begins to document historic

---

* Sadly, Prof. Robert Ward, who was co-author of the final chapter in the first edition, passed away in early 2011. We sincerely miss his insights and help with the book.

focusing events and the federal government's episodic responses to them, outlining the foundation of the government's eventual involvement in emergency management on a sustained basis.

Chapter 3 continues this documentation with a discussion of the Great Mississippi Flood of 1927, the Dust Bowl drought of the 1930s, and explosions that occurred in Texas City after World War II. Together, these two chapters provide insight into how emergency management progressed from a largely unorganized effort reliant on local citizens and voluntary organizations to an organized movement that resulted in the Federal Disaster Relief Act of 1950. Butler also shows how the events of the first half of the century laid the organizational groundwork for a new federal emergency management system.

In Chapter 4, Keith Bea tackles the period from 1950 to 1978, ending with the recommendations that resulted in the creation of FEMA. As Bea demonstrates, emergency management continued to evolve during this period, supported by legislation giving federal agencies authority over disaster response and relief. The federal government's role expanded because of new threats to the nation—not only natural disasters but also the perceived threat of nuclear attack from the Soviet Union. Emergency management at all levels of government began expanding its focus to include civil defense readiness for enemy attacks, environmental and human-induced disasters, and public health emergencies. By the end of the 1970s, federal policy makers and administrators had assumed a dominant role in emergency management.

In Chapter 5, Richard Sylves focuses on the development of the emergency management field from the advent of FEMA in 1979 to 2001, when the terrorist attacks on 9/11 changed the nature and scope of emergency management. As Chapter 5 illustrates, this period was characterized by a growing involvement of the federal government, as seen in the number of presidential disaster declarations issued, and by a complex emergency management response system that was based on intergovernmental and interorganizational cooperation and coordination.

Chapter 6 discusses the changes in federal emergency management after the terrorist attacks of 9/11, noting both the intended and unintended consequences of actions taken during the response and recovery periods. John Harrald describes the many changes in policy, authority, and organization that occurred, particularly at the federal level. He also discusses the new emergency management system that evolved, with particular attention to two new components: the National Response Plan and the National Incident Management System.

As already noted, 2005 was a monumental year for emergency management. Thus, Chapter 7 covers just this one year as Melanie Gall and Susan Cutter discuss the three catastrophic hurricanes in the fall of 2005. From an emergency management perspective, these hurricanes and the initial response to them provided a startling indication of the problems and deficiencies of the national, state, and local systems, systems that many people assumed had been enhanced in the four years since 9/11. Considering the many developments that have occurred in the last few years, the authors have substantially revised this chapter and also offer their perspectives on changes that have and have not taken place during that time.

Chapter 8 is a new one, added to discuss and analyze the BP oil spill about one year after it happened. The response and recovery efforts were different from those usually undertaken for declared national disasters and managed by FEMA under the Stafford Act. Some of those differences were

- The decision to handle the federal response by means of the National Contingency Plan rather than the Stafford Act's presidential declaration powers and the involvement of FEMA as the lead agency

- The designation of the BP corporation as the "responsible party," thereby giving it a major role in management and requiring it to assume most of the costs (direct and indirect)

- A focus on the long-term environmental and ecological damages, the full extent and costs of which will probably not be determined for several years or decades to come.

In Chapter 9 Patrick Roberts, Robert Ward, and Gary Wamsley provide a summary of and commentary on the previous chapters and offer a perspective on what the history of disasters means for the future of emergency management. And in the final chapter, they discuss the field of emergency management in the larger context of public administration, highlighting key teaching points for the reader and extracting essential lessons to offer insights into emergency management practices.

Until we know what systems and methods have been developed and what learning has occurred, we cannot successfully create the body of knowledge and professional practices needed for the events and demands of the twenty-first century. This book is designed to provide emergency management professionals with information about the foundation of our emergency management approaches. Better understanding of the basis on which common assumptions are made, as well as of the problems and mistakes that have been made over the past century, can provide these professionals with the tools they need to improve the system and its many parts.

The Limitations of Writing about Recent History

Finally, a few words about the inherent imitations of writing about recent history: We have bravely proceeded to try to explain major events of the past five to ten years, knowing that in actuality it takes many years—perhaps even a decade or two—to gain a broad perspective on past major disasters and their far-reaching consequences. We have done our best in this short time frame.

Three of the chapters (6, 7, and 8) are focused on relatively recent events (e.g., Hurricane Katrina and the BP oil spill), the complete dimensions and ramifications of which are not yet known. As a result, those chapters cannot be as fully developed as the earlier ones, but as new information becomes available in the coming years, future writers will be able to address these incidents from a broader perspective.

For recent disaster events, the usual sequence of information resources is news media accounts, agency and organizational reports, magazine and journal articles, and finally—perhaps a year or two later—books. As has been noted, the authors have relied heavily on secondary sources, augmented where possible by personal contacts and experience. No efforts were made to obtain new primary information—for example, from interviews, questionnaires, or other inquiries. Moreover, each author has not only a disciplinary specialty but also a specific geographic base, which may have affected his or her selection of resources. For example, those in the Washington, D.C., metropolitan area may have the advantage of greater access to national news sources and to persons in decision-making positions or in key support functions, but this may also result in the disadvantage of a Washington-based perspective.

In closing, I want to go back to the initial discussion about the already historic events that occurred in just the first ten years of this century and the suggestion that they be viewed as a challenge to those charged with responsibility for emergency management in the decades ahead. These events underscore the need to think and plan more expansively about emergency management. In short, to effectively function in the twenty-first century, public officials and others responsible for emergency management will have to think in bolder, broader, and more comprehensive concepts and terms than they have in the past. Critical thinking and decision-making skills need to be enhanced, and more attention must be given to strategic thinking and foresight. The goals must be to anticipate rather than react to future disasters, and to develop the leadership skills, talents, and training for future emergency managers.

Endnotes

1 Without getting into an involved discussion of the definition of a catastrophic event, suffice it to say that all three of these events were quite unusual, with many surprising aspects, and very costly—each estimated to have caused at least $20 billion in damage.

2 Emergency management professionals and disaster scholars define *catastrophe* as a very large event that surpasses local and regional capabilities for response or recovery, and *disaster* as a less severe event, although it, too, might require outside (i.e., federal government) assistance; see E. L. Quarantelli, "Emergencies, Disaster and Catastrophes Are Different Phenomena," Preliminary Paper 304 (Newark: Disaster Research Center, University of Delaware, 2000), at udel.edu/DRC/Preliminary_Papers/pp304.pdf.

3   Rutherford H. Platt, *Disasters and Democracy: The Politics of Extreme Natural Events* (Washington, D.C.: Island Press, 1999).

4   Claire B. Rubin and Judith Colle, *Major Terrorism Events and Their U.S. Outcomes (1988–2005)* (Fairfax, Va.: Public Entity Risk Institute, 2006).

5   In his analysis of industrial disasters, James K. Mitchell defines *surprise* as "unprecedented" and writes, "Nothing quite like [the surprise has] ever occurred before in the same or similar contexts"; see James K. Mitchell, *Long Road to Recovery: Community Responses to Industrial Disaster* (New York: United Nations Press, 1996), 11.

6   Erik Larson, *Isaac's Storm: A Man, a Time, and the Deadliest Hurricane in History* (New York: Random House/Vintage Books, 1999); John M. Barry, *Rising Tide: The Great Mississippi Flood of 1927 and How It Changed America* (New York: Simon and Schuster, 1997).

7   Examples include Platt, *Disasters and Democracy;* William Waugh, *Living with Hazards, Dealing with Disasters* (New York: M. E. Sharpe, 2000); and Richard T. Sylves and William L. Waugh Jr., *Disaster Management in the U.S. and Canada: The Politics, Policymaking, Administration and Analysis of Emergency Management* (Springfield, Ill.: Charles C. Thomas, 1996).

8   See the time lines developed by Claire B. Rubin & Associates at disaster-timeline.com.

9   In his 1997 book *After Disaster: Agenda Setting, Public Policy, and Focusing Events* (Washington, D.C.: Georgetown University Press), Thomas Birkland was among the first people to use the term *focusing events* to refer to disasters that had an impact on emergency management policy or practice; the term has been further developed in the timeline charts and related reports developed by Claire B. Rubin & Associates.

10   Claire B. Rubin, Irmak Renda-Tanali, and William Cumming, *Disaster Time Line: Major Focusing Events and U.S. Outcomes (1979–2005)* (Arlington, Va.: Claire B. Rubin & Associates, 2006), at disaster-timeline.com; Claire B. Rubin, Irmak Renda-Tanali, and William Cumming, *Terrorism Time Line: Major Focusing Events and U.S. Outcomes (2001–2005)* (Arlington, Va.: Claire B. Rubin & Associates, 2006), at disaster-timeline.com; and Rubin and Colle, *Major Terrorism Events and Their U.S. Outcomes.* See also Birkland, *After Disaster.*

11   See Michele Landis Dauber, *The War of 1812, September 11th, and the Politics of Compensation,* Public Law Working Paper No. 74 (Palo Alto, Calif.: Stanford Law School, 2003), papers.ssrn.com/sol3/papers.cfm?abstract_id=480703; and David A. Moss, "Courting Disaster? The Transformation of Federal Disaster Policy since 1803," in *The Financing of Catastrophe Risk,* ed. Kenneth A. Froot (Chicago: University of Chicago Press, 1999).

12   There also are federal response plans, such as the National Contingency Plan, for dealing with oil spills, industrial accidents, and hazardous materials incidents; these are beyond the scope of this book.

Chapter 2

Focusing Events in the Early Twentieth Century: A Hurricane, Two Earthquakes, and a Pandemic

David Butler

Prior to World War II, there was no overarching legislation or policy at any level of government driving emergency and disaster management in the United States. Rather, policy, legislation, and practice typically were created in response to individual disasters. The federal government's involvement was almost always disaster specific, usually delayed, and varied in the services provided. Sociologist Gary Kreps writes that prior to 1950 "there was no permanent federal program of disaster assistance to states and localities in the United States. Private voluntary agencies, such as the American National Red Cross, the Salvation Army, and many others, bore the primary responsibility for disaster relief; and state and local governments coped as best they could with disaster impacts."[1]

Federal disaster relief was also inconsistent. Political scientist Peter May writes, "The guiding criterion for deciding an appropriate [federal] relief level was the precedent established by previous disaster relief provisions."[2] Indeed, "between 1803 [when Congress first provided any kind of disaster relief] and 1947, Congress enacted 128 pieces of special disaster-specific legislation.... When army (or beginning in the 1880s, Red Cross) representatives arrived on the scene of a disaster, they generally found ad hoc local or regional relief committees collecting funds and relief supplies, and performing recovery efforts."[3] May provides an analysis of the 128 pieces of legislation prior to 1947 and notes that their aims and approaches changed over time, with disaster assistance becoming increasingly generous.[4]

Despite the frequency of event-specific federal legislation, the government did not view disaster response and relief as a federal responsibility. "More often than not, the federal government provided no assistance at all in the aftermath of disaster," concludes David Moss in his analysis of the federal government's disaster policy.[5] Like other domestic social needs, disaster assistance was considered the responsibility of the states or, more often, local governments, charities, and other social institutions such as churches. Geographer and legal scholar Rutherford Platt also notes that the "reduction of vulnerability to natural hazards ('mitigation') was accomplished, if at all, through actions taken individually or at the local level prior to the 1930s."[6]

Platt further comments that government was not involved in providing direct assistance to disaster victims. "Before 1950, disaster assistance was viewed as the moral responsibility of neighbors, churches, charities, and communities—not the federal government," writes Platt. "Furthermore, disasters tended to be viewed as unavoidable 'acts of God,' which, by definition, transcend the power of government to prevent."[7] Federal legislation was enacted and programs created for mitigation of only one type of hazard: floods (especially on the Mississippi River). As early as the mid-eighteenth century, the federal government, through the U.S. Army Corps of Engineers, was involved in flood control and the maintenance of navigable waterways.

Given the lack of any overriding federal mandates in the first half of the twentieth century, studying the evolution of emergency management during this period requires examining landmark incidents rather than surveying federal legislation or policy. Specifically, such an examination should look at (1) the precipitating physical event, prior planning and preparedness (if any), response, and recovery; (2) the long-term effects on society, policy, and practice; and (3) the resulting changes in American consciousness and attitudes toward disasters and their management. This includes examining the questions and lessons each disaster poses for modern emergency management.

While there were numerous disasters in the early twentieth century, only a few stand out as historic events affecting the course of American emergency management—or, as discussed in Chapter 1, as *focusing events*. The ones examined in this chapter are the 1900 Galveston Hurricane, the 1906 San Francisco and 1933 Long Beach earthquakes, and the 1918–1919 flu pandemic. The Great Mississippi Flood of 1927, the dust storms of the 1930s, and the 1947 Texas City explosions are discussed in Chapter 3. Careful study of these events reveals issues, successes, mistakes, and lessons to be learned, which are elucidated for the benefit of current and future emergency managers, as well as for researchers and consultants who share their concerns. Collectively, the studies of these disasters could make up their own textbook in emergency management.

Nineteenth-Century Disaster Response

Of course, the United States experienced many natural disasters prior to 1900.[8] Perhaps most common were floods along the major waterways that formed the backbone of the nation's transportation network. As the country became increasingly urban and the populace more concentrated, floods and other natural occurrences became more destructive to both people and the built environment. The two best-known disasters of the late nineteenth century were urban catastrophes: the Chicago Fire of 1871, in which approximately 300 people died and 90,000 were rendered homeless, and the Johnstown (Pennsylvania) Flood of 1889, which resulted in more than 2,000 deaths.[9] Another notable event, the Great Peshtigo Fire of October 1871, raged across northeastern Wisconsin and upper Michigan at the same time as the Chicago fire. Both fires resulted in part from the same meteorological conditions—heat and dryness—that pervaded the upper Midwest at the time, but the Peshtigo fire took an estimated 1,500 lives—five times as many as the more famous Chicago conflagration. Additional notable disasters of the late nineteenth century include the forest fires that raged through Michigan in 1881;[10] the flooding of the Ohio and Mississippi Rivers in 1884; the hurricane that hit the Sea Islands, South Carolina, in 1893; and the Great Blizzard of 1888, which left between two and five feet of snow across much of northern New Jersey, eastern New York, and western New England and resulted in roughly 400 deaths.[11]

The sheer magnitude of events, such as the 1889 flood of Johnstown, Pennsylvania, shown here, raised awareness of the potential devastation to communities and influenced some government officials to begin to reconsider the ad hoc approach to disaster response. Photo courtesy of E. Benjamin Andrews, *History of the United States*, volume V. New York: Charles Scribner's Sons, 1912.

All these disasters are historically important for at least three reasons. First, these natural disasters marked the first American Red Cross response, resulting in a formal charter by the federal government to provide disaster response and recovery.[12]

The American Red Cross

Founded by Clara Barton in 1881, the American Red Cross (ARC) was chartered by Congress in 1900 and again in 1905 to carry out responsibilities delegated by the federal government. Among other things the original charter called for the ARC to manage a system of national and international relief in time of peace; to apply the same system in mitigating the sufferings caused by pestilence, famine, fire, floods, and other great national calamities; and to devise means for preventing disasters and "to promote measures of humanity and welfare of mankind." At the time, these mandates for domestic aid and disaster prevention were unique to the ARC. Red Cross organizations in other nations were typically concerned only with aid to victims of combat.

The ARC's early work included aiding victims and workers in the floods of the Mississippi and Ohio Rivers in 1882 and 1884, the Texas famine of 1886, the Florida yellow fever epidemic in 1887, an earthquake in Illinois in 1888, and the 1889 Johnstown Flood.

The relationship between the government and the American Red Cross is unique. The ARC is an independent, nonprofit, tax-exempt, charitable institution, but unlike other congressionally chartered organizations, it has the legal status of "a federal instrumentality"; that is, it is bound by its charter to carry out responsibilities delegated to it by the federal government. These responsibilities currently include

- Fulfilling the provisions of the Geneva Conventions, to which the United States is a signatory, assigned to national societies for the protection of victims of conflict

- Providing family communications and other forms of support to the U.S. military

- Maintaining a system of domestic and international disaster relief, including mandated responsibilities under the National Response Plan coordinated by the Federal Emergency Management Agency.

On the national level, in the first half of the twentieth century the Red Cross—not the federal government—had the lead responsibility for emergency relief operations. The formal relationship between that organization and the federal government may have given Americans the impression that the federal government had responsibility for managing all phases of disaster, from pre-disaster mitigation to post-disaster recovery, but the ARC is not a federal agency, nor does it receive regular federal appropriations. It relies on public contributions and cost-recovery charges for most of its services, but it seeks federal funding when extreme costs surpass charitable contributions. According to former Red Cross official Roy Popkin, in recent years, "as government programs have expanded, the Red Cross role in individual family assistance has diminished, particularly in larger disasters receiving a presidential declaration and federal funds."[1] Today, the ARC remains the only nonprofit organization identified in federal disaster legislation.

Source: American Red Cross website at redcross.org/museum/history/timeline.asp.

1 Roy S. Popkin, "The History and Politics of Disaster Management in the United States," in *Nothing to Fear: Risks and Hazards in American Society*, ed. Andrew Kirby (Tucson: University of Arizona Press, 1990), 105.

A second reason that these major catastrophes are significant is, quite simply, because they have become a prominent part of American history and cultural lore. As such, they inform modern American thought and attitudes regarding disasters. For example, modern fire suppression systems and urban design reflect lessons learned and fears reinforced by the Chicago Fire of 1871; current dam safety laws can be traced in part to the Johnstown Flood of 1889.

A third reason that these disasters have been singled out is that, when examined closely, each demonstrates, implicitly or explicitly, areas in which disaster management could be improved—in preparedness, warning, response, recovery, and/or long-term mitigation. Moreover, each demonstrates the many dimensions that combine to create a disaster: local geography, human settlement and activity patterns, political and cultural characteristics, and planning and response systems. Thus, these early disasters can help us to identify the corresponding areas of understanding that might enable us to better deal with disasters: physical science (e.g., hydrology, meteorology, and geology), engineering, organizational management, public administration, social structure and human behavior, and psychology.

The great catastrophes of the early twentieth century have shaped our cultural and governmental attitudes toward disaster even further. Beginning with the Galveston Hurricane of 1900, these events have demonstrated many ways and means of dealing with disasters—including experimentation, innovation, and improvisation—and draw attention to specific problems and areas on which government and society could focus resources and efforts to lessen their toll.

The Galveston Hurricane of 1900

The 1900 Galveston Hurricane, which made landfall on September 8, remains the deadliest disaster in U.S. history. The exact number of deaths was never determined, in part because bodies were buried on land and at sea or cremated en masse immediately following the storm. But at least 6,000 people and perhaps as many as 12,000—one of every six Galveston citizens—lost their lives in the disaster.[13]

The U.S. Weather Bureau in Washington, D.C., began sending to its Galveston office warnings of an approaching storm as early as September 4. Although the precise evolution of the storm is unknown, apparently the less severe tropical storm that swept over Cuba on September 4 and 5 exploded into a major hurricane as it passed over the warm water of the Gulf of Mexico. The storm moved north of Key West on September 6 and then, rather than turning to the northeast as the U.S. Weather Bureau had predicted, it continued on its westward path, gaining strength as it went. By the evening of September 7, large, slow swells were creating huge surf along the beaches in and near Galveston. The next morning, people gathered to watch the sea. The early morning skies remained only partly cloudy and winds were not yet strong, so few people took heed of the storm warnings issued by the local weather bureau.

Floodwaters began to creep into Galveston early in the day on September 8, and by midmorning the train tracks into town were flooded. The rain began in earnest in the early afternoon, and a steady northeasterly wind was blowing. By 5:00 p.m., the Galveston weather bureau was recording sustained hurricane force winds. But it was water, not wind, that presented the greatest problem. The low-lying island of Galveston was inundated by a storm surge of over 15 feet. At one point, the sea rose 4 feet in just four seconds. The encroaching waters acted like a riverine or flash flood, compiling and pushing debris inland, each row of structures adding more mass to the mountain of wreckage as buildings were pushed off their foundations. By the end of the surge, more than 3,600 homes were destroyed. Although the actual magnitude of the storm is not known, the damage and a storm surge of 15.5 feet has led the National Oceanic and Atmospheric Administration to estimate that it was a Category 4 hurricane (defined as a storm with winds of 131 to 155 mph and a storm surge of 13 to 18 feet).

The vulnerable location of Galveston, the denial of the hurricane hazard, and an inadequate warning and evacuation system all contributed to the devastation caused by the hurricane and storm surge that struck the city in 1900. Photo courtesy of the National Oceanic and Atmospheric Administration.

Prior History, Preparedness, Response, Reconstruction, and Mitigation

Prior to the hurricane, Galveston was a thriving city of more than 40,000, one of the wealthiest cities in the country and the most important seaport in Texas. More than 70 percent of the U.S. cotton crop passed through Galveston, and some 1,000 ships called on the port annually.[14]

The 1900 storm should not have been unexpected; "hurricanes had periodically raked the Gulf of Mexico coast—at least eleven times in the nineteenth century. Yet the inhabitants [of Galveston] denied the threat to their island community."[15] Indeed, since its founding in 1839, Galveston had weathered numerous storms and dodged many others, but in no case had it faced a direct hit. The result was widespread complacency among the city's leaders and residents.

Erik Larson points out that in 1875 and 1886, through wind and storm surge, hurricanes destroyed the thriving port of Indianola on Matagorda Bay, approximately 120 miles southwest of Galveston.[16] The first hurricane killed 176 people; the second compelled survivors to abandon the town.

The Indianola situation should have forewarned Galveston's leaders. Whereas Indianola was in the corner of a protective bay and shielded by barrier islands, Galveston—an unprotected island with its highest point only 8.7 feet above sea level—was clearly more vulnerable. Indeed, Galveston's leading citizens perceived Indianola as an object lesson and launched an effort to construct a seawall to protect the island, but the campaign languished. Soon, development increased Galveston's vulnerability to storms as sand dunes along the shore were removed to fill low-lying areas in the city, removing what little barrier there was between the Gulf of Mexico and downtown Galveston. By 1900 Galveston was completely unprepared for a hurricane—both psychologically and physically.

By all accounts, the immediate aftermath of the hurricane was horrific. During the storm and immediately after, victims had only each other to rely on for medical care, shelter, food and clothing, search and rescue, and locating and burying the dead. There were many, many bodies amid the debris.[17]

Help soon arrived. The U.S. Army sent soldiers, tents, and food. Larson writes, "The train-ferry *Charlotte Allen* brought a thousand loaves of bread from Houston. The steamer *Lawrence* brought one hundred thousand gallons of fresh water." When Clara Barton, the president of the American Red Cross, arrived on the scene, she telegraphed home, "Situation not exaggerated."[18] The recovery operations, particularly the recovery and disposal of bodies, continued for weeks.

As with disasters even today, the outpouring of donations sometimes proved as much a burden as a blessing. "The Red Cross gave out food and clothing, but found much of its supply of donated clothing unusable, either too warm for the climate or too shabby, clearly the discards of distant souls who believed survivors

A Note from Galveston

John D. Blagden was a U.S. Weather Bureau meteorologist on temporary assignment in Galveston when the hurricane hit. This excerpt from a letter to his family in Duluth, Minnesota, was written one day after the storm.

"There is not a building in town that is uninjured. Hundreds are busy day and night clearing away the debris and recovering the dead. It is awful. Every few minutes a wagon load of corpses passes by on the street.

"The more fortunate are doing all they can to aid the sufferers but it is impossible to care for all. There is not room in the buildings standing to shelter them all and hundreds pass the night on the street…. The City is under military rule and the streets are patrolled by armed guards…. I understand four men have been shot today for robbing the dead. I do not know how true it is for all kind of rumors are afloat and many of them are false. We have neither light, fuel or water. I have gone back to candles. I am now writing by candlelight.

"A famine is feared, as nearly all the provisions were ruined by the water which stood from six to fifteen feet in the streets and all communication to the outside is cut off…. We had warning of the storm and many saved themselves by seeking safety before the storm reached here. We were busy all day Thursday answering telephone calls about it and advising people to prepare for danger. But the storm was more severe than we expected."

Source: Casey Edward Greene and Shelly Henley Kelly, *Through a Night of Horrors: Voices from the 1900 Galveston Storm* (College Station: Texas A&M University Press, 2000), 15–19.

were in no position to be picky," writes Larson. "Someone donated a case of fancy women's shoes, but all 144 shoes were for the left foot, samples once carried by a shoe-company traveler."[19]

Unlike Indianola's leaders, Galveston officials decided to rebuild after the hurricane. Just a decade earlier, the city had rejected the construction of a seawall, but it now adopted the idea. Considered a modern engineering marvel, the wall took almost sixty years to complete. It rises 15.5 feet above sea level and is constructed with an advance barrier of granite boulders 27 feet wide. Beyond constructing a barrier, Galveston's engineers physically elevated the city, using dredged sand to raise the city by as much as 17 feet. More than 2,100 buildings were raised in the process.[20]

There are limits to what can be achieved with such structural mitigation measures, however. In 1915, another hurricane struck Galveston. Its wind and 12-foot storm surge resulted in the deaths of 275 people. Although the death toll was significantly lower than it was in 1900, in dollar terms, the 1915 hurricane resulted in almost as much damage as the 1900 storm.[21]

Following the 1900 hurricane, Galveston officials approved the construction of a seawall to protect the city—an idea that had been rejected ten years earlier. Today the Galveston coast is protected by a 7-mile-long, 15.5-foot-high seawall. Photo courtesy of the Federal Emergency Management Agency/Bob McMillan.

Hubris, Denial, and Complacency

One way to study emergency management is to look at disaster events and learn what went right and what went wrong. Each of the disasters discussed here holds many lessons for modern emergency management. Galveston, as much as any of the other tragedies, demonstrates what is, perhaps, the most fundamental lesson of emergency management: the danger of hubris, denial, and complacency.

As already discussed, there was much evidence indicating that Galveston could be struck by a severe hurricane. For various reasons—psychological, social, and economic—the people of Galveston, and particularly those responsible for the city's welfare and safety, ignored the warning signs. Erik Larson is particularly critical of the U.S. Weather Bureau: he cites the agency's territorial jealousies, the centralized command and control in the Washington headquarters office, the inability of the agency to recognize its own shortcomings and gaps in knowledge, and a reluctance to issue warnings and share information. His book about the hurricane, *Isaac's Storm,* recounts the response of Isaac Cline, head of Galveston's weather bureau at the time, who personified many of his agency's faults. According to Larson, Cline was a scientist who "believed he understood weather in ways others did not." He adds, "Hubris infused the text just as it infused the age," and cites an 1891 *Galveston News* article in which Cline argued, "[H]urricanes could not as a rule strike Texas [and] no greater damage may be expected here from meteorological disturbances than in any other portions of the country."[22]

According to Larson's account, Cline rejected the need for a protective seawall and dismissed the storms that had struck Indianola earlier. Cline "belittled hurricane fears as the artifacts of 'an absurd delusion.' He was especially confident about storm surges. 'It would be impossible,' [Cline] wrote, 'for any cyclone to create a storm wave which could materially injure the city.'"[23]

Other accounts are less critical of Cline.[24] They, and Cline's own report, say that he issued a hurricane warning without authorization from Washington. He is also credited with personally going to the Galveston beach on the morning of September 8 to warn the people gathered there to leave the beach and evacuate the city.

Cline was not alone in minimizing the threat of a hurricane. Although there was a civic movement in Galveston to construct a protective seawall after the 1886 Indianola hurricane, the idea eventually died out as complacency quickly returned. Even following the 1900 hurricane, the editor of the *Galveston Tribune* called the belief that Galveston is subject to severe storms a "mistake."[25] Willis Moore, head of the U.S. Weather Bureau, believed the Galveston hurricane to be a "freak of nature": "'Galveston should take heart,' he wrote, 'as the chances are that not once in a thousand years would she be so terribly stricken.'"[26] Nature proved him wrong. The city was hit by another powerful hurricane just fifteen years later.

It is easy in hindsight to see that Galveston was in danger in 1900, but even today Galveston remains one of the major population areas on the Gulf Coast endangered by hurricanes. Many climatologists argue that global warming and the consequent increases in water temperature and sea level have put the region at greater risk than ever before. But regardless of climate changes, the risk is greater simply because many more people live there today than in 1900. Hazard experts Roger Pielke and Daniel Sarewitz explain, "[T]he number and scale of disasters worldwide has been rising rapidly in recent decades because of changes in society, not global warming. In the case of hurricanes, the continuing development and urbanization of coastal regions around the world accounts for all of the increases in economic and human losses that we have experienced."[27]

Since 1900, at least fifty-five storms of Category 3 or stronger have struck the continental United States. As more and more people settle along coastal areas, the risk of serious loss of life increases. More than 13 million people live in counties bordering the Gulf Coast, and millions more are immediately inland. In 1900 there were fewer than a million. Are the people there today aware of how often hurricanes strike and what dangers they face? Are the communities along the Gulf Coast better prepared for a hurricane than they were in 1900? Is the United States adequately prepared with its satellite technologies, modern communications, better construction, and improved transportation? Do people assume that because we have been struck by major hurricanes (Katrina and Rita) within the past decade, another major storm must be decades away? As the Galveston hurricane—and many of the other disasters of the early twentieth century—demonstrates, such hubris, denial, and complacency seem to be the heralds of disaster.

The San Francisco Earthquake and Fires of 1906

Shortly before dawn on April 18, 1906, almost 300 miles of the northern end of the San Andreas Fault ruptured, resulting in an earthquake later estimated to be of magnitude 7.8.[28] The epicenter was along the coast near Daly City, just southwest of San Francisco, but the earthquake was felt from southern Oregon to south of Los Angeles and inland as far as central Nevada. In just 45 to 60 seconds, the quake inflicted damage throughout Northern California. Santa Rosa, a community to the north of San Francisco, was particularly affected, as were San José and Stanford University to the south, but the event became known in American culture as the Great San Francisco Earthquake.[29]

Fires caused by ruptured gas lines, broken electrical lines, damaged and fallen chimneys, spilled lanterns, and other incendiary hazards (including arson by property owners to secure insurance payments) erupted immediately. In an eyewitness account, Jack London describes the scene:

> On Wednesday morning at a quarter past five came the earthquake. A min-
> ute later the flames were leaping upward. In a dozen different quarters
> south of Market Street, in the working-class ghetto, and in the factories,
> fires started. There was no opposing the flames. There was no organization,
> no communication. All the cunning adjustments of a twentieth-century city
> had been smashed by the earthquake. The streets were humped into ridges
> and depressions and piled with debris of fallen walls. The steel rails were
> twisted into perpendicular and horizontal angles. The telephone and tele-
> graph systems were disrupted. And the great water mains had burst. All the
> shrewd contrivances and safeguards of man had been thrown out of gear by
> thirty seconds' twitching of the earth crust.[30]

With many burst water lines and the fire alarm system knocked out by the quake, emergency responders were unable to quench the fires that erupted. The San Francisco Earthquake became the Great San Francisco Fire. Over the next three days, many smaller fires, feeding on the debris of structures dynamited in a failed effort to form firebreaks, joined in one great firestorm. The flames raged for three days, obliterating 4.7 square miles of the central city and destroying more than 28,000 buildings.[31]

Prior Events

Earthquakes and fires were not new to San Francisco. Native Americans in the area shared stories of earthquakes with early European explorers. In 1812, half of the missions in Southern California were damaged by an earthquake and the state's first earthquake deaths were recorded.[32] Subsequent quakes of magnitude 6.5 or greater occurred in or near San Francisco in 1836, 1838, 1865, and 1868. Then a period of relative calm ensued, with minor quakes becoming a common and therefore less alarming occurrence. Several major conflagrations also had destroyed parts of the city during its early days as a gold rush boomtown: San Francisco had one devastating fire in 1849, three in 1850, and two more in 1851. Decades later the city remained highly vulnerable to fire. One writer describes the structures in the city as "shacks and lean-tos and hastily cobbled together cuboids likely to burn or fall down at the slightest excuse.... The houses on Telegraph Hill and Russian Hill and where the Italians gathered in North Beach were almost all made entirely of wood."[33]

Many people warned that the situation in San Francisco was dire. Dennis Sullivan, the city's fire chief, argued for years "that the city was a tinderbox waiting to be struck."[34] (Sullivan's recommendations for an improved water distribution system and fire service were not implemented, and the Great Fire of 1906 proved him correct in his predictions. He died four days after the conflagration from injuries sustained in the earthquake.) In October 1905, the National Board of Fire Underwriters rated the probability of a major fire in San Francisco (even without an earthquake) as "alarmingly severe" and declared that the city's water supply system was structurally in such poor shape that the hydrants would be unable to extinguish a fire. The report went on to say that "San Francisco has violated all underwriting traditions and precedent by not burning up."[35]

The Devastation

For financial reasons, powerful and moneyed residents of San Francisco tried to have the 1906 disaster identified as a fire, not an earthquake. Insurance companies and potential investors were more likely to perceive fire as a manageable hazard, whereas an earthquake was seen as a capricious "act of God." At the time, the federal government estimated that only between 3 percent and 10 percent of the damage in San Francisco was directly attributable to the earthquake.[36] Subsequent studies have revised this estimate,[37] but researchers continue to attribute the primary cause of property damage in San Francisco to the fires.[38]

In addition, 225,000 of San Francisco's residents were rendered homeless. "[T]he great majority of these last were men, women, and children…seeking refuge from the calamity," writes Simon Winchester in his account of the event, "and thus they were American *refugees*. Not until the migrations enforced by the midwestern miseries of the Dust Bowl would such wretchedness be seen again."[39] And perhaps not again until 2005, when Hurricane Katrina devastated New Orleans and its environs.

In some areas, including Stanford University, the shaking from the 1906 earthquake did cause substantial damage. The most dramatic destruction due to shaking occurred among poorly built brick and wood-frame structures on wetlands and in tidewater areas that had been filled in to create new ground.[40] Earthquake engineers now recognize such "unconsolidated soils" as prone to liquefaction, making it particularly hazardous ground on which to build. In the 1989 Loma Prieta earthquake, for instance, the most heavily damaged areas of San Francisco were in the Marina District, built in part on refuse from the 1906 quake.

Although fire was responsible for most of the property damage in San Francisco, the earthquake and falling structures were responsible for a far greater proportion of deaths and injuries. Initially, the commander of the U.S. Army relief operations reported 498 deaths in San Francisco, but a city subcommittee formed to determine the death toll increased this number to 674. Years later, San Francisco archivist Gladys Hansen began to question these figures because her research showed that many deaths had not been counted. Although Chinatown had been virtually obliterated, for example, only twelve Asian names appeared on the subcommittee's list of deaths. After extensive research, Hansen concluded that at least 3,000 people had died, making it by far the deadliest earthquake in U.S. history.[41]

Fires raged throughout the city following the 1906 San Francisco Earthquake. Photo courtesy of the US Army Center of Military History.

Response and Recovery

As in any large disaster, the ability of government and the military to improvise solutions to problems and establish mechanisms of response and control where none had previously existed was a key element of the response. Although martial law was never officially declared, military from local bases were either asked to take on or simply assumed the role of keepers of the social order and protectors of property. Without standing orders regarding how the military should respond to what was essentially a civil matter, Brig. Gen. Frederick Funston, interim commander of the U.S. Army's Pacific Division based in the San Francisco Presidio at the time of the quake, quickly contacted the mayor and committed his soldiers to help maintain civil order.

Soldiers, police, "special police," and vigilantes were instructed to tolerate no civil disobedience or unrest and to shoot "looters" on sight. The incidence of such shootings has been debated and remains unclear; estimates range from single digits to more than 500.[42]

Equally improvisational were the actions of Lt. Frederick Freeman of the U.S. Navy. Also acting without orders and supervision, he organized his men to protect the city's dock areas from fire, actions that many people believe saved the waterfront. This not only enabled victims to evacuate by ferry, but also made it possible for goods and supplies to be shipped into the city.

The earthquake disabled the city's water supply (which, according to the National Board of Fire Underwriters, would have been inadequate anyway). Lacking water but feeling that something had to be done, city leaders and the military decided to use explosives to blast firebreaks.

Immediately following the disaster, San Francisco's mayor Eugene Schmitz established a "committee of fifty" to oversee the recovery and rebuilding of the city. The extragovernmental committee was composed of prominent, wealthy citizens, and ultimately it usurped the power of the city's elected board of supervisors. The committee was replaced a month later by a "committee on reconstruction," but the original subcommittee on finance and its chairman, James Phelan, retained control of all relief and redevelopment funds.

As the fires abated, three players—the Red Cross, the U.S. military, and the committee of fifty—emerged to take care of the dispossessed. Author Philip L. Fradkin notes that "the Red Cross had the expertise, the army had the manpower, and Phelan had the money [because he was president of Relief and Red Cross Funds]."[43] A vast relief effort was mounted almost immediately and lasted more than three years. Within two weeks, an estimated 268,000 persons were fed in a single day. Refugees were initially housed in army tents or makeshift shelters and then in semipermanent camps constructed by the U.S. Army.

The citizens of San Francisco—particularly the wealthy and the power-ful—moved quickly (perhaps too quickly) to rebuild the city. San Francisco was essentially reconstructed by 1910 and hosted the Panama-Pacific International Exposition just five years later to celebrate both the opening of the Panama Canal and the revival of San Francisco.

Mistakes Made and Lessons Learned

As much as any other disaster in the twentieth century, the 1906 earthquake revealed the problems and mistakes that often surround a major catastrophe.[44] The lessons learned relate to the following issues:

- **Denial of risk and vulnerability.** There was ample historical evidence that Northern California was at risk for both earthquakes and fires, but local leaders ignored or denied the risk.[45]

- **Shoddy construction.** At the time of the earthquake, San Francisco was evolving from a shoddily built boomtown and industrial city to a well-constructed and better organized community. Although some of the new buildings in the financial district and wealthy areas were strong enough to withstand earthquakes, others were not.[46] The reinforced brick and masonry walls of San Francisco's new city hall—the grandest structure in the city—crumbled when the earthquake hit, leaving a dome precariously perched on the remaining skeleton of the structure. In a subsequent report, the U.S. Geological Survey (USGS) called the city hall "a monument of bad design and poor materials and workmanship."[47] This was but one of thousands of structures that proved vulnerable to fire and earthquake.

- **Poor planning.** Beyond the vulnerability of individual structures, the city itself, with its narrow streets, crowded buildings, and inadequate infrastruc-ture, was a disaster waiting to happen, particularly in the poorer neighbor-hoods. Ironically, Daniel Burnham, the renowned Chicago architect and planner who had been retained prior to the earthquake to develop a plan for the city, had presented his plan to the San Francisco Board of Supervisors in the fall of 1905. The freshly printed final edition was delivered to city hall on the afternoon of April 17, 1906, but all copies burned in the fires of the next three days.[48]

- **Ineffective fire control.** Despite advice in 1905 from Fire Chief Sullivan and others, San Francisco failed to upgrade its firefighting capabilities, including its water distribution system. The result, according to earthquake experts Charles Scawthorn, Thomas O'Rourke, and F. T. Blackburn, was "the greatest single fire loss in U.S. history…. The National Board of Fire

Underwriters concluded that even under normal conditions the multiple simultaneous fires would probably have overwhelmed a much larger department, such as New York's, which had three times the apparatus."[49]

- **Law enforcement and the military response.** Immediately following the earthquake, the mayor and other local leaders made law enforcement a priority. The city mobilized to prevent anarchy and looting. In addition to the San Francisco police, the U.S. military, the National Guard and state militia, special police, vigilantes, and others joined in local law enforcement efforts. (Similar circumstances prevailed in Galveston after the hurricane.)[50] "This plethora of armed groups with no central coordination and little supervision, each reporting to a separate command structure, created a considerable amount of confusion and led to tragedy," writes Lucien Canton in a 2006 discussion of the 1906 disaster. "There are numerous reports, some anecdotal, of men in uniform being drunk, looting, forcing others into labor, and even committing murder."[51] Although martial law was not officially imposed, most citizens assumed it to be in effect.

San Francisco City Hall, April 1906. The U.S. Geological Survey called the building "a monument of bad design and poor materials and workmanship." It was just one among thousands of structures that crumbled during the 1906 earthquake. Photo courtesy of the National Geophysical Data Center/W. C. Mendenhall, U.S. Geological Survey.

Looting and Lawlessness in a Disaster

Modern social scientists have questioned the fear of looting following a disaster, citing it as one of several disaster myths (along with other behaviors and fears, such as panic, post-event shock that renders survivors unable to act, and the need to quickly bury the dead to prevent contagion). Careful analysis of disasters demonstrates that looting does happen in some cases, depending on several factors including the affected population's social and economic circumstances prior to the disaster. Moreover, what constitutes *looting,* as opposed to simple survival actions or the protection of one's own property, remains a question.

Philip Fradkin is particularly critical of this aspect of the city's response to the 1906 earthquake and fires:

"The exaggerated concern about looting led to the extreme solution: to summarily kill suspects of any crime. It was one of the principal tragedies of the disaster. [Mayor] Schmitz set in motion one of the most infamous and illegal orders ever issued by a civil authority in the country's history.

"All later accounts by both officials and private citizens emphasized that looting was minor or nonexistent.... In any case, how was looting to be defined? Citizens pillaging drugstores for medical supplies for the injured? Others seeking food for hungry families from stores that were about to be burned? Well-dressed residents sifting through the ruins of the mansions and Chinatown? Or army troops pawing through boxes of shoes in the middle of the street?...The determination was subjective and made in a moment. No one publicly questioned the order that substantially infringed upon the few civil liberties that existed at the time and cost the lives of an undetermined number of innocent citizens.

"One resident of San Francisco observed, 'The division of authority between army and municipality brought some terrible results.... The military was called in to take partial command; the citizens did not know whom they were to obey, and certainly the military subordinates and guards were not made to understand the limits of their authority. The consequences were tragic.... Preserve us from our preservers was the cry of many of us.'"[1]

1 Quoted in Philip L. Fradkin, *The Great Earthquake and Firestorms of 1906: How San Francisco Nearly Destroyed Itself* (Berkeley: University of California Press, 2005), 65, 67–68.

In the end, the wave of lawlessness feared by the mayor and his advisers failed to materialize. There were some incidences of looting, and several people assumed to be looters were shot by authorities, but some researchers argue that many of these people may have been trying to salvage their own possessions.[52]

Beyond the question of the legality (not to mention the morality) of the mayor's actions lies a larger issue regarding the imposition of martial law and role of the military in disaster response. Canton observes:

The use of military personnel to maintain public order is always fraught with peril. The Posse Comitatus Act of 1878 prohibits the use of military personnel for law enforcement functions without the specific authorization of Congress.... [M]ilitary personnel are neither trained nor permitted by the law to perform law enforcement functions, and most local authorities would prefer not to see the military in this role. Absent the use of the military, how would San Francisco deal with such a situation in 2006?[53]

The Posse Comitatus Act and the use of the military in disaster response are discussed further in Chapter 10.

- **Disaster relief.** Recovery efforts in San Francisco demonstrated the problems inherent in getting supplies to victims. "As in the tale of the Sorcerer's Apprentice, for a time there was no turning off the flood of material goods and cash," writes Fradkin. He adds, "As with any large-scale, hastily organized relief effort, this one was plagued by too much of one thing (flour), not enough of another (suitable clothes), and delays in getting food and clothing into the hands of needy refugees." He further notes that a survey of the relief effort determined that much of the donated clothing and other donated goods were of very poor quality, simply unacceptable, and "more or less of a burden on the Red Cross."[54] Still, in the 1906 disaster, one area in which the military was particularly effective was providing aid to victims. The organization and efficiency of the military proved essential in establishing temporary shelter and managing supplies.

  The time and expense involved in sorting "in-kind" donations and the influx of unsolicited goods to a disaster site remain problems that sometimes hinder, rather than help, recovery. As a result, in recent years the Red Cross and other nonprofit agencies, the government, and emergency managers have increasingly stressed money as the preferred form of donation.

- **Poor and ethnic populations.** At the time of the earthquake, San Francisco was an industrial, commercial port city with a large working class and many impoverished residents. One-third of the population had been born outside the United States; another third were first-generation Americans.

  It has long been noted that less affluent groups are differentially affected in disasters. Poor residents often can afford to live only in the most vulnerable locations and in less sturdy structures: in San Francisco at the turn of the nineteenth century, for instance, new immigrants crowded into wood-frame buildings prone to fire in areas of filled land prone to liquefaction. In addition, poorer individuals and families invariably have fewer resources, and therefore fewer choices, both to respond to and to recover from a disaster than do their more affluent counterparts.

  Further, institutions established to aid recovery were sometimes designed (albeit inadvertently) to assist white, middle-class individuals to the exclusion of others. In some cases, overt racism exacerbated obstacles to recovery. All these factors affected response efforts in San Francisco. Fradkin states simply that "who would suffer most was preordained." He also notes that poorer segments of the community were at a disadvantage in dealing with insurance companies: "Those people who needed cash immediately did not know how the system worked and were unable to exert political and legal pressure received the lowest returns on their policies."[55]

As it is today, the San Francisco of a century ago was home to large ethnic populations, particularly Chinese and Japanese immigrants. An estimated 14,000 to 25,000 Chinese Americans lived in the city, and almost all were forced to flee after the earthquake and fires decimated Chinatown. Although most moved to other parts of California or back to China, "a few hundred made the unwise choice of remaining in San Francisco."[56] This was unwise because those who remained faced additional hardships and racial discrimination. Whites objected to the presence of Asians in the refugee camps, forcing the latter to move to ever more remote camps and leaving their property vulnerable to being ransacked. Because the oligarchy of the city perceived Chinatown as a blight on the city and as coveted real estate, the city's leaders devised a plan to permanently relocate the population. *The San Francisco Call* issued a proclamation:

> Strike while the iron is hot. Preserve this fine hill for the architecture and occupancy of the clean and moderate Caucasian. We now hold the situation in the hollow of our hand. We have but to say the word and fine edifices will in the future grace that commanding slope, filched from us by the insidious, gradual occupation of the Mongol.[57]

"There was still a powerfully racist element to San Francisco," explains Winchester, "and not a few thought the fires a blessing. Now many residents breathed quietly, the Chinese could push off elsewhere, and the slums… could be replaced by office buildings or houses for more respectable folks."[58] However, the effort to relocate the Chinese population failed because of political and economic pressure from Washington, the Chinese government, and local Chinese businesses and property owners. Nearly two years after the disaster, an estimated 15,000 Chinese residents had returned to the city.

The San Francisco catastrophe underscores an important lesson reiterated in the analysis of almost every other disaster in this chapter: In the multiethnic culture that is the United States, emergency management—in preparedness, warning, response, recovery, and long-term mitigation—must take into account the language, culture, desires, and fears of the many and diverse populations it serves.

• **Reconstruction and rebuilding.** San Francisco moved quickly to rebuild after the 1906 fires but continued to do so without a plan. The plan that had been developed by Burnham a few years earlier was reprinted, but the city never adopted this—or any other—comprehensive building plan. To the powerful of San Francisco, it was more important to resume business and reestablish the tax base as quickly as possible. As a result, the city was allowed to rebuild and grow much in the same haphazard way that it had before the devastation of 1906. Fradkin writes,

> The "upbuilding," as the physical reconstruction of San Francisco was called, proceeded with great speed, without any plan, and with only slight regard for the congestion and shoddy building practices that magnified the scale of the natural disaster. Recovery was eventually gained, but at great cost to forests, horses [scores were literally worked to death in the recovery and reconstruction], people, democracy, and future public safety.... In the end...San Francisco [remained] highly vulnerable to natural disasters.[59]

Efforts to strengthen building codes were mostly defeated, although the city did pass a new ordinance in 1909, after most of the rebuilding was complete.[60] In addition, in the summer of 1906, the city passed legislation requiring new buildings to be able to withstand a wind force of 30 pounds per square foot, but as the impact of the disaster faded in the following decades, this standard was cut in half. It would take additional earthquakes—Santa Barbara in 1925 and Long Beach in 1933—to prompt the state of California to pass laws mandating safe construction based on standards related to earthquakes.[61]

San Francisco made more progress addressing water distribution needs. It might have disregarded the need for a more effective water distribution system had it not been for economic pressure from interests beyond the city. The insurance industry demanded that a high-pressure system be implemented, as Sullivan had called for prior to the earthquake. As a result, in 1908 the city engineer proposed the construction of an auxiliary water supply system, which was funded through a $5.2 million bond issue and was largely completed by 1912.[62] In their discussion of lessons learned from the event, Scawthorn and colleagues detail the much-improved water distribution system, but their conclusions regarding the city's ability to fight fires are sobering:

The building stock west of Van Ness, to and including Pacific Heights, is mainly wood frame and is virtually intact, as it was in 1906—large wood-frame buildings of three to four stories in height, a conflagration hazard. The area east of Van Ness Avenue, to Stockton Street, including Telegraph Hill, was completely burned off in 1906. In the rush to rebuild, it was reconstructed virtually as it was, recreating the conflagration hazard that previously existed.

With occasional high winds, narrow streets and densely built wood-frame buildings of three to four stories in height, this section of San Francisco today is as significant a conflagration hazard as it was in 1906.[63]

- **Denial following the quake.** Those who were in charge of the reconstruction of San Francisco denied, or at least minimized, the effects of the earthquake. As mentioned earlier, local financial and real estate interests felt that portraying the disaster as an earthquake would deter outside investment in the city and hinder the availability of insurance. Reporter Charles Smith writes, "Realizing that the vast destruction cast a pall on both prospects and property values, business leaders quickly grasped the wisdom of excising 'earthquake' from their pronouncements, replacing it with the less frightening (and more insurance-worthy) 'Great Fire' of 1906."[64] Hence, for years, the San Francisco disaster was referred to as the Great San Francisco Fire, with no reference to the earthquake that was at its root.

San Francisco—The Archetype, the Reality, and the Risk

A small number of American catastrophes have become legendary, a part of the country's collective cultural lore. In this regard, the 1906 San Francisco Earthquake surpasses the Johnstown Flood and rivals the Dust Bowl as a national event etched in memory, evoking images of the human struggle against catastrophe. As Ted Steinberg says, "The 1906 San Francisco earthquake is arguably the event that defines calamity in the popular imagination. It is the Big One that lurks in the back of the American mind."[65] (It has now certainly been joined by the events of September 11, 2001, and Hurricane Katrina.)

Becoming legend has both negative and positive consequences. On the one hand, it can mean that reality is supplanted by anecdote and myth. On the other, it means that the event, and therefore similar events, becomes part of public awareness. In their analysis of the impact of the 1906 earthquake on public policy, Jeanne Perkins and her colleagues point out that the San Francisco earthquake set the stage for research and subsequent state and federal measures to reduce seismic hazards. It provided both a historical example and concrete data to support mitigation efforts. As they state:

> Because of the 1906 earthquake, California state and local governments no longer consider earthquakes and their effects as acts of God, beyond human control. These events are considered inevitable; impacts are compared to other natural disasters and understood through targeted scientific investigations.[66]

Indeed, only two years after the earthquake, University of California geologist Andrew Lawson and his colleagues published the *Report of the State Earthquake Investigation Commission on the California Earthquake of April 18, 1906,* which remains perhaps the most comprehensive study of a seismic event in the United States and a baseline for post-earthquake analysis. The quake also led to the formation in 1906 of the Seismological Society of America "for the acquisition and diffusion of knowledge concerning earthquakes and allied phenomena, and to enlist the support of the people and the government in the attainment of these ends."[67]

In terms of legislation, California did not act until three decades later, following the Long Beach earthquake of 1933. However, although intervening earthquakes were often the precipitating events and more proximal causes of change, researchers suggest that virtually all later California programs and legislation can be traced in part to information and insights derived from the Great San Francisco Earthquake of 1906.[68] Perkins and colleagues cite not only the Seismological Society of America but also the first Uniform Building Code seismic provisions, the Field and Riley acts (discussed below), the Association of Bay Area Governments' Earthquake Program, California's Joint Legislative Committee on Seismic Safety, the Alquist-Priolo Earthquake Fault Zoning Act, the 1973 Hospital Seismic Safety Act, the California Seismic Safety Commission, and the National Earthquake Hazards Reduction Program, which was established more than seventy years later (discussed further in Chapter 4). Robert Reitherman traces an entire lineage of earth scientists and earthquake engineers whose progenitors first became involved in these fields after the 1906 earthquake; he further posits that the Great San Francisco Earthquake established the credibility of the study of earthquakes in the United States.[69]

Analyses of San Francisco's vulnerability today are sobering. In 2003, a report of the USGS and other scientists concluded that "there is a 62 percent probability of at least one magnitude 6.7 or greater quake, capable of causing widespread damage, striking somewhere in the San Francisco Bay region before 2032."[70] In 2006, in preparation for the centennial commemoration of the Great San Francisco Earthquake, a report was published outlining the present-day consequences of an earthquake of the magnitude of the 1906 event:

> The current population of this Northern California region is about ten times what it was in 1906, and the replacement value of buildings is about 500 times greater. Despite improvements in building codes and construction practices, the growth of the region over the past 100 years causes the range of estimated fatalities, approximately 800–3,400 depending on time of day and other variables, to be comparable to what it was in 1906. The forecast property loss to buildings for a repeat of the 1906 earthquake is in the range of approximately $90–120 billion; 7,000–10,000 commercial buildings in the region are estimated to be closed due to serious damage; and about 160,000–250,000 households calculated to be displaced from damaged residences. Losses due to fire following earthquake, as well as losses to utility and transportation systems, would be in addition to these estimates.[71]

"A major quake can occur in any part of this densely populated region," warned the USGS in 2003. "Therefore, there is an ongoing need for all communities in the Bay region to continue preparing for the quakes that will strike in the future."[72]

The Great Influenza Pandemic of 1918

Experts do not agree on the origins of the Great Influenza Pandemic of 1918, but some suspect that it began with an outbreak of flu in southwestern Kansas in the spring of that year. Initially, the influenza virus may have been passed from birds to humans directly or through an intermediary host, such as pigs. In any event, the virus became deadly when it mutated into a form directly transmissible from human to human.[73]

The influenza progressed in waves over the next several years, but the second and third outbreaks—the most serious—occurred during the fall and winter of 1918–1919. By then, the virus had mutated into a virulent form. The explosive and deadly outbreak was unlike anything the world had seen in more than five centuries. At the time, *Science* magazine reported, "The epidemics now occurring appear with electric suddenness, and, acting like powerful, uncontrolled currents, produce violent and eccentric effects. The disease never spreads slowly and insidiously. Wherever it occurs, its presence is startling."[74]

The historical setting made the disease's transmission almost impossible to control. Specifically, the entry of the United States into World War I resulted in young men from around the country being concentrated in large training facilities, where they were housed in proximity to one another and then transported to other parts of the country and, ultimately, overseas. In a sense, the war created a system for distributing the disease across the country and around the world—and later, bringing it back to the United States once again.

As mentioned, the disease spread in waves, with the most severe outbreaks occurring during the fall and early winter of 1918–1919, and less severe episodes occurring in the months and years that followed. The flu was unusual not only in its virulence but also in its sudden onset and rapid course. It could incapacitate and kill a victim within hours, and it could blanket an entire city in only a few days. It was also unique in the pattern of its morbidity: Besides infants and elderly—the usual victims of flu—the 1918–1919 outbreak was particularly deadly for young adults. The high mortality rate was due in large part to the flu's alarming tendency to produce fatal secondary pneumonia.[75]

In 1918 and 1919, the influenza pandemic caused more deaths than had occurred during the previous four years in World War I. Once the virulent strain spread across the world, it killed at least 25 million people in just six months. An estimated 5 percent of India's population died. The death rate was especially high for indigenous peoples in areas such as Alaska, southern Africa, and the South Pacific, where entire villages perished.

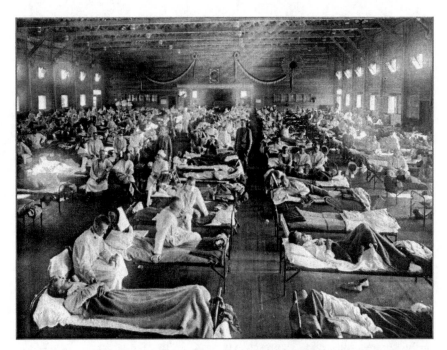

Camp Funston, Kansas, was the site of one of the first major flu epidemics. Photo courtesy of the National Museum of Health and Medicine, Armed Forces Institute of Pathology, Washington, D.C.

The disease also spread through Europe. In May 1918, one of the more severe early outbreaks of the disease hit Spain, where an estimated 8 million people contracted the virus. While other countries discouraged or even censored mention of the disease because leaders feared that it would incite panic or hurt morale and/or wartime production, Spain publicized it widely. As a result, the pandemic became popularly known as the "Spanish flu."

By the time the disease had subsided, an estimated 500 million people—one-third of the world's population—had been infected and an estimated 2.5 to 5 percent of the world's population had died.[76] In absolute numbers, more lives were lost to the 1918–1919 pandemic than to any other disease. In terms of percentages, it was the worst health disaster since the Black Death in the fourteenth century.

Between 500,000 and 675,000 Americans lost their lives to the pandemic—ten times more than died on the World War I battlefields. The virus killed 195,000 in October 1918 alone, making that month the deadliest in U.S. history. The average lifespan in the United States declined by ten years as a result.[77]

Researchers Jeffery Taubenberger and David Morens note that the impact of the pandemic went beyond 1918–1919: "All influenza A pandemics since that time, and indeed almost all cases of influenza A worldwide…have been caused by descendants of the 1918 virus…making the 1918 virus indeed the 'mother' of all pandemics."[78] According to these researchers, variants of the disease still survive today.

An Eyewitness Account

The following excerpt from a letter written by an unknown soldier at Camp Devens, near Boston, demonstrates the deadly grip the pandemic had on the 50,000 men living there:

"These men start with what appears to be an ordinary attack of La Grippe or Influenza, and when brought to the Hospital, they very rapidly develop the most vicious type of Pneumonia that has ever been seen. Two hours after admission they have the mahogany spots over the cheek bones, and a few hours later you can begin to see the Cyanosis extending from their ears and spreading all over the face, until it is hard to distinguish the coloured men from the white. It is only a matter of a few hours then until death comes, and it is simply a struggle for air until they suffocate. It is horrible. One can stand it to see one, two or twenty men die, but to see these poor devils dropping like flies sort of gets on your nerves. We have been averaging about 100 deaths per day....

"It takes special trains to carry away the dead. For several days there were no coffins and the bodies piled up something fierce, we used to go down to the morgue (which is just back of my ward) and look at the boys laid out in long rows. It beats any sight they ever had in France after a battle. An extra long barracks has been vacated for the use of the Morgue, and it would make any man sit up and take notice to walk down the long lines of dead soldiers all dressed and laid out in double rows."

Source: N. R. Grist, *British Medical Journal* (December 22–29, 1979): 1632.

Preparedness and Response

At the time of the 1918 influenza outbreak, the United States had a broad and competent health infrastructure that included national and local public health agencies as well as a seemingly adequate supply of doctors, nurses, and hospitals. Nevertheless, the system was soon overwhelmed by the Great Influenza Pandemic. Hospitals, particularly those in military camps, had far too few beds to accommodate the massive numbers of sick in the fall of 1918. Furthermore, the war had depleted the number of available doctors and nurses.

Initially public health agencies reacted by denying the threat. U.S. Surgeon General Rupert Blue, for instance, "did, literally, less than nothing: he blocked relevant research." Although Blue published warnings about the flu, "he made no preparations whatsoever to try to contain it. Even after it began to show evidence of lethality…neither he nor his office attempted to gather information about the disease anywhere in the world. And he made no effort whatsoever to prepare the Public Health Service for a crisis."[79] Only when the crisis could not be denied did Blue finally react, asking for money from Congress to hire 5,000 doctors for emergency duty for a month.

Although the disease was first manifest in military installations, the military seemingly also failed to recognize the scope of the problem. It ignored the need to curtail troop movements or quarantine the sick, contributing to the rapid spread of the disease.

Compounding poor preparedness and a reluctance to address the problem was the fact that there was neither a vaccine to prevent the disease nor a serum to treat it. When the epidemic broke out, a great deal of effort was spent to determine the origin. The etiological agent was unknown, but it was thought to be airborne bacteria. Although early on some researchers suspected a virus (the true cause), that agent was only determined conclusively years later.[80]

As the epidemic spread and leaders were forced to acknowledge the scope of the disease, the U.S. response was multifaceted, involving both public health measures and medical and scientific efforts to treat, understand, and develop medicines to counteract the disease. The public health measures undertaken in cities and towns throughout the nation as well as within military installations were directed toward inhibiting the transmission of the pathogen, whatever it might be. Since the microbe was thought to be airborne, these measures sometimes involved prohibiting or limiting public assembly by closing theaters, saloons, restaurants, and sometimes schools and by limiting attendance at places of worship and even funerals.

Some state and local health agencies mandated the quarantine of infected individuals. To the extent possible, hospitals separated patients from one another. Authorities also recommended various measures that individuals should take to prevent infection. For example, many health authorities advocated wearing gauze masks, which local Red Cross volunteers spent much time making, and San Francisco issued a trial ordinance requiring the entire population to wear the masks. All these measures required a major public information campaign, and both federal and local health agencies, as well as the American Red Cross, launched education campaigns using leaflets and posters to inform the public of recommended practices.

Many of the public health measures had some basis in science, but many were just commonsense notions regarding personal health and hygiene. In the end, it is questionable whether any of the measures did much to control the spread of the disease. An article in the December 1918 *British Medical Journal* lamented the inability to stem its tide: "Every town-dweller who is susceptible must sooner or later contract influenza whatever the public health authorities may do; and that the more schools and public meetings are banned and the general life of the community dislocated the greater will be the unemployment and depression."[81]

Across the United States, the Red Cross became the lead organization at the local level to deal with the epidemic. The organization had grown tremendously as a result of the war effort. The number of local chapters increased from 107 in 1914 to 3,864 in 1918; during these years, membership grew from 17,000 to more than 20 million Americans. The Red Cross was involved in everything from making gauze masks to locating and recruiting nurses to provide home care. Indeed, "15,000 Red Cross nurses, dietitians, and others were recruited to work in military camps, hospitals, coal fields, munitions plants, and shipyards, where they remained until the epidemic finally subsided in the spring of 1919."[82] But it became increasingly difficult to meet the domestic need for doctors and nurses during a time of war:

> Since the medical practitioners were away with the troops, only the medical students were left to care for the sick. Third- and fourth-year classes were closed and the students assigned jobs as interns or nurses.... The shortage was further confounded by the added loss of physicians to the epidemic. In the U.S., the Red Cross had to recruit more volunteers to contribute to the new cause at home of fighting the influenza epidemic. To respond with the fullest utilization of nurses, volunteers and medical supplies, the Red Cross created a National Committee on Influenza. It was involved in both military and civilian sectors to mobilize all forces to fight Spanish influenza.[83]

It is unrealistic to think that the medical researchers of the day could have developed medicines in time to control the pandemic or diminish its devastating effects. If an outbreak as ferocious as the 1918 epidemic were to break out today, many experts say that it is unlikely that scientists would be able to develop a vaccine—and the pharmaceutical industry mass-produce it—quickly enough to control the disease. Furthermore, because of the virulence and explosiveness of the 1918 disease, research had to proceed faster than most scientists would have liked. Controls could not always be established, results confirmed, or conclusions verified. Nevertheless, researchers worked furiously to develop a vaccine that would inhibit the bacterial causes of secondary pneumonia, seen as the proximal cause of death. The resulting vaccines had some prophylactic efficacy, but they had no effect once infection had set in. Ultimately, scientists found neither a palliative to relieve the symptoms of the disease nor a cure to prevent its deadly consequences.[84]

Current Concerns, Future Threats, and the Role of the Emergency Manager

The Great Influenza Pandemic of 1918–1919 is significant because, like the San Francisco Earthquake, it has become part of American history, culture, and consciousness. Like the other disasters discussed in this chapter, it was an archetype and baseline for events that followed.

The pandemic poses several critical questions for modern society and today's emergency managers:

- Could a similar epidemic occur today?

- What would be the likely consequences?

- What role should emergency managers play in responding to such an event?

Researchers agree that the answer to the first question—could a similar epidemic recur—is yes. "[S]ince it happened once, analogous conditions could lead to an equally devastating pandemic," conclude Taubenberger and Morens.[85] Much earlier, in an article published in the *British Medical Journal,* N. R. Grist wrote:

> Epidemic influenza remains the biggest and unconquered acute threat to human health, inflicting damage and death far beyond familiar notification data. The impact of influenza A is particularly severe during periodic pandemics owing to novel antigenic variants which override immunity from experience of earlier subtypes. *It is salutary to remember that we do not really understand why the devastating pandemic of 1918–19 was so severe, and that we cannot therefore be confident that our modern medical measures would succeed against a similar future challenge* [emphasis added].[86]

Such fears informed the concern that peaked in 2005–2006 about a possible H5N1 bird flu epidemic and the even greater concern in 2009–2010 regarding the H1N1 (swine) flu. In *The Great Influenza: The Story of the Deadliest Pandemic in History,* John M. Barry goes further, pointing out that we need to address not only the potential consequences of a pandemic but also the effects of more moderate annual outbreaks of the flu:

> The threat of H5N1 (bird flu) has…focused the minds of scientists and public health officials around the world. They are quietly, and sometimes not so quietly, warning those with the power to spend money that, if they do not prepare for a pandemic now, some time in the near future an investigative commission will write the equivalent of a 9/11 Commission Report, asking why they failed to act. Only this time, instead of a few thousand dead, the toll will be in the millions…. Influenza has to be seen as a lethal threat. A pandemic would prove more deadly than even a major bioterrorism attack, and it is more likely to occur. In addition according to the CDC [Centers for Disease Control and Prevention], every year influenza kills 36,000 Americans, almost triple the country's AIDS death tolls, and…despite medical advances influenza's annual death toll is trending up, not down.[87]

Similarly, at the time of the bird flu pandemic, experts Caroline Ash and Leslie Roberts state that research on the bird flu virus was essential not only for that current problem but for future outbreaks as well. "An energetic response to H5N1 does not have to be alarmist," they write. "We can marshal existing concern about this particular strain of avian influenza to build a long-lasting international infrastructure to monitor and thwart threats from such emerging infections."[88]

The concern regarding the H5N1 bird flu virus that spread across Asia, as well as that regarding the H1N1 outbreak, reflects the fear that many scientists and medical professionals have of the recurrence of a pandemic as deadly as the 1918 flu. While bird flu has infected only a limited number of people, more than half of those have died from the disease; specifically, "on December 9, 2010, the WHO [World Health Organization] announced a total of 510 human cases which resulted in the deaths of 303 people since 2003."[89] So far, transmission of this type of flu has been almost entirely from birds to humans. Scientists worry that a human-to-human strain will evolve and a worldwide pandemic will follow. In the case of the H1N1 swine flu, the concern is that the relatively mild disease will mutate into a much more deadly form.

Such an event could have devastating consequences. Despite the lack of understanding (or perhaps because of it) regarding the origins and evolution of the 1918 virus, Taubenberger and Morens conclude:

> Even with modern antiviral and antibacterial drugs, vaccines, and prevention knowledge, the return of a pandemic virus equivalent in pathogenicity to the virus of 1918 would likely kill [more than] 100 million people worldwide. A pandemic virus with the (alleged) pathogenic potential of some recent H5N1 outbreaks could cause substantially more deaths.[90]

These researchers provide a partial answer to the second question posed earlier: What would be the likely consequences? Clearly, a virus like the 1918 virus would result in unprecedented loss of life, but even a less severe strain of flu could have major consequences. The World Health Organization estimates that a milder virus (akin to a strain that appeared in 1968) would kill between 2 and 7.4 million people worldwide. The Centers for Disease Control and Prevention (CDC) estimates that a mild virus would result in 89,000 to 207,000 deaths in the United States.[91] Moreover, because of the global nature of our modern culture, a pandemic would affect the world economy and our transportation systems far more drastically than in 1918–1919. Researchers warn that a pandemic would quickly overwhelm national and international health care systems and severely disrupt the economy. (Conversely, some people speculate that the Internet could ameliorate some of these problems because it would enable many people to work and communicate in isolation.)

In many respects a massive quick-onset, virulent epidemic is similar to other disasters. It results in the death of large numbers of people with little warning. The ensuing response requires planning, coordination, information sharing, and the management of many people. In this light, the answer to the last question regarding the role of an emergency manager is clear. Emergency managers have the experience, knowledge, and skills necessary to deal with the disruption that an outbreak would cause to the social structure. Emergency managers would be called on to share that expertise, but they would be part of a much larger team addressing the problem.

In the early 1900s, epidemics and other widespread health disasters were not included with natural disasters as phenomena that could be addressed by a common "emergency management system," primarily because such a system had not yet emerged. There was no person called a *professional emergency manager*. Today, however, an epidemic or other mass health problem is recognized as an emergency issue. Planning for such an eventuality involves the broad range of agencies and institutions that could contribute to its management, including hospitals, physicians, local health departments, the CDC, government officials and agencies at all levels, news media, and emergency management professionals. Indeed, the National Response Plan (NRP), which was superseded in 2008 by the National Response Framework (NRF; see Chapter 8), stated:

> No single entity possesses the authority, expertise, and resources to act unilaterally on the many complex issues that may arise in response to a disease outbreak and loss of containment affecting a multijurisdictional area. The national response requires close coordination between numerous agencies at all levels of government and with the private sector.[92]

The NRF itself, which was built upon the NRP "establishes a comprehensive, national, all-hazards approach to domestic incident response,"[93] and expressly addresses the need for coordination to combat biological incidents and public health threats through its "Emergency Support Function #8 – Public Health and Medical Services Annex."

Various people and institutions are responsible for preventing outbreaks of influenza and other communicable diseases. Researchers at private companies have joined public health agencies to develop vaccines and to stockpile antiviral medications to contain an epidemic should one break out.[94] But researchers caution that it is "almost impossible to produce, distribute, and administer hundreds of millions of doses, and possibly a billion or more, within six months after the emergence of a new pandemic virus."[95]

Thus, if an outbreak occurred, a wide range of individuals and organizations—emergency managers, Red Cross volunteers, media, and government officials and agencies at the federal, state, and local levels—would be needed to manage everything from triage, to feeding and sheltering victims, to the dissemination of public information. To address a coordinated management effort, the federal government has drafted a Health and Human Services Pandemic Influenza Plan and a National Strategy for Pandemic Influenza.[96]

To a certain extent, the role of the modern emergency manager in health emergencies is clear: to prepare for systemic failure due to widespread illness and deaths from the flu or other pandemic diseases. At the same time, until an actual outbreak occurs, the precise nature of the emergency manager's role will remain uncertain. Emergency managers will have to work in concert with other professionals to address previously unknown circumstances. This is almost always the case with disasters, and effective response requires prior planning, coordination, and communication among the many people and organizations involved so that those unknown consequences and events can be quickly and efficiently addressed. Unlike other disasters, however, a major health emergency could last for months, with the impact spreading across communities throughout the nation or even the world. As a result, the network of professionals called upon to respond could be extensive and the need for prior planning and coordination correspondingly large.

The Long Beach Earthquake of 1933

On March 20, 1933, at 5:54 p.m., an earthquake of approximately 6.3 magnitude struck Southern California. "When the quake hit we all scrambled to get out the back door," recalls Arthur G. Porter, an Orange County resident. "I tried several times before I could get up off the sofa, and then as we stood (or, rather attempted to stand) near the rear kitchen door, our garage appeared to be shaking just as if it were on the end of a rug shaken by hand."[97]

Much smaller and more localized than the Great San Francisco Earthquake, the Long Beach quake killed about 120 people, making it the deadliest earthquake in Southern California history. The Southern California Earthquake Center reports that more than two-thirds of the deaths occurred "when people ran outside and were struck by falling bricks, cornices, parapets, and building ornaments."[98]

But things could have been worse. Records show that 75 percent of Long Beach's schools sustained extensive damage. "Brick buildings with unreinforced masonry walls, including many of the school buildings in Long Beach and surrounding areas, failed catastrophically," write Susan Fatemi and Charles James in their account of the Long Beach quake. "If the earthquake had struck a few hours earlier, when school was in session, the loss of life would have been appalling."[99]

As in San Francisco twenty-seven years earlier, the military responded with troops, supplies, and food kitchens. Martial law was not declared, but the presence of soldiers led many Long Beach residents to think that the city was under martial law.

The Consequences: California Recognizes Its Seismic Risk

The Long Beach quake is significant as the focusing event that led the state of California to adopt legislation addressing its seismic hazard. In 1933, just one month after the earthquake, California passed the Safety of Design and Construction of Public School Buildings Act (known as the Field Act because it was authored by state legislator Don C. Field). The Field Act regulates the construction or reconstruction of school buildings and the inspection of existing school buildings through a state agency independent of local political influence. Six years later, the Garrison Act strengthened the requirements by mandating that school buildings constructed prior to 1933 and found by inspectors to be unsafe be updated to the California Building Code.

In 1933, the California Assembly also adopted the Riley Act, which required all California local governments to have a building department and inspect new

Many buildings with unreinforced masonry, like the Jefferson Junior High School shown here, were severely damaged during the earthquake that struck Long Beach in 1933. This disaster led directly to state legislation mandating seismic safety in school construction. Photo courtesy of U.S. Geological Survey/ Capt. T.J. Maher.

construction, and mandated that all new structures be designed to withstand a horizontal acceleration of 0.02 times the acceleration due to gravity.

Disaster Management as a Historical, Evolutionary Process

Although it was the proximal event, the Long Beach earthquake constituted just one of a series of events—social, political, and programmatic, as well as seismic—that ultimately increased and reshaped public awareness regarding the earthquake threat in California. In 1925 a moderate earthquake struck in Santa Barbara, killing thirteen people. Robert Olson concludes that this event sustained, if not rekindled, interest in earthquake engineering and seismic building codes, in part because it alerted insurers to their potential liability. Perkins and colleagues agree that the "1925 earthquake also prompted the initial public recognition that earthquakes were a California problem, not a San Francisco problem."[100]

Because the Long Beach earthquake occurred just eight years later, it renewed attention to the lessons learned in the Santa Barbara quake. Olson writes, "Above all, the [Long Beach] earthquake forever closed the 'window of denial' by forcing business and public recognition that California was seriously threatened by earthquakes."[101] As a consequence, in 1933, unlike in 1906, scientists and engineers were ready to use the earthquake to argue that Californians faced a serious threat from future seismic events. These seismologists and earthquake engineers embarked on a vigorous public relations campaign that succeeded in painting the Long Beach earthquake as a manifestation of a general hazard rather than an isolated occurrence.[102]

In an immediate sense, by building on the experience of the 1906 and 1925 quakes, the Long Beach earthquake helped engender a heightened awareness of and improved response to the problems posed by poorly designed, poorly constructed, unreinforced masonry structures in seismic areas. In a broader sense, the event ushered in the modern era of state and federal involvement in earthquake hazard mitigation.

It is tempting to point to the 1933 earthquake as *the* event that launched California's (and, by extension, the nation's) concern with seismic safety, but this denies the historical, evolutionary process of disaster management. The Long Beach disaster would not have resulted in significant change had the San Francisco and Santa Barbara quakes not come before it. Those earlier disasters laid the groundwork—through research and innumerable smaller institutional and policy changes—for the major legislation passed by the state government following the Long Beach quake. This California legislation, in turn, laid the groundwork for national awareness and federal legislation many years later (as discussed in Chapters 3 and 4).

Policy makers and emergency managers work not only in a social, political, and geographical context but also in a historical context. Their actions and concerns are part of a decades-long effort to safeguard the lives of people subject to disasters. Awareness of that history can help to facilitate both the formation of sound policy and the creation of effective practice in dealing with hazards. For instance, true to the evolutionary process of hazard management, the 1933 Field Act has been updated many times; as a result, no California school covered by the Field Act has failed in an earthquake.[103]

Endnotes

1   Gary A. Kreps, "The Federal Emergency Management System in the United States: Past and Present," *International Journal of Mass Emergencies and Disasters 8*, no. 3 (1990): 281.

2   Peter J. May, *Recovering from Catastrophes: Federal Disaster Relief Policy and Politics* (Westport, Conn.: Greenwood Press, 1985), 18.

3   Roy S. Popkin, "The History and Politics of Disaster Management in the United States," in *Nothing to Fear: Risks and Hazards in American Society*, ed. Andrew Kirby (Tucson: University of Arizona Press, 1990), 106. For more thorough surveys of early federal involvement, see also May, *Recovering from Catastrophes,* and David A. Moss, "Courting Disaster? The Transformation of Federal Disaster Policy," in *The Financing of Catastrophe Risk,* ed. Kenneth A. Froot (Chicago: University of Chicago Press, 1999), 312 ff.

4   May, *Recovering from Catastrophes.*

5   Moss, "Courting Disaster?" 312.

6   Rutherford H. Platt, *Disasters and Democracy: The Politics of Extreme Natural Events* (Washington, D.C.: Island Press, 1999), 1.

7   Ibid., 2.

8   The disasters of the late nineteenth and early twentieth centuries have been studied in detail and written about many times. The accounts here rely on both primary sources and the studies derived from these sources. The reader is encouraged to consult these earlier works; many are classics in the study of disasters and emergency management.

9   Karen Sawislak, *Smoldering City: Chicagoans and the Great Fire, 1871–1874* (Chicago: University of Chicago Press, 1995); Chicago Historical Society/Northwestern University, "The Great Chicago Fire and the Web of Memory," chicagohs.org/fire/index.html; David McCullough, *The Johnstown Flood* (New York: Simon & Schuster, 1987); and Johnstown Area Heritage Foundation, "Johnstown Flood Museum," jaha.org/FloodMuseum/history.html.

10   Stephen J. Pyne, *Fire in America: A Cultural History of Wildland and Rural Fire* (Seattle: University of Washington Press, 1997), provides a detailed discussion of these conflagrations, citing the 1871 fire as the worst forest fire in U.S. history. See also Deana C. Hipke, "The Great Peshtigo Fire of 1871," peshtigofire.info.

11   Paul J. Kocin and Louis W. Uccellini, *The Cases,* vol. 2 of *Northeast Snowstorms,* AMS Meteorological Monographs 32, no. 54 (Boston, Mass.: American Meteorological Society, November 2004): 304–308.

12   For a more thorough discussion of these events, see the American Red Cross website, redcross.org/museum/history/timeline.asp, from which much of this information is taken.

13   For discussion and various estimates of the death toll, see Edward N. Rappaport and Jose Fernandez-Partagas, "The Deadliest Atlantic Tropical Cyclones, 1492–Present," at the National Hurricane Center, nhc.noaa.gov/pastdeadly.html.

14   "The 1900 Storm: Triumph and Tragedy," *Galveston County Daily News,* 2011, 1900storm.com/storm/storm2.lasso.

15   Philip L. Fradkin, *The Great Earthquake and Firestorms of 1906: How San Francisco Nearly Destroyed Itself* (Berkeley: University of California Press, 2005), 19.

16   Erik Larson, *Isaac's Storm: A Man, a Time, and the Deadliest Hurricane in History* (New York: Random House/Vintage Books, 1999), 81–84.

17   Casey Edward Greene and Shelly Henley Kelly, *Through a Night of Horrors: Voices from the 1900 Galveston Storm* (College Station: Texas A&M University Press, 2000), 15–19.

18   Larson, *Isaac's Storm,* 244.

19   Ibid., 256.

20   John H. Lienhard, Engines of Our Ingenuity, "No. 865: Raising Galveston" uh.edu/engines/epi865.htm.

21   Jerry D. Jarrell, Max Mayfield, and Edward N. Rappaport, "The Deadliest, Costliest, and Most Intense United States Hurricanes from 1900 to 2000 (and other Frequently Requested Hurricane Facts)," NOAA Technical Memorandum NWS TPC-1 (National Oceanic and Atmospheric Administration [NOAA], 2001), Table 3A, aoml.noaa.gov/hrd/Landsea/deadly/.

22   Larson, *Isaac's Storm,* 79–80.

23   Ibid., 84.

24   See, for example, Texas State Historical Association, "Galveston Hurricane of 1900," tshaonline.org/ handbook/online/articles/ydg02. For Cline's official report, see NOAA History, "Galveston Storm of 1900," history.noaa.gov/stories_tales/cline2.html.

25   Fradkin, *Great Earthquake and Firestorms,* 19.

26   Larson, *Isaac's Storm,* 272.

27   Roger A. Pielke Jr. and Daniel Sarewitz, "Managing the Next Disaster," *Los Angeles Times,* September 23, 2005, sciencepolicy.colorado.edu/admin/publication_files/resource-1770-2005.37.pdf.

28   Earthquake magnitude is a logarithmic measure of earthquake size. In simple terms, this means that at the same distance from the earthquake, the shaking will be 10 times as large during a magnitude 5 earthquake as during a magnitude 4 earthquake. The total amount of energy released by the earthquake, however, goes up by a factor of 32. There are many different ways that magnitude is measured from seismograms because each method only works over a limited

range of magnitudes and with different types of seismometers. For more information, see the U.S. Geological Survey (USGS) glossary, earthquake.usgs.gov/learn/glossary.

29   The data in this paragraph are from earthquake.usgs.gov/regional/nca/1906/18april/index.php; Fradkin, *Great Earthquake and Firestorms;* and Simon Winchester, *A Crack in the Edge of the World: America and the Great California Earthquake of 1906* (New York: HarperCollins Publishers, 2005). See also the Virtual Museum of the City of San Francisco, 'The Great 1906 Earthquake and Fire," sfmuseum.org/1906/06.html.

30   As quoted in John Carey, *Eyewitness to History* (New York: Avon Books, 1987), 418–419.

31   Throughout this chapter and the next, the author avoids citing dollar amounts for damage. Even using supposed scales and algorithms, it is virtually impossible, for example, to compare the destruction in San Francisco in 1906 with that in New Orleans in 2005. (In a sense, it also may be demeaning to disaster victims to call one event "more costly" than another.) For further discussion, see Fradkin, *Great Earthquake and Firestorms,* 346; and Winchester, *Crack in the Edge of the World,* 288n.

32   Fradkin, *Great Earthquake and Firestorms,* 9.

33   Winchester, *Crack in the Edge of the World,* 228–229.

34   Quoted in ibid., 229.

35   As cited in Fradkin, *Great Earthquake and Firestorms,* 37, 237.

36   Winchester, *Crack in the Edge of the World,* 288.

37   Stephen Tobriner, "An EERI Reconnaissance Report: Damage to San Francisco in the 1906 Earthquake: A Centennial Perspective," *Earthquake Spectra* 22, no. S2 (2006): S38.

38   Charles Scawthorn, Thomas Denis O'Rourke, and F. T. Blackburn, "The 1906 San Francisco Earthquake and Fire: Enduring Lessons for Fire Protection and Water Supply," *Earthquake Spectra* 22, no. S2 (2006): S136, sparisk.com/documents/06Spectra1906SFEQandFire-EnduringLessons CRSTDOFTB.pdf.

39   Winchester, *Crack in the Edge of the World,* 302.

40   See Tobriner, "EERI Reconnaissance Report."

41   Gladys Hansen, "Who Perished: A List of Persons Who Died as a Result of the Great Earthquake and Fire in San Francisco on April 18, 1906" (San Francisco: San Francisco Archives, 1980), sfmuseum.org/ perished/index.html; and Gladys Hansen and Emmet Condon, *Denial of Disaster: The Untold Story and Photographs of the San Francisco Earthquake and Fire of 1906* (San Francisco: Robert A. Cameron, 1989). For further information regarding Hansen's analysis and a more general discussion concerning the number of lives lost because of the earthquake, see Fradkin, *Great Earthquake and Firestorms,* 190–191.

42   For different views and estimates, see Winchester, *Crack in the Edge of the World,* 309; Fradkin, *Great Earthquake and Firestorms,* 140ff.; and Lucien G. Canton, "San Francisco 1906 and 2006: An Emergency Management Perspective," *Earthquake Spectra* 22, no. S2 (2006): S159–S182.

43   Fradkin, *Great Earthquake and Firestorms,* 205, 207.

44   For an excellent analysis of the response to this disaster and a summary of lessons learned, see Canton, "San Francisco 1906 and 2006," who also draws parallels between the 1900 Galveston Hurricane and Hurricane Katrina in New Orleans in 2005.

45   New Orleans's vulnerability to a devastating hurricane and flooding was similarly identified prior to Hurricane Katrina. Disaster sociologist Shirley Laska wrote in November 2004 about a major hurricane striking New Orleans: "Should this disaster become a reality, it would undoubtedly be one of the greatest disasters, if not the greatest, to hit the United States, with estimated costs exceeding 100 billion dollars. According to the American Red Cross, such an event could be even more devastating than a major earthquake in California. Survivors would have to endure conditions never before experienced in a North American disaster." See Shirley Laska, "What If Hurricane Ivan Had Not Missed New Orleans?" *Natural Hazards Observer* 29, no. 2 (2004): 6.

46   See Tobriner, "EERI Reconnaissance Report," for a thorough analysis of various kinds of structural failure due to the earthquake.

47   As cited in Winchester, *Crack in the Edge of the World,* 285.

48   Ibid., 357–358.

49   Scawthorn, O'Rourke, and Blackburn, "1906 San Francisco Earthquake and Fire," S135, S139.

50   Fradkin, *Great Earthquake and Firestorms,* 19.

51   Canton, "San Francisco 1906 and 2006," S172.

52   Ibid., S172–S173. Of the situation in New Orleans following Hurricane Katrina in 2005, Canton writes: "The impression given by the media was that there was wide-scale looting. But there is a significant difference between the criminal act of stealing for personal gain and the actions of a disaster victim seeking essential supplies or a property owner salvaging whatever he or she can. Many of the reports of looting in San Francisco following the 1906 catastrophe were later found to be unsubstantiated, as appears may now be the case in Hurricane Katrina."

53   Ibid., S173.

54   Fradkin, Great Earthquake and Firestorms, 186, 206, 207.

55   Ibid., 59, 235.

56   Ibid., 289.

57   Ibid., 295.

58   Winchester, Crack in the Edge of the World, 330.

59   Fradkin, Great Earthquake and Firestorms, 197.

60   Tobriner, "EERI Reconnaissance Report"; and Jeanne B. Perkins et al., "A Retrospective on the 1906 Earthquake's Impact on Bay Area and California Public Policy," Earthquake Spectra 22, no. S2 (2006): S237–S259.

61   Charles Smith, "What San Francisco Didn't Learn from the '06 Quake," San Francisco Chronicle, April 15, 2006, sfgate.com/cgi-bin/article.cgi?f=/c/a/2006/04/15/HOGQ9I7P2T1.DTL; and Ted Steinberg, Acts of God: The Unnatural History of Natural Disaster in America (New York: Oxford University Press, 2000), 36–37.

62   Scawthorn, O'Rourke, and Blackburn, "1906 San Francisco Earthquake and Fire," S145.

63   Ibid., S146.

64   "Smith, "What San Francisco Didn't Learn."

65   Steinberg, Acts of God, 25.

66   Perkins et al., "Retrospective on the 1906 Earthquake's Impact," S237.

67   Perry Byerly, "History of the Seismological Society of America," seismosoc.org/inside/history/byerly_history.php.

68   Perkins et al., "Retrospective on the 1906 Earthquake's Impact."

69   Robert Reitherman, "The Effects of the 1906 Earthquake in California on Research and Education," Earthquake Spectra 22, no. S2 (2006): S207–S236.

70   USGS, "Is a Powerful Quake Likely to Strike in the Next 30 Years?" USGS Fact Sheet 039-03 (2003), walrus.wr.usgs.gov/infobank/programs/html/factsheets/pdfs/2003_0039_FS.pdf. Note that this report has been updated and is superseded by Edward H. Field, Kevin R. Milner, and the 2007 Working Group on California Earthquake Probabilities, "Forecasting California's Earthquakes; What Can We Expect in the Next 30 Years?" USGS Fact Sheet 2008-3027 (2008), pubs.usgs.gov/fs/2008/3027/. In the study reported there, however, the probability of a magnitude 6.7 quake in the San Francisco region in the next 30 years remains 63 percent.

71   Charles A. Kircher et al., "When the Big One Strikes Again: Estimated Losses due to a Repeat of the 1906 San Francisco Earthquake," Earthquake Spectra 22, no. S2 (2006): S297.

72   USGS, "Is a Powerful Quake Likely to Strike?"

73   For further discussion of potential origins, see Jeffery K. Taubenberger and David M. Morens, "1918 Influenza: The Mother of All Pandemics," Emerging Infectious Diseases 12, no. 1 (2006): 15–22, cdc.gov/ncidod/EID/vol12no01/05-0979.htm; John M. Barry, The Great Influenza: The Story of the Deadliest Pandemic in History (New York: Penguin Books, 2005), 456 ff.; and PBS, "Secrets of the Dead," pbs.org/wnet/secrets/previous_seasons/case_killerflu/index.html.

74   As cited in Barry, Great Influenza, 313.

75   See Molly Billings, "The Influenza Pandemic of 1918" (June 1997; modified February 2005), virus.stanford.edu/uda.

76   Taubenberger and Morens, "Mother of All Pandemics." As with most large disasters, accurate numbers are difficult to determine. Early estimates indicated that the pandemic resulted in 21 million deaths worldwide, but experts today believe that it killed at least 50 million and perhaps as many as 100 million people. For further information about problems inherent in identifying the correct number, see Board on Global Health, The Threat of Pandemic Influenza: Are We Ready?

Workshop Summary, ed. Stacey L. Knobler et al. (Washington, D.C.: National Academies Press, 2005); and Barry, *Great Influenza,* 396 ff. For statistics regarding deaths worldwide, see Barry, *Great Influenza,* 359–365.

77   See PBS, "Timeline: Influenza across America in 1918," pbs.org/wgbh/americanexperience/features/timeline/influenza; and Barry, *Great Influenza,* 238.

78   Taubenberger and Morens, "Mother of All Pandemics."

79   Barry, *Great Influenza,* 309, 310.

80   See "The Medical and Scientific Conceptions of Influenza," virus.stanford.edu/uda/fluscimed.html.

81   Quoted in "The Public Health Response," virus.stanford.edu/uda/fluresponse.html.

82   American Red Cross Museum, "Natural Disasters and War Continue to Command Red Cross Attention," redcross.org/museum/history/00-19_b.asp.

83   Billings, "Influenza Pandemic of 1918."

84   The first drugs to ameliorate influenza symptoms were introduced in the latter part of the twentieth century, when several antiviral drugs were approved by the U.S. Food and Drug Administration for the treatment of flu. In 2000, one of those drugs (oseltamivir, better known by its trade name Tamiflu) was approved as an influenza *preventative.* There remains no drug that is able to eliminate the symptoms of flu (fever, aching joints, headache, etc.); most drugs merely reduce the duration of the disease by one day—and only if administered within the first two days of onset.

85   Taubenberger and Morens, "Mother of All Pandemics."

86   N. R. Grist, *British Medical Journal* (December 22–29, 1979): 1632.

87   Barry, *Great Influenza,* 455–456.

88   Caroline Ash and Leslie Roberts, "Influenza: The State of Our Ignorance," *Science* 312, no. 5772 (2006): 379, sciencemag.org/content/312/5772/379.full?sid=e384fd66-2adc-41ed-88e6-816b919eb1b2.

89   For a country-by-country breakdown of these numbers, see the World Health Organization, "Cumulative Number of Confirmed Human Cases of Avian Influenza A/(H5N1) Reported to WHO," who.int/csr/disease/avian_influenza/country/cases_table_2010_12_09/en/index.html.

90   Taubenberger and Morens, "Mother of All Pandemics."

91   Barry, *Great Influenza,* 452.

92   "Incident Annexes," dhs.gov/xlibrary/assets/NRP_FullText.pdf, BIO-3 (no longer available online since the National Response Plan has been replaced by the National Response Framework).

93   Department of Homeland Security, *Introducing...National Response Framework* (January 2008), 2, fema.gov/pdf/emergency/nrf/about_nrf.pdf.

94   For a discussion of many of the issues involved, see *Science* 312, no. 5772 (April 21, 2006), sciencemag.org/content/312/5772.toc, particularly the article by Derek J. Smith, "Predictability and Preparedness in Influenza Control," sciencemag.org/content/312/5772/392.full.

95   Barry, *Great Influenza,* 454–455.

96   See U.S. Department of Health and Human Services (HHS), *HHS Pandemic Influenza Plan* (Washington, D.C., November 2005), hhs.gov/pandemicflu/plan; and Homeland Security Council, *National Strategy for Pandemic Influenza: Implementation Plan* (Washington, D.C., May 2006), hosted.ap.org/specials/ interactives/wdc/documents/pandemicinfluenza.pdf. The federal government also maintains a website managed by HHS, pandemicflu.gov, that provides current information and "one-stop access" to U.S. government flu information.

97   Anaheim Colony Historic District, "Orange County and the 1933 Earthquake," anaheimcolony.com/Disaster/quake.htm.

98   Southern California Earthquake Center, "Long Beach Earthquake: 70th Anniversary," scec.org/education/030310longbeach.html.

99   Susan Fatemi and Charles James, "The Long Beach Earthquake of 1933" (National Information Service for Earthquake Engineering, University of California, December 8, 1997), nisee.berkeley.edu/long_beach/long_beach.html.

100 Robert A. Olson, "Legislative Politics and Seismic Safety: California's Early Years and the 'Field Act,' 1925–1933," *Earthquake Spectra* 19, no. 1 (2003):111–131; Perkins et al., "Retrospective on the 1906 Earthquake's Impact," S246.

101 Olson, "Legislative Politics and Seismic Safety," 117.

102   Carl-Henry Geschwind, "Earthquakes and Their Interpretation: The Campaign for Seismic Safety in California, 1906–1933" (Ann Arbor, Mich.: UMI Dissertation Services, 1996), 197, as cited in Olson, "Legislative Politics and Seismic Safety," 115.

103   Fatemi and James, "Long Beach Earthquake of 1933."

Chapter 3

The Expanding Role of the Federal Government: 1927–1950

David Butler

As communities in the United States recovered from one disaster after another, there was a growing body of knowledge about what response and recovery looked like. There was also a growing understanding that the needs of communities and their victims exceeded local capacity. The Great Mississippi Flood of 1927 and the drought that plagued the Dust Bowl for several years during the 1930s captured the attention of the nation. Each of these events demonstrated that disasters and their effects do not respect state boundaries; the financial effects of the drought that plagued the southern Great Plains during the Depression rippled across the nation.

Throughout this period, federal government response continued to be reactive and focus driven, but it was becoming increasingly common. From 1933 to 1937, disaster relief legislation emerged as part of President Franklin D. Roosevelt's New Deal administration. Beginning in 1934, Congress authorized the Reconstruction Finance Corporation to grant loans to rebuild public facilities damaged by disasters. Subsequent legislation in 1937 created the Disaster Loan Corporation. These programs eventually evolved into the Small Business Administration disaster loan program, which still exists today.

This chapter looks at three major disasters: the Great Mississippi Flood; the drought and storms that became known as the Dust Bowl; and the Texas City explosions, which occurred just after World War II. The explosions in Texas City captured the nation's attention not only because of the sudden onset and immediate death toll, but also because the event vividly demonstrated the risk that accidents and other human-induced threats pose to communities. The chapter explores why and how these disasters became focusing events. In particular, the discussion examines how these events prompted the federal government, as well as state and local governments, to take a greater role in disaster prevention, response, and recovery—a gradual transformation that resulted in the passage of major federal disaster legislation in 1950.

The Great Mississippi Flood of 1927

Communities along the Mississippi have been involved in flood control—primarily levee construction—since 1726, when residents of New Orleans began building levees to protect the city from the rising river. The federal government's involvement dates back to 1824, when the U.S. Supreme Court ruled in *Gibbons v. Ogden* that it was constitutional for the federal government to finance and construct river improvements. Within two months of the ruling, Congress had appropriated funds and authorized the U.S. Army Corps of Engineers (USACE) to remove certain navigation obstructions from the Ohio and Mississippi Rivers. As flooding of the Mississippi River basin continued in the ensuing decades, the federal government—primarily through USACE—became increasingly involved in flood control efforts. In the Swamp Land Acts of 1849 and 1850, for example, Congress transferred "swamp and overflow land" along the lower Mississippi River from federal ownership to state governments on the condition that the states use revenue from the sale of the lands to build levees and drainage channels. In 1850, Congress commissioned two surveys of the Mississippi River delta, "with such investigations as may lead to determine the most practicable plan for securing it from inundation."[1] These surveys ultimately led to a federal policy of using levees—and only levees—to control flooding.

Continued flooding of the river led in 1879 to the creation of the Mississippi River Commission to regulate and coordinate the efforts of the many private and local entities, such as levee districts, that were independently trying to control the river. According to the Association of State Floodplain Managers (ASFPM), "To some, 1879 marked the turning point in the long battle to garner federal support for flood control. From that time forward, Congress gradually increased federal government responsibility to develop flood control throughout the nation."[2]

By 1890, the entire lower Mississippi valley from St. Louis to the Gulf of Mexico had been divided into state and local levee districts. In 1926, just one year before the Great Flood, USACE publicly declared that the levee system would prevent future floods in the Mississippi River basin—an assertion that would quickly prove false.

Beginning in 1926 the Mississippi drainage basin, which stretches from New York to Montana and includes tributaries in thirty-one states and southern Canada, received unprecedented precipitation. Heavy rains began in the summer and continued through the winter. On April 16, 1927, a 1,200-foot section of the levee collapsed thirty miles south of the confluence of the Ohio and Mississippi Rivers, flooding 175,000 acres. In the days to come, much of the levee system

The refugee camp at Vicksburg, Mississippi, was a relatively pleasant camp on high ground. Many refugees lived in such camps for months with inadequate shelter and food until the waters of the Great Mississippi Flood of 1927 receded. Photo courtesy of the National Oceanic and Atmospheric Administration.

along the lower Mississippi failed, affecting areas in Arkansas, Illinois, Kentucky, Louisiana, Mississippi, Missouri, and Tennessee. By May, the Mississippi River south of Memphis, Tennessee, spanned sixty miles.

As in all great catastrophes, the exact numbers of deaths, injuries, and homeless people resulting from the flood, as well as the precise amount of destruction, is uncertain. The American Red Cross reported 246 deaths, but the actual toll may have been several times greater. An estimated 700,000 people were rendered homeless, and more than 300,000 victims spent several months in more than 150 Red Cross camps hastily constructed following the flood. Another 300,000 people received food and other assistance outside the camps. Approximately 200,000 buildings were damaged or destroyed, and at least 20,000 square miles of land (or as much as 27,000 square miles, by some accounts) were flooded. In a comprehensive history of flooding in the United States, the ASFPM called the 1927 flood of the Mississippi River "the greatest natural disaster to befall [the United States] in terms of total human misery and suffering."[3]

The Response

Kevin R. Kosar, a Congressional Research Service analyst, describes the federal government's response to the 1927 flood:

> [It] was a mixture of pre-New Deal minimalist federal governance and… "governing by network." The federal government would make no immediate appropriations to the affected area. Instead, it would utilize federal resources and coordinate networks of federal, state, private, and not-for-profit organizations to deliver relief services. The President's Cabinet would direct the relief effort in close consultation with the American National Red Cross…. Thus, flood response policy was centralized, but its execution was decentralized.[4]

In *Rising Tide: The Great Mississippi Flood of 1927 and How It Changed America,* John M. Barry recounts two stories regarding how two different communities—Greenville, in the delta cotton-growing region of Mississippi, and New Orleans, farther downriver—responded to the flood.[5] Each is instructive because of the light it sheds on American history and the lessons it offers for today's emergency managers.

In Greenville, African Americans were compelled, sometimes at gunpoint, to maintain the levees protecting the town. More than 13,000 African Americans around Greenville were evacuated to the crest of an unbroken levee and stranded there for days without food or clean water, even as boats arrived to evacuate white women and children. Meanwhile, armed members of the National Guard patrolled the levee and refused to allow anyone to enter or leave without a pass. In the town itself, whites stayed on the upper floors of offices and hotels, while African Americans were crowded into warehouses, mills, and stores. A report of the Colored Advisory Commission describes the plight of these people:

> We found numerous instances where the colored people, as a result of years of living under a semi-peonage system, in many communities were afraid to ask for the things to which they were entitled under the Red Cross. In every community we visited we found some colored people of this type and many times their fear caused them a great deal of suffering.[6]

As the flood approached New Orleans, the city's rich and powerful residents (including Isaac Cline, head of the New Orleans weather bureau and previously the head of the weather bureau in Galveston at the time of the 1900 hurricane) had thirty tons of dynamite detonated to breach a levee downriver so that pressure would be relieved on the city's levees. The New Orleans oligarchs promised to compensate the trappers and other rural inhabitants inundated by the breach, but they all but reneged on this promise and paid no reparations to local residents. Moreover, the breach turned out to be unnecessary; major breaks upstream had already relieved pressure and minimized the risk.

The American Red Cross carried most of the financial burden of recovery from the flood and normally would have been responsible for managing relief

Greenville, Mississippi, April 27, 1927. Photo courtesy of the National Oceanic and Atmospheric Administration.

operations. Given the enormity of the flood, however, President Calvin Coolidge named Secretary of Commerce Herbert Hoover to head a quasi-governmental commission that included cabinet members and representatives of the American Red Cross. With near-absolute authority to call on the resources of federal departments as well as other state and local entities and the private sector, Hoover oversaw and coordinated the response—the biggest disaster relief effort in U.S. history to date.[7] The response blended federal, state, local, and private resources and was generally regarded as efficient and successful.

The concentration of power, combined with minimum accountability at all levels, caused problems, however. African American sharecroppers fared the worst. In some cases, relief and recovery supplies were given to the landowners for whom the sharecroppers worked, some of whom charged the sharecroppers for the supplies. Compounding these problems, Hoover had political ambitions—his eye was on the presidential nomination in the upcoming 1928 elections—and he was determined that any unsatisfactory conditions that might occur be hidden from public scrutiny. He used his influence and promises of future political patronage to African American community leaders to keep the media from learning about the deplorable situation in the refugee camps. His subsequent election was largely due to the positive publicity and praise he received from managing

The Mississippi levee below New Orleans was dynamited to reduce pressure on the levees within the city. However, the action was unnecessary (upstream breaches had already minimized the risk to the city) and resulted in the flooding of poor trappers and other rural residents downstream. Photo courtesy of the National Oceanic and Atmospheric Administration.

the flood response. But he failed to keep his promises to African Americans; as a result, their allegiance began to shift from the Republican to the Democratic Party.

The flood, then, had an impact not only on disaster management but also on the political and social fabric of the nation. Barry concludes his examination of the 1927 Great Mississippi Flood as follows:

> [The flood] penetrated to the core of the nation, washed away surface, and revealed the nation's character. Then it tested that character and changed it. It marked the end of a way of seeing the world, and possibly the end of that world itself.... It shifted perceptions of the role and responsibility of the federal government—calling for a great expansion—and shattered the myth of a quasi-feudal bond between Delta blacks and the southern aristocracy.... It accelerated the great migration of blacks north. And it altered both southern and national politics.[8]

The Effect of the Great Mississippi Flood on Federal Floodplain Management

The 1927 flood demonstrated the inadequacies of the federal government's "levees-only" policy. Moreover, whereas flood management had been viewed primarily as a local issue, the Mississippi Flood demonstrated the limitations of an approach that relied on local governments, levee districts, and private efforts, and the public began to warm to the idea of a federal flood control program to address flooding in the Mississippi River basin and protect their lives and property. After all, the 1927 flood involved drainage from far outside the lower Mississippi valley. Federal legislators further recognized "that locals were unable to finance effective flood control measures and that local governments were already making enormous contributions to flood control."[9]

In the Flood Control Act of 1928, Congress abandoned the levees-only approach. The act provided for a partnership between the federal and local governments for the construction and maintenance of control structures. But while the federal allocation was significant—more than local governments had paid for flood control during the previous 200 years—the legislation held far greater significance: "The law set a precedent of direct, comprehensive, and vastly expanded federal involvement in local affairs," explains Barry. "In the broadest sense, this precedent reflected a major shift in what Americans considered the proper role and obligations of the national government, a shift that both presaged and prepared the way for far greater changes that would soon come."[10] Congress appropriated $10 million for relief and reconstruction associated with the 1927 flood, but it spent thirty times this amount—$300 million—the following year on flood control projects along the lower Mississippi.

Federal involvement continued to expand in the ensuing years. In the wake of devastating floods in New England and the Ohio River basin, Congress passed the Flood Control Act of 1936, declaring "flood control a 'proper' federal activity in the national interest" and establishing a national policy of flood control.[11] The legislation passed easily—in part because, in the midst of the Great Depression, it supported numerous public works programs. The legislation launched

> a two-pronged attack on the problem of reducing flood damages. On one side, the Department of Agriculture would develop plans to reduce runoff and retain more rainfall where it fell. On the other, the Corps [of Engineers] would develop engineering plans for downstream projects. In theory, the plan required cooperation between the two agencies but included no mechanism to ensure coordination. In reality, the major work fell to the Corps.[12]

Not surprisingly, more flooding led to more legislation. Congress passed additional flood control acts in 1938 and 1941, authorizing more construction and increasing the federal cost share for dams and reservoirs to 100 percent. Between 1936 and 1952, Congress appropriated more than $11 billion for flood control projects.

However, some floodplain managers, engineers, and scholars realized that this reliance on engineering and construction to mitigate floods was, in its own way, a policy as narrow-minded (and dangerous) as the earlier levees-only approach of USACE. Studies demonstrated that, despite structural measures to control floods, monetary losses continued to grow. Critics warned that with the country's increasingly urban population, the national flood damage potential was growing faster than structural solutions could control.[13] As one researcher writes, "Federal flood control projects in fact often made matters worse by providing a false sense of security that attracted new development to floodplains."[14] Thus, critics called for a broader approach that considered all possible means to mitigate flooding, including land use planning, zoning, restrictions on the use of land in flood zones, flood proofing, and insurance.

A few members of President Roosevelt's administration espoused these ideas in the 1930s. Perhaps the best known was Gilbert White, a young geographer from the University of Chicago, who in his PhD dissertation described the prevailing national policy as "essentially one of protecting the occupants of floodplains against floods, of aiding them when they suffer flood losses, and of encouraging more intensive use of floodplains."[15] White advocated taking a broader approach. "Dealing with floods in all their capricious and violent aspects," he stated, "is a problem in part of adjusting human occupancy to the floodplain environment so as to utilize most effectively the natural resources of the floodplain, and at the same time, of applying feasible and practicable measures for minimizing the detrimental impacts of floods."[16]

It took several decades for such ideas to be embraced, but today they influence and shape the approach to flood control at all levels of government. For example, the National Flood Insurance Program, administered by the Federal Emergency Management Agency (FEMA), requires local governments to institute effective floodplain management measures, and USACE now considers a wider range of approaches than just structural measures, such as levees and dams, to reduce flood losses. Still, the economic, social, institutional, and political forces that lead people to live in floodplains (and governments and government agencies to promote structural "solutions") remain powerful and intractable. An equitable national flood control policy has yet to be devised and instituted.

Management Implications for Emergency Managers

Like most other great disasters of the twentieth century, the 1927 flood exposed problems and inequities in society. Wealthy white citizens fared far better than African Americans and other poor minorities. The manifold reasons for this differential effect are not always attributable to blatant racism or abuse of power, however. Rather, wealthier residents in almost any community tend to live in places that are less vulnerable to natural hazards and in structures that are better able to withstand the damage wrought by such hazards. In addition, wealthier citizens have more resources to respond to and recover from an event. They have cars in which they can leave when a threat occurs, and they can afford other means of transportation if needed. They have friends and family in other parts of the community, state, or nation with the means to take them in. Their jobs are likely to be secure; and they have savings, insurance, and other resources to fall back on if work is disrupted. Moreover, they know how government agencies work, and they have relationships with banks and other financial institutions should they need to obtain loans or other financing.

The response and recovery issues following Hurricane Katrina in 2005, discussed in detail in Chapter 7, reveal that the issues of class and race that emerged during events of almost a century ago are still very much a part of the American social fabric. The fundamental lesson for emergency managers is clear: Any plans for preparedness, warning, evacuation, response, recovery, or long-term mitigation, as well as any actions, must consider *all* members of a community. This includes not only ethnic minorities but other groups as well—women, children, the disabled, the elderly, those with limited proficiency in English, and individuals housed in institutions such as hospitals or prisons. These people cannot or will not respond to the information and actions directed toward able-bodied, middle-class citizens with all the resources that "able-bodied" and "middle-class" imply. A modern emergency manager must consider the needs of the entire community.

The Dust Bowl

The 1930s Dust Bowl was a different species of disaster. It did involve some horrific dust storms that would qualify today as quick-onset events requiring immediate emergency response. Lawrence Svobida, who wrote an eyewitness account of the Dust Bowl in Kansas, describes these dust storms:

> A cloud is seen to be approaching from a distance of many miles. Already it has the banked appearance of a cumulus cloud, but it is black instead of white, and it hangs low, seeming to hug the earth. Instead of being slow to change its form, it appears to be rolling on itself from the crest downward. As it sweeps onward, the landscape is progressively blotted out. Birds fly in terror before the storm, and only those that are strong of wing may escape. The smaller birds fly until they are exhausted, then fall to the ground, to share the fate of the thousands of jack rabbits which perish from suffocation.[17]

Yet, overall, the Dust Bowl was a slow-onset disaster with very deep-seated ecological and social origins and widespread consequences. Researcher Richard A. Warrick compares it to more common disasters: "As opposed to the three-minute impact time of an earthquake, or the two-day impact time of a hurricane, the impact of a drought can cover many years. In addition, it is difficult to state precisely when the effects and their associated 'costs' begin, or when they cease."[18] In his award-winning analysis, historian Donald Worster maintains that the Dust Bowl was the worst ecological catastrophe in U.S. history.[19]

Severe drought and soil erosion first occurred in the Great Plains in eastern Montana and the Dakotas at the start of the 1930s. While drought was widespread during this decade and struck every state in the Union except Maine and Vermont, historians generally define the Dust Bowl as the drought that plagued the southern Great Plains—specifically, southwestern Kansas, southeastern Colorado, northwest New Mexico, and the panhandles of Oklahoma and Texas—from the early 1930s to 1940. The Oklahoma panhandle was at the center of the Dust Bowl, which encompassed almost 100 million acres. By 1935, the landscape there had become, in the words of one reporter, "'a vast desert, with miniature shifting dunes of sand.'"[20] By 1938, the peak year for wind erosion, 10 million acres had lost at least the upper five inches of topsoil and another 13.5 million acres had lost at least two and a half inches. The average acre lost more than 400 tons of dirt. The soil drifted; in some cases it blew so far to the east that plumes of dust were witnessed in the skies over the Atlantic shore. At its height, the Dust Bowl involved sixty to seventy dust storms per year.

Aside from being an ecological and economic catastrophe, the blizzards of sand and dirt presented a major health hazard. Many people contracted upper respiratory diseases. Among the most vulnerable were the elderly and infants. To help handle the health risks, the Red Cross set up six emergency hospitals in Colorado, Kansas, and Texas and staffed them with its own nurses.

Thus, like the 1918 flu pandemic, the Dust Bowl severely affected human beings. To a lesser degree it affected structures and other personal property, although clearly one type of personal property—the land itself—was severely damaged. Hence, the effects can be classified as environmental as well as social and economic.[21]

Dust storms, like this one approaching Stratford, Texas, plagued areas throughout and beyond the Midwest in the 1930s. Photo courtesy of the National Oceanic and Atmospheric Administration.

The ongoing drought devastated crops, and the people of the Great Plains, namely farmers, suffered accordingly. The social and economic systems on which the farmers depended and which depended on them—from banks and businesses to schools and families—suffered as well. The severe economic hardship that resulted from the Dust Bowl uprooted many families in and beyond Oklahoma, who migrated in search of a livelihood. Some settled in a nearby county; more moved thousands of miles away. Thus, the effects of the drought rippled across the United States.

Because the Dust Bowl occurred during the Depression and because its effects were integrated into the regional and national economy, it is impossible to accurately estimate its economic consequences. The National Drought Mitigation Center (NDMC) calls the Dust Bowl one of the greatest economic disasters in the history of the United States but says that "determining the direct and indirect costs is a difficult task because of the broad impacts of drought, the event's close association with the Great Depression, the fast revival of the economy with the start of World War II, and the lack of adequate economic models for evaluating losses at that time."[22] Worster concludes that "the financial cost of the 1934 drought alone amounted to one-half the money the United States had put into World War I. By 1936, farm losses had reached $25 million a day, and more than 2 million farmers were drawing relief checks."[23]

The Dust Bowl was unique in at least one other way. Perhaps in large part because it came on top of the Great Depression, it soon passed into American culture through John Steinbeck's *The Grapes of Wrath,* the photographs of Dorothea Lange, the songs of Woody Guthrie, and other works, all of which told the story of the crisis and its victims. The Dust Bowl was soon seen as a landmark social crisis that revealed social inequities and failures in the prevailing economic system and, perhaps, in humanity itself. Unsurpassed by subsequent events, the Dust Bowl of the 1930s remains the archetypical drought disaster.

The Causes of the Dust Bowl

Many researchers have identified the "causes" of the widespread drought that became known as the Dust Bowl. But experts reach different conclusions, depending in part on whether they define the Dust Bowl as a climatological event, an agricultural failure, a socioeconomic problem, or an ecological catastrophe, and on how they define the "cause" of such an event. Computer modeling undertaken by scientists at the National Aeronautics and Space Administration, for example, focuses on changes in surface temperatures of the Pacific and Atlantic Oceans and on the resulting synergistic effects.[24] Although there was substantial local variability, precipitation decreased markedly in the central United States during the 1930s. In Boise City, Oklahoma, the annual precipitation averaged over 19 inches

Dust buried farms and equipment, killed livestock, ruined crops, and increased the misery of the Depression. Photo courtesy of the U.S. Department of Agriculture.

(2 inches above normal) from 1926 to 1930, but averaged just 11.65 inches from 1931 to 1936. A change of 7 inches in a humid climate may be hardly noticeable, but in a marginal ecological zone like the southern Great Plains, it can—and did—make the difference between a bumper wheat harvest and a disaster.

But the 1930s Dust Bowl was more than a simple climatological event; it was a social disaster with social origins. As with any disaster, where and how people live makes them more or less vulnerable to the physical hazard. Worster points to a number of human actions that contributed to this particular disaster. Agricultural practices—including the destruction of natural grasslands; overgrazing of the range; tillage of poor, marginal soils; and the reduction of agriculture in the region to a single crop (winter wheat)—that worked in more humid regions of the United States proved destructive to the more fragile land of the southern Great Plains. Native grasses were replaced by wheat fields, undermining the Great Plains ecosystem. Dry-land wheat farming had been practiced extensively in the region for less than thirty years when the Dust Bowl hit, and the farmers lacked experience with changes in precipitation.[25] Unwise land use practices were fueled by the desire to maximize production and profits at the expense of taking a long-term view of the effects. Simply put, these agricultural practices led to greater exposure of the soil to wind erosion.

Another contributing factor was the increased use of machinery, including tractors, combines, and disk plows. The disk plow, in particular, increased the vulnerability of soil to erosion much more than the lister, or double-sided plow, which it had replaced. But there was a far greater impact: the widespread use of machinery, along with improved varieties of wheat, led to the cultivation of more and more land—including marginal land. This, in turn, increased the land's exposure to erosion. It also created ever-larger harvests. The increased production (including a bumper crop in 1931) caused a marked drop in the price of wheat. Thus, a destructive cycle emerged: increasing production led to declining prices, which led to even more production. In the race to survive, agricultural producers abandoned soil conservation practices and cultivated increasingly marginal land. Further exacerbating the problem was the need for farmers to increase their profits in order to pay for the capital equipment they needed to increase production. In sum, efficient methods led to overproduction and a drop in prices, which led to even more production.

An Eyewitness Account

When I knew that my crop was irrevocably gone I experienced a deathly feeling which, I hope, can affect a man only once in a lifetime. My dreams and ambitions had been flouted by nature, and my shattered ideals seemed gone forever. The very desire to make a success of my life was gone; the spirit and urge to strive were dead within me. Fate had dealt me a cruel blow above which I felt utterly unable to rise.

— Lawrence Svobida

Source: PBS, American Experience, "Surviving the Dust Bowl," pbs.org/wgbh/amex/dustbowl.

Social and cultural factors further contributed to the disaster. Tenant farming, for instance, created an arrangement in which decisions were made by people who had no permanent interest in the land. Most tenant farmers sought to maximize their annual yield and had little concern for the potential long-term effects on the soil. Further, tenant farmers tended to be a migratory population, moving from farm to farm. Many had no attachment to or understanding of the land they toiled. An increasing number of farms were owned by "suitcase farmers," who lived and worked elsewhere and visited their land only during planting and harvesting—if at all. Finally, agribusiness had taken hold in the area. Corporations working the land on a large scale sought primarily to maximize profits.

Collectively, these social circumstances alienated farmers from the land they worked, and they lost their connection to it. Examining deeper causes of the Dust Bowl, Worster argues that this alienation was a direct result of the American culture and economic system. "The Dust Bowl," he writes, "was the inevitable outcome of a culture that deliberately, self-consciously, set itself that task of dominating and exploiting the land for all it was worth."[26] He goes on to claim that the Dust Bowl was a direct result of the American economic system—capitalism. "It came about because the expansionary energy of the United States had finally encountered a volatile, marginal land, destroying the delicate ecological balance that had evolved there," he explains. "What brought [farmers] to the region was a social system, a set of values, an economic order. There is no word that so fully sums up those elements as 'capitalism.'"[27]

Yet it would be a mistake to place the blame solely on capitalism or broader aspects of the American culture. Droughts have occurred in many places where capitalism is not the prevailing economic principle. In fact, Worster himself notes that drought occurred in the Soviet Union in 1921–1922 and again in 1932–1934, resulting in widespread famine and the deaths of millions of people. A situation much like the Dust Bowl also occurred in the Soviet Union from 1954 to 1965, when, in an effort to massively increase wheat production, the country plowed almost 100 million acres in Kazakhstan and eastern Russia. Subsequent drought led to severe wind erosion and the destruction of the land.

In a 1986 article, Harry C. McDean questions Worster's conclusions, noting that the circumstances of the American Dust Bowl were unique in both time and place.[28] McDean argues that the Dust Bowl was not the inevitable result of a capitalist society. Throughout time, farmers in the United States and elsewhere have adopted systems and practices that are more sympathetic to the land. In other capitalist agrarian regions, ecological disaster has not occurred.

Regardless, Worster's analysis contains an essential truth about disasters: the catastrophe is the sum of a physical hazard and a complex social structure that put residents (some more than others) at risk. Any society, culture, or economic system that heedlessly seeks to maximize production without concern for either the welfare of the land or the safety of its inhabitants can and will suffer similar catastrophes. Furthermore, the penalty for such folly will be manifest first where the environment is fragile and resources are limited.

Prior Events, Response, and Recovery

The dry period that led to the Dust Bowl was not unprecedented. Droughts had occurred in the southern Great Plains in 1892 and 1912; at that time, however, the sod had not yet been "busted" and native grasses for the most part remained intact, so the soil was less vulnerable to erosion. Droughts have also occurred since the Dust Bowl. The area experienced a more severe drought (by climatological measures) in the mid-1950s, and major dry periods continue to this day.

The response to the severe dust storms of the 1930s was much like the response to any sudden-onset emergency, but the response to the overall drought at the individual, local, and national levels was different. Worster describes the reaction of those who lived in the affected region:

> The pattern of reaction among plainsmen went something like this: fail to anticipate drought, underestimate its duration when it comes, expect rain momentarily, deny that they are as hard hit as outsiders believe, defend the region against critics, admit that some help would be useful, demand that the government act and act quickly, insist that federal aid be given without strings and when and where local residents want it, vote for those politicians who confirm the people's optimism and pooh-pooh the need for major reform, resent interference by the bureaucrats, eagerly await the return of "normalcy" when the plains will once more proceed along the road of steady progress.[29]

Despite the denial of a recurring hazard and the sense of frontier independence that was prevalent in the area at the time, the severe economic hardship brought about by the drought during the Depression changed the general attitude regarding aid. More than 20 percent of rural families received federal relief during the Dust Bowl. Moreover, the federal government's role shifted. The NDMC explains:

> [M]any measures were undertaken to relieve the direct impacts of droughts and to reduce the region's vulnerability to the dry conditions. Many of these measures were initiated by the federal government, a relatively new practice. Before the 1930s drought, federal aid had generally been withheld in emergency situations in favor of individual and self-reliant approaches. This began to change with the development of the Great Depression in the late 1920s and the 1933 inauguration of President Franklin Delano Roosevelt. The Depression helped "soften deep-rooted, hard-line attitudes of free enterprise, individualism, and the passive role of the government," thus paving the way for Roosevelt's New Deal programs, which in turn provided a framework for drought relief programs for the Great Plains.[30]

As the Depression and drought continued, the federal government adopted a wide-ranging and long-term approach. Federal drought relief programs provided emergency supplies, cash, and livestock feed and transport to maintain the basic functioning of livelihoods and farms and ranches; established health care facilities and supplies to meet emergency medical needs; established higher tariffs, government-based markets for farm goods, and loan funds for farm market maintenance and business rehabilitation; and provided the supplies, technology, and technical advice needed to research, implement, and promote appropriate land management strategies.[31]

Roosevelt's administration established numerous agencies and programs to address the hardships of the Great Depression. The plethora of agencies and programs involved in the federal response, however, often resulted in contradictory goals and approaches, interagency conflicts, and competition for funds.

Among the first actions Roosevelt took was the creation of the Agricultural Adjustment Administration (AAA), which probably had a greater effect on farmers in the Dust Bowl than any other federal program. The AAA's principal approach to the problems created by the drought was to create "planned scarcity" by reducing agricultural production. To accomplish this, the AAA managed a program whereby wheat farmers could receive payments for not planting part of their previously productive land. From 1933 to 1937, these payments for not working the land provided many Dust Bowl farmers with their only source of income.[32] They also laid the groundwork for today's federal farm policy, which involves a complex and often controversial system of price supports and subsidies.

Initially, the federal government focused on general economic problems. For instance, the Farm Credit Administration, created in 1933, was charged with refinancing farm mortgages and making low-interest production and marketing loans to farmers. As the drought progressed, however, the administration began to directly address issues related to agriculture and land use. On June 9, 1934, Congress approved President Roosevelt's comprehensive $525 million drought program, making funding available for emergency livestock and feed programs, seed purchase, the purchase of submarginal lands, relief for farmers, and assistance for displaced residents. In August, the federal government formed the Drought Relief Committee chaired by the secretary of the U.S. Department of Agriculture (USDA) and with members from other federal agencies responsible for providing relief. Subcommittees were established to carry out specific tasks, including drought area designation, livestock purchase, and feed provision.

The Taylor Grazing Act of 1935 and the subsequent land use project represented further efforts on the part of the federal government to reverse the damage done to the land by overuse and to purchase submarginal lands in order to return them to their natural state. Such actions further increased direct federal government involvement in the stewardship of the land. At the same time, the USDA's Soil Conservation Service (SCS) worked with private citizens to help them preserve and manage their land for greater productivity. The Civilian Conservation Corps—another New Deal program designed to provide jobs—worked with the SCS to conduct soil conservation projects, including the creation of shelterbelts, which entailed the planting of rows of trees to decrease wind erosion.

The federal government continued to seek ways to provide relief to those affected by the drought. In January 1935, the administration formed the Drought Relief Service to coordinate relief activities, including the purchase of cattle in designated drought-affected counties. More than half the animals were deemed unfit for consumption and destroyed; the remaining cattle were given to the Federal Surplus Relief Corporation for food distribution to needy families. An account of the program concludes, "Although it was difficult for farmers to give up their herds, the cattle slaughter program helped many of them avoid bankruptcy.

The government cattle buying program was a God-send to many farmers, as they could not afford to keep their cattle, and the government paid a better price than they could obtain in local markets."[33]

On April 8, 1935, President Roosevelt signed the Emergency Relief Appropriation Act, which earmarked $4.8 billion for the creation of government assistance programs. Prior to this legislation, most New Deal programs provided relief payments to qualified applicants, but this act ushered in a new approach by requiring many aid recipients to work on public projects. Several new employment programs, including the Works Progress Administration and the National Youth Administration, were put in place to provide jobs.

Federal Disaster Mitigation

Flood control and New Deal programs represented the first federal disaster mitigation policies. By the end of the Depression, one out of every three or four farmers in the area affected by the Dust Bowl had accepted government relief at one time or another, "with tenants represented most heavily and smaller operators more common than large ones."[34] In short, federal policy regarding the drought and its economic consequences soon became a mix of disaster relief and disaster mitigation or prevention.

Some of the programs that took seed during the Depression continue today. The NDMC notes that the Roosevelt era "marked the beginning of large-scale

The federal government initiated a host of new programs to help Dust Bowl farmers deal with drought. Here, a Civilian Conservation Corps worker is planting seedling trees to form a shelterbelt to prevent soil erosion. Photo courtesy of the National Oceanic and Atmospheric Administration.

aid [and] also ushered in some of the first long-term, proactive programs to reduce future vulnerability to drought."[35] Federal agencies, including the Natural Resources Conservation Service, which evolved from the SCS, continue to promote crop diversity, crop rotation, the use of irrigation, the enlargement of reservoir capacity, and other soil conservation measures. Moreover, crop insurance and other measures to mitigate the effects of a drought are widely available. These programs have played a fundamental role in reducing the vulnerability of the nation to drought.

Given the many factors that contributed to the Dust Bowl, one might question whether any of the actions perceived as "solutions" were in reality long-range answers to the fundamental problems that led to that event. Some analysts argue that the actions were simply stopgap measures that delayed the desecration and eventual desertification of large tracts of the Great Plains. To avoid future calamities, the tendency to deny the hazard and the fragility of the soil, the fierce independence that prevented some farmers from heeding advice regarding agricultural practices, and, above all, the tendency to maximize short-term production and profit would have to be counterbalanced by a deeper understanding of and appreciation for the land itself. These ideas took hold among some government leaders during the 1930s. Worster writes:

> A few of Roosevelt's administrators soon began to see that something more was required: a more far-reaching conservation program that would include social and economic changes. Some officials, therefore, began to call for major revisions in the faulty land system; others emphasized new agronomic techniques, rural rehabilitation, more diversified farming, or extensive grassland restoration. But their common theme was that staying meant changing. The Dust Bowl, in this evolving government view, must be explained as a failure in ecological adaptation—as an absence of environmental realism.[36]

A comprehensive plan to achieve such adaptation was prepared by the Great Plains Drought Area Committee and presented to President Roosevelt in December 1936. The 194-page *The Future of the Great Plains: Report of the Great Plains Committee* provided possible strategies—both social and environmental—for overcoming the Dust Bowl and preserving the region.[37] It pointed out some of the fundamental cultural attitudes and economic assumptions that had led to land destruction in the southern Great Plains: the domination of the nature ethic, with the corollary view of natural resources as raw material to be exploited and used; the belief in the inexhaustibility of those natural resources; and the convictions that an owner could do as he liked with his property, that market forces should control production, and that industrial farming represented the way to maximum utility. The report failed to address these underlying causes in its conclusions, however. In an evaluation of the report published fifty years later, geographer Gilbert White writes:

> The committee was perspicacious in listing attitudinal obstacles to readjusting the system of social controls and incentives. It did not know how to gauge their weights in relation to the possible benefits from altering state and federal policies and procedures and it assumed its recommendations would be put into practice. It felt unable to recommend basic modifications in the economic and political organization of the nation.[38]

Worster sees many of the New Deal approaches to the Dust Bowl as failures. "Neither the federal land-use planners nor the ecologists made a lasting impact on the region.... The return of dust-bowl conditions in the 1950s demonstrated, or should have demonstrated, the inability of a technical assistance program by itself to reform the old ethos."[39]

Worster is somewhat more positive when discussing present-day federal policy:

> Even free-market fundamentalists have come around to agree with pro-government planners...that aggressive farming must be controlled to prevent another thirties-style disaster. They have admitted that wind erosion is a human-caused problem and that its solution lies in grassland restoration on a large scale. The nation cannot, it is now agreed on all sides, depend on the farmer's economic self-interest to bring back the grass or prevent erosion. Pragmatism has triumphed over ideology.[40]

White offers a more optimistic viewpoint. He points out unexpected developments—including the creation of high-yield, drought-resistant hybrid species of wheat and corn, and the development of central-pivot irrigation that draws water from massive subterranean aquifers below the Great Plains—that have made continued widespread, highly productive agriculture possible in the region. But White cautions that those living in the Great Plains—and the emergency managers who work there—should be vigilant about the possibility of further problems. The water pumped from the Ogallala Aquifer to irrigate the Plains is a finite resource, warns White, and there is no guarantee that another technological fix can be found once this water is depleted. Questions about whether the region can continue its current agricultural production and whether the area will be affected by a future severe drought remain unanswered.[41]

Drought and Emergency Management

What does the Dust Bowl imply for today's emergency managers? Those managers may not be directly involved in answering broader questions regarding resource management, but they will be involved in planning for, responding to, and mitigating the immediate problems and longer-term social consequences of a severe drought.

In the last few decades, interest in planning for drought has increased at all levels. Whereas only three states (Colorado, New York, and South Dakota) had drought plans in 1980, today thirty-eight states either have such a plan in place or are in the process of developing one. In several states, the plans are maintained by the state offices of emergency management.

The NDMC's website provides information (including a ten-step guide) designed for emergency managers to use to develop a drought plan, which, it says, should be based on three main components: monitoring and early warning, risk assessment, and mitigation and response.[42] The site includes copies of existing state drought plans, which adopt a number of approaches to address the problem. Which specific approaches are appropriate depends on local circumstances, but many of the approaches require the knowledge, skills, and authority of an emergency manager. Indeed, the ability to conduct the planning process itself may be one of those essential skills.

Texas City Explosions, 1947

On April 16, 1947, a freighter containing more than 2,000 tons of ammonium nitrate caught fire and exploded in the port of Texas City. The blast—comparable to a two- to four-kiloton nuclear weapon—knocked people off their feet in Galveston, ten miles from Texas City, and shattered windows in Houston, more than forty miles from the explosion. Two small planes flying over Texas City were knocked from the sky, and numerous fires ensued among the crude oil and petrochemical facilities surrounding the docks. Fire reached another freighter loaded with ammonium nitrate and sulfur, causing it to explode sixteen hours after the first blast. At least 581 people were killed and 3,500 injured in what is still considered the worst industrial accident in U.S. history.

Preparedness and Response

The Texas City catastrophe was not without precedent. Perhaps the most devastating industrial explosion ever occurred on December 6, 1917, in Halifax Harbor, Nova Scotia, Canada, when a Norwegian vessel collided with a French munitions ship carrying more than 2,500 tons of explosives. The explosion—the largest human-induced detonation before the atomic bomb—leveled more than half a square mile and damaged virtually every building in Halifax. The blast killed more than 1,500 people outright; hundreds more would die in the hours and days to come. An additional 9,000 people were injured, not only by the blast itself but also by the debris and glass from Halifax's crumbling buildings.[43] Another devastating accident involving ammonium nitrate and ammonium sulfate occurred on September 21, 1921, at a BASF chemical and fertilizer plant in Oppau, Germany, when a silo exploded, killing between 400 and 600 people and injuring more than 2,000.[44]

Hence, port safety and the hazard posed by ammonium nitrate were recognized issues at the time of the Texas City catastrophe. The loading of this chemical compound was prohibited in Galveston, but Texas City officials seemed unaware of the risks it posed. Author Angus Gunn describes the scene at the port:

> Within a one-square-mile area beside the docks were six oil-company complexes, eleven warehouses, and several other installations and residential blocks. Fire-prevention experts assured the port authorities that only one-fifth of this area was in danger of a serious fire and that existing precautions would be adequate to cope with such an eventuality.... [T]his thinking should have changed when large quantities of ammonium nitrate fertilizer began to be shipped from Texas City in 1946.[45]

All twenty-eight members of Texas City's volunteer fire department were killed in the initial blast—more in one day than were killed in any previous fire in the United States. With no local firefighters to stem the ensuing blaze, as many as 200 volunteers from as far away as Los Angeles battled the fires for a week.

Convergence, Spontaneous Organization, and Improvisation

Immediately following the explosion, medical personnel, law enforcement officers, and other responders—some called in by authorities, others of their own accord—began to converge on the scene. The city's auditorium was transformed into a roughshod first-aid center to cope with the casualties. In his book on the 1947 disaster, author Hugh W. Stephens notes, "within an hour, doctors, nurses, and ambulances began arriving unsummoned from Galveston [and] state troopers and law enforcement officers from nearby communities helped Texas City's... police force maintain order and assisted in search and rescue."[46] These rescue workers were joined by news reporters, federal investigators, relief organization volunteers, and a host of others.

In Texas City, as in most disasters, both the immediate on-scene responders and those who converged on the disaster site in the hours and days that followed organized themselves into functional groups. And, as with almost any other disaster of significant size, responding to the Texas City explosion required improvisation. The first responders were those people near the blast who suffered no or inconsequential injuries, so these survivors could lend assistance to others who needed help. They were quickly joined by other altruistic, self-sacrificing citizens of the city, who improvised search and rescue strategies. Representatives from the oil companies, warehouses, and other organizations at the docks rushed to the scene and sent their organizations' firefighters to help. An assistant to the mayor, who was put in charge of coordinating the city's response, describes the scene:

> At first there were little groups doing separate jobs.... There were many [people] standing around who seemed to want to help but did not know what to do. They were glad to follow any reasonable instructions. These separate crews started out working on their own, but they began to get together when they would come up against big jobs.[47]

Any such activity undertaken by people who suddenly find themselves in the midst of a disaster is clearly improvised. But a sudden-onset disaster requires that those at more removed levels of responsibility and authority also improvise an appropriate response. Even the most comprehensive response plan cannot predict the precise pattern of a disaster or foresee all the elements that will be involved.

The actions undertaken by Texas City police chief William Ladish illustrate this point. The explosion threw Ladish to the ground as he stood in his office more than a mile from the explosion, and it knocked out the police radio. Upon finding that the radio was inoperable, he "ran to the telephone exchange through glass-littered streets filling with dazed and bleeding people [and] placed a call to the Houston Police Department, where he talked to Captain W. M. Simpson."[48] Ladish told Simpson of the explosion in the harbor and requested that Simpson send fifty officers and all available ambulances. He then returned to city hall, where he ordered his officers to establish roadblocks and seal off the dock areas. He sent the few remaining men of his seventeen-man department to the docks "with no more direction than advice to assist in any way possible and use anybody who would help."[49]

Immediately following the disaster, the "emergency managers" in Texas City—including the assistant to the mayor and Chief Ladish—had to deal with the convergence of well-intentioned volunteers as well as curious onlookers and the local media. They quickly put spontaneously organized groups to constructive use. In a larger sense, the emergency managers had to improvise in order to deal with an unexpected and unprecedented situation, using whatever resources they could amid overwhelming disarray and uncertainty.

Liability and Compensation

Following the Texas City explosions, the first-ever class action lawsuit was filed against the U.S. government on behalf of 8,485 victims. A district court found the government responsible because "the explosion resulted from negligence on the part of the Government in adopting the fertilizer export program as a whole, in its control of various phases of manufacturing, packaging, labeling and shipping the product, in failing to give notice of its dangerous nature to persons handling it and in failing to police its loading on shipboard."[50] The U.S. Fifth Circuit Court of

Appeals overturned the decision, however, maintaining that the U.S. government had the right to exercise its own discretion in vital national matters. On June 8, 1953, the Supreme Court upheld the Appeals Court's decision (346 U.S. 15), concluding that the Federal Tort Claims Act clearly exempted "the failure to exercise or perform a discretionary function or duty" and that the government's actions were discretionary. As the twentieth century progressed, however, the responsibility of public organizations—or more specifically, their liability in a disaster—would become an increasingly salient issue for emergency managers.

After the lawsuit was decided, Congress enacted a special appropriation for victims' relatives—yet another ad hoc appropriation in response to a specific event. "At the time, Congress occasionally appropriated funds for flood relief, but only on a case-by-case basis," writes Stephens.[51] He goes on to emphasize the lack of a centralized response or recovery agency:

> No equivalent of today's Federal Emergency Management Agency existed to rush personnel and resources to the scene and provide emergency housing and grants for individuals and businesses under the aegis of a presidential disaster declaration. Rather, relief and recovery activities went forward in a decentralized manner; volunteer agencies, churches, companies, individuals, and, to a lesser extent, municipal, county, and state governments assumed or shared most of the burden.... Longer-term rehabilitation fell to volunteer organizations, particularly the Salvation Army, Volunteers of America, and the Red Cross.[52]

The ad hoc approach to relief and recovery resulted in inconsistencies—both in the funding provided to disaster victims and in the ways that this funding was distributed. As discussed in the following chapters, the federal government tried to remedy these problems in the decades to come through overarching disaster legislation. Several federal government agencies, most notably FEMA, were created to improve disaster response, but even today, major disasters almost inevitably result in disaster-specific appropriations.

Responsibility

In hindsight, it is relatively easy to see many of the conditions, decisions, and actions that led to the Texas City catastrophe. Stephens proposes that "the event originated from complacency about hazardous materials; the close physical proximity of docks, petrochemical facilities, and residences; and an absence of preparation for a serious industrial emergency."[53] Angus Gunn adds that, despite USDA warnings and prior explosions, local railway managers, ships' masters, and others involved in leading port operations simply failed to recognize the risks posed by the transportation of ammonium nitrate. (Texas City did not have a port authority overseeing its operations.) Those who could have—or should have—taken responsibility failed to enact or coordinate safety measures that would protect the city. Stephens calls the lack of governmental oversight of the transportation of hazardous materials (particularly the U.S. Coast Guard's failure to play a role) and the concomitant lack of oversight of dock operations a "sin of omission."[54]

The Texas City disaster had a subtle but profound impact on disaster management in the United States as it changed the way people thought about disaster preparedness. "This [may have been] the beginning of a shift away from an essentially passive, reactive posture toward a more active, anticipatory mode," writes Stephens. "Clearly some individuals came to understand that when hazardous materials were at issue, the public interest required a community-wide effort to mitigate the worst effects of disaster and prepare response measures beforehand."[55] In the end, the tragedy of Texas City provided the impetus for fundamental improvements in preparedness and response for industrial catastrophes, not only locally but at the state and national levels as well.[56]

Complex System Failures

The Texas City catastrophe might be considered an example of a new category of human-caused disaster resulting from the failure of complex systems. Although industrial accidents were common with the advent of the Industrial Revolution at the outset of the nineteenth century, complex human-caused disasters became increasingly common in the latter half of the twentieth century. Such disasters are the consequence of increasing industrialization, technological advances, increased residential development near industrial areas, and, particularly, complex industrial/human systems and processes in which cataclysmic risk is not immediately apparent and, thus, judgment and decision making are inadequate. In short, these are disasters resulting from hazards *created* by humankind. Indeed, major catastrophes resulting from advanced technologies; the storage, transportation, and use of hazardous materials; and complex industrial systems have become hallmarks of the disaster history in the late twentieth century.[57]

In *Normal Accidents: Living with High-Risk Technologies,* a classic account of such disasters, Charles Perrow discusses the risk of "tight coupling" in which "processes happen very fast and can't be turned off, the failed parts cannot be isolated from other parts, or there is no other way to keep the production going safely."[58] Perrow explains that in recent years, accidents have been increasingly caused by

> interactive complexity in the presence of tight coupling, producing a system accident. We have produced designs so complicated that we cannot anticipate all the possible interactions of the inevitable failures; we add safety devices that are deceived or avoided or defeated by hidden paths in the systems. The systems have become more complicated because either they are dealing with more deadly substances, or we demand they function in ever more hostile environments or with ever greater speed and volume.[59]

Perrow demonstrates that we cannot foresee all the possible interactions in complex systems that might lead to catastrophic failure:

> The argument is basically very simple. We start with a plant, airplane, ship, biology laboratory, or other setting with a lot of components (parts, procedures, operators). Then we need two or more failures among components that interact in some unexpected way. No one dreamed that when X failed, Y would also be out of order and the two failures would interact so as to both start a fire and silence the fire alarm. Furthermore, no one can figure out the interaction at the time and thus know what to do.... This interacting tendency is a characteristic of a system, not of a part or an operator.[60]

In the case of Texas City, the individuals overseeing the port failed to recognize the additional risks resulting from a change in the system: the introduction of ammonium nitrate as cargo. Moreover, even those officials who knew that the hazardous material was passing through the port could not foresee the many ways in which its transportation could result in a disaster.

Implications for Emergency Management

The lessons for emergency managers are sobering. The first unavoidable conclusion is that not all disasters can be foreseen, much less mitigated. Even if people settle away from a floodplain, construct sturdier buildings in seismic zones, or design better evacuation systems for hurricanes, in an increasingly complex, interconnected society other risks remain—risks that will inevitably manifest themselves as catastrophes. Even those measures specifically designed to mitigate disasters can lead to failures that cannot be anticipated (consider, for example, the failure of flood control structures during and after Hurricane Katrina).

Hence, emergency managers must plan and prepare for the unexpected. "Preparing for the unexpected" might sound like an oxymoron, but it is essential. Although the specific hazards posed by and to some systems may not be clear, it is important to predict as many potential *consequences* of system failure as possible. How the Internet will collapse may not be known, for instance, but the resulting disruption to communication networks and those who use these networks (individuals, businesses, government, etc.) can be anticipated to some extent. Flexibility can and should be built into response plans, and improvisation in response is not only inevitable but essential.

Perhaps the most glaring problem shown by the Texas City example involved the lack of oversight and management regarding the transportation of hazardous materials. This lack of planning resulted in a failure to recognize the hazard and contributed to the second explosion. Additionally, those responding to the accident—from doctors to firefighters, from the Red Cross to the military—confronted myriad complicated issues and decisions, and their efforts were hampered by inefficient and ineffective communication and a general lack of coordination among responding agencies. Moreover, the failure to identify the clear roles and responsibilities of the many agencies involved resulted in inadequate damage assessment. Other communication problems involved the media: the lack of a clear plan for communicating with the public contributed to widespread rumors and bad information.

Other problems related to medical aid and mass casualty management with regard to triage, transportation, care, and tracking injured and displaced individuals. Again, the sudden convergence of people and donations on the disaster scene wreaked havoc. And in the longer term, victims faced inadequate sanitation and homelessness, as well as issues involving the recovery and reconstruction of the community and compensation for losses.

Again, although the specific event—in this case, two massive explosions—may not have been foreseeable, most, if not all, of these problems could have been ameliorated through prior planning.

Ultimately—and beyond planning for such specific difficulties—emergency managers must appreciate that risks are constantly changing. New and more complex systems, with their attendant hazards, are appearing at an accelerating rate. In addition, the populations at risk are continually shifting in size, composition, distribution, and vulnerability. Modern emergency managers must repeatedly reevaluate the situation and adapt preparedness, warning, response, recovery, and mitigation to emerging hazards.

Disaster authority E. L. Quarantelli warns that regardless of the current situation, the future will be different. "As the world continues to industrialize and to urbanize, it is continually creating conditions for *more and worse disasters,*" he writes. "Both social processes…will increase the number of potential disaster agents and enlarge the vulnerabilities of communities and populations that will be at risk."[61] Quarantelli outlines five factors that will contribute to an increase in potential disaster agents:

- Accelerating incidents of accidents and mishaps in the chemical and nuclear areas

- Technological advances that reduce some hazards but make some old threats more dangerous

- New versions of old and past dangers, such as urban droughts

- The emergence of innovative kinds of technologies, such as computers and bio-genetic engineering, whose breakdowns will present distinctively new dangers

- An increase in multiple or synergistic disasters resulting in more severe environmental consequences.[62]

As we prepare for an era in which there will certainly be more disasters, many of which may be complex and unanticipated, emergency managers can nevertheless look to the past for lessons to guide them.

1900-1950: A Summary and Lessons Learned

The first half of the twentieth century was marked by numerous catastrophes, only a few of which have been covered in the last two chapters. At the time, there were no unified federal or (in most cases) state or local response and/or recovery programs. Nor were there federal government programs (with the exception of flood control programs) in place to minimize hazards. With no coordinated government response or recovery programs, the primary responsibility for victim aid fell to the American Red Cross.

Many of the major disasters of the early twentieth century quickly became part of the historical basis and national consciousness that informed the emerging, evolving practice of emergency management in the United States. In almost every case, the catastrophes discussed in these chapters demonstrated deficiencies—if not failures—in preparedness, response, recovery, and long-term mitigation. Mitigation was particularly lacking, and similar disasters, with similar consequences, occurred again in many of the same communities. In some cases, the disasters also exposed deep problems in the American social structure—problems relating to race, poverty, and social inequality, and extending to the economic system and our system of government.

A survey of U.S. disasters from 1900 to 1950 reveals at least four significant truths:

- **Disasters happen with greater frequency than most people think.** At least thirty-two hurricanes of Category 3 or stronger struck mainland U.S. from 1900 to 1950. At least seventy-five earthquakes of magnitude 5.3 or greater struck California during the same period. Flu outbreaks cause approximately 36,000 deaths annually. The U.S. Geological Survey lists thirty-two "significant" floods occurring in the United States in the twentieth century, seven prior to 1950. Flooding of some kind somewhere in the United States results in loss of life and property every year. Similarly, drought occurs almost annually somewhere in the country, and, as mentioned in the discussion of the Dust Bowl, severe droughts continue to occur every few years. Finally, technological/human-caused disasters are an increasing nightmare in this modern age, constantly evolving with new forms and new risks.

- **Disasters are soon forgotten and their causes often denied.** Disasters tend to be denied, or at least conveniently forgotten, by both ordinary citizens and political leaders. Despite the frequency of disasters, no one can ever say exactly when or where one will occur. Therefore, nationally and locally, they tend to be overlooked relative to more pressing concerns. Galveston was rebuilt, only to be struck by another devastating hurricane fifteen years later. The oligarchs of San Francisco overtly censured mention of the seismic risk in their city so that it could be rebuilt, and it was struck again in 1989. The victims of the Dust Bowl attributed the massive dust storms and their subsequent misfortunes to "acts of God" as capricious as tornadoes, rather than to unsound agricultural practices; the region experienced an even worse drought two decades later. Today, the population of the American West continues to grow disproportionately relative to most of the rest of the country, despite a scarcity of water.

Rather than denying the risks, one of the ways that an emergency manager can improve his or her work is to look at previous disasters, consider what happened, and anticipate similar circumstances. One of the great mistakes that an emergency manager can make is to assume, "It can't happen again," "It won't happen here," or "I'm ready." If a close study of disaster history tells us anything, it tells us that it can, it will, and you're not.

- **Mistakes are often repeated.** It should be striking to anyone examining twentieth-century disasters how the tragic response to Hurricane Katrina reflects similar failures in 1900, 1906, 1918, 1927, 1930, 1947, and beyond. These include not only the failure to recognize the hazards and anticipate their consequences, but also recurring mistakes in response involving such factors as failure to deal with incapacitated, poor, and/or ethnic minorities, inability to manage unwanted relief supplies, failure to improvise needed actions, and inability to manage converging responders. They also include failures to recognize and deal with disaster myths such as alleged looting, anarchy, and the need for martial law. Often compounding these problems are poor communication and inadequate coordination. These failures can continue into recovery, during which rich and powerful business interests in a community often assume control, and communities are quickly rebuilt without consideration of the hazards that brought them down in the first place or any planning to mitigate future disasters.

- **Past disasters affect present-day disaster management.** Despite society's propensity to look the other way, past disasters can and should inform disaster management policies and practices. As discussed in more detail in subsequent chapters, government at all levels has taken steps to address the hazards that occurred prior to 1950. The recurrence of hurricanes, for instance, has led to measures at the national level, including the establishment of the National Hurricane Center, as well as at the local level, where some communities in hurricane-prone regions have strengthened building codes and adopted zoning ordinances to direct settlement away from areas that are most vulnerable. Similarly, earthquake hazards are now addressed by national programs, such as the National Earthquake Hazards Reduction Program, and by state and local legislation in California and other states. At the federal level, the National Flood Insurance Program addresses flood losses, while floodplain management has become an increasing concern of state and local governments.[63] At the same time, many state governments have put plans in place to deal with drought, while the NDMC offers information and technical assistance to both develop such plans and deal with drought generally. The Centers for Disease Control and Prevention and other federal agencies, as well as their counterparts at the state and local levels, are actively working to limit possible future flu pandemics. And finally, modern technological hazards are the focus of the Comprehensive Environmental Response, Compensation, and Liability Act; the Emergency Planning and Community Right-to-Know Act (also known as the Superfund Amendments and Reauthorization Act [SARA] Title III), and other major pieces of legislation that encourage and support knowledge about and management of hazards at both the national and local levels. In addition, for all these hazards, the federal government has established policies, programs, and agencies to deal with the attendant problems.

The numerous mistakes notwithstanding, there were also major successes in disaster management in the early 1900s, resulting in disasters averted, risks mitigated, and improved response that saved lives and reduced property damage. Such successes can be hard to measure, but it is important to recognize that the field of disaster management is evolving, building on the base of knowledge and experience of those who have come before.

By looking at failures and successes in past disasters and identifying the patterns that emerge, emergency managers and others can anticipate responses and problems that will arise with present-day disasters and plan accordingly. The consequences of disasters can be ameliorated by clearly identifying local hazards and the vulnerable populations and environments. The intersection of these two sets of data represents the overall risk to a community. Such risk analysis can then help inform a set of plans to deal with the various hazards. Each plan should address preparedness (including warning and evacuation when necessary), response, and recovery, as well as the long-term measures that can be undertaken to either reduce the hazard or minimize vulnerability.

The early-twentieth-century events discussed in this chapter and the one before it set the stage for an increased role by the federal government in all aspects of disaster management. The federal government has continued to react, through legislation and appropriations, to individual major disasters and catastrophes up to the present day.[64] Over time, however, both private institutions and government agencies have increasingly recognized the need for better, more consistent, and proactive approaches to disaster management beyond event-based response. One result has been the advent of a new profession—emergency management—charged with overseeing disaster-related tasks at all levels of government.

Endnotes

1   Association of State Floodplain Managers (ASFPM), *The Nation's Responses to Flood Disasters: A Historical Account* (Madison, Wis.: ASFPM, 2000), 5.

2   Ibid., 6.

3   Ibid., 9. The ASFPM report was published prior to Hurricane Katrina, which has perhaps eclipsed the 1927 flood.

4   Kevin R. Kosar, *Disaster Response and the Appointment of a Recovery Czar: The Executive Branch's Response to the Flood of 1927,* CRS report RL33126 (Washington, D.C.: Congressional Research Service, 2005), 4.

5   John M. Barry, *Rising Tide: The Great Mississippi Flood of 1927 and How It Changed America* (New York: Simon & Schuster, 1997).

6   PBS, *American Experience,* "Fatal Flood," pbs.org/wgbh/amex/flood.

7   David A. Moss, "Courting Disaster? The Transformation of Federal Disaster Policy," in *The Financing of Catastrophe Risk,* ed. Kenneth A. Froot (Chicago: University of Chicago Press, 1999), 308.

8   Barry, *Rising Tide,* 422.

9   ASFPM, *Nation's Responses to Flood Disasters,* 9.

10   Barry, *Rising Tide,* 407.

11   Nicole T. Carter, *Flood Risk Management: Federal Role in Infrastructure,* CRS report RL33129 (Washington, D.C.: Congressional Research Service, 2005), 2.

12   ASFPM, *Nation's Responses to Flood Disasters,* 11.

13   These concerns were not new. Nineteenth-century studies, including one of the aforementioned 1850 studies, pointed out that the flood problem along the Mississippi River was as much a problem of increased occupancy of the floodplain as it was of increased flooding.

14   Rutherford H. Platt, *Disasters and Democracy: The Politics of Extreme Natural Events* (Washington, D.C.: Island Press, 1999), 6.

15   Gilbert F. White, *Human Adjustment to Floods: A Geographic Approach to the Flood Problem in the United States* (PhD diss., University of Chicago, 1942), 32.

16   Ibid., 2. White is considered the father of modern floodplain management because of his advocacy of a broad range of human adjustments to floods.

17   Lawrence Svobida, *Farming the Dust Bowl: A First-Hand Account from Kansas* (Lawrence: University Press of Kansas, 1986).

18   Richard A. Warrick et al., *Drought Hazard in the United States: A Research Assessment* (Boulder: University of Colorado, 1975), 28.

19   Donald Worster, *Dust Bowl: The Southern Plains in the 1930s* (New York: Oxford University Press, 2004).

20   Robert Geiger, *Washington Evening Star,* April 15, 1935, as quoted in ibid., 29.

21   See the National Drought Mitigation Center (NDMC) website (drought.unl.edu) for analyses of each of these dimensions, as well as extensive information on the phenomenon of drought and drought planning, monitoring, and mitigation.

22   NDMC, "What Is Drought?," drought.unl.edu/DroughtforKids/WhatisDrought.aspx.

23   Worster, *Dust Bowl,* 12.

24 National Aeronautics and Space Administration, "NASA Explains 'Dust Bowl' Drought" (March 18, 2004), nasa.gov/centers/goddard/news/topstory/2004/0319dustbowl.html.

25 NDMC, "What Is Drought?"

26 Worster, *Dust Bowl*, 4.

27 Ibid., 5.

28 Harry C. McDean, "Dust Bowl Historiography," *Great Plains Quarterly* 6 (Spring 1986): 117–127.

29 Worster, *Dust Bowl*, 28.

30 NDMC, "What Is Drought?"

31 Warrick et al., *Drought Hazard in the United States*, 37; NDMC, "What Is Drought?"

32 PBS, *American Experience*, "Surviving the Dust Bowl," pbs.org/wgbh/amex/dustbowl/sfeature/newdeal.html.

33 PBS, *American Experience*, "Timeline: Surviving the Dust Bowl, 1931–1939," pbs.org/wgbh/americanexperience/features/timeline/dustbowl.

34 Worster, *Dust Bowl*, 133.

35 NDMC, "What Is Drought?"

36 Worster, *Dust Bowl*, 41–43.

37 Morris Cooke et al., *Report of the Great Plains Drought Area Committee*, August 27, 1936, Hopkins Papers, Box 13, Franklin D. Roosevelt Library, Hyde Park, N.Y., newdeal.feri.org/hopkins/hop27.htm.

38 Gilbert F. White, "The Future of the Great Plains Re-visited," *Great Plains Quarterly* 6 (Spring 1986): 93.

39 Worster, *Dust Bowl*, 229.

40 Ibid., 248.

41 White, "Great Plains Re-visited."

42 See NDMC, "What Is Drought?"

43 Many scholars mark the Halifax explosion as the beginning of modern social science research into disasters. Samuel Henry Prince, a curate in an Anglican church in Halifax, studied the effects of this traumatic event on the victims. His resulting 1920 doctoral thesis is generally regarded as the first in-depth sociological study of a disaster and its consequences.

44 See "Die Explosion von Oppau," wortlastig.de/text/oppau.htm.

45 Angus Gunn, *Unnatural Disasters: Case Studies of Human-Induced Environmental Catastrophes* (Westport, Conn.: Greenwood Press, 2003), 46.

46 Hugh W. Stephens, *The Texas City Disaster, 1947* (Austin: University of Texas Press, 1997), 4.

47 Quoted in ibid., 50.

48 Ibid., 43.

49 Ibid.

50 See *Dalehite v. United States*, 346 U.S. 15 (1953), caselaw.lp.findlaw.com/scripts/getcase.pl?court=us&invol=15&vol=346.

51 Stephens, *Texas City Disaster*, 103.

52 Ibid.

53 Ibid., 1.

54 Ibid., 18.

55 Ibid., 114.

56 The next time the United States witnessed a policy-changing disaster of this magnitude was in 1984, when a deadly gas leak at a Union Carbide plant in Bhopal, India, resulted in approximately 3,400 deaths and countless disabilities.

57 Gunn provides succinct analyses of thirty-four such disasters in *Unnatural Disasters*.

58 Charles Perrow, *Normal Accidents: Living with High-Risk Technologies* (New York: Basic Books, 1984), 4.

59 Ibid., 11–12.

60   Ibid., 4.

61   E. L. Quarantelli, "Disaster Planning, Emergency Management, and Civil Protection: The Historical Development and Current Characteristics of Organized Efforts to Prevent and to Respond to Disasters," Disaster Research Center Preliminary Paper 227 (Newark: University of Delaware, 1995), 22.

62   Ibid., 22.

63   ASFPM has grown steadily and, as of 2011, had 14,000 members and thirty-two state chapters.

64   See Claire B. Rubin, Irmak Renda-Tanali, and William Cumming, *Disaster Time Line: Major Focusing Events and Their Outcomes* (1979–2005) (Arlington, Va.: Claire B. Rubin & Associates, 2006), disaster-timeline.com.

Chapter 4

The Formative Years: 1950–1978

Keith Bea

Prior to World War II, reactive disaster relief and response generally constituted the primary approach to emergencies and their consequences. The decentralized and largely uncoordinated activities described in the preceding chapters depended on voluntary private and local efforts to meet the immediate needs of disaster victims and communities. When the threats of that war ceased, academicians and policy makers recognized a wealth of interdisciplinary knowledge that could provide the basis for establishing policies to manage both the consequences of disasters and the conditions that might ease their impacts. Part of this process involved sorting out the complex responsibilities of federal and nonfederal entities before and after catastrophes.

Over nearly three decades, from 1950 to 1978, the nature of emergency management changed significantly. During those years, policy makers and administrators addressed several parallel concerns, including civil defense readiness for enemy attacks, hazard reduction before and recovery from natural disasters, the identification and typing of different threats, and the management of technological and environmental disasters stemming from human-caused events. (A fourth concern, public health emergencies associated with diseases, remained outside the developing policy field of emergency management.) By the end of the 1970s, as federal policy makers and administrators assumed a dominant role that could not have been imagined in 1950, emergency management had become the primary responsibility of a single federal agency.

1950–1963: Civil Defense and Natural Disasters

Natural disasters have always challenged societies. While World War II dominated governmental efforts prior to 1945, floods, hurricanes, and earthquakes continued to take lives and destroy property. In 1950, with the advent of the Cold War, some of the tools used to manage "acts of God"—for example, sheltering in safe havens, providing essential goods, and evacuating civilians at risk—were found to be applicable to events of a less celestial nature, such as air raids and enemy attacks.

Civil defense—the protection of civilian centers in case of enemy attack—has an erratic history of popular and governmental support in the United States. State and local civil defense organizations developed during World War II largely to involve civilians in the war effort. Concerns regarding air attacks led federal civil defense administrators and state officials to develop civil protection policies and plans as well as a loose network of organizations. Nationwide, civil defense involved as many as 800,000 individuals in the Ground Observer Corps, whose participants watched the skies from 16,000 observation posts.[1]

Some states subsequently enacted legislation to expand civil defense responsibilities to include all disasters, regardless of their cause. For example, the California Disaster Act added and amended provisions in 1943, 1945, 1950, and 1951 that authorized the state Office of Civil Defense to undertake broad preparedness functions. The statute, as amended, noted, "The state has long recognized its responsibility to provide for preparedness against disasters that may result from such calamities as flood, fire, earthquake, pestilence, war, sabotage, and riot."[2]

In the early 1950s, the threat of nuclear attack by the Soviet Union built upon previous concerns that coastal states might be vulnerable to enemy strikes by air or sea (from Germany on the East Coast or from Japan on the West Coast, including Alaska). Congress developed national security policies that augmented federal powers but did not specifically address concerns of the home front. To fill this gap, many states adopted civil defense laws, developed mutual aid agreements, and designated civil defense directors to develop plans for civilian protection and sheltering. However, many people argued that without assistance and guidance from the federal government, they could not be expected to address the nuclear threats associated with enemy attack. The outbreak of military action in Korea in June 1950, frustration with a dearth of federal activity, and other factors led President Harry Truman and the 81st Congress to act. After extensive hearings, Congress passed the Civil Defense Act of 1950 (CDA), which President Truman signed into law on January 12, 1951 (P.L. 81-920).[3]

In keeping with the assumption that primary responsibility for civil defense rests with individuals and communities supported and guided by plans developed by local governments and their states, the CDA continued past practices that recognized state sovereignty and historical limitations on federal intervention in domestic security matters. Among the principal features of the CDA were the following:

- The definition of *civil defense,* which included emergency repairs to or restoration of "vital utilities and facilities destroyed or damaged by any such attack" as well as preparation for an attack.

- Establishment of the Federal Civil Defense Administration (FCDA) and a Civil Defense Advisory Council composed of state, local, and citizen representatives.

- Authority for the FCDA administrator to prepare civil defense plans and programs for the nation, coordinate federal activities with states and border countries, encourage states to develop interstate mutual aid compacts, and provide grants to states for civil defense activities.

- Authority for the president to proclaim, or Congress to establish by concurrent resolution, the existence of a "state of civil defense emergency" in response to an attack or threatened attack upon the United States. During such an emergency, the president could direct federal agencies to provide personnel and other aid to the states, including work essential to save lives and property. Such an emergency declaration would terminate when the president by proclamation, or Congress by concurrent resolution, noted the end of the emergency.

In 1950, President Truman established the FCDA in the Office of Emergency Management to create the means to "promote and facilitate" civil defense and encourage mutual aid compacts "to meet emergencies or disasters from enemy attacks which cannot be adequately met or controlled by the local forces."[4]

Civil Defense

As ultimately defined by the U.S. Department of Defense, civil defense is a function directly associated with wartime threats, not natural disasters. The Office of Civil Defense defines *civil defense* as "all activities and measures designed or undertaken (1) to minimize the effects upon the civilian population and Government caused, or which would be caused by an attack on the United States, (1) to deal with the immediate emergency conditions which would be created by any such attack, and (3) to effectuate emergency repairs to, or the emergency restoration of vital utilities and facilities destroyed or damaged by any such attack."

Source: U.S. Department of Defense, Office of Civil Defense, "Abbreviations and Definitions of Terms Used in Civil Defense Training" (January 1971), as cited in Amanda Dory, *Civil Security: Americans and the Challenge of Homeland Security* (Washington, D.C.: Center for Strategic and International Studies, 2003), 10.

The Federal Disaster Relief Act of 1950

In 1950 Congress passed the Federal Disaster Relief Act (P.L. 81-875), the most significant general federal disaster assistance policy adopted in the nation's history to that date.[5] Whereas concerns with nuclear attack and the escalation of the war in Korea were obvious triggers for action on civil defense, no single catastrophic disaster served as the catalyst for this legislation. Debating the bill, members of Congress noted that the acceptance of the proposal reflected a recognition that more than $3 million had been appropriated since 1948 for "emergency purposes" to help victims of flooding along the Columbia and Red Rivers. One congressman noted, "The primary purpose of the pending legislation is to provide a general congressional policy in respect to federal disaster relief."[6]

Enactment of the Federal Disaster Relief Act is notable for three reasons. First, it established ongoing (permanent) authority for federal action. Victims of floods, along with state and local governments, no longer had to wait until Congress met, debated, and acted upon a reported need. Rather, Congress authorized federal assistance for future events so that just one person—not hundreds of lawmakers—could decide that a disaster warranted the distribution of funds. Second, the statute shifted responsibility from Capitol Hill to the White House. The president had authority for deciding when the federal government would provide assistance and which agencies would be involved. (President Truman assigned the task of implementing the new disaster relief policy to the Housing and Home Finance Administration [HHFA], which had been established in 1947.) Third, the legislation committed the federal government to provide specific types of limited assistance following a disaster, as well as certain help before a disaster occurred, including actions to foster the development of state and local disaster plans.

The 1950 Federal Disaster Relief Act maintained that the federal government was not responsible for disaster relief and that federal aid would be limited to temporary, emergency repairs. It specified, for instance, that federal funding could be available for the emergency repair of state and local buildings but not for their replacement. The legislation authorized the availability of federal aid in a "coordinated" fashion—both internally as well as with nonfederal entities, such as the American Red Cross and state and local governments. The president had discretion over federal funding for disaster relief, but the federal government would maintain an arm's-length stance and defer to state authority, responding only to gubernatorial requests for assistance. The act continued a policy that had been established in 1949, whereby a governor requesting federal aid had to certify that "reasonable" amounts of nonfederal resources had been dedicated to the response effort.

The record of debate on the bill indicates that the legislation was not politically controversial. The bill "is directed to every state in the Union," declared one legislator. "There is no danger of this bill not passing."[7] A prescient member of Congress might have added as well that any appropriations that the legislation authorized were in no danger of congressional rejection. Disasters, then and now, have broad constituencies.

Administration of Civil Defense and Disaster Relief Policies

In one year, through enactment of the CDA and the Federal Disaster Relief Act, Congress and President Truman agreed to establish two parallel tracks for the management of emergencies. By 1953, however, the split between civil defense and disaster relief had closed administratively (and temporarily), as the FCDA bore responsibility for administering policies for both functions.[8] To fulfill its primary mission of providing limited federal assistance for the repair and replacement of public facilities damaged in disasters, the FCDA reached a formal understanding with the American Red Cross to set out joint responsibilities for disaster relief.

In addition to delegating responsibility to the FCDA for administering the policies prescribed by the two acts, President Truman assigned emergency functions to six federal agencies: the Departments of Defense, Commerce, Agriculture, and Health, Education and Welfare, along with the General Services Administration and HHFA. The administrative complex at the federal level then grew when he established the Office of Defense Mobilization to take on responsibility for "coordinating all major federal emergency preparedness programs except civil defense."[9]

The administrative structure at the federal level continued to change in subsequent years. In 1958, President Dwight Eisenhower opted "for coordinating and conducting the interrelated defense mobilization and civil defense functions" by consolidating various relevant functions into the Office of Defense and Civilian Mobilization, later renamed the Office of Civil and Defense Mobilization (OCDM).[10] In 1961, President John F. Kennedy separated civil defense from disaster relief functions through an executive order that transferred civil defense functions to the Department of Defense, which established the Office of Civil Defense (OCD) to administer those functions. The following year, he made the Office of Emergency Planning (OEP), located in the executive office of the White House, responsible for emergency planning and preparedness, coordination of federal emergency functions, dispersal of essential facilities in the event of enemy attack, and disaster relief.

Intergovernmental Relationships in Civil Defense

During World War II the federal government had become increasingly involved in mobilization, resource allocation, and crisis planning activities. Enactment of the CDA in 1950 built on that trend by establishing federal authority over certain aspects of the task of protecting the civilian population from emergencies. Implementation of the new authority, however, proceeded in half steps. The federal government was criticized "for its seeming evasion of responsibility for civil defense," wrote historian Harry B. Yoshpe: "Milwaukee Mayor Frank P. Zeidler voiced the belief of many mayors that 'it is the basic philosophy of the defenders of the nation to consider the people in the cities as indefensible, and to write them off.'"[11] Other local and state officials, however, decried the involvement of Washington in matters that historically were the responsibility of the states. Perhaps because of this struggle to strike a balance between federal and state authority, the CDA remained unchanged for eight years and civil defense remained on the back burner of policy implementation. That the threat of any enemy attacks, while widely discussed in the media and popular culture, never materialized also contributed to the inertia.

By comparison, natural disasters continued to strike, and administrators and policy makers at all levels of government recognized that the management of emergencies required action. Some states, such as California and New York, had a long history of preparing for and responding to disasters as part of their civil defense mission, largely perhaps because of their open borders and potential vulnerability to enemy attacks by air or sea. Other states continued to rely primarily on voluntary and charitable organizations, religious institutions, and private resolve without modifying their policies.[12] All recognized the need for emergency management, but the underlying policy remained a matter to be resolved.

In 1958, seeking to resolve the federalism dilemma, Congress enacted Public Law 85-606. The statute vested responsibility for civil defense jointly in the federal government, the states, and local governments, with the federal government providing "necessary direction, coordination, and guidance." State plans funded through federal grants would be consistent with the "national plan." With the urging of the FCDA, most states gradually enacted civil defense legislation largely based on models developed by the federal agency or the changes enacted by other legislatures.

The federal government's reliance on the plans of nonfederal entities presented an interesting paradox: a national policy built upon decentralized actions. The question remained whether a confederated approach would be the most effective way to carry out the federal government's policies. At the request of the FCDA, a research team associated with the Disaster Research Center located at Ohio State University (now at the University of Delaware) looked into the capabilities, authorities, and resources of nonfederal civil defense agencies and found wide variance among them. By the late 1960s, the researchers concluded, local civil defense organizations "had little or no legitimacy among other community emergency groups" and had little impact on missions associated with enemy attacks.[13] Of greater significance were the activities of those organizations concerned with preparation for natural disasters. While the parallel tracks of civil defense and disaster relief often did not intersect at the federal level, community organizations recognized the need for convergence in their approaches to these two types of risk.

The Federal Government's Role in Disaster Response

Within a year of enactment of the 1950 Federal Disaster Relief Act, Congress began a decades-long process of restructuring and expanding its policies regarding disaster assistance.[14] Following flooding in the Midwest, it amended the legislation to include authority for the president to provide temporary housing or emergency shelter for disaster victims. It also increased the mortgage insurance limit for the reconstruction of a home after a disaster. Other changes to the 1950 legislation that were made during the next decade included authorization for the federal government to distribute surplus Korean War equipment and supplies to disaster areas, and expansion of federal disaster relief assistance to state governments and U.S. protectorates and territories.

In conjunction with President Truman, Congress also broadened federal involvement by addressing the disaster relief needs of the private sector. Through the Small Business Act of 1953 (P.L. 83-163), the newly established Small Business Administration (SBA) was authorized to provide loans to help victims of floods and other disasters. Like the Federal Disaster Relief Act, the 1953 law delegated to the executive branch—in this case, the SBA administrator—responsibility for determining whether assistance would be provided. The funding made loans available not only for small businesses but also for individuals for "housing for personal occupancy by the borrower."[15]

Disaster Declaration and Funding

Relatively few significant disasters occurred in the years following the Federal Disaster Relief Act, and no civil defense emergencies were declared. In 1952, President Truman issued a report to Congress summarizing the funding provided under authority of the 1950 law. The initial $31 million appropriated in 1952 more than met the needs created by floods in Illinois, Kansas, Missouri, and Oklahoma and by a blizzard in South Dakota.

The federal government also provided assistance through other means. After a 1952 flood, for instance, it provided temporary housing assistance in Kansas through the HHFA's statutory authority. It spent more than $4 million on the purchase of 1,515 trailers, the development of sites, and disposal of the trailers when they were no longer needed. In his report to Congress, President Truman wrote, "Temporary stop-gap housing operations will continue until the need has been met, and until the families so housed have found other means of more permanent housing."[16] This report marks one of the first incidences in which the president exercised the discretionary authority for disaster relief that Congress had granted in the 1950 legislation.

From 1950 to 1964, the federal government issued 174 disaster declarations, resulting in total expenditures of almost $275 million (Table 4–1). By comparison, Congress had appropriated more than $450 million for civil defense planning from FY 1951 through 1958.[17] Of significant note, neither disaster declarations nor separate congressional appropriations were issued for the 1957 Asian flu pandemic, an emergency outside the realm of other natural disasters. The tunnel vision that went into the classification of emergencies (human caused, acts of God, diseases) resulted in specialization and, unfortunately, inaction when certain catastrophes fell through the bureaucratic cracks. The pandemic, which was one of the deadliest catastrophes of its time, causing almost 70,000 deaths in the United States, was one of those oversights. Still, even without federal initiatives, aid was forthcoming from Washington. Throughout the nation, federal and nonfederal health officials provided limited supplies of vaccines available to prevent the spread of the disease.[18]

Consideration of the third appropriation for the emergency fund (P.L. 82-326) in 1952 gave rise to debate about whether Congress could dedicate funds for specific disasters or whether this authority should remain with the executive office. In the end, Congress rejected an attempt to target the appropriated funds, setting a precedent that has lasted throughout the decades. Today, if Congress wants to specify catastrophe assistance to a particular area or need, funds are appropriated to specific departments or agencies, such as the Departments of Agriculture, Transportation, or Housing and Urban Development (HUD), in addition to the entity responsible for administering the Disaster Relief Fund.[19]

The Alaska Earthquake of 1964

For years, federal lawmakers and administrators could not reach agreement on the scope of the civil defense program. By the mid-1960s, federal civil defense was perceived primarily as a warning and shelter program, with the costs of sheltering proving too expensive for Congress. Advocates of a strong civil defense program claimed that it was grossly underfunded and contended that it would be of little help in the event of an attack. Protests against nuclear proliferation and the Vietnam War combined to keep civil defense and preparedness on the back burner. In a 1969 directive, President Richard Nixon called for federally funded construction to include shelters. Other than that modification, civil defense policy remained unchanged and the program continued to be funded at low levels.

On March 27, 1964, an event occurred that changed federal disaster relief policy radically. When seismographs in the relatively new state of Alaska registered an earthquake measuring a record 8.4 on the Richter scale, all sectors of the state were seriously disrupted. Within minutes, thousands of people lost their homes and 114 people lost their lives. According to a field report, "Seismic sea waves swept the Pacific Ocean from the Gulf of Alaska to Antarctica; they caused extensive damage in British Columbia and California and took 12 lives in Crescent City, California, and 4 in Oregon.... The entire earth vibrated like a tuning fork."[20] A few days after the quake, President Lyndon Johnson established the Federal Reconstruction and Development Planning Commission for Alaska. He charged the commission with

Year	Number of Presidential Disaster Declarations	Types of Disasters Resulting in a Presidential Declaration	Expenditures, in Current Dollars	Expenditures, in Constant (2005) Dollars
1953	13	Tornadoes, floods, a forest fire, and salmon industry failure in Alaska	$2,634,677	$15,945,210
1954	16	Tornado, floods, hurricanes, an earthquake, and salmon industry failure in Alaska	$9,243,419	$55,305,289
1955	17	Tornadoes, floods, hurricanes, a volcanic eruption, and salmon industry failure in Alaska	$16,778,942	$99,529,224
1956	15	Tornadoes, floods, hurricanes, a wind storm, and a forest fire	$4,528,272	$26,172,038
1957	15	Tornadoes, floods, a hurricane, and a tidal wave	$13,272,808	$73,927,466
1958	6	Tornadoes, floods, and a hurricane	$4,900,749	$26,494,749
1959	6	Floods and Hurricane Dot	$5,071,637	$26,995,774
1960	11	Tornadoes, floods, earthquake and volcanic eruption, tidal waves, fires, and Hurricane Donna	$8,939,326	$47,016,598
1961	11	Tornadoes, floods, fire, and Hurricane Carla	$12,735,062	$66,036,976
1962	21	Tornadoes, floods, storms, two chlorine barge accidents, high tides, and Typhoon Karen	$50,851,736	$260,750,893
1963	19	Floods, storms, drought and impending freeze, Typhoon Olive, and Hurricane Cindy	$11,438,070	$57,924,568
1964	24	Floods; droughts; earthquake; seismic sea wave; Typhoon Louise; and Hurricanes Cleo, Dora, and Hilda	$134,387,260	$672,545,214
Total	174		$274,781,958	$1,428,643,999

Table 4-1. Annual Major Disaster Statistics and Incidents, 1953–1964.

Source: Nominal expenditure data from U.S. House of Representatives (1974), 23, fema.gov/news/disasters.fema. A more recent source of information about presidential declaration details is at peripresdecusa.org/mainframe.htm.

developing "coordinated plans for federal programs which contribute to reconstruction and to economic and resources development in Alaska and...appropriate action by the federal government to carry out such plans."[21]

Two features of the Alaska Commission bear noting. First, although it did not include state or local representatives, it was charged with cooperating with the state to develop reconstruction plans and make recommendations for programs, projects, and legislation. Second, President Johnson took the unusual step of appointing a senator, Clinton P. Anderson of New Mexico, as the commission chair. This link between the legislative and executive branches facilitated action on legislation (notably, appropriations) and ensured that Congress was actively involved in the reconstruction and planning process.

The Johnson administration's prompt action led to significant results. Congress appropriated $23.5 million to help the new state rebuild essential facilities and, in precedent-setting fashion, to replace lost tax revenue (P.L. 88-451).[22] The 1964 statute also changed the cost share normally applied to the reconstruction of federal-aid highways by authorizing the forgiveness of loans. In short, a host of federal agencies—the SBA, U.S. Army Corps of Engineers, Federal Aviation Agency, Department of the Interior, and the Federal Housing Administration,

Downtown Anchorage after the 1964 earthquake. Before the earthquake the sidewalk on the left was at street level on the right. The Alaska earthquake resulted in an unprecedented federal government response. Photo courtesy of the U.S. Geological Survey.

among others—were engaged in Alaska's recovery. This approach—using existing funding streams and programs to expedite the delivery of assistance—continues to be used today. The urgent needs that must be met in a disaster do not allow for lengthy debate or consideration of administrative options.

Six months later, President Johnson furthered the work of the Alaska Commission through the Federal Field Committee for Development Planning in Alaska. Like the commission, the field committee was composed of federal officials in Alaska. Congress charged the committee with cooperating with state representatives, overseeing Alaska's, and ensuring that the economic and resource development plans reflected federal, state, and local policies. President Johnson and the administration officials strove to respect the sovereignty of the new state and the prerogatives of its elected representatives.

Hurricane Betsy, 1965

Less than a year after the earthquake in Alaska, disaster struck across the continent. After bedeviling forecasters with unpredictable travel plans, Hurricane Betsy crossed the Florida Keys and southern Florida, entered the Gulf of Mexico, and sped toward New Orleans. The limited technology of the 1960s made tracking the storm challenging. As reported by one federal official, "Because of the storm's erratic behavior, prepositioning of regional staffers in the field became a guessing game."[23] The peripatetic path of the hurricane as graphed in 1965 (precomputer graphics) is presented in Figure 4–1.

Hurricane Betsy had long-lasting and record-breaking impacts. It resulted in seventy-six deaths and destroyed much property in the southeastern United States. Causing more than $1 billion in damage (roughly $8 billion in 2005 dollars), it established a new benchmark for catastrophic destruction.

However, familiarity with the consequences of the Alaska earthquake and an awareness of the reach of the hurricane had led to greater disaster wisdom. Members of Congress and others recognized that the policy framework for disaster relief that had been built in 1950 could be expanded to accommodate more complex emergencies and situations. Thus, more than 138,000 Red Cross and federal government representatives were assigned to provide relief to hurricane-stricken areas.[24] Federal agencies, including the OCD and the OEP, worked with state and local civil defense agencies, the media, and nonprofit organizations to meet the needs of disaster victims. But perhaps the most noteworthy aspect of the response to Hurricane Betsy was the direct involvement of President Johnson, who took it upon himself to monitor the actions of federal agencies and mandated that federal personnel (including the director of OEP) remain in the stricken area to oversee relief operations. Thus, President Johnson modeled a new role for the president as an active and engaged emergency manager.

To help address the needs of victims, Congress passed the Southeast Hurricane Disaster Relief Act (P.L. 89-339). This legislation realized the need for assistance beyond that that authorized in the Federal Disaster Relief Act of 1950 and provided longer-term assistance than previous legislation had offered, in part by authorizing the sale of temporary housing directly to victims. Yet another important component of the relief act required HUD to examine the need for a national flood insurance policy. The 1964 law also expanded upon loan forgiveness provisions that had been enacted for Alaska by allowing business or property owners to cancel up to $1,800 of loans provided to restore or replace damaged or destroyed property. The loan forgiveness measure was continued in additional disaster relief legislation over the next five-year period.[25]

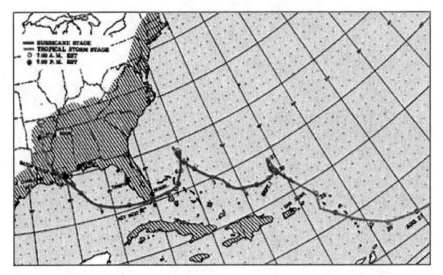

Figure 4–1. The track of Hurricane Betsy, which made landfall in South Florida on September 8 and in Louisiana in September 9, 1965.

Courtesy of the U.S. Department of Commerce, Environmental Science Services Administration, Weather Bureau, "Hurricane Betsy, Preliminary Report with Advisories and Bulletins Issued," September 15, 1965.

Policy Revisions

Again, the lessons from the Alaska earthquake, Hurricane Betsy, and other disasters in the mid-1960s were not lost on policy makers in Washington. Judging from the number of presidentially declared disasters, the risks from major emergencies appeared to be mounting. The basic assistance provided through the authority of the 1950 statute appeared sufficient for "normal" disasters. However, blockbuster catastrophes like the Alaska earthquake and Hurricane Betsy, especially in light of such trends as the development of larger and more expensive urban centers, the growing development of flood-prone areas (notably the shores), and enhanced expectations for government action, contributed to public calls and support for an increased federal role—an important indicator that disaster relief was a win-win option for policy makers. Photo opportunities, federal largess to victims (sometimes regardless of need), and an awareness that suffering could be alleviated brought significant changes to federal law.

New Orleans following Hurricane Betsy. The 1965 hurricane prompted Congress to pass legislation addressing the long-term needs of victims and calling for HUD to examine the need for a national flood insurance policy. Photo courtesy of the National Oceanic and Atmospheric Administration/R. Vetter, American Red Cross.

As a result, Congress renewed its interest in the federal government's role in disaster relief. In two important measures, lawmakers established new categories of assistance to individual victims of disasters and to state and local governments. Through the Disaster Relief Act of 1966 (P.L. 89-796), Congress made the most significant changes in policy in sixteen years. The statute authorized federal agencies to provide loans at below-market rates for as long as forty years, extended aid to unincorporated communities in rural areas, and created a new category of eligibility for public colleges and universities damaged by disasters. In addition, the 89th Congress took steps to improve administrative issues associated with federal disaster relief by linking civil defense warning systems with threats from natural disasters (a forerunner of the "dual-use" or "all-hazards" concepts developed later) and authorizing the president to coordinate federal assistance efforts.

The second major piece of legislation that passed at this time was the National Flood Insurance Act of 1968 (NFIA; P.L. 90-448). While federal flood insurance had been discussed several times in the past, studies had been completed—including one undertaken by HUD in 1966—that measured the viability of a federal insurance program based on a federal subsidy in high-risk flood zones. The NFIA authorized the federal government to provide flood insurance to property owners on the condition that local governments adopt regulations specifying that the insurance would be provided only if the applicant communities adopted land use regulations. With the NFIA, the federal government's role expanded through a back door into land use regulation and policy, an area normally vested in local government.

The 1968 legislation led to the creation of the National Flood Insurance Program (NFIP), a program based on the premise that private property owners would pay for future disaster losses (at least partially) through premiums. Significant changes to the NFIA were subsequently adopted, including a 1973 requirement that federally backed mortgages include flood insurance coverage (Flood Disaster Protection Act of 1973, P.L. 93-234).

In 1969, Congress broadened the Disaster Relief Act of 1966 with Public Law 91-79. This legislation

- Allowed disaster victims to use unoccupied federal housing and units held by local public housing authorities

- Authorized the president to lease manufactured homes and to make food coupon allotments available

- Provided unemployment assistance related to a disaster for up to one year

- Provided funding to states and localities for the removal of debris from private property when removal was in the public interest

- Expanded eligibility for public assistance, including the repair of state and county roads and the suppression of fires that could turn into major disaster conflagrations

- Provided authorizing grants to states for the improvement of comprehensive disaster relief plans and the establishment of agencies for that purpose.[26]

The far-reaching changes authorized by the 1969 legislation were scheduled to expire in 1970, leaving the 91st Congress to scramble for a more permanent solution. For the first time, Congress considered replacing the foundation laid by the 1950 Federal Disaster Relief Act with a more complex system. President Nixon summarized his concerns in a special message to Congress:

> The last Presidential special message on the subject of disaster assistance was written 18 years ago. Since that time, this program has grown in a piecemeal and often haphazard manner, involving over 50 separate congressional enactments and executive actions. This slow development process has created a complex program, one which has a number of gaps and overlaps and needs increased coordination. It is time for new legislation and executive action to make our federal disaster assistance program more effective and efficient.[27]

Renewed concerns led to the first omnibus legislation on disaster relief. The Disaster Relief Act of 1970 (P.L. 91-606), which superseded the 1950 statute, established a "superstructure" of policy and administrative guidance, with a growing emphasis on aid to individuals. It continued some of the policies that had been in place since 1950, including

- Maintenance of lead coordination by a federal officer to ensure the cooperation of federal agencies

- Delegation to the president of authority for disaster determination

- Provision of federal equipment, supplies, and personnel

- Funding for state planning assistance

- Prohibition of the duplication of federal disaster assistance (such as through insurance payments)

- Specification of disaster loan interest rates

- Unemployment assistance

- Assistance in debris removal

- Funding for the suppression of fires that could become major disasters

- Funding for the repair or replacement of state and local public facilities.

However, the Disaster Relief Act of 1970 might be considered almost revolutionary in that it dramatically expanded the federal role in both the pre- and post-disaster time periods, adding such new authorities and limitations as

- Detailing federal personnel to disaster areas through "emergency support teams"

- Recognizing the role of nongovernmental organizations

- Restricting the use of federal aid for the reconstruction of public facilities to conditions that existed immediately before the disaster struck

- Giving reconstruction work and contract preference to firms and individuals based in the stricken area

- Authorizing federal agency heads to waive procedures (but not conditions) for assistance

- Ensuring that disaster aid be provided in a nondiscriminatory manner

- Providing assistance before a dangerous condition reaches catastrophic levels

- Augmenting emergency communication and transportation systems

- Repairing or replacing damaged or destroyed federal facilities

- Providing temporary housing assistance of a general nature, at no charge, for a year after the disaster (not solely through the provision of leased manufactured homes) and providing mortgage and rental payments for individuals facing eviction or foreclosure

- Providing legal assistance to lower-income families

- Authorizing grants to local governments to replace revenue streams disrupted by the disaster.

The Disaster Relief Act of 1970 also implicitly addressed pre-disaster mitigation and preparedness needs by ordering the Office of Emergency Preparedness (previously the Office of Emergency Planning, but renamed by President Johnson in 1968) to investigate "additional or improved plans, procedures, and facilities… necessary to provide immediate effective action to prevent or minimize losses of publicly or privately owned property and personal injuries or deaths which could result from fires (forest and grass), earthquakes, tornadoes, freezes and frosts, tsunamis, storm surges and tides, and floods, which are or threaten to become major disasters."

Administrative Changes

From 1966 through 1970, Congress evaluated legislative options concerning the scope of federal assistance. The debate did not explicitly raise questions about which level of government—federal or state—should have primary administrative responsibilities. Despite the presumption that federal aid supplemented state and local efforts, federal officials made decisions in many critical areas concerning how resources would be allocated and what commitments the states would need to make. Moreover, to ensure that federal officials coordinated activities after each disaster, Congress required the president to appoint a federal coordinating officer, who would be responsible for establishing field offices and working with state, local, and nongovernmental entities to ensure that disaster victims obtained the assistance to which they were entitled. Administrative "ownership" of the emergency management process shifted from Congress and the Capitol to the president and the OEP staff.

As was the case in other policy areas, state and local officials expressed dissatisfaction with the federal bureaucracy and the complexities of the emergency management process. In 1972, federal and state officials reviewed administrative procedures to determine how the complex mix of federal, state, local, and private responsibilities would converge at the scene of a disaster. In general, review of the responses to major catastrophes indicated that constraints on state and local authorities often hampered the ability of those authorities to respond.

Administrative responsibility for the Disaster Relief Act in its various forms rotated over the decades from one entity to another. From its establishment in 1961, the OEP (both before and after its name change) had responsibility for carrying out the provisions of the 1950 Federal Disaster Relief Act and subsequent legislation. In 1973, however, as part of a larger effort to reduce the centralization of authority in the White House, President Nixon abolished the OEP and transferred the responsibility for disaster relief administration to HUD, the General Services Administration, and the Department of the Treasury, thereby limiting the involvement of the president and his immediate staff.[28]

The decision to move primary authority from the White House into the domain of administrative agencies has been the focus of extensive analysis.[29] For example, an investigation conducted in response to coordination difficulties after Hurricane Andrew struck the U.S. coast in 1992 concludes that "the location and relationship of an emergency management agency to the institutional presidency and the President have always been variable and problematic."[30] While there is no definitive answer as to the extent to which the president should be involved in emergency management functions, events have shown that when responses to *catastrophic* disasters involve decisions made by, or with the support of, the president, their outcomes tend to be superior to those of responses handled solely by administrative channels.

Disaster Declarations and Funding

Federal funding data clearly indicate the federal government's increasing commitment to disaster assistance. A comparison of the figures in Table 4–2 below with those in Table 4–1 illustrates the growth in federal expenditures over the two decades since the 1950 Federal Disaster Relief Act. This growth may be associated with an increase in the number of catastrophic disasters that occurred over this period, as well as with the states' growing realization that federal funds were a relatively low-cost resource. The data arguably support the former perspective: although there were fewer disasters from 1965 to 1970 than there were during the twelve years prior to 1965, federal expenditures doubled, a result that is to be expected after large-scale events.

Despite the expenditures for the largest, most severe disasters, funds were not always allocated for catastrophic losses. As in the previous decade, the most deadly catastrophe to occur between 1965 and 1970 did not result in a major disaster declaration. It occurred in December 1968 when a pandemic associated with the Hong Kong flu spread throughout the United States, resulting in almost 34,000 deaths.[31]

Year	Number of Presidential Disaster Declarations	Types of Disasters Resulting in a Presidential Declaration	Expenditures, in Current Dollars	Expenditures, in Constant (2005) Dollars
1965	24	Tornadoes, floods, storms, water shortage, earthquake, and Hurricane Betsy	$88,378,156	$434,804,781
1966	10	Tornadoes, floods, storms, typhoon, and high tides	$10,765,330	$51,854,806
1967	10	Tornadoes, floods, storms, forest fires, Typhoon Sally, and Hurricane Beulah	$28,826,139	$134,509,804
1968	18	Tornadoes, floods, storms, ice storm, Typhoon Jean, and Hurricane Gladys	$14,219,629	$64,078,255
1969	28	Tornadoes, floods, storms, landslide, and Hurricane Camille	$231,666,874	$998,345,932
1970	16	Tornadoes, floods, fires, ice jams, and Hurricane Celia	$94,062,792	$384,359,429
Total	106		$467,918,920	$2,067,953,007

Table 4-2. Annual Disaster Statistics and Incidents, 1965–1970.

Source: Nominal expenditure data from U.S. House of Representatives (1974), 23, FEMA.gov/news/disasters.fema.

Focusing Events of the Early 1970s

Like Hurricane Betsy and the Alaska earthquake in the 1960s, other events in the 1970s served to focus attention on federal policy gaps. On February 9, 1971, in California's San Fernando Valley area, an earthquake measuring 6.5 on the Richter scale resulted in sixty-five deaths and roughly $500 million in damage. The earthquake also wreaked significant damage on public and private nonprofit hospitals. Congress responded with legislation that expanded the disaster relief structure (P.L. 92-209), making private nonprofit hospitals eligible for repair and reconstruction grants (not loans).

In mid-June 1972, Hurricane Agnes made landfall on the Gulf Coast and moved north along the East Coast to North Carolina, where it traveled back over water into the Atlantic, recharged its batteries, and then struck the United States again, causing severe flooding in Virginia, Maryland, and Pennsylvania (Figure 4–2). The storm resulted in fifty deaths, caused more than $2 billion in property damage, and—like the earthquake in 1971—forced policy makers to address gaps in disaster relief coverage. By August, Congress and President Nixon agreed that the federal government would play a greater role in disaster response and recovery, thereby further involving it in what had been state responsibilities. One former official of the American Red Cross noted that federal aid provided after Hurricane Agnes resulted in a decrease in individual and family assistance provided by that nonprofit organization.[32] The federal government passed legislation (P.L. 92-385) that increased the practice of partial loan forgiveness (including an increase in the cap on forgiveness to $5,000 and an interest rate of 1 percent) and expanded the purposes for which loans could be provided to include refinancing mortgages on affected property at subsidized rates. In addition, following the pattern established by the previous year's legislation, the 1972 act authorized the provision of grants to private nonprofit educational institutions that had been damaged or destroyed by Hurricane Agnes.

The 1972 legislation is notable not only because it expanded the federal government's role, but also because it included a congressional mandate for a study of federal disaster policies:

> The President shall conduct a thorough review of existing disaster relief legislation as it relates to emergency loans and housing loans administered by the Farmers Home Administration of the United States Department of Agriculture, and not later than January 31, 1973, he shall transmit to the Committee on Agriculture and Forestry of the Senate and the Committee on Agriculture of the House of Representatives a report containing specific legislative proposals for the comprehensive revision of such legislation in or to (1) adjust the benefits and the coverage available to persons affected by disasters; (2) improve the execution of the program by simplifying and eliminating unnecessary administrative procedures; and (3) prevent the misuse of benefits made available under the program (86 Stat. 559).

The 1971 earthquake that struck the San Fernando Valley caused over $500 million in property damage, such as that which occurred when the Veterans Administration Hospital collapsed, as shown here. Photo courtesy of the U.S. Geological Survey.

By enacting this legislation, Congress aimed to construct a continuing omni-bus disaster relief program based on systematic procedures that would not require significant policy changes from one "unparalleled" or "truly devastating" disas-ter to another. The charge to improve the delivery of federal disaster assistance brought attention to the administration of disaster aid, which had received rela-tively little attention prior to this. This mandate laid the groundwork for the most extensive revision of federal policy to date in 1974 and, of great importance to those concerned with administration, presaged the establishment of the Federal Emergency Management Administration (FEMA) in 1979.

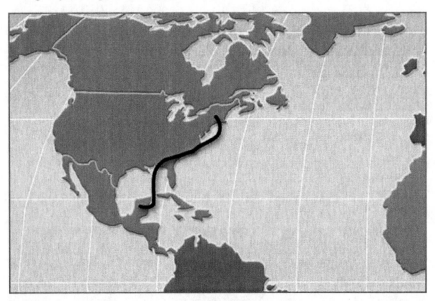

Figure 4–2. The track of Hurricane Agnes, 1972. This hurricane caused severe inland flooding in Virginia, Maryland, Pennsylvania, New Jersey, and neighboring states. Two months later, the federal government passed new disaster legislation.

An Expanding Federal Mission

In 1973, President Nixon submitted a report to Congress that sought to reorient federal disaster policy to ensure that state and local governments, not the federal government, would exercise the lead role in emergency management. The Nixon administration sought a new policy direction, including greater reliance on insur-ance and hazard mitigation, but Congress disagreed. The Disaster Relief Act of 1974 (P.L. 93-288) was not a radical departure from past legislation; it continued to expand the range of federal disaster assistance and preparedness authority. It required communities receiving federal disaster assistance to create mitigation plans. It also removed the flood insurance mandate.

Even more than past statutory additions to the 1950 authority, the 1974 legislation vested greater authority in the president. It authorized the president to establish a federal program of disaster preparedness that cut across agency boundaries and to build an emergency communications system with federal and private resources. In addition, the statute authorized the president to provide federal assistance to repair public facilities and provide limited assistance to individuals. While it strengthened the premise that federal aid supplemented, not replaced, state and local authority (by establishing requirements that gubernatorial requests had to provide details on state resource commitments), this point was a policy pronouncement with little teeth.

Many of the categories of assistance that had been adopted in earlier legislation were carried over in 1974, but some important changes were made. These included

- Addition of a new classification, "emergency," allowing a lower level of federal assistance when the president determined that, although overwhelmed, state and local governments did not require a "major disaster" declaration

- Removal of references to specific administration officials (notably the administrator of the Federal Disaster Assistance Administration), replacing them with authorization for presidential action

- Removal of the requirement that applicant states commit an equal share of the costs to receive federal assistance for preparedness grant development, and inclusion of a new emphasis on disaster prevention (precursor to the hazard mitigation authority enacted in 1988)

- Consolidation of all disaster administration provisions into one title (Title III)

- An added requirement that state contributions be a "significant proportion" of the "reasonable expenditures" requirement to ensure that federal aid supplemented, rather than supplanted, state resources

- Addition of a section that imposed civil and criminal penalties on those who defrauded the government or misapplied funds

- Authorization for the president to ensure that supplies and material needed for reconstruction would be available in the disaster area

- Exemption of public facility restoration activities from environmental review requirements established in the National Environmental Policy Act of 1969

- Enhancement of provisions requiring that restored public and private structures be repaired or rebuilt pursuant to building codes and standards

- Expansion of federal assistance for the repair of public facilities, including recreational facilities (previously excluded from eligibility), and allowance for "in-lieu" grants to be provided so that communities could elect to rebuild new facilities to replace destroyed facilities that were no longer desired

- Replacement of grants with loans to provide funds to communities that lost revenue streams, but with authority granted to the president to cancel loan repayment requirements should communities be unable to meet operating budgets within three years

- Expansion of housing assistance for minimal repairs to make damaged housing habitable, along with authority to authorize the transfer of manufactured homes to disaster victims

- A new individual and family grant program to replace loan forgiveness provisions enacted in previous years

- New crisis counseling authority to ensure that mental health assistance would be available to disaster victims

- Authorization for the president to establish a disaster preparedness program, provide technical assistance to the states for the development of "comprehensive plans and practicable programs for preparation against disasters," and award grants to states for the development and maintenance of disaster plans.

The need for the 1974 legislation became apparent the very month that it was signed into law. On April 3 and 4, a series of 148 tornadoes struck thirteen states, resulting in more than three hundred deaths and hundreds of millions of dollars in property losses.[33] The new and expanded categories of individual and family assistance that had been included in the 1974 legislation were put to use in the states that had been affected by this record-setting tornado event.

Civil Defense in the Early 1970s

Federal civil defense policy remained on the back burner throughout the 1970s. In 1973, the Department of Defense adopted a dual-use policy, whereby civil defense activities could also be used to prepare for natural disasters, and the parallel tracks of civil defense and natural disaster management began to merge into the broader concept of emergency management. This policy led to new responsibilities for the Defense Department, such as funding emergency preparedness applications submitted by state and local governments, administering emergency warning and communications systems, and building an intergovernmental network to reduce catastrophic losses. These responsibilities differed from the department's central military mission, and the funding requests submitted to Congress suggest that the

The tornado that struck Xenia, Ohio, on April 3 was the deadliest and most destructive of the series of 1974 storms that resulted in more than three hundred deaths in thirteen states. This was the first major disaster to fall under the Disaster Relief Act of 1974. Photo courtesy of the Department of Homeland Security.

Defense Department was an unwilling guardian of civil disaster preparedness. In 1976, the department recommended a reduction in aid to local governments and encouraged Congress to amend the Civil Defense Act (CDA) to require that state and local governments use federal civil defense funding only to prepare for nuclear attacks. Congress rejected that recommendation and instead amended the CDA to allow the use of the civil defense "structure" for disasters "other than disasters caused by enemy attack" (P.L. 94-361).

Despite the urging of Congress, funding for civil defense and administrative authority languished; however, the protection of the civilian population from nuclear attack took a new direction. The Nuclear Civil Protection Planning effort, also known as crisis relocation planning (CRP), emphasized disaster preparedness by establishing plans to quickly relocate civilians (given sufficient warning) from high-risk areas and to shelter them in place when they could not be evacuated.[34] But by this time, policy administrators had a hard time "selling" the concept of nuclear threats to a jaded public. CRP suffered from unrealistic expectations and lack of public (and congressional) support, and it faded from practice.

Carter Administration Initiatives

While much of the emphasis since 1950 had been on the substance of legislation and the type of assistance to be provided in the case of emergencies, federal officials continued to wrestle with the question of leadership. Concern about the adequacy of emergency preparedness spurred a joint congressional committee to undertake a comprehensive survey of federal activities. From results of the survey sent to federal agencies in July 1976, a joint congressional committee came to the following conclusion:

> As regards civil emergency preparedness for natural and man-made disasters or economic disruptions, analysis disclosed that government activity in this area is far more substantial than is generally realized but also suffers from the lack of high-level attention, organizational diffusion, inadequate foresight and coordination, weak or misdirected funding, and the absence of a comprehensive approach to what is basically a homogenous group of planning and programmatic functions. The delegation of authorities, in particular, has led to a situation in which authority is not commensurate with responsibilities. Here the problem is still further complicated by the fact that, unlike industrial mobilization, government at all levels—federal, regional, state and local—is involved, placing adequate coordination at a premium, if measures are to be useful in terms of protecting life and property.[35]

State and local officials also evinced displeasure with the mix of federal emergency management authorities, arguing that their policies and practices were confusing and cumbersome. As a result, the Council of State Governments and the National Governors Association (NGA) developed a new policy framework that included a "comprehensive approach to emergency preparedness planning."[36] Through these organizations, as well as other channels, the states asked President Jimmy Carter to establish a more centralized federal emergency management administrative mechanism. In a multivolume study released by the NGA concerning the status of emergency management among the states and territories, the authors expressed concern about a "lack of a national policy for the management of natural, man-made, and attack emergencies."[37] In their view, the lack of an overarching federal policy regarding disaster mitigation, preparedness, response, and recovery, when coupled with the dispersion of responsibilities among numerous federal agencies, hampered the ability of states to manage disaster situations. Having multiple agencies involved also made it more difficult for states to access the wide range of federal assistance that was available.[38]

In August 1977, President Carter mandated a study of federal preparedness and response to natural, accidental, and wartime emergencies. The problems identified by the study's authors included redundancy, a lack of clarity about federal emergency preparedness programs and planning efforts, confusion about jurisdictions and boundaries of responsibilities, and lack of accountability. The report's main recommendation focused on the need for a new federal entity to administer many of the federal emergency management authorities.[39] (Certain authorities would remain with the SBA and Department of Agriculture because their services were targeted to the clients helped by those federal entities on a continual basis.)

President Carter responded by establishing FEMA, under Reorganization Plan Number 3 of 1978, giving it responsibility over a wide range of functions, including emergency preparedness, civil defense, disaster relief, emergency communications, flood and crime insurance, fire prevention, and continuity of government. The agency was created on April 1, 1979, with four main components: the Federal Disaster Assistance Administration and the Federal Insurance Administration, both transferred from HUD; the Defense Civil Preparedness Agency, transferred from the Department of Defense; and the U.S. Fire Administration, transferred from the Department of Commerce.[40]

Year	Number of Presidential Disaster Declarations	Types of Disasters Resulting in a Presidential Declaration	Expenditures, in Current Dollars	Expenditures, in Constant (2005) Dollars
1971	16	San Fernando earthquake, floods, and Hurricane Edith	$214,436,787	$834,550,498
1972	47	Storms, floods, Tropical Storm Agnes, and toxic algae in coastal waters	$713,889,127	$2,653,063,731
1973	45	Storms, urban fire, dam collapse, tornadoes, and landslides	$173,800,498	$618,635,675
1974	45	Floods, tornadoes, freeze in salmon spawning area, and Hurricane Carmen	$250,000,000	$829,951,909
1975	37	Storms, tornadoes, floods, and Tropical Storm Eloise	$206,000,000	$619,458,209
1976	29	Storms, floods, and Typhoons Marie, Pamela, and Therese	$362,000,000	$1,015,309,802
1977	21	Ice conditions, shrimp loss, dam collapse, storms, and floods	$294,000,000	$767,122,608
1978	24	Storms, flooding, and Tropical Storm Carmen	$461,000,000	$1,126,990,925
Total	264		$2,675,126,412	$8,465,083,356

Table 4-3. Annual Major Disaster Statistics and Incidents, 1971-1978.

Source: Nominal expenditure data from U.S. House of Representatives (1974), 23, fema.gov/news/disasters/fema.

During the Carter presidency, the Disaster Relief Fund continued to be a growing source of assistance and cost to the federal treasury. Table 4–3 presents information on the major disaster declarations issued from 1971 through 1978. By the end of that period, the federal role in emergency management had reached even higher levels of funding than those previously summarized.

The Downside of Technology

This book deals only briefly with environmental hazards and disasters, yet these are an important element of emergency management history.[41] The greater interest in scientific progress and the answers found in technological innovation presented the nation with opportunities and risks. In the 1970s, new categories of catastrophes became evident—those caused by human error or malfeasance and involving chemicals or other toxic agents. The first major event occurred in the Midwest in the early 1970s, when a contractor sprayed waste oil containing hazardous chemicals, including dioxin, on roads around Times Beach, Missouri. Flooding raised awareness that there were serious environmental consequences of this action. Following years of investigation, Congress ultimately enacted legislation to provide relocation and other aid after environmental emergencies.

The second major human-caused disaster of the 1970s was a chemical disaster around Love Canal, in upstate New York. Love Canal brought the dangers of an environmental catastrophe to the nation's attention. The disaster was years in the making, as a chemical company had used an old canal as a dumping ground for waste products. The neighborhood had an extremely high rate of cancer and an alarming number of birth defects. Children at the neighborhood 99th Street School were constantly ill. Beginning in 1978, Lois Gibbs, president of the Love Canal Homeowners' Association, led an effort to investigate community concerns about the health of its residents. Her discovery of chemicals in the adjacent canal began a three-year fight to prove that the toxins buried by Hooker Chemical, a subsidiary of Occidental Petroleum, were responsible for the environmental disaster.

This was a new type of disaster as the homeowners were opposed not only by Occidental Petroleum but also by government officials, who argued that the chemicals had been successfully contained within the former landfill. Since residents could not prove that the chemicals on their property had come from Hooker's disposal site, they could not prove liability. Throughout the legal battle, homeowners continued to ail, but they were unable to sell their property to move away from the land they believed was poisoning them. The 99th Street School, which was located within the former boundary of the Hooker Chemical landfill site, was closed and demolished, but neither the school board nor the chemical company would accept liability.

The media picked up the story, making it national news. This made it even more difficult for public officials to deny that toxic chemicals were affecting the health of Love Canal's residents. President Carter used the emergency authority granted in the 1974 disaster relief legislation to relocate families from the area. The Environmental Protection Agency sued Occidental Petroleum, and in 1995 Occidental's officials agreed to provide financial restitution ($129 million). In all, the event made it clear to emergency management professionals and policy makers that additional policies were needed to prepare for and respond to such environmental emergencies.

Conclusion: The Emergence of Disaster Policy

During the nineteen years covered by this chapter, the federal government expanded its involvement in a number of domestic policy areas, including education, housing, health care, and income support. National goals in these and other areas were established; new policies and programs directed billions of dollars toward state and local governments; and federal policy makers realized that such actions resulted in public support. In general, more federal government assistance and involvement served as the mantra for the nation. Measured in constant dollars, federal appropriations for disaster relief were seventy times more in 1978 ($1.1 billion) than in 1953 ($16 million). Over this period, federal disaster relief legislation became more complex and targeted a greater number of communities, organizations, and people. More types of assistance were authorized, greater discretion was granted to the executive branch, and more organizations were chartered to conduct emergency management activities.

Several specific areas of disaster response are worth noting:

- **Response capabilities and requirements.** There were no federal requirements to ensure that disaster response and relief efforts would be coordinated or delivered in accordance with specified standards. Rather, the 1950 Federal Disaster Relief Act required merely that federal agency officials "cooperate to the fullest extent possible" with one another, with state and local governments, and with the Red Cross. By 1978, Congress required that the president "coordinate" the response activities of federal agencies and form emergency support teams to be deployed to a major disaster area.

- **Public facilities.** In 1950, Congress authorized the president to help local governments by "making emergency repairs to and temporary replacements of" public facilities. By 1978, legislation had been enacted to (1) pay for the repair of transportation infrastructure; (2) replace, repair, restore, or reconstruct state and local government public facilities (including airports, recreational facilities, and parks); (3) replace, repair, restore, or reconstruct private nonprofit facilities that provided specified services, such as hospitals; and (4) provide cash grants in lieu of restoring, replacing, repairing, or rebuilding state and local facilities. The federal government could—and did—use this authority to replace municipal and state structures destroyed during a disaster. Local governments also could receive loans for the loss of taxes and other revenues, and loan forgiveness policies protected localities from defaulting on these loans.

- **Aid to individuals.** A much wider range of federal government assistance was available to individuals and families in 1978 than in 1950. The 1950 Federal Disaster Relief Act authorized federal agencies to provide equipment, supplies, and personnel to state and local governments, and, through the American Red Cross, to distribute food and medicine to individual victims; however, it did not expressly authorize direct assistance to victims of a disaster. By 1978, federal temporary housing assistance was available for individuals and families affected by a disaster. The federal government also covered the costs of installing essential utilities to temporary mobile homes when it was in the public interest. In addition, the federal government was authorized to provide unemployment assistance to people put out of work by a disaster, grants (of up to $5,000) to victims to help them meet immediate needs, food coupons and surplus food, legal services for low-income victims, and crisis counseling assistance.

Regarding the federal government's approach to hazard mitigation and disaster prevention, the following areas had been strengthened between 1950 and 1978:

- **Preparedness.** Although the 1950 Disaster Relief Assistance Act specified the intent of Congress "to foster the development of such state and local organizations and plans to cope with major disasters," the legislation did not authorize or appropriate funding for that purpose. The CDA of 1950, by comparison, did provide funding for a federal preparedness infrastructure (the Federal Civil Defense Administration and the Civil Defense Advisory Council), the construction of facilities, and the purchase of necessary material, but this funding was targeted at preparing for an enemy attack, not natural disasters. By 1978, Congress had amended the CDA to authorize the use of such funds on a dual-use basis: to prepare for the threat of enemy attack *and* for natural disasters.

- **Mitigation.** Prior to 1950, the term *hazard mitigation* was rarely, if ever, used, and mitigation activities were not a focus of federal policy. By 1978, however, Congress had specified that federal disaster preparedness programs should include mitigation; allowed technical assistance to be used for "hazard reduction, avoidance, and mitigation"; required that public facilities that were replaced or repaired be compliant with building codes and standards; and required that state and local governments receiving funds assess "natural hazards" in their jurisdiction and act to "mitigate such hazards, including safe land-use and construction practices" in accordance with federal standards.

For almost thirty years the federal government had, at different times, inched toward a policy that gave administrators a superior and determinative role in emergency management. At times during that period, federal policy received a hard push from nature, such as the Alaska earthquake or Hurricane Betsy. Periodically, members of Congress or administration officials nudged federal policy in a different direction. By 1978, however, experience had shown that coordination of federal and nonfederal action, not dispersion, was the best approach. Increasing presidential grants of authority and discretion was one element of this approach. The institutionalization of policy in one entity, as discussed in the next chapter, was another.

Endnotes

1   Bruce D. Callander, "The Ground Observer Corps," *Air Force Magazine* 89 (February 2006): 80–83, afa.org/magazine/feb2006/0206GOC.pdf.

2   Earl Warren, *Legislation Affecting Civil Defense and Disaster* (Sacramento: State of California, 1951).

3   Congress also enacted the Defense Production Act of 1950 (P.L. 81-932) to ensure that the nation's industrial production would be allocated to meet military and civilian needs in the event of threats to national security.

4   Executive Order no. 10186, *Federal Register* 15 (December 5, 1950): 8557.

5   Precedents to this legislation included P.L. 80-233, which authorized the president to transfer surplus federal property to the Federal Works Agency to alleviate suffering and damage from floods; P.L. 80–785, the first law to appropriate funding for disaster relief without specifying a specific disaster; and P.L. 81-266, which established an emergency fund to help state and local governments and other agencies provide relief following a natural disaster.

6   The debate on the legislation is set forth in the *Congressional Record* (August 7, 1950), 11895–11915.

7   Ibid., 11905.

8   While the FCDA was charged with administrative responsibilities for civil defense in the CDA, the 1950 disaster relief statute referred solely to presidential authority. President Truman delegated responsibility for administering P.L. 81-875 to the FCDA by executive orders (10346 and 10427). The FCDA was charged with preparing federal emergency plans and given authority for disaster relief administration.

9   Gary A. Kreps, "The Federal Emergency Management System in the United States: Past and Present," *International Journal of Mass Emergencies and Disasters* 8, no. 3 (1990): 277.

10   Dwight D. Eisenhower, "Message of the President, Reorganization Plan No. 1 of 1958," U.S. Code Home, law.justia.com/codes/us/title5a/5a_4_62_2_.html.

11   Harry Beller Yoshpe, *Our Missing Shield: The U.S. Civil Defense Program in Historical Perspective*, Contract No. DCPA 01-79-C-0294 (Washington, D.C.: Federal Emergency Management Agency, 1981), 27, dtic.mil/cgi-bin/GetTRDoc?AD=ADA099634&Location=U2&doc=GetTRDoc.pdf.

12   Note, for example, the confluence of organizations involved in the response to the 1927 Mississippi River floods.

13   E. L. Quarantelli, *Local Emergency Management Agencies: Research Findings on Their Progress and Problems in the Last Two Decades* (Newark: Disaster Research Center, University of Delaware, 1988), 2, putnam.lib.udel.edu:8080/dspace/bitstream/handle/19716/498/PP126 .pdf?sequence=3.

14   See Roy S. Popkin, "The History and Politics of Disaster Management in the United States," in *Nothing to Fear: Risks and Hazards in American Society,* ed. Andrew Kirby (Tucson: University of Arizona Press, 1990), 109–113.

15   While the Federal Disaster Relief Act and the Small Business Act marked the development of a new, expanded federal role, not all federal disaster relief legislation of the early 1950s proved to be successful. Congress passed the Federal Flood Insurance Act (P.L. 84-1016) in 1956 but never appropriated funds for its implementation. The act would have established the first federally backed disaster insurance program, but its implementation failed, largely because costs were not identified and it also had no mitigation provisions.

16   Information derived from the U.S. House of Representatives, "Message from the President of the United States, Report Covering Expenditures Appropriated to the President for Federal Assistance in Major Disaster Areas," House Document 434, April 22, 1952.

17   Yoshpe, Our Missing Shield, 164.

18   See "Pandemics and Pandemic Threats since 1900," pandemicflu.gov/general/ historicaloverview.html.

19   In 1992, for example, Congress appropriated $45 million to HUD "for community development activities in areas impacted by Hurricane Andrew, Hurricane Iniki, or Typhoon Omar" (P.L. 103-50); the nearly $3 billion appropriated to FEMA for disaster relief and the $432 million appropriated to the SBA for disaster loans were to be used more generically "for disaster relief" (P.L. 102-368) and "for the cost of disaster assistance loans" (P.L. 102368), respectively.

20   Wallace R. Hansen, The Alaska Earthquake, March 27, 1964: Field Investigations and Reconstruction Effort, Geological Survey Professional Paper 541 (Washington, D.C.: U.S. Government Printing Office, 1966), 1.

21   Executive Order 11150, Federal Register 29 (April 4, 1964): 4789. Congress supported the presidential directives by appropriating funds, forgiving loan repayment requirements, and authorizing federal assistance for the repayment of mortgages in legislation (P.L. 88-451).

22   In the Disaster Relief Act of 1970, Congress followed this precedent by including a provision for grants to local communities to replace taxes and other funding streams that were disrupted by a major disaster.

23   From a report by Pete Craig, public information officer for OCD Region 3 (undated, available in Tab D, file 397-HB, National Archives holdings).

24   Office of Emergency Planning, Hurricane Betsy: Federal Action in Disaster (Washington, D.C.: Executive Office of the President, 1966), inside front cover.

25   "In 1965, the 30-year maturity was made standard for all SBA disaster loans, and, in addition, SBA was authorized to suspend payment of principal and interest for 5 years. A major turning point occurred in 1965 with the establishment of an $1,800 forgiveness provision for victims of Hurricane Betsy. The cancellation feature was made permanent in 1969 and was increased to $2,500 in the Disaster Relief Act of 1970." U.S. House of Representatives, After Disaster Strikes: Federal Programs and Organizations, 93rd Cong., 2nd sess., 1974, 18.

26   This provision is the first hazard mitigation mandate authorized by Congress in disaster relief legislation, outside of flood prevention legislation. The first use of the term mitigation occurred in the Disaster Relief Act of 1974 (PL 93-288).

27   Richard Nixon, "Special Message to the Congress on Federal Disaster Assistance, April 22, 1970," Public Papers of the Presidents of the United States: Richard Nixon (Washington, D.C.: U.S. Government Printing Office, 1971), 129.

28   In 1996, President Clinton extended ex officio cabinet membership to James Lee Witt, director of FEMA. However, primary administrative authority remained in FEMA, an independent agency outside of the White House. See "Telephone Remarks to the National Emergency Management Association Meeting," Weekly Compilation of Presidential Documents 32 (February 26, 1996), 380–381.

29   For example, see Richard T. Sylves and William L. Waugh Jr., eds., Disaster Management in the U.S. and Canada: The Politics, Policymaking, Administration and Analysis of Emergency Management (Springfield, Ill.: Charles C. Thomas Publisher, 1996).

30   Gary L. Wamsley et al., Coping with Catastrophe: Building Emergency Management System to Meet People's Needs in Natural and Manmade Disasters (Washington, D.C.: National Academy of Public Administration, 1993), 22.

31   "Pandemics and Pandemic Threats since 1900."

32   Popkin, "History and Politics of Disaster Management."

33   "Tornado Super Outbreak, April 3, 1974," april31974.com.

34   See Defense Civil Preparedness Agency, *Protection in the Nuclear Age* (Washington, D.C.: U.S. Department of Defense, 1977).

35   U.S. Joint Committee on Defense Production, *Annual Report 1976,* vol. 1, 95th Cong., 1st sess., House Report 95-352 (1977), 20.

36   See Council of State Governments, *Comprehensive Emergency Preparedness Planning in State Government* (Lexington, Ky.: Council of State Governments, 1976); and National Governors' Association (NGA), *1978 Emergency Preparedness Project and Comprehensive Emergency Management: A Governor's Guide* (Washington, D.C.: NGA, 1978).

37   NGA, *Emergency Preparedness Project Final Report* (Washington, D.C.: NGA, 1978), xi.

38   As part of the project, the NGA issued summary information on federal policies; it also took the lead in identifying policies at the state and federal levels on domestic terrorism, a topic that few people had on their radar.

39   President's Reorganization Project, *Federal Emergency Preparedness and Response Historical Survey* (Washington, D.C.: U.S. Office of Management and Budget, 1978).

40   Executive Order 12127, 44 *Federal Register* (March 31, 1979): 19367.

41   For an example, see Susan L. Cutter, *Living with Risk* (London: Edward Arnold Publishers, 1995), which addresses the history and impact of chemical accidents and policy responses.

Chapter 5

Federal Emergency Management Comes of Age: 1979-2001

Richard T. Sylves

This chapter begins with an overview of emergency management at the federal level and examines the historical period between the creation of the Federal Emergency Management Agency (FEMA) in 1979 and the terrorist attacks of September 11, 2001. FEMA's place in the executive branch and within the federal system is explored. This is followed by an examination of the importance of presidents in emergency management and an analysis of how presidents have used their disaster declaration authority to shape federal emergency management and, indirectly, the profession of emergency management. One section takes up the science and technology of disaster; a second describes the growing importance of public infrastructure in emergency management; a third furnishes an overview of federal disaster laws from 1979 to 2001; and a fourth acknowledges how the profession of emergency management has advanced. The chapter offers an overview of the major disaster-focusing events that transpired during the period and ends with a summary and set of observations.

The Creation and Maturation of FEMA

In 1979, President Jimmy Carter issued two executive orders (E.O. 12127 and E.O. 12148) to implement Reorganization Plan No. 1 of 1978, which merged disparate disaster-related responsibilities into the new Federal Emergency Management Agency.[1] FEMA absorbed several other agencies, including the Federal Insurance Administration, the National Fire Prevention and Control Administration, the National Weather Service Community Preparedness Program,[2] the Federal Preparedness Agency of the General Services Administration, and the Federal Disaster Assistance Administration activities from the U.S. Department of Housing and Urban Development (HUD). The Defense Civil Preparedness Agency within the U.S. Department of Defense was also transferred to FEMA, thus assigning FEMA major civil defense duties.[3]

From its inception, FEMA has addressed all phases of emergency management: mitigation, preparedness, response, and recovery, a paradigm developed by the National Governors Association in the late 1970s.[4] In so doing, it has worked with a host of agencies and organizations, including state and local emergency management agencies, the American Red Cross and other voluntary organizations, and private corporations, particularly its contractors. It has also worked with various federal agencies that have statutory authorities for emergency management duties, or have people or resources for response and recovery operations.

Until it became part of the U.S. Department of Homeland Security (DHS) on March 1, 2003, FEMA was an independent federal administrative agency with no commerce clause regulatory powers.[5] Over the years, it proved to be especially adept at mobilizing contractors and temporary workers to meet most of the nation's disaster management needs. While its full-time 1979–2001 workforce never exceeded four thousand, the agency relied on paid reservists and trained volunteers, private contractors with disaster knowledge, and nonprofit organizations as circumstances dictated. FEMA's emergency response and recovery capabilities relied heavily on the agency's ability to mobilize and work cooperatively with the people of other federal agencies working under the various emergency response plans in effect between 1979 and 2001, most particularly the Federal Response Plan (FRP). The FRP emerged in 1989 and was used well into the 1990s.[6]

FEMA's duties gradually broadened as the agency came to address a growing range of natural and human-caused disasters. From 1979 to 1992, FEMA assisted state and local governments in their response to several major hurricanes, earthquakes, a great many floods, severe storms, and winter blizzards, as well as a volcanic eruption (1980) in Washington State. During this period, FEMA also assumed primary responsibility for the Cold War federal civil defense preparedness initiatives of Presidents Jimmy Carter, Ronald Reagan, and George H. W. Bush.[7]

In the mid- to late 1990s, several major disasters—including the Great Midwest Flood (1993), California's Northridge earthquake (1994), and a series of highly destructive hurricanes—as well as a host of smaller-scale disasters tasked emergency managers and response organizations. Moreover, the World Trade Center truck bombing of 1993 and the Murrah Federal Building truck bombing in Oklahoma City in 1995 signaled an escalation of terrorist activity inside the United States.

Nonetheless, 1993–2000 were "golden years" for FEMA. By the mid-1990s, FEMA's performance and image had improved to such an extent that both the public and many members of Congress, whether Democrat or Republican, came to hold a positive image of the agency.[8] FEMA was judged by many to be successful during President William J. Clinton's administration, owing much to the leadership of its appointed director, James Lee Witt. Although Witt was a close friend of the president, having served in Clinton's gubernatorial administration in

Arkansas, his appointment was not merely one of political patronage; Witt had experience in county emergency management and as a local elected official. This made him an ideal candidate for the job.

In 1996, President Clinton extended ex officio cabinet membership to Witt, thus underscoring Clinton's high regard for Witt and his recognition of the importance of disaster management. FEMA, though a small, independent agency outside of the White House, came to carry "the flag" for emergency managers throughout the United States. Indeed, the positive publicity and concomitant presidential promotion of the agency even enticed officials from several nations to seek advice from FEMA administrators about how their nations could form or improve their own emergency management.

Terrorism emerged as a major concern of federal emergency management in the twentieth century. Shown here, search and rescue crews hunt through the debris following the Oklahoma City bombing on April 19, 1995. Photo courtesy of the Federal Emergency Management Agency.

FEMA's Place in Policy, Intergovernmental Relations, and the Presidency

FEMA has always been very much an instrument of presidential power. Presidents often call on the agency to address calamities that may escalate to become disasters.[9] The President's Disaster Relief Fund, administered by FEMA, provides the president with an emergency spending account, subject to fiscal-year limitations, to address federal disaster spending needs. The fund also helps pay for expenses incurred in coping with unusual or acute problems not funded adequately, or at all, by other federal programs.[10]

One chief reason why FEMA remains deeply beholden to the Oval Office is that the agency has always had a small, politically weak, and sometimes feuding clientele. Meeting the needs of a constituency that includes emergency management professionals, first-responder organizations, state and local government agencies, relief organizations, private insurance companies, and individual disaster victims is a monumental job. These groups tend to perceive FEMA's mission differently and thus do not always agree on what FEMA's priorities should be:

- The nation's emergency managers, public safety directors, and firefighters, working mostly at the state or local level, strongly support FEMA in almost every case,[11] as do nonprofit organizations that qualify for FEMA funding in declared disasters or emergencies or that work closely with FEMA personnel.

- Governors, mayors, city managers, and county executives typically champion federal emergency management but at times tend to be critical of FEMA as well.

- Property insurance corporate officials are generally enthusiastic about federal efforts in disaster loss reduction, but they tend to be suspicious that the federal government, perhaps with FEMA's encouragement, will nationalize certain lines of the insurance they sell and maintain. Insurers and FEMA generally agree on the need to promote disaster mitigation, but each sometimes disagrees on what and how this should be done.

- Major construction firms, the building trades, and economic development interests benefit from post-disaster, federally subsidized reconstruction, but between disasters, these groups often perceive FEMA as a de facto regulator that sometimes impedes economic development in the interest of public safety.

Although these sources of agency clientele support are critical to maintaining FEMA's organizational and political life, their collective political power is far less than that of interest groups working in many other federal policy arenas. For example, U.S. Department of Health and Human Services clientele, such as the American Medical Association, the American Hospital Association, health maintenance organizations, and similar interest groups, have vastly greater political influence in Congress than do FEMA clientele.[12] Many of FEMA's clientele are prevented from lobbying Congress by conflict-of-interest laws, tax rules that put nonprofit contributions in jeopardy of losing deductibility if the organization lobbies, and laws that restrict lobbying by public employees.

Disasters are, by definition, phenomena that cause widespread destruction and distress. They are assumed to be infrequent, and this is often so for any specific locality. People who survive disasters and who receive aid from FEMA—or from any government agency at any level—seldom go on to champion emergency management. Although disasters unquestionably affect the perceptions of voters, regardless of whether they have directly experienced a disaster, disasters rarely affect how people vote in elections.[13] According to Kevin Arceneaux and Robert Stein, "Whether citizens blame the government depends on their level of political knowledge…. Although many individuals attribute blame to the government, it does not affect their voting decision for mayor unless they blame the city in particular."[14] Yet there have been some notable exceptions in which elected or appointed officials bungled the preparation for, or response to, a disaster, and they later suffered negative electoral or political consequences owing to their disaster mismanagement. The key takeaway here is that grassroots public support for emergency management, even among former disaster victims who received government relief in some form, is temporary, vacillating, and politically diffuse.

Intergovernmental Relations in Disaster Response

From 1979 through 2001, emergency management in the United States was largely based on shared authority, not on a top-down, command-and-control system. In the U.S federal system of government, national and state governments have different but often overlapping responsibilities. Most federal agencies, including the Department of Defense, cannot simply dictate what state or local officials must do in the emergency management arena. American federalism entrusts state government with "reserved powers" and spheres of jurisdiction. States shoulder considerable emergency management duties and responsibilities in their own right.

FEMA's mission and the federal government's involvement in emergency management have always been complicated further by the role that local governments play. It is local governments—cities, towns, counties, etc.—that have primary responsibility for preparing for disasters and the evacuation of residents. Many mitigation activities, including zoning and building codes, remain under the purview of municipal and county governments. In addition, local governments manage the response to, and recovery from, a disaster. Localities are sometimes aided by their state governments. In turn, states and localities are sometimes aided by the federal government, but only under certain emergency conditions. This federal assistance is conditioned on the expectation that state and local authorities are overwhelmed by the disaster. Considerable controversy has arisen over what "overwhelmed" actually means when a disaster condition is alleged.

The typical process for federal government involvement in response operations is for the governor of the disaster-stricken state to ask the president to declare a major disaster or emergency for the state and its affected counties. The president considers information about the damage zones within counties and localities affected by the disaster and within the state as a whole, as well as ongoing human suffering and loss, before approving or turning down the governor's request.[15] FEMA is a major channel through which such information is supplied to the president. Under customary policy, the federal government comes to the assistance of a state government only when the president determines that the state and local resources are overwhelmed by, or incapable of addressing, a disaster. The policy has long been open to interpretation by successive presidents such that each president has been free to judge whether the criteria have been met.

Thus, emergency management in the United States requires coordination and cooperation among local, state, and federal government agencies as well as among the many private organizations involved in preparing for and responding to a disaster. It also sometimes involves a presidential determination that events warrant presidential declarations of major disaster or emergency.

FEMA's Role in Intergovernmental Partnerships

FEMA's intergovernmental relationship with states and localities through the 1990s was primarily through Performance Partnership Agreements/Cooperative Agreements (PPA/CAs) with state offices of emergency management, an initiative that gained momentum mid-decade. In 1995 then FEMA director James Lee Witt declared, "A centerpiece of our reinvention is changing the way in which we do business with the states by empowering them through Performance Partnerships."[16] A PPA/CA is analogous to a contract between FEMA and state officials regarding the outcomes expected from funding support. Such agreements provided a way to pass funds through state offices of emergency management to local offices of emergency management.

FEMA asked each state to integrate disparate programs into a multiyear, risk-based agreement that would be signed by the president and the governor. With these performance partnerships, FEMA and state officials hoped to achieve mutually agreed-upon performance outcomes while building emergency management capacity. Witt envisioned these agreements as a method for creating "more objective Disaster Declaration criteria based on each state's unique capabilities."[17]

The political relevance of PPA/CAs resides in how effectively these agreements were originally negotiated and implemented. Because states could afford to commit only limited resources to emergency management, governors and state emergency managers needed federal government support, particularly after a disaster. Correspondingly, although FEMA's resources were meager and subject to considerable fluctuation from one administration to the next, the agency could leverage those limited resources in modest ways. In some respects, FEMA guidance and resources encouraged commitment to emergency management from the governor, state legislature, and local community. FEMA was thus credited with helping to build up or improve state and local emergency management capacity.

During the Clinton administration, at a time when FEMA's funding and personnel grew, the agency sought to reduce the administrative burden imposed on state programs and officials by simplifying procedures for requesting aid and by offering states more flexibility. For example, to quickly facilitate FEMA-state coordinative relations when disasters were imminent or transpiring, the agency routinely dispatched a representative to the staff of the governor whose state was, or was likely to be, affected.

FEMA also worked out a new memorandum of understanding with each state emergency management agency. Government officials usually negotiate memoranda of understanding (MOUs), and although they usually abide by such agreements, the agreements are considered voluntary and so lack the force of

The Emergency Management Assistance Compact

In 1992, when Hurricane Andrew devastated Florida, it became apparent that even with federal resources, states would need to call upon one another in times of emergencies. As a result, the Southern Governors' Association cooperated with Virginia's Department of Emergency Services to develop and adopt a state-to-state mutual aid agreement.

In 1995, the EMAC member-state governors voted to open membership to the mutual aid agreement to any state or territory that wished to join. The broadened agreement, the Emergency Management Assistance Compact (EMAC), was administered by the National Emergency Management Association. In 1996, EMAC became national law (P.L. 104-321), making it the first national disaster compact since the Civil Defense Compact of 1950 to be ratified by Congress.

EMAC is a mutual aid agreement and partnership among states designed to help them collectively and cooperatively address the constant threat of disaster. Participating states join forces to help one another when they need it most, whenever disaster threatens. Through EMAC, a disaster-stricken state can request and receive assistance from other member states quickly and efficiently, resolving two previously contentious issues: liability and reimbursement. States are not required to assist other states if they are unable to do so.

Since being approved in law, EMAC has been ratified by fifty states, Puerto Rico, the U.S. Virgin Islands, and the District of Columbia. The only requirement for joining is that a state's legislature ratifies the language of the compact.

In 2004, EMAC proved its worth during the response to Hurricanes Charley, Frances, Ivan, and Jeanne, deploying more than 800 state and local personnel from thirty-eight states (including one nonmember state, California). The cost was approximately $15 million in personnel, equipment, and National Guard expenditures. In 2005, in response to Hurricanes Katrina and Rita, EMAC member states deployed a total of 65,929 personnel to Alabama, Florida, Louisiana, Mississippi, and Texas.

Source: Emergency Management Assistance Compact website, emacweb.org.

law. Nonetheless, MOUs helped clarify for emergency circumstances who would do what, how it would be paid for, and how liability and responsibility would be apportioned.

Mutual aid agreements (MAAs) are another tool of intergovernmental relations. When governments and their agencies set forth MAAs, the agreements are negotiated as legal contracts. Agencies may draw up agreements for reciprocal assistance under certain conditions or may set out contingent acquisition agreements between providers, vendors, and contractors. From 1979 to 2001, MAAs among public, private, and nonprofit organization officials became a common instrument for coordinating disaster response. MAAs between government agencies and between governments themselves proliferated in the 1980s and 1990s. Among the most influential MAAs in disaster response is the Emergency Management Assistance Compact (EMAC), by which states have pledged their support for one another (see sidebar on the previous page). In 1996, EMAC gained the force of law (P.L. 104-321) when it was ratified by Congress.

Presidential Disaster Declarations

Presidential declarations matter. They stand as milestones in American history because they demonstrate how the federal government relates to its people and governments in times of emergency or disaster. Presidential declarations of major disaster or emergency unlock a host of resources, most importantly money, which aid in disaster relief and rebuilding. In a sense, the record of declarations demonstrates the resilience of the nation to a host of calamities, some foreseeable and others impossible to anticipate. Presidential declarations also perform metaphorically as "national shock absorbers," helping federal, state, and local governments cope with rapid-onset calamities that are greatly unforeseen or unprecedented, that may produce massive primary and secondary consequences, or that may produce national and international repercussions.

U.S. presidents since Harry S Truman have made decisions regarding the declaration of major disasters (beginning in 1951) and emergencies (beginning in 1974). Each president's declarations reveal something about that president as a person, as a public executive, and as a politician. The record of disaster declarations also says something about each president's view of federal-state relations, policy position on disasters, use of declarations as an instrument of political power, and view of disasters within the broader context in which he governed. Because FEMA begins its primary and most visible work only at the initiative of the president, understanding much of the history of emergency management requires examining presidential disaster declarations.

Declaration Types

There are two types of federal disaster declarations that state governors may seek: major disaster declarations and emergency declarations. Both require presidential approval, and both authorize the president to provide federal disaster assistance. However, the cause of the declaration and type and amount of assistance differ.

Major disaster declaration: The president can make a major disaster declaration for any natural event—including any hurricane, tornado, storm, high water, wind-driven water, tidal wave, tsunami, earthquake, volcanic eruption, landslide, mudslide, snowstorm, or drought, or, regardless of cause, fire, flood, or explosion—that the president believes has caused damage of such severity that it is beyond the combined capabilities of state and local governments to respond. This type of declaration may also apply to human-caused or technological disasters, including acts of terrorism or war. A major disaster declaration provides a wide range of federal assistance programs for individuals and public infrastructure, including funds for both emergency and permanent work.

Emergency declaration: An emergency declaration can be made for any occasion or instance when the president determines that federal assistance is needed. Emergency declarations usually supplement state and local efforts in providing emergency services, such as the protection of lives, property, public health, and safety, or to lessen or avert the threat of a catastrophe in any part of the United States. The amount of emergency assistance is, by law, not to exceed $5 million per single event unless the president reports to Congress that more than $5 million will be spent, as has often happened under a great many emergency declarations in recent decades.[1]

Source: Federal Emergency Management Agency, fema.gov/media/factsheets/declarations.shtm.

1 *Robert T. Stafford Disaster Relief and Emergency Assistance Act, as amended, and Related Authorities*, FEMA 592, June 2007, Section 502 of the Stafford Act, 42 U.S.C. 5192, fema.gov/pdf/about/stafford_act.pdf. The key provision is as follows: "Except as provided in paragraph (2), total assistance provided under this title for a single emergency shall not exceed $5,000,000." Paragraph 2 stipulates, "The limitation described in paragraph (1) may be exceeded when the President determines that—(A) continued emergency assistance is immediately required; (B) there is a continuing and immediate risk to lives, property, public health or safety; and (C) necessary assistance will not otherwise be provided on a timely basis." Paragraph 3 covers the presidential reporting requirement: "Whenever the limitation described in paragraph (1) is exceeded, the President shall report to the Congress on the nature and extent of emergency assistance requirements and shall propose additional legislation if necessary" (53).

Disaster Declarations and Presidents

Presidential declarations constitute a record—albeit a crude one subject to influence by political factors—of human suffering and losses attributable to various natural and human-caused forces. The growth in the number and types of declarations during the latter part of the twentieth century reflects increasing human and physical property losses and costs. Generally, natural disasters in the United States seem to be killing or injuring fewer people, perhaps because of improved mitigation and warning, while damaging more property and public infrastructure, which is increasingly expensive to repair or replace.[18] Conversely, from 1979 through

2001, human-caused disasters, especially those caused by terrorism, increased in frequency, number of deaths produced, and degree of devastation.

Table 5-1 provides information about presidential declarations of major disasters and emergencies for ten presidents, from May 1953 to September 2005. While the table does not include information about the nature of the declared disasters and emergencies, or about how they differed from those events leading to requests that were turned down, it illustrates the pattern of gubernatorial requests and, in broad terms, presidential decision making.

Stated simply, from 1953 to 1969, Presidents Dwight Eisenhower, John F. Kennedy, and Lyndon Johnson averaged about 1.3 major disaster declarations per month; from 1989 to 2005, Presidents George H. W. Bush, Bill Clinton, and George W. Bush averaged 3.9 major disaster declarations per month. Between these two periods, the average number of major disaster declarations tripled. The increase in major disaster declarations after 1989 appears to be unrelated to the political party of the president; there is also no statistical evidence that presidents of one political party accept a greater percentage of gubernatorial requests than those of another.

The number of disaster declaration requests that presidents turned down is also an important consideration. As shown in the table, presidents from Eisenhower through Reagan turned down between 30 and 37 percent of the gubernatorial requests, with the sole exception of Carter, who rejected 45 percent of the requests

Presidential Administration	Dates	Number of Presidential Disaster Declarations			
		Major Disaster[1]	Emergency	Total	
Eisenhower	5/2/53–1/21/61	106	N/A	106	
Kennedy	1/21/61–11/20/63	52	N/A	52	
Johnson	11/21/63–1/21/69	93	N/A	93	
Nixon	1/21/69–8/5/74	195	1	196	
Ford	8/5/74–1/21/77	76	23	99	
Carter	1/21/77–1/21/81	112	59	171	
Reagan	1/21/81–1/21/89	184	9	193	
G.H.W. Bush	1/21/89–1/21/93	158	2	160	
Clinton	1/21/93–1/21/01	380	68	448	
G.W. Bush	1/21/01–9/22/05	247	98	345	
All	5/2/53–9/22/05	1,603	260	1,863	

Table 5-1. Approvals and Turndowns: Gubernatorial Requests for Presidential Disaster Declarations, 1953–2005.

Sources: Data regarding the number of presidential declarations: Federal Emergency Management Agency, at fema.gov; Declaration Assistance Records and Information System, June 1997, Federal Emergency Management Information System, December. U.S. Department of Homeland Security (DHS), Emergency

for major disaster declarations and 39 percent of those for emergency declarations. It is ironic that Carter, who was a former governor and the leader who officially made FEMA a reality, turned down more requests than any other president from 1953 to 2011.

Richard Nixon was the first president to make a declaration of emergency, but he did this only once—for the effects of a drought that occurred in the U.S. Virgin Islands. Before he resigned in 1974, Nixon had rejected fifteen of the sixteen requests for emergency declarations. Most of these rejections occurred because the requesting governors sought them to cover marginal or ineligible events. Later presidents were more disposed to granting gubernatorial requests for emergency declarations, perhaps because governors eventually learned how to make more appropriate and qualifying requests.

Perhaps the most striking aspect of the data shown in Table 5–1 is the tremendous decline in rejection rates for both major disaster and emergency requests after 1989. Presidents G. H. W. Bush and Clinton each turned down roughly 21 percent of the requests for major disaster declarations they received. G. W. Bush has a 16 percent turndown rate for major disasters; both he and Clinton (and President Barack Obama) rejected even fewer of the requests for an emergency declaration. Over the fifty-one years depicted in the table, 44 percent of all the requests made for a presidential declaration of a major disaster or emergency came in the last

Number of Requests Turned Down			Percentage of Requests Turned Down		
Major Disaster	Emergency	Total	Major Disaster	Emergency	Total
55	N/A	55	34.2	N/A	34.2
22	N/A	22	29.7	N/A	29.7
49	N/A	49	34.5	N/A	34.5
102	15	117	34.3	93.8	37.4
35	7	42	31.5	23.3	29.8
91	37	128	44.8	38.5	42.8
96	16	112	34.3	64.0	36.7
43	3	46	21.4	60.0	22.3
103	13	116	21.3	16.0	20.6
46	12	58	15.7	10.9	14.4
642	103	745	28.6	28.4	28.6

Preparedness and Response Directorate, Justification of Estimates FY04 March 2003; 9/11/01–9/22/05 turndown data from a letter to author from Sen. Carper re: DHS Freedom of Information (FOI) Request 9/22/05. Date of declaration checked for each administration to the day.

1 Presidential declarations of major disasters began in 1953.

The accident at Three Mile Island nuclear power plant near Harrisburg, Pennsylvania, helped to convince President Carter to launch the Federal Emergency Management Agency (FEMA), which consolidated the functions of several existing federal agencies and programs. Photo courtesy of National Archives and Records Administration.

sixteen years. Clearly, for governors, seeking presidential disaster and emergency declarations has become a "growth industry."

Some disasters, particularly those that are truly catastrophic, profoundly affect presidents and often impel them to transform disaster-related rules and policy. Hurricane Andrew in 1992 challenged both G. H. W. Bush (at the close of his term) and Clinton (in 1993 and beyond) to make major reforms in federal emergency management. The 9/11 terrorist attacks exhorted G. W. Bush to quickly redirect his administration's primary mission to one of countering terrorism. As discussed in the next chapter, a major result of this policy change was that federal emergency management became enmeshed with and dominated by the primacy of terrorism consequence management.

The 1979 nuclear accident at Metropolitan Edison's Three Mile Island nuclear power plant, located just south of Harrisburg, Pennsylvania, is another example of an event that changed policy. Although the incident did not warrant a presidential declaration of a major disaster, it did convince Carter to expedite FEMA's formation and operations. The U.S. Nuclear Regulatory Commission had managed public warning and evacuation so badly during the crisis that the president reassigned some of the commission's off-site radiological emergency preparedness duties to FEMA.[19]

Disaster Declarations for New and Old Hazards or Problems

Presidents sometimes redefine and broaden the types of events that officially constitute a disaster. Carter's 1979 presidential declaration of a major disaster in and around Love Canal, a neighborhood of Niagara Falls, New York, was not only unprecedented but also controversial. Using FEMA to buy out homes in the contamination zone and, in turn, pay for relocation costs of those displaced was a novel action.

Similarly, the 1982 news report that residents of the small town of Times Beach, Missouri, might be suffering ill effects from the spraying of dioxin on local roads—spraying authorized by the state transportation department—contributed to changes in the nation's policy on abandoned hazardous waste.[20] Just as he did in the toxic waste incident that had occurred in Love Canal, President Carter asked FEMA to provide help and resources to affected Missourians.

In 1984, when a hazardous chemical accident at an American company in Bhopal, India, killed several thousand people, President Reagan and Congress worked to reduce the risk of a similar chemical plant disaster in the United States. The resulting statute, SARA Title III,[21] called for the provision of appropriate emergency public warning, evacuation planning, community preparedness, and emergency medical and public health response. All of this added to FEMA's emergency management portfolio.

In April 1986, the explosion of and radiation release from the Chernobyl nuclear power plant in the Soviet Republic of Ukraine—an event that, according to a UN agency, killed twenty-eight in the first three months[22] and exposed thousands more to potential cancer-inducing radiation doses over a broad expanse of northern and eastern Europe—again impelled the United States to take heed. The Chernobyl disaster pressed policy makers to ask the U.S. Nuclear Regulatory Commission to reexamine the adequacy of U.S. nuclear power plant reactor design and, along with FEMA, investigate the adequacy of nuclear power plant emergency preparedness.[23]

Beyond these cases, presidents sometimes use their disaster declaration powers to address certain anomalous events or problems. For example, in 1980, when Cuban president Fidel Castro launched the Mariel "boatlift" that allowed thousands of Cubans to escape to the United States, President Carter issued an emergency declaration to reimburse Florida for the costs incurred in serving and processing the refugees.[24] This action assigned FEMA a unique management task that required cooperation with various state and federal agencies—among them, the U.S. Immigration and Naturalization Service and federal investigative agencies, both responsible for separating Cuban incarcerated criminals from innocent Cuban refugees.

Some twenty years later, President Clinton approved New York State governor George Pataki's request for a presidential declaration of a major disaster following discovery of an outbreak of the West Nile Virus in neighborhoods surrounding New York City's Kennedy Airport. The federal funds were to help cover pesticide spraying and public health costs. This action created another new category of presidentially declarable disaster.[25] It was also a precursor of how emergency managers might be asked to address biological and bioterrorism incidents in the future.

Declarations for immigration emergencies, abandoned hazardous waste threats, and fast-spreading invasive insect-borne diseases set precedents that led governors to conclude that they could legitimately seek presidential declarations to cover these types of calamities in the future. Repeated gubernatorial requests for presidential declarations to cover relatively small, mundane, marginal, or seemingly localized emergencies sometimes convinced presidents to declare certain types of incidents that had not usually warranted such declarations before. Indeed, repeated requests for presidential declarations to cover unremarkable snowstorms, severe storms, and minor tornado damage, as well as minor hazardous materials emergencies and urban-wildland intermix fires that destroy few homes or structures, all pressed Presidents Clinton, G. W. Bush, and later Obama to accede. They each routinely issued declarations for seasonal blizzards, localized flooding, zero-fatality tornadoes that damaged fractions of neighborhoods, wildfires that burned into sparsely settled areas, and more—events that their predecessors from Eisenhower to Reagan had seldom declared major disasters.

Terrorism Declarations

As mentioned, terrorism gradually emerged as a major new concern of federal emergency management in the latter part of the twentieth century. The United States has a long history of dealing with terrorists and terrorism, but the first presidential disaster declaration for a terror-caused incident occurred after the 1993 truck bomb attack on the World Trade Center. Two years later, another presidential disaster declaration went to the State of Oklahoma and Oklahoma City for a terror bombing committed by American Timothy McVeigh and an accomplice. This was the first disaster in which FEMA officials had to work closely with the Federal Bureau of Investigation, which was assigned responsibility for apprehending the perpetrators.

Disaster Declarations and Presidential Philosophy

The trend toward "nationalizing" disaster management functions and creating a national response plan in which federal, state, and local authorities work in tandem was under way well before the terrorist attacks of September 11, 2001, and the era of homeland security. Disaster declarations were becoming increasingly frequent before President Reagan took office in 1981, but the upward trend was suspended during Reagan's tenure. During the sixteen years that Presidents Eisenhower, Kennedy, and Johnson were in office, there was an average of 15.6 disaster declarations per year; during the next twelve years and the administrations of Nixon, Ford, and Carter, this average jumped to 31.9 declarations. However, the Reagan administration averaged only 23.0 disaster declarations per year.

So why did this change occur? What caused the average number of disaster declarations to decrease during the Reagan years? While this may have been the result of an unusual period of quiescence and good fortune, it is difficult to discern any highly significant disaster event during this period. The decrease may also have stemmed from the Reagan administration's attitudes toward governance. Reagan's political ideology held that states too often relied on the federal government for help in matters they could easily address on their own and that the federal government needed to be less intrusive in matters traditionally left to state and local government. This "new federalism" may have discouraged governors from requesting federal government assistance. A catchword of the Reagan era was "devolution" of certain federal responsibilities back to the states and localities.

President George H. W. Bush, serving from 1989 through 1992 and a Reagan conservative himself (he was Reagan's vice president for two terms), issued many more presidential disaster declarations on average than did his predecessor. Declaration numbers escalated from 1993 through 2000, when President Clinton occupied the Oval Office. During this interval, federal activity in disaster management grew in almost every respect. Natural and human-caused disasters—many routine but several others catastrophically large—challenged the government's system of disaster management. Governors grew accustomed to receiving assistance from the federal government for major and minor disasters and emergencies. In addition, Presidents G. H. W. Bush and Clinton, as well as Congress, seemed more receptive to greater federal involvement in emergency management, a realm that had not long before been perceived as the responsibility of local and state government.

Presidential Discretion, Public Money, and Disaster Declarations

The flexibility to decide what constitutes a disaster is essential in an era when the nation faces new threats, some of which are nearly impossible to predict. In his work on presidential character, James David Barber observes, "People look to the President for reassurance, a feeling that things will be all right, that the President will take care of his people."[26] Having the authority to declare a major disaster or emergency allows the president to reassure the nation that steps are being taken and to provide significant disaster assistance. Yet it is the president's ability to use discretion in making disaster declarations that leads some people to allege that such decisions are made on politically expedient grounds.

When a president issues approval for unique primary incidents, a precedent is set. States take notice. If there are events or circumstances that approximate the new "disaster" type, governors then look for opportunities to request a presidential declaration. Thus, presidential administrations must be careful to consider the long-term fiscal and administrative implications of adding new categories of disaster or emergency to the list of approved declarations.

When major disaster declaration requests are considered, it appears that governors since 1988 have had a much better chance of securing approval of their requests than governors who served from 1953 through 1988. What explains the higher rates of approval for these requests? Clearly, that would be the broad range of declaration authority given to presidents, particularly in the November 1988 Robert T. Stafford Disaster Relief and Emergency Assistance Act (P.L. 100-707) as well as the Homeland Security Act of 2002 (P.L. 107-296).[27]

Some experts contend that the lack of clear and meaningful criteria for recommending disaster declarations has resulted in presidents directing "federal funds to...states that do not need assistance, while ignoring the legitimate needs of others."[28] This is not to suggest that presidents are intentionally denying federal disaster relief to deserving states, but rather that disasters are becoming "politically constructed" phenomena. FEMA's efforts to establish firm criteria for recommending the approval or denial of a presidential disaster declaration request have been thwarted on several occasions. Congress specifically prohibits FEMA from denying federal assistance solely by virtue of an arithmetic formula or sliding scale, such as one based on state income and population.[29] However, FEMA has published in the *Code of Federal Regulations* factors that are considered in evaluating declaration requests; while Congress hoped such indicators might discourage excessive gubernatorial requests, they may have instead set forth thresholds that, when met or passed, constitute the disaster entitlement that some have posited.[30]

Since the late 1980s, immense news media disaster and emergency coverage, as well as a new governmental emphasis on pre-event mobilization, may also have encouraged presidents to issue both major disaster and emergency declarations with less hesitation. A president's declaration of emergency mobilizes federal emergency managers and makes assistance available in the event of a disaster. Presidents thus use emergency declarations to demonstrate their leadership skills. Immediately before and during a disaster, emergency declarations put the federal government in the business of saving lives, conducting search and rescue, protecting property, and more. Emergency declarations also authorize federal spending prior to the approval of a declaration of major disaster.

Table 5–2 displays the most expensive major disasters by year for FEMA from 1979 to 2001, and Table 5–3 shows overall FEMA expenditures. Despite considerable year-to-year fluctuation, FEMA's spending in terms of the most costly disasters per year shows a marked upward trend. During the Reagan administration, no single major disaster declaration exceeded $215 million in 2003 constant dollars. During the first Bush's presidency, however, California received more than $1.2 billion from FEMA following the Loma Prieta earthquake and Florida received almost $2.2 billion following Hurricane Andrew.

President Clinton's most expensive disaster declarations by year were the Northridge earthquake in 1994 (almost $7 billion to California in 2003); Hurricane Georges in 1998, an event that raked Puerto Rico and resulted in more than $2 billion in FEMA 2003 constant dollar funding; and Hurricane Floyd in 1999 (discussed below). The FEMA disaster declaration cost grouping for the Great Midwest Flood of 1993 (which combines payouts to all states granted major

The News Media and Disasters

In the late twentieth century, television news-gathering capabilities mushroomed. Smaller cameras, satellite uplinks that allow remote broadcasts, trucks equipped for live filming and editing, and massive growth in local news broadcasting capacity combined to revolutionize television news. Moreover, the proliferation of camcorders and the ubiquity (in both time and space) of CNN made television news a twenty-four-hour-a-day, seven-day-a-week phenomenon. Indeed, in 1993 a report of the National Academy of Public Administration referred to the rise of "camcorder politics" and the "CNN Syndrome."[1]

News media coverage has played a major role in shaping the "social construct" of disaster. Disasters are immensely newsworthy, and many are epically visual. Disasters and emergencies almost invariably qualify as "breaking news." They often embody high drama with almost universal viewer interest, and many newscasters have built their careers covering disaster events. Some of the increase in presidential disaster declarations may be directly attributable to television news coverage; this is because media coverage of disasters and emergencies imposes political pressure on the president to demonstrate concern and offers a unique opportunity to demonstrate assertiveness, compassion, and strong decision-making skills. Public officials tend to use the news media to demonstrate their sympathy for disaster victims and to decry slow emergency response and relief efforts.

The power of television news images is so great that disaster managers have been known to deploy emergency people and resources to areas filmed by television news teams. Disaster sociologists point out that for many people, the social construct of what a specific disaster is comes from the images they witness as television viewers. The negative is that today's news media is driven by snapshot images and attention-getting headlines. As a result, most stories focus on highly dramatic incidents like looting. Viewers may get the impression of complete mayhem, where such chaos is in fact the exception to an otherwise orderly response and recovery operation.

1 Gary L. Wamsley et al., *Coping with Catastrophe: Building an Emergency Management System to Meet People's Needs in Natural and Manmade Disasters* (Washington, D.C.: National Academy of Public Administration, 1993).

Declaration Number	Date of Declaration	State/Territory	Event	
598	9/13/79	Alabama	Hurricane Frederic	
615	2/21/80	California	Severe storms, mudslides, and flooding	
640	5/27/81	Montana	Severe storms and flooding	
651	1/7/82	California	Severe storms, flood, mudslides	
677	2/9/83	California	Coastal storms, floods, slides	
705	5/15/84	Kentucky	High winds, tornadoes, and flooding	
753	11/7/85	West Virginia	Severe storms and flooding	
758	2/21/86	California	Severe storms and flooding	
799	10/7/87	California	Earthquake and aftershocks	
808	1/8/88	Hawaii	Severe storms, mudslides, and flooding	
845	10/18/89	California	Loma Prieta Earthquake	
883	11/26/90	Washington	Severe storms and flooding	
927	12/13/91	American Samoa	Hurricane Val	
955	8/24/92	Florida	Hurricane Andrew	
995	7/9/93	Missouri	Severe storms and flooding	
1,008	1/17/94	California	Northridge Earthquake	
1,067	9/16/95	Virgin Islands	Hurricane Marilyn	
1,134	9/6/96	North Carolina	Hurricane Fran	
1,193	12/17/97	Guam	Typhoon Paka, torrential rains, wind	
1,247	9/24/98	Puerto Rico	Hurricane Georges	
1,292	9/16/99	North Carolina	Hurricane Floyd	
1,345	10/4/00	Florida	Severe storms and flooding	
1,391	9/11/01	New York	Fires and explosions, terrorist attack	

Table 5-2. Most Expensive Major Disaster Declarations, 1979-2001.

1 FEMA spending. This number represents the money spent from the Disaster Trust Fund, which includes spending under FEMA-approved mission assignment by other federal agencies but does not include monies spent from non-FEMA federal agency accounts. State and local government expenditures (including matching funds) and private and insurance costs (including claims paid under federal insurance as part of the National Flood Insurance Program) are also not included in this figure.

disaster declarations for the flood) stands at about $1.33 billion in 2003 constant dollars.[31] (These disasters are discussed further beginning on page 142.) More recent disasters, such as the 9/11 terror attacks and Hurricane Katrina, have cost the federal government even more.

FEMA Relief, Current Dollars[1]	FEMA Relief, Constant (2003) Dollars[2]	President Issuing Declaration
186,058,159	470,727,142	Carter
89,802,346	200,259,232	Carter
4,491,650	9,073,133	Reagan
29,168,478	55,420,108	Reagan
115,982,094	214,566,874	Reagan
17,455,772	30,896,716	Reagan
110,119,852	188,304,947	Reagan
54,912,707	92,253,348	Reagan
44,944,829	72,810,623	Reagan
5,303,893	8,221,034	Reagan
836,483,340	1,237,995,343	G.H.W. Bush
50,215,305	70,803,580	G.H.W. Bush
96,729,580	130,584,933	G.H.W. Bush
1,654,328,135	2,167,169,856	G.H.W. Bush
279,903,635	355,477,616	Clinton
5,584,845,418	6,925,208,318	Clinton
493,757,789	597,446,925	Clinton
431,390,378	504,726,742	Clinton
148,496,747	170,771,259	Clinton
1,915,593,338	2,164,518,771	Clinton
689,564,680	758,521,148	Clinton
602,937,350	645,142,964	Clinton
8,616,595,410	8,961,259,226	G.W. Bush

2 Assistance made to state and county governments.

From the mid-1980s to the present, the growth in declarations and the resulting larger federal disaster expenditures have partly been a result of presidential decisions to expand the definition of what constitutes a disaster or an emergency. It is also true that traditional types of disasters have increased in number and in magnitude of loss over the same period. Many factors account for this. First, urban sprawl often leads to development in hazard zones; throughout the country, the numbers of people and structures situated along coastlines and estuaries vulnerable to flooding and hurricane devastation have increased significantly.[32] Second, changes in natural forces—for example, patterns of temperature extremes and precipitation changes,

Year	FEMA Spending (in millions of dollars)
1989	1,436
1990	1,194
1991	410
1992	2,805
1993	1,910
1994	8,145
1995	1,463
1996	2,453
1997	1,869
1998	4,014
1999	1,982
2000	786
2001	12,470

Table 5–3. FEMA Total Disaster Declaration Spending, All Types and Categories, 1989–2001.

Source: PERI, DHS-FEMA spending totals by year as of 7/31/06; see peripresdecusa.org (last accessed January 14, 2012).

effects from high-density human settlement and deforestation, and the vagaries of change in weather patterns—may also increase human vulnerability to disaster as well as levels of disaster damage. Finally, many structural mitigation works built in the last century, such as dams, bridges, and levees, have not been properly funded or maintained, putting them at increased risk of failing.

From Civil Defense to Homeland Security

Civil defense against nuclear attack was a significant part of Carter's and Reagan's Cold War foreign policy. The Reagan administration convinced Congress to increase defense spending, particularly for new generations of nuclear weaponry and an antiballistic missile defense system. Dual-use requirements mandated that to receive federal civil defense funding for civilian use, federal, state, and local emergency managers must supply an acceptable civil defense justification. Consequently, FEMA was drawn into national security matters through its civil relocation program, sheltering programs, and continuity-of-government program.

In early 1989, as the Berlin Wall came down and the Cold War came to a close, civil defense lost its support in Congress, in the Department of Defense, and in the National Security Council. State and local governments were gradually freed of the restraints imposed by dual-use requirements of federal disaster funding. These conditions had often frustrated and confounded emergency managers, who recognized that natural and technological disasters unrelated to superpower conflict deserved more of their attention and expertise.

Between the end of the Cold War in 1989–1990 and the beginning of the War on Terrorism, initiated by the attacks on the World Trade Center and the Pentagon in 2001, terror attacks in the United States were addressed domestically as crimes and internationally as surgical military strikes on terrorist compounds. In 1993, Arab Islamist terrorists ignited a car bomb with 1,500 pounds of nitrate fuel in the World Trade Center's parking garage, killing six people and injuring more than a thousand. The devastation could have been far worse because the bombers had intended to bring down both the North and South Towers. In 1995, the bombing of the Alfred P. Murrah Federal Building in downtown Oklahoma City, planned and carried out by Americans Timothy McVeigh and Terry Nichols, resulted in 168 deaths and more than 800 injuries, becoming at that time the deadliest domestic terrorist attack in nation's history.

Terrorist attacks outside the United States further fueled concerns about the nation's preparedness. In 1995, Aum Shinrikyo, a Japanese religious group, released sarin nerve gas into the Tokyo subway in five coordinated attacks, killing twelve people and injuring nearly a thousand others. The 1996 bombing of U.S. barracks in the Khobar Towers in Saudi Arabia and the 1998 bombings of U.S. embassies in Kenya and Tanzania reignited public fears about the threat of terrorist attack. For the first time also, emergency management began to consider in earnest weapons of mass destruction.[33]

Clearly, even before the 9/11 terrorist attacks, domestic disaster management began to be displaced by the nation's growing concerns about terrorism.[34] When in 1996 the Nunn-Lugar-Domenici Weapons of Mass Destruction Act became law, its principal aim was to reduce domestically and internationally the threat of new and old weapons of mass destruction.

Some policy makers and emergency management professionals argued that the devastation from human-made disasters, particularly those inflicted to instill terror, would far exceed the damage wreaked by natural disasters. At the same time, disaster researchers increased their emphasis on the need for improved disaster mitigation and reduced vulnerability—an idea that found receptive audiences among the public and various political leaders.[35] Federal efforts aimed at encouraging states and communities to mitigate or prevent disasters and thus to identify and reduce disaster vulnerability would later provide a gateway for federal policy makers and homeland security authorities to draw state and local officials into the business of terrorism awareness and prevention.

The Science and Business of Disasters

During the last several decades of the twentieth century, emergency management grew as an intellectual and multidisciplinary enterprise. Significant advances in hazards research—most particularly in meteorology, seismologic studies, and physical geography, as well as in the building sciences, climate change research, and environmental studies—gave credibility to disaster research.[36] These advances coincided with, and often were made possible by, a number of major technological innovations: advances in high-speed computing and massive data storage, the development of personal computers and sophisticated computer software, civilian use of satellite telemetry of data about the atmosphere and surface of the Earth, and geographic information system (GIS) technology. John C. Pine's *Technology in Emergency Management* deftly explores the role of technology in emergency planning, response, recovery, and mitigation, covering GIS and global positioning system tools, including remote sensing.[37]

The social sciences also made major contributions to the field through the work of disaster sociologists, political scientists, economists, social geographers, demographers, and urban planners. The National Research Council's *Facing Hazards and Disasters: Understanding Human Dimensions* is an excellent edited compilation of the social scientific research produced in the last thirty-five years.[38]

In the 1990s, FEMA developed HAZUS, a computer-based earthquake simulation applicable and adaptable to most of the nation, and distributed it free of charge through its website. HAZUS and its successor, HAZUS-MH, are powerful risk assessment software programs for analyzing potential losses from earthquake. HAZUS-MH also models loss from wind and flood disaster agents.[39] The results of HAZUS research have been used to mitigate the effects of disasters and improve preparation for, response to, and recovery from such events.

Indeed, many segments of the nation's academic community, often in cooperation with scholars outside the United States, received government support for disaster research through the National Science Foundation, the National Oceanic and Atmospheric Administration (NOAA), the U.S. Environmental Protection Agency, the U.S. Geological Survey, the National Institute of Standards and Technology, the U.S. Army Corps of Engineers, FEMA, and others. FEMA also made a significant contribution to the expansion of seismic engineering science and disaster loss estimation. This intellectual maturation of the field has helped advance emergency management from an occupation to a profession.[40]

The intellectual and technological advances of the 1980s and 1990s gave rise to a disaster services business sector composed of consultants, contractors, for-profit businesses, and nonprofit organizations. The development of emergency management as a profession also meant greater dependence on a skilled and educated workforce, thus diminishing the need for large numbers of untrained volunteers who had performed disaster response and recovery operations in the past.

As state emergency management agencies, in conjunction with their local government counterparts, became adept at skillfully designing requests for presidential disaster declarations, federal involvement in state and local emergency management expanded. State and local governments often lacked the full capacity to meet the physical and social demands of disaster recovery and so used federal disaster funding to pay for-profit and nonprofit contractors to serve many of these functions. Private sector firms were retained to repair or replace public infrastructure, and nonprofits endeavored to meet a host of other disaster-related human needs, including emergency housing, employment counseling, and short-term health and family services.

Public Infrastructure and Disasters

From 1979 through 2001, questions like these emerged: How is public infrastructure defined in disaster-related legislation? Who pays for the repair of infrastructure following a disaster? Are buyouts and relocations replacing engineered disaster mitigation, such as flood levees and flood control works?

Since 1979, emergency management in the United States has become increasingly involved in issues related to public infrastructure: highways and roads; bridges; ports; airports; flood control works; water, sewer, and other utility systems; electrical systems; natural gas distribution networks; telephone and cable systems; and public buildings and facilities. With the astounding growth of the Internet and the World Wide Web, and the resulting advances in the range and depth of information technology, communications infrastructure has also become a major new concern for emergency managers. The maintenance of routers and hubs, and the protection of transmission devices ranging from hard lines to fiber-optic cables, cell towers, and wireless instruments, are now emergency management priorities. The perpetuation of connectivity has become a paramount concern, particularly as public and private emergency managers have grown dependent on the availability of the Internet and communications networks before, during, and after disasters. Economic and social dependence on these communications and information pathways has convinced political leaders of the importance of "cyber security." Computer hackers who disrupt Internet usage are recognized as potential terrorists and purveyors of disaster. Since the early 1990s, disasters or emergencies that damaged—or threatened to damage—any of these critical systems have been a new area of responsibility for FEMA.

In many respects, FEMA's effectiveness in disaster management has been judged in terms of how quickly public infrastructure is restored after a disaster. Americans have become accustomed to virtually uninterrupted delivery of services; a power outage, even for just a few hours, is considered by those affected to be a "disaster" or "emergency." The loss of Internet availability and connectivity has serious economic and social implications. As a result, federal agencies, as well as state and local politicians, have come to recognize FEMA's role in addressing infrastructure needs following a disaster.

While disaster mitigation had become a mandate set forth in law in 1974, it was not until the Northridge earthquake in January 1994 that FEMA was authorized to fund public infrastructure repairs beyond the restoration of the original structures. Repairing or replacing infrastructure often costs millions—even billions—of dollars. Following the devastation of the earthquake and its aftershocks, the California Freeway overpasses were rebuilt at great public expense to be able to withstand far more powerful seismic shocks in the future.[41]

FEMA was not the only federal agency with a growing role in meeting disaster-related public infrastructure needs. The U.S. Army Corps of Engineers has a long history in the construction, operation, and maintenance of dams, levees, revetments, and nonstructural disaster mitigation works. It also owns, operates, and maintains other massive infrastructure, including lock systems, navigable waterways, bridges, and ports. Consequently, it has played an important role in the nation's emergency management system, particularly during the 1980s and 1990s.

The Rise of Disaster Mitigation

From 1979 through 2001, emergency management took on the challenge of preventing or reducing disaster-related losses by identifying hazard risks capable of producing disasters or emergencies and by attempting to address these risks. Project Impact (discussed beginning on page 141) represented a high point in federal disaster mitigation. By law, policy, and custom, however, land use control in the United States is a responsibility of local government, and such activity sometimes generated local political opposition because it portended "federal zoning."[42]

Nonetheless, disaster mitigation—emergency management work between disasters—came to assume an increasing and enduring importance in emergency management at all levels of government. Emergency management officials of the period stressed that disaster mitigation and prevention is everyone's responsibility, something to be practiced in homes, schools, and workplaces. In many ways, the diffusion of disaster mitigation knowledge did much to advance public awareness of emergency management and catalyze public action.

In the 1980s and 1990s, FEMA led efforts to reduce recurring disaster losses. Its Federal Insurance Administration (FIA) managed the National Flood Insurance Program (NFIP), which Congress had established in 1968. The FIA's Unified Program for Floodplain Management established national goals and set strategies to reduce losses and protect natural resources. The NFIP worked with local governments to design programs and pass legislation and ordinances to discourage unsafe construction in flood zones. Local governments had to agree to participate in the program in order for property owners to qualify for NFIP's low-cost flood insurance. In essence, the NFIP was an early FEMA mitigation program. Homeowners whose domiciles were subject to recurring flood loss sometimes petitioned FEMA to buy their properties or to relocate them (at government expense) to safer locations. The subsequent era of FEMA residential home buyouts may have had its origins in the assistance provided to those who were displaced by the abandoned waste contamination of Love Canal in Niagara Falls, New York, and to residents of the small Missouri community of Times Beach (both mentioned previously), which was relocated with FEMA funds following its contamination by the hazardous substance dioxin.[43]

The Law and Policy of Disaster Management

As discussed in the preceding chapter, the Disaster Relief Act of 1950 (P.L. 81-875) provided "an orderly and continuing means of assistance by the federal government to states and local governments in carrying out their responsibilities to alleviate suffering and damage resulting from major disasters."[44] This 1950 law and the Stafford Act of 1988 stipulate that the governor of an affected state must formally ask the president to declare a major disaster or emergency. If the request is granted, the federal government will then provide disaster assistance "to supplement the efforts and available resources of state and local governments in alleviating the disaster."[45] The governor must provide specific information on the severity and magnitude of the disaster and on the amount of state and local resources that will be committed. The president has significant discretion over whether the disaster or emergency is of sufficient severity and size to warrant federal disaster or emergency assistance. Since enactment of the Disaster Relief Act of 1950, presidents have always guarded their authority to declare a major disaster or emergency and have never delegated it to FEMA or any other federal agency.

Any funds appropriated by Congress for disaster relief supplement the efforts and resources of state and local governments. The portion paid by the federal government can vary from 75 percent to 100 percent, depending on whether the president elects to waive all or most of the state's matching requirement. Such a determination rests on the circumstances of the state and local governments affected. From 1979 to 2001, federal disaster outlays spiraled upwards as disaster declarations tended to grow in number and cost and the federal government increased its funding of state and local disaster response and recovery costs.[46]

The president's Disaster Relief Fund is important because it allows the president to provide immediate assistance to cover the expense of deploying federal personnel, equipment, and resources to a disaster-stricken area. It also provides direct assistance to state and local governments and to victims and their families, pays a share of the cost of food and shelter, and frees funds to begin debris clearance and otherwise restore life to normal.[47]

The Disaster Relief Act of 1974 (P.L. 93-288) empowered presidents to issue declarations of emergency, "defined as any event determined by the president to require federal assistance,"[48] as stipulated by the Stafford Act. Emergencies tend to be of less magnitude and scope than major disasters. Emergencies involve a federal government response to protect lives and property when a disaster is imminent, ongoing, or immediately past—often before or during the period in which a major disaster declaration request is being considered. Many emergency declarations apply for a period of hours or days, and they may precede the issuance of major disaster declarations. Thus, presidents sometimes issue emergency declarations to facilitate pre-disaster mobilizations for events that could become major disasters.[49]

Emergency declarations differ from major disaster declarations in several significant ways. When requesting a major disaster declaration, governors are required to prove need and submit estimated disaster loss information, but this is not required for an emergency declaration request. As a result, a declaration of emergency tends to be more subjective than a declaration of disaster. Emergency declarations sometimes stretch the rule that states must lack the capacity to recover on their own to qualify for a presidential declaration. In times when state and local budgets are tight, an emergency designation offers a flexible path for states to secure help from the federal government for less than catastrophic occurrences. Snowstorms, windstorms, and minor flooding are the most common types of events that receive emergency declarations.[50]

In April 1986, FEMA proposed changing both the process for declaring major disasters and the criteria for eligibility for federal assistance. These proposed changes would have decreased the federal share of disaster costs from 75 percent to 50 percent, and states would have been required to meet more stringent economic criteria to receive federal aid. These proposals were withdrawn after they were strongly opposed in Congress, and they were not reflected in the adoption of the Stafford Act in 1988.[51]

In September 1993, a Clinton administration National Performance Review report concluded that federal disaster assistance was too generous and too frequent, and conjectured that states might perceive the federal government as their "first-line resource in every emergency."[52] Echoing past recommendations, the report urged the development of objective criteria that could be used to make decisions about disaster declarations; however, both the administration and Congress took no action on this.

Hazard Mitigation Law and Policy

Mitigation consists of pre-disaster activities that involve the assessment of risk and lessen the potential effects of disasters; increasingly, it also involves post-disaster activities to reduce potential damage from future disasters.[53] The 1988 Stafford Act authorized disaster mitigation in the form of post-disaster federal assistance dedicated directly to proposed disaster mitigation projects on both the state and local levels. Federal funds could be used to acquire destroyed or damaged properties. Rebuilding in high-hazard zones was to be discouraged, and reconstruction was to include measures to reduce exposure to hazard risks. The Stafford Act also authorized the allocation of up to 10 percent of FEMA's public assistance grants for hazard mitigation projects that were cost-effective (as determined through a cost-benefit analysis) and that would substantially reduce the risk of future damage, hardship, loss, and suffering. The act established FEMA's Hazard Mitigation Grant Program, which would make grants to state and local governments and to certain nonprofit organizations to implement long-term hazard mitigation measures following a president declared disaster.[54]

In a 1993 National Academy of Public Administration (NAPA) report titled *Coping with Catastrophe*, the authors reviewed the devastation caused by Hurricane Andrew in South Florida and concluded that FEMA had not successfully integrated disaster mitigation into its mission. The report asserts, "FEMA has been ill-served by congressional and White House neglect, a fragmented statutory charter, irregular funding, and the uneven quality of its political executives appointed by past presidents."[55] In response, Witt undertook a major reorganization of FEMA and its five directorates, the FIA, and the U.S. Fire Administration and its ten regional offices.

In 1993, major flooding of the Mississippi River pointed out lapses in disaster mitigation policy for flood disasters. To address this need, Congress amended the Stafford Act to increase federal support for relocating flood-prone properties and increased the amount of hazard mitigation funds available post-disaster from 10 to 15 percent of all of FEMA's disaster spending on each major disaster declaration that a state received.[56] In addition, the act increased from 50 to 75 percent the federal share of state and local costs of mitigation activities approved by FEMA as eligible; clarified acceptable conditions for the purchase of damaged homes and businesses; required the complete removal of such structures; and dictated that the purchased land be dedicated "in perpetuity for a use that is compatible with open space, recreational, or wetlands management practices."[57]

The Disaster Relief Act of 1974 included the first explicit congressional requirement for hazard mitigation as a prerequisite for disaster assistance. Section 406 (which remains in effect today as Section 409 of the 1988 Stafford Act) requires state and local governments receiving aid to agree that "the natural hazards in the areas in which the proceeds of the grants or loans are to be used be evaluated and appropriate action taken to mitigate such hazards, including safe land use and construction practices, in accordance with [federal] standards."[58]

In October 1997, FEMA launched Project Impact to protect against and reduce the impacts of natural disasters before they happen. The project sought to build disaster-resistant communities through public-private partnerships, and it included a national public awareness campaign and outreach to community leaders. FEMA encouraged localities to assess the risks they face, identify vulnerabilities, and take steps to prevent disasters and reduce disaster-related losses. Congress appropriated $30 million for Project Impact for fiscal year (FY) 1998 and $25 million for FY 1999.

With the goal of having at least one Project Impact community in every state by September 30, 1998, Project Impact was piloted in Deerfield Beach, Florida; Pascagoula, Mississippi; and Wilmington, North Carolina. By December 2000, roughly two hundred localities had joined the program. The program was then canceled in 2001 by the G. W. Bush administration.

In support of FEMA's growing emphasis on mitigation, Congress approved and President Clinton signed the Disaster Mitigation Act of 2000 (P.L. 106-390), giving FEMA authority to establish a program of technical and financial assistance for enhanced pre-disaster mitigation to state and local governments. FEMA was to help state and local governments develop and carry out pre-disaster hazard mitigation measures designed to reduce injuries, loss of life, and damage and destruction of property, including damage to critical public services and facilities. To be eligible for pre- and post-disaster federal funding, the act required "local governments to identify potential mitigation measures that could be incorporated into the repair of damaged facilities."[59] Local governments were encouraged to engage in hazard mapping, planning, the development of land use regulations and building codes, and other mitigation activities.[60] The law also upgraded the 1974 requirement for post-disaster mitigation plans by requiring that states prepare a comprehensive program for pre-disaster emergency and disaster mitigation before they could receive post-disaster declaration funds from FEMA.

Focusing Events of the Era 1979–2001

As in previous decades, several very major disasters occurred between 1979 and 2001 that altered federal emergency management and the laws empowering FEMA and other disaster management agencies. Earthquakes, including those in northern (1989) and southern (1992) California; several hurricanes; and the Great Midwest Flood of 1993 all generated new or amended federal, state, and local laws. These cumulative experiences constantly underscored the need for improvements in disaster mitigation, preparedness, response, and recovery.

Earthquakes

Earthquakes, like other sudden-onset/no-notice disasters, often temporarily overwhelm the emergency response and recovery capacity of state and local governments, businesses, nonprofit organizations, and individuals. The human and economic losses inflicted by an earthquake and its consequences sometimes require a great deal of help from governments, organizations, and people outside the affected area. As a result, dealing with earthquake threat and destruction has been addressed in national policy and federal law. The federal government is expected to step in to provide basic humanitarian aid to the devastated areas.

Generally speaking, California is a heavily populated and politically powerful state that is highly prone to damaging earthquakes, so the history of federal earthquake policy is very much intertwined with California's earthquake experience. Because it is the most populous state, California has a very large congressional delegation and commensurate political influence, something that has helped it to shape the nation's earthquake policy.

In 1977, Congress determined that many states are vulnerable to earthquake hazards and that a national policy was needed to address earthquake as a major natural hazard.[61] As a result, Congress passed the National Earthquake Hazards

The National Earthquake Hazards Reduction Program

Since its creation in 1977, the National Earthquake Hazards Reduction Program (NEHRP) has been an integral part of the federal government's approach to earthquake mitigation and preparedness, supporting research, planning, and response activities. NEHRP works through four participating agencies—FEMA, the U.S. Geological Survey (USGS), the National Science Foundation (NSF), and the National Institute of Standards and Technology (NIST)—as well as with state governments, academia, and the private sector to minimize risk to life and property from future earthquakes. It also sets forth external grant programs funded through FEMA, the USGS, and NSF. NEHRP's primary goals are to make structures safer, to inform the public more effectively, and to advance seismic mitigation. This entails

- Understanding, characterizing, and predicting seismic hazards

- Improving model building codes and land use practices

- Learning risk reduction through post-earthquake investigation and analysis

- Developing improved design and construction techniques

- Promoting the dissemination and application of research results.

From the program's inception until 2004, when leadership was assumed by NIST, FEMA was the lead agency. Each year, FEMA provided project grants through its state cooperative agreements program. The state matching requirement ultimately rose to 50 percent, and, as mentioned in the mitigation section above, a share of federal-state funding had to be used for mitigation activities.

Two of NEHRP's significant accomplishments have been the development of seismic resistance standards for new construction and for strengthening existing buildings in earthquake-prone areas. FEMA's work under NEHRP facilitated the creation of the Federal Response Plan, which, until its replacement by the National Response Plan in December 2004, provided the basic framework for coordination of federal disaster relief work among federal departments and agencies.

Source: Richard T. Sylves, "Earthquakes," in *Handbook of Emergency Management*, ed. William L. Waugh Jr. and Ronald J. Hy (Westport, Conn.: Greenwood Press, 1991).

Reduction Act of 1977 (P.L. 95-124). This act and its implementing program, the National Earthquake Hazards Reduction Program (NEHRP), support federal, state, local, and private research and planning to reduce the risks to life and property resulting from earthquakes in seismic risk areas.[62]

NEHRP has provided the framework for a national earthquake policy. When FEMA was created in 1979, it was charged with coordinating that program. In 1990, after the Loma Prieta quake of the previous year, Congress reauthorized the National Earthquake Hazards Reduction Act and called for seismological risk assessments to be used in emergency planning, public regulations, building design, insurance ratings, and more.[63]

Before its absorption into DHS in March 2003, FEMA had a National Earthquake Mitigation Program Office within its Mitigation Directorate, producing manuals and guidance documents that continue to serve as the basis for seismic safety codes. Several other federal government agencies also played critical roles in earthquake mitigation. The U.S. Geological Survey has long been in the business of producing

Declaration Number	FEMA Disaster Relief Program	State	Date Event Began	Event	
682	Public Assistance, Individual Assistance	California	5/5/83	Coalinga Earthquake	
694	Public Assistance, Individual Assistance	Idaho	10/28/83	Earthquake	
799	Public Assistance, Individual Assistance	California	10/1/87	Earthquake and aftershocks	
845	Public Assistance, Individual Assistance	California	10/17/89	Loma Prieta Earthquake	
943	Public Assistance, Individual Assistance	California	4/25/92	Earthquake and aftershocks	
947	Public Assistance, Individual Assistance	California	6/28/92	Earthquake and aftershocks	
985	Public Assistance	Oregon	3/25/93	Earthquake	
1,004	Public Assistance	Oregon	9/20/93	Earthquakes	
1,008	Public Assistance, Individual Assistance	California	1/17/94	Northridge Earthquake	
1,342	Public Assistance, Individual Assistance Mitigation Assistance	California	9/3/00	Earthquake	
1,361	Public Assistance, Mitigation Assistance	Washington	2/28/01	Nasqualie Earthquake	

Table 5-4. Presidential Declarations of Major Disaster for Earthquakes, 1983–2001.

1 FEMA spending. This number represents the money spent from the Disaster Trust Fund, which includes spending under FEMA-approved mission assignment by other federal agencies but does not include monies spent from non-FEMA federal agency accounts. State and local government expenditures (including matching

earth science data, calculating earthquake probabilities, and supporting land use planning and engineering design as well as emergency preparedness. For many years, the National Science Foundation has promoted construction siting, fundamental geotechnical engineering design, and structural analysis, in part through its Centers for Earthquake Engineering Research. FEMA worked with the National Institute of Standards and Technology (NIST) and state and local officials, model building code groups, architects, engineers, and others to ensure that the latest advances in scientific and engineering research were incorporated into building codes, standards, and practices. (In 2004, the NIST became the lead agency for NEHRP.)[64]

Table 5–4 lists presidential disaster declarations issued for earthquakes between 1983 and 2001. President Reagan made just three earthquake declarations, the first for a highly publicized but only moderately destructive seismic event in and around Coalinga, California, in 1983. The Coalinga earthquake caused extensive local property damage but no loss of life. Due in part to the media attention the event received, Coalinga's mayor was successful in convincing California

Date of Disaster Declaration	Costs, Current Dollars[1]	Cost, Constant (2003) Dollars[2]	Number of Counties Covered	President Issuing Declaration
5/5/83	3,716,909	6,876,281	2	Reagan
11/18/83	975,902	1,805,418	3	Reagan
10/7/87	44,944,829	72,810,622	2	Reagan
10/18/89	836,483,340	1,237,995,343	12	G.H.W. Bush
5/4/92	13,088,116	17,145,431	1	G.H.W. Bush
7/2/92	19,827,277	25,973,732	2	G.H.W. Bush
4/26/93	9,275,832	11,780,306	4	Clinton
10/15/93	2,877,056	3,653,861	1	Clinton
1/17/94	5,584,845,418	6,925,208,318	3	Clinton
9/14/00	8,939,407	9,565,165		Clinton
3/1/01	177,656,954	184,763,232		G.W. Bush

funds) an private and insurance costs (including claims paid under federal insurance as part of the NFIP) are also not included in this figure.

2 Assistance made to state and county governments

governor George Deukmejian, who, in turn, convinced President Reagan, to grant Coalinga state and presidential disaster declarations, respectively.[65] President G. H. W. Bush also issued three major disaster declarations for earthquakes, including one for the state of California following the Loma Prieta earthquake. President Clinton provided California with a major disaster declaration for the Northridge trembler in 1994.

The Loma Prieta Earthquake

The earthquake struck northern California over an area stretching from Monterrey Bay to points north of San Francisco on October 17, 1989; it caused widespread damage as far as fifty miles away from its epicenter. In Oakland, a major segment of the Admiral Nimitz Freeway collapsed, crushing vehicles and killing forty-one motorists; a fifty-foot span of the upper deck of the San Francisco–Oakland Bay Bridge also collapsed, interrupting a major corridor between San Francisco and the East Bay; gas lines were severed, and fires erupted in residential buildings.[66] Loma Prieta was the first earthquake to result in more than $1 billion in FEMA spending.

The Loma Prieta quake, named for its epicenter, occurred just before the third game of the 1989 World Series between the Oakland Athletics and the San Francisco Giants. Because the television crews assigned to cover the game immediately turned their attention to the quake and its immediate aftermath, the Loma Prieta quake became the first earthquake to be, in effect, televised live. In some respects, the television coverage of the damage in the Bay Area influenced the federal and state

The Loma Prieta earthquake of October 17, 1989, resulted in extensive damage to infrastructure—particularly elevated highways and bridges—and was the first earthquake to result in more than $1 billion in FEMA spending. This photo shows a collapsed building and burned area in San Francisco's Marina District. Photo courtesy of the U.S. Geological Survey/C. E. Meyer.

response to the disaster: some analysts concluded that state disaster managers sent their first response personnel and resources to areas that had received immediate and sustained coverage. For this reason, some believe that the federal and state disaster response may have been slower to Watsonville, Santa Cruz, and other communities south of San Francisco, which had sustained heavy loss of life and major property damage but did not have the benefit of early television coverage.

The government response to the Loma Prieta earthquake was generally lauded, but controversy continued regarding how to provide appropriate and reasonably priced residential earthquake insurance to Californians.[67] The disaster also raised issues of mitigation and underscored the importance of protecting bridges, elevated roads, and other infrastructure. The collapse of the bridge in Oakland demonstrated the urgency of retrofitting highway structures to withstand seismic shaking.

For the G. H. W. Bush administration, the devastation wrought by the earthquake in the Bay Area and along the coast demonstrated some lessons learned. Owing largely to television news coverage, federal emergency management had become highly visible, exhaustively critiqued, and immensely newsworthy. Vice President Dan Quayle's visit to damaged areas of San Francisco revealed that it was politically counterproductive to visit disaster areas before adequate federal disaster relief had arrived.

The Northridge Earthquake

The Northridge earthquake of January 17, 1994, owing to its impact on the massively developed and densely populated greater Los Angeles area, was the most destructive U.S. earthquake in the 1983–2001 period. It stood as FEMA's most expensive disaster until the terror attacks of September 11, 2001. As of July 31, 2006, FEMA funding in all categories for the Northridge quake totaled $6.97 billion—almost three times as much as FEMA spent on Hurricane Andrew ($1.66 billion for Florida and $147 million for Louisiana).[68] Prior to the Loma Prieta quake, no single disaster had cost more than $1 billion (even with control for inflation) of Disaster Relief Fund monies, but the Northridge earthquake began an era of intermittent multibillion-dollar federal disaster payouts.[69]

The Northridge earthquake occurred along a thrust fault and did most of its damage in the San Fernando Valley and other areas of Los Angeles. As with Loma Prieta, the Northridge event drew protracted national news coverage, often broadcast live with the anchorperson in the disaster-affected area. Political and partisan differences between President Clinton and Governor Pete Wilson were overcome quickly, and cooperation between FEMA and California's Office of Emergency Services (OES) in the response and recovery was generally efficient and effective.

Federal response to the 1994 Northridge earthquake was remarkable also because it introduced many new applications of information technology. For the first time, FEMA's inspectors used handheld computers to send and receive reports,

The Northridge earthquake was the first seismic event to strike directly under a major U.S. city since the 1933 Long Beach quake. The quake caused widespread damage, including the collapse of major freeways, parking structures, and office and residential buildings. Retrofits of masonry buildings helped reduce loss of life, however, and hospitals suffered less structural damage than in the 1971 San Fernando earthquake. Photo courtesy of the Federal Emergency Management Agency.

which allowed them to instantly communicate information gathered on field visits to homes and other damaged structures whose owners or occupants sought federal assistance. FEMA and California's OES officials generated prodigious numbers of GIS-produced maps, which helped them to survey their progress in building inspection. Such maps provided multiple information layers showing damage patterns and infrastructure problems. Use of cell phone technology further facilitated field operations and did so in unprecedented ways.[70]

A post-disaster rebuilding controversy arose over the costs of rebuilding Los Angeles–area hospitals. In March 1996, FEMA announced that it would provide nearly $1 billion in a new mitigation effort to strengthen the structural integrity of four local hospitals damaged by the Northridge earthquake. This decision came after a heated dispute between FEMA and California officials. When thousands of large, medium, and small businesses objected to the high cost of rebuilding under the new, tougher codes, California relented and waived the new code requirements for private sector entities, but the state kept the new requirements for public structures—those that would be built with a 90/10 federal/state cost-sharing scheme. President Clinton had waived the 75/25 federal/state match in favor of the 90/10 federal/state match.[71] The hospitals and other government and nonprofit enterprises eligible for federal funding would have to comply with the new, tougher building codes.

At first FEMA complained that California's post-quake building code changes were unfair to the federal government. FEMA officials argued that most of the hospitals required less rebuilding and structural upgrades than specified in the new codes. But FEMA director James Lee Witt quickly realized the potentially serious nature of this stance. Facing strong political opposition from top state officials and the embarrassment of opposing an admittedly expensive but strong mitigation effort, Witt agreed that FEMA would pay its share—amounting to $831 million—to rebuild the hospitals.[72] A press release offered FEMA's new take on the issue:

> [T]hrough comprehensive consultation with the state and the hospitals, FEMA provided the most cost-effective funding package that would ensure that these buildings will be able to operate after another major earthquake. This new mitigation effort is providing the means to repair or replace damaged buildings. More importantly, these funds will enable hospitals to build their facilities to stronger structural standards to withstand future earthquakes.[73]

Improving the ability of hospitals to withstand an earthquake would not only reduce the need to evacuate patients but also improve post-disaster operation by enabling these facilities to continue operation at a time when victims are in most need of help.

Hurricanes

Many nations are vulnerable to tropical windstorms. In the Pacific, these weather disturbances are most often called typhoons; in South Asia, they are called cyclones; in the North Atlantic, they are hurricanes. Hurricanes are huge, cyclonic, low-pressure storms.

Hurricanes are perhaps the type of disaster most familiar to Americans. Hurricane Andrew (1992) taught Florida residents "that hurricanes were not freak instances or random acts of nature: Floridians learned that humans and their institutions made decisions that had an important influence on whether a community did or did not suffer substantial damage from hurricanes."[74] Hurricanes also have helped to shape federal, state, and local emergency management, particularly in states along the Gulf of Mexico and the Atlantic seaboard.[75]

Before the mid-twentieth century, it was difficult to forecast or track hurricanes. The limits of meteorological analysis and technology also limited hurricane preparedness and response efforts. Since the early 1980s, coastal communities have come to benefit from ever-improving hurricane tracking and landfall projections, as well as from increasingly better scientific information and advice provided to emergency managers. These advances are the result of many factors, including major advances in weather forecasting due in large part to ever-expanding computing capacity; and an improved ability to follow tropical weather systems using satellites, radar, long-range hurricane reconnaissance aircraft, weather reports from ships at sea, and data from mid-ocean weather-monitoring buoys.[76]

But tracking the storm is just the beginning of preparedness. Emergency managers must decide on, announce, and help manage public evacuation. Part of this requires that they alert people to relocate to shelters. Disaster evacuation and sheltering have been increasingly problematic for emergency managers.

At the local level, pre-disaster hurricane-related politics involve decisions about zoning and setback regulations, code enforcement, beach preservation and dune protection, open space requirements, and a host of other concerns that affect a community's protection from or vulnerability to hurricanes. As a hurricane looms, authorities must decide whether to call for an evacuation and whether this evacuation will be voluntary or compulsory—decisions that have dramatic economic and political implications. The responsibilities of the state include promoting and disseminating hurricane forecasts and tracking information, helping local jurisdictions effect evacuation and sheltering when needed, maintaining utility infrastructures, conducting damage assessment, and facilitating post-hurricane reconstruction.

The Hurricane Preparedness Planning Program, as it was known prior to FY 1994, consisted mainly of support for studies of coastal areas to help state and local emergency management agencies in evacuation planning. In the Disaster Relief Act of 1974, FEMA was authorized to issue grants to state agencies to help them pay for the cost of developing emergency preparedness plans. States were to share some of this funding with their local governments, which would also use it to develop hurricane preparedness plans.[77] The U.S. Army Corps of Engineers played a role in managing and funding research studies, while the National Weather Service supported the development of hurricane storm-surge models for coastal areas. Overall, the emphasis was on protecting the at-risk population from storm surge and coastal flooding, forces that had historically produced the most hurricane-related deaths.

Over fifteen years, the Hurricane Preparedness Planning Program produced hurricane evacuation studies for most of the nation's coastal areas vulnerable to hurricanes. (Many of these studies need to be updated to take into account population growth and new development.) The evacuation plans that state and localities developed with support of these program funds were used in South Carolina when Hurricane Hugo struck in September 1989 and in Florida for Hurricane Andrew in August 1992.

As in other disasters, hurricanes have proven to be focusing events that have changed public opinion, political priorities, and public policy. For instance, following Hurricanes Hugo, Andrew, and Floyd, the insurance industry and some government officials stepped up their efforts to enact new zoning regulations and strengthen building codes to minimize the damage wreaked by a hurricane. Retrofitting existing structures to better withstand wind and water, and relocating

The National Hurricane Program

The National Hurricane Program (NHP), which was established in 1985, continues to provide support for hurricane research and activities. Housed under FEMA's Mitigation Division, NHP conducts and supports many projects and activities that help protect communities and their residents from hurricane hazards. The program also conducts assessments and provides tools and technical assistance to state and local agencies in developing hurricane evacuation plans.

NHP is a multiagency partnership involving FEMA, the National Oceanic and Atmospheric Administration, the National Weather Service, the U.S. Department of Transportation, the U.S. Army Corps of Engineers, and several other federal agencies. Annual funding goes for FEMA's hurricane program activities and a grant program that subsidizes state funds for hurricane preparedness and mitigation activities.

Source: FEMA, "National Hurricane Program," fema.gov/plan/prevent/nhp/index.shtm.

other structures away from the most hazardous areas, continue to be increasingly attractive tools in hurricane preparedness and mitigation policy.

Hurricane Hugo

In September 1989, millions of people throughout the Caribbean and the eastern United States watched in amazement as Hurricane Hugo traveled thousands of miles without losing intensity. Late at night on September 17, the hurricane slammed into the islands of Guadeloupe and Montserrat with winds of 140 miles per hour, killing twenty-one people and leaving another twelve thousand homeless before heading toward the U.S. Virgin Islands; there, it left thousands more people homeless and resulted in $2 billion in damages. Widespread looting forced President G. H. W. Bush to dispatch military police to St. Croix to restore order.

By midday of September 19, Hugo had reached Puerto Rico. High seas and sustained winds of 125 miles per hour resulted in the death of twelve people. More than thirty thousand Puerto Ricans lost their homes. Although Hugo was weakened somewhat as it crossed the mountains of Puerto Rico, it gained in size and intensity as it headed northwest over the warm waters of the Gulf Stream. By the time it hit the U.S. mainland on September 21, it had grown into a Category 4 storm, with sustained winds of 135 miles per hour.

By any estimation, Hurricane Hugo was a devastating storm. But it could have been far worse. Most residents had complied with the mandatory evacuation order issued for the barrier islands. Moreover, the bulk of Hugo's devastation was in relatively rural areas north of Charleston, South Carolina. Unfortunately, despite all media coverage and advanced warnings, Hugo's human toll was high: fifty-seven deaths in the mainland United States and another twenty-nine in

U.S.-owned Caribbean islands. The storm caused $7 billion of damages in the mainland United States, making it the most costly hurricane up to that time. An additional $3 billion in damages was reported in the Caribbean.[78]

Saundra K. Schneider examined the response to and recovery from Hurricane Hugo in the Caribbean, South Carolina, and North Carolina and the public's reaction to the federal government efforts. Her review brings to light some organizational failures, most particularly for South Carolina.[79]

The state of North Carolina had engaged in extensive emergency management training before the disaster, employed full-time professionals trained in emergency management, and allocated more state money for disaster management than the other states affected by Hurricane Hugo. Emergency response procedures, which incorporated a bottom-up approach, worked as planned, with FEMA and other federal agencies supplementing local and state efforts, and the state government acting as the liaison between the federal and local levels. North Carolinians generally reacted positively to the management of recovery operations in their state, and state politicians had favorable opinions about FEMA and other federal agencies following the hurricane.

The Atlantic House Restaurant at Folly Beach, South Carolina, before and after Hurricane Hugo. These buildings not withstanding, structures built to National Flood Insurance Program standards performed well. Photo courtesy of the National Oceanic and Atmospheric Administration/National Hurricane Center.

South Carolina's experience was less positive, however. The state allocated proportionally less money to disaster preparedness procedures and staffing than had North Carolina, resulting in problems regarding procedures and duties in the aftermath of Hurricane Hugo. Although a state emergency management team was already in place, shortly before Hugo made landfall Governor Carroll Campbell appointed an ad hoc emergency management team to provide additional knowledge and experience during response and recovery operations. This led to confusion about whom to contact at the state level and proved frustrating for local and federal emergency personnel. The two state emergency management groups duplicated efforts and actions.

The bottom-up emergency response plan failed in South Carolina. Many local governments had little knowledge of emergency management procedures. Consequently, some localities improperly reported damage, which delayed the receipt of assistance. State and local government officials joined the public in criticizing response efforts and directed blame to the federal government.

Hurricane Hugo also reinforced the need for and effectiveness of strict building requirements. In the midst of the devastation wrought by the hurricane, the buildings that adhered to NFIP requirements held up well, demonstrating the effectiveness of those requirements.

Hurricane Andrew

In August 1992, just two years after Hurricane Hugo's record-breaking devastation, Hurricane Andrew ripped through the Caribbean and into Florida's Atlantic coast, leaving a path of destruction across South Florida. The U.S. death toll was twenty-three; three other people were killed in the Bahamas. Hurricane Andrew caused $26.5 billion in damage in the United States, of which $1 billion occurred in Louisiana and the rest in South Florida. The vast majority of the damage in Florida was due to winds: NOAA's National Hurricane Center measured a peak

Hurricane Andrew, which was one of only three Category 5 hurricanes to strike the United States in the twentieth century, became the most costly hurricane in U.S. history. FEMA's slow response to this event was partly responsible for marked changes in the agency in the following years. Photo courtesy of the National Oceanic and Atmospheric Administration.

gust of 164 miles per hour, while a 177-mile-per-hour gust was measured at a private home.[80]

Hurricane Andrew taught emergency managers and political leaders many lessons. In an unpublished draft paper for the International Hurricane Research Center, Stephen Leatherman writes:

> The shoddy building practices and fraudulent inspections in South Florida were fully disclosed, resulting today in Florida having the best building codes (e.g., High Velocity Hurricane Zone codes) in the nation. Arguably, the most important fallout from Hurricane Andrew was changes in the insurance industry, an industry that had previously relied upon historical payouts to set actuarial rates. Andrew was a wake-up call to an industry that absorbed catastrophic losses and often had to make full payouts for replacement of damaged houses and furnishings. Since Andrew, the insurance industry has engaged in computer modeling to set insurance rates. However, hurricane insurance rates have soared by over 300 percent in South Florida since Andrew.[81]

President G. H. W. Bush appointed Secretary of Transportation Andrew Card rather than FEMA director Wallace Stickney to manage the emergency response operations in Florida. (One explanation has been that Stickney had asked Bush not to put him in charge for health reasons.) When political leaders make such major changes in emergency management leadership, it indicates distrust in FEMA's leadership and operating procedures. When Card showed up in Florida leading the president's newly impaneled task force on Hurricane Andrew recovery, he inadvertently slowed FEMA's response by insisting that "FEMA personnel distribute money directly to storm victims without going through the lengthy assessment and verification processes."[82]

Hurricane Floyd

In October 1999, Hurricane Floyd traveled up the eastern seaboard, inflicting damage in the mid-Atlantic and northeastern states. Floyd made landfall in North Carolina and caused the worst flooding in the state's history. Over $100 million in disaster assistance was provided to more than seventy-two thousand North Carolina residents.

Floyd, at one time a Category 5 hurricane that was four times larger than Hurricane Andrew, prompted the largest evacuation in U.S. history. From Miami to North Carolina, more than three million people attempted to flee from coastal areas, clogging highways and overwhelming other resources. Residents of Charleston, South Carolina, many of whom remembered the twenty-foot storm surge generated by Hugo in 1989, tried to escape inland to the state's capital city, Columbia. Cars caught up in the slow-moving, bumper-to-bumper traffic on I-26 stalled; many families were stranded for as much as twelve hours without food, water, or toilets in the late summer heat. The media picked up the story, blaming

As shown here, Hurricane Floyd caused extensive inland flooding, particularly in the Carolinas. Of the fifty-six people who died in the hurricane, fifty drowned in the floodwaters. Photo courtesy of the Federal Emergency Management Agency/Dave Gatley.

the state for failing to have an adequate evacuation plan. Some analysts believe that the negative coverage was a factor in Governor Jim Hodges's defeat in his 2002 bid for reelection in South Carolina.[83]

Although Floyd was only a Category 2 hurricane when it made landfall in North Carolina, it caused $5 billion in damage. Fifty-six people were killed outright, largely because of inland freshwater flooding. At the time, FEMA's flood maps were grossly out of date. The explosive development in North Carolina over the two previous decades had made the rivers vulnerable to flash flooding in areas that were perceived to be outside of hazard zones. The rain inundation in the state caused major flooding, enveloping entire towns in some places.

Again, the hurricane proved to be a focusing event that called attention to the inadequacies of the emergency preparedness system. As a result of Hurricane Floyd, FEMA finally recognized the inadequacy of its flood maps. North Carolina became the first state to embrace the new technology of airborne laser mapping, which offered far greater accuracy in mapping hurricane storm surge.[84]

Floods

History demonstrates that floods have long been a major cause of property damage in the United States. Since 1950, presidents have issued more disaster declarations for floods than for any other category of disaster event. In fact, almost half (47 percent) of the presidential major disaster declarations between 1953 and 2001 were for floods (663 flood disaster declarations). Prior to 1990, flood disasters usually accounted for the largest component of federal disaster relief funding, but over the next decade, FEMA federal disaster fund spending on earthquakes and hurricanes each overtook the spending for floods.

The total number of gubernatorial requests for weather-related incidents steadily increased in the 1980s and 1990s. FEMA spent $25.4 billion for declared disasters during the last decade of the twentieth century; flooding resulting from severe storms cost the agency more than $7.3 billion during this time.[85]

NOAA estimated that the Great Midwest Flood of 1993 cost $15–$20 billion. FEMA's share of these costs was $1.17 billion, excluding claims paid out by FEMA's NFIP.

The Great Midwest Flood of 1993

In the summer of 1993, continuous rain fell across the midwestern United States. Most of the Midwest received more than 12 inches of precipitation; parts of Iowa, Kansas, Minnesota, Missouri, and Nebraska got more than 24 inches of rain; and an estimated 38.4 inches fell on East-Central Iowa—amounts that were from two to four times the average amount of rainfall. The continuous rainfall saturated the soil and engorged rivers and streams. As rivers overflowed and dams and levees failed, the result was the largest and most damaging flood event in recorded U.S. history. Damages totaled $15 billion and at least forty-eight people died.[86] Thousands of people evacuated and many never returned to their flood-ravaged homes. Ninety-five river gages generated the highest flood crests ever recorded at their locations. The large area that was affected by flooding and the length of time over which the rainfall occurred made the flood a seminal event.

In his book covering the event, Rich Tobin writes that the Great Midwest Flood "provided evidence that the nation has not yet reached an accommodation between nature's periodic need to occupy her floodplains and the present human occupancy and use."[87] Only about one in ten structures affected by the flood were covered by flood insurance policies. President Clinton declared 534 counties in nine states to be federal disaster areas. At one point, every county in the state of Iowa was covered under a presidential declaration of major disaster owing to flooding and its affects. Direct federal assistance exceeded $4.2 billion, and an additional $621 million in disaster loans was provided to individuals and businesses.[88]

In a comprehensive evaluation of the Great Flood, Stanley Changnon identifies the main issues that confronted decision makers during the recovery process:

- Whether to repair or reconstruct the hundreds of damaged flood-control levees (or other structural/protective measures in future floods) and who would pay for permitted repairs

- Whether to permit repair or rebuilding of thousands of substantially damaged structures so they could again be inhabited

- Whether to commit community planning and financial assistance to develop alternative mitigation strategies to the typical repair/rebuild scenario

- Whether to use risk insurance as a type of mitigation tool.[89]

The Midwest floods were one of the first major challenges of Clinton's revamped FEMA, and the agency was widely praised for its management of the response. Witt made sure that FEMA proactively addressed the disaster under a

> new policy that it would no longer wait for states to ask for damage assessment teams.... Witt sent regional staffs out before the flooding became serious to help states apply for disaster assistance; had them prepare preliminary damage assessments before President Clinton's formal disaster declaration; directed FEMA workers to respond immediately to any state requests; and anticipated requests rather than waiting for the state to tell FEMA what they needed. Witt's FEMA never lost focus....[90]

The winter following the floods, the Clinton administration convened the Interagency Floodplain Management Review Committee to conduct a comprehensive review of floodplain management. The committee's recommendations, in its report *Sharing the Challenge: Floodplain Management into the 21st Century* (referred to as the *Galloway Report*, after the committee's chair, Gerald E. Galloway Jr.), called for shared responsibility for floodplain management among federal, state, and local governments. It also recommended restrictions on development in floodplains. The committee criticized the lack of national flood insurance policies in communities affected by the Great Midwest Flood and noted that overly generous federal disaster assistance has the potential to reduce individual responsibility to self-protect against disasters.[91]

In September 1993, Witt issued a memo stating that the Hazard Mitigation Grant Program would be used for property acquisition and residential relocation. This was important for two reasons: first, few believed that homeowners would voluntarily sell their homes and relocate on a mass scale (although, to the surprise of many after the Great Flood, they did, for the first time in history, and some 14,000–20,000 structures moved out of the floodplain); and second, Witt was getting tremendous pressure to rebuild failed levees throughout the Midwest. In the memo he contended that levees are the purview of U.S. Army Corps of Engineers and that FEMA would "not" do levees.[92]

Professionalization of Emergency Management

Emergency management as a profession continued to expand and grow in knowledge base and experience from 1979 to 2001. Its rise as a profession was

A total of 534 counties in nine states received federal disaster declarations owing to the damage caused by the Great Midwest Flood of 1993. This prompted the Clinton administration to call for a comprehensive review of floodplain management. Photo courtesy of the Federal Emergency Management Agency/Andrea Booher.

important: the constantly improving state and local administrative capacity to better document disaster losses may have been a factor in the era's increased number of presidential disaster declarations.[93] This growing capacity, in addition to automated damage measurements, might have meant that the federal government was increasingly able to validate a state's needs when the federal government's assistance was requested;[94] it would suggest that presidents became better able to make decisions about disaster and emergency declarations. In August 2001, however, the U.S. General Accounting Office cited inadequate declaration criteria and a host of FEMA/state information management problems, including inadequate staffing and training.[95]

Owing to advances in information technology, state emergency managers at the close of the twentieth century were likely better able to document disaster loss than they were in the 1970s. State and local governments became more expert in using information technology to document disaster losses and more proficient in proving their need for federal assistance, which gave them a stronger factual basis for requesting a presidential disaster declaration. This may have contributed to the trend in declining turndowns of requests for federal assistance. Thus, they enjoyed a liberal provision of federal disaster relief from a variety of federal agencies, including FEMA. By 2001, state and local governments could count on federal help to pay for "debris removal, repair, restoration, or replacement of public facilities"; community disaster loans to cover shortfalls in local tax revenue owing to a disaster; and coverage of a major share of their emergency response costs.[96]

Conclusions

The president's role in emergency management grew in importance over the period of 1979 to 2001. In 1980, President Reagan at first planned to dismantle FEMA, viewing it as an unnecessary Carter-era organization. However, as soon as Reagan had to confront a series of small disasters, some of them caused by humans, he walked back his dismantlement plans, recognizing the unique role assumed by the agency. FEMA leaders over the Reagan years ranged from capable to irresponsibly poor. Regrettably, when confronted with Hurricane Andrew's devastation in 1992, President G. H. W. Bush circumvented FEMA and formed a hurricane task force led by Secretary of Transportation Andrew Card. In 1989, he had appointed Transportation Secretary Samuel Skinner to assume the same leadership role in managing recovery from the Northridge earthquake. Steven Daniels and Carolyn Clark-Daniels conclude,

> The bypassing of the official disaster agency by various presidents had a number of serious consequences. The first was the inevitable duplication of effort. Despite presidential intervention, FEMA and its predecessors nevertheless retained both the inclination and the statutory requirement to intercede on behalf of disaster victims. The separate presidential and agency response efforts unavoidably wasted resources. The second consequence was the management of disaster response and recovery by less qualified personnel. The White House staff invariably had much less emergency management experience than permanent agency employees. As a result, each administration that relied heavily on presidential preemption of disaster recovery had a much longer learning curve than administrations that relied on a permanent disaster agency, such as FDAA [Federal Disaster Assistance Administration] or FEMA.[97]

Clark and Daniels eloquently add, "One of the major differences between the Bush and Clinton administrations was the level of support provided by the president to disaster management. Bush's disaster response was largely reactive and bypassed the existing disaster management structure. Clinton's disaster management policy was more proactive and politically sensitive. Clinton also improved FEMA's political stature by emphasizing the lead disaster role of the agency and its director, and by raising the FEMA director to cabinet status. One former state emergency management official argued, 'Witt's greatest impact was the fact that he linked FEMA to the executive branch, the Executive Office of the President, and the president. Witt had access.'"[98]

Some experts maintain that, in an era of devolution and decentralization of government, U.S. disaster policy became an increasingly centralized responsibility of the federal government.[99] Yet during the closing decades of the twentieth century, emergency management was profoundly shaped by what state and local governments did or did not do.[100] Many states and localities promoted and facilitated their emergency management capacities and launched pre-disaster mitigation programs.

Federal assistance for disaster victims also grew considerably from 1979 to 2001, although this growth was not substantial during the Reagan years. Grants for individuals and families, temporary housing aid, provisions for mobile home use, and disaster unemployment assistance became part of the disaster relief provided after an event. The federal government also funded legal services for the poor, crisis counseling, and mental health assistance programs for disaster victims. Small Business Administration disaster loans were issued to applicant homeowners and businesses.

The Great Midwest Flood of 1993, the nationwide increase in severe storm-related disasters, and mounting hurricane devastation have led environmental hazard researchers, including many in the meteorological and physical geography communities, to contend that there have been an unusually large number of hydro-meteorological disasters.[101] Many of these researchers maintain that we are experiencing more temperature and precipitation extremes (high and low) than ever before, some as manifestations of climate change. Others see the escalating costs of disasters as evidence of more expansive, expensive, and disaster-vulnerable communities and structures.[102]

FEMA was born in an era in which civil defense against nuclear attack was of strategic importance. As the cry for civil defense lost urgency, civilian emergency management took on increased significance. In 1993, however, just as civil defense had faded from the emergency manager's "radar screen," the World Trade Center was bombed, thus renewing concern about civil defense and emergency preparedness.

In contradistinction, the era included major advances in disaster sciences and information technology, which both advanced and complicated emergency management. An increasing number of researchers and politicians, along with the public, have begun to understand that disasters emanate not simply from natural forces, but also from human causes and human-tolerated vulnerabilities. New tools, including information technology, GIS, global positioning systems, and advanced individual and mass communication devices, as well as portable computing via laptops and palmtops, have become increasingly available. To master their use, emergency managers have had to acquire new knowledge and skills, further advancing their profession.[103]

The era also saw strides in disaster mitigation, as public, private, and non-profit organizations began to take disaster vulnerability and mounting disaster losses more seriously than ever before. Major insurers, a sophisticated network of government disaster researchers, and scientific and engineering experts within academia are now using technological advances to study and counteract where possible a wide variety of hazards and disaster agents.

In both a social and political sense, Americans have become increasingly aware of the growing range of natural and human-caused disaster agents they face, and they are less tolerant of preventable disaster-caused losses. Elected policy makers have grown to expect federal, state, and local emergency managers to serve as disaster protectors, preventers, evacuation directors, shelter managers, responders, rescuers, relief distributors, restorers, and agents of government-funded post-disaster recompense.

Media coverage of disasters and emergencies, often provided in "live shots" or near real time, have made Americans (and the world) almost instantly aware of disasters and human tragedies in other parts of the nation and across the globe. NAPA's conclusion in its 1993 report was prescient: camcorder politics and the CNN effect have thoroughly permeated emergency management.[104] Arguably, media coverage of disasters and emergencies did more to change the political and managerial world of emergency management from 1979 to 2001 than almost anything else—a trend that has escalated. Americans watched their televisions in horror as the events of 9/11 unfolded before their eyes.[105]

At the close of the century, communities were much better prepared for a disaster than they were when FEMA was first established, but the federal government's role has continued to evolve. Partnerships between and among federal, state, and local governments, private sector businesses, and nonprofit organizations address the needs that were made evident by the Loma Prieta and Northridge earthquakes; by Hurricanes Hugo, Andrew, and Floyd; by the Great Midwest Flood, and by other disasters big and small. Emergency management has become "big business" and a growth industry in every sector.

From March 1979 until March 2003, FEMA operated as an independent federal agency. It then floated in a sea of departments and agencies, many of which dwarfed the agency in workforce size, budget authority, and political clout. The agency sank or swam as a function of how it was perceived by the president in office and how its appointed leaders managed their jobs. Subsequent chapters explain how FEMA has, since 2003, been subsumed within the Department of Homeland Security. According to FEMA chief of staff Jason McNamara, FEMA remains intact, has its biggest workforce to date, and has recaptured a positive reputation.[106] In many ways, the FEMA personnel of 1979–2003 built the foundation for and pioneered, with successes and failures, the world and profession of current emergency managers.

Endnotes

1   Executive Order No. 12127 of March 31, 1979, essentially created FEMA; see 3 C.F.R. 1979 Comp., 376, fas.org/irp/offdocs/eo/eo-12127.htm. Executive Order No. 12148, enacted on July 20, 1979, transferred and reassigned duties to the newly formed agency; it also directed FEMA to develop a plan to outline how the agency would cooperate and respond to a nuclear emergency. In response, FEMA established the Federal Radiological Emergency Response Plan; see fas.org/irp/offdocs/EO12148.htm.

2   Although this transfer was in the plan, it was officially canceled in 1982, and FEMA never acquired the National Weather Service Community Preparedness Program.

3   Henry B. Hogue and Keith Bea, *Federal Emergency Management and Homeland Security Organization: Historical Developments and Legislative Options* (Washington, D.C.: Congressional Research Service [CRS], Library of Congress, June 1, 2006); George D. Haddow, Jane A. Bullock, and Damon P. Coppola, *Introduction to Emergency Management,* 4th ed. (Burlington, Mass.: Elsevier Butterworth-Heinemann, 2011), 6.

4   B. Wayne Blanchard, *Background "Think Piece" for the Emergency Management Roundtable Meeting, EMI March 5–6, 2007, on What Is Emergency Management? And What Are the Principles of Emergency Management,* draft (Emmitsburg, Md.: Emergency Management Institute, FEMA, Department of Homeland Security, March 2, 2007), 18, google.com/url?sa=t&sou rce=web&ct=res&cd=2&url=http%3A%2F%2Ftraining.fema.gov%2FEMIWeb%2Fedu%2Fdocs% 2Femprinciples%2FEM%2520Roundtable%2520Background%2520Think%2520Piece .doc&ei=4cJwSsvSHY-vlAfx6pjsCg&rct=j&q=five+phases+of+emergency+management&usg=AF QjCNEk_yLu3dp1t3zlYcBN_z9xnJdhOA.

5   "About FEMA, What We Do," fema.gov/about/.

6   Richard T. Sylves, *Disaster Policy and Politics: Emergency Management and Homeland Security* (Washington, D.C.: CQ Press, 2008), 62–63.

7   Ibid., 48–51.

8   R. Steven Daniels and Carolyn L. Clark-Daniels, *Transforming Government: The Renewal and Revitalization of the Federal Emergency Management Agency,* Presidential Transition Series (Arlington, Va.: PricewaterhouseCoopers Endowment for the Business of Government, April 2000), fema.gov/pdf/library/danielsreport.pdf.

9   Emergency management professionals differentiate between smaller-scale emergencies, which are limited in time, space, and effect, and disasters, which have a broader, more severe impact and require more response and recovery resources. The differentiation between a disaster and an emergency stems from the enabling Stafford Act, as well as from usage among disaster professionals. A catastrophe is defined as a rare event that surpasses most expectations as well as the ability of state and local governments to respond, and hence it becomes a historic event.

10 Sylves, *Disaster Policy and Politics,* 62. See also Francis X. McCarthy, *Federal Stafford Act Disaster Assistance: Presidential Declarations, Eligible Activities, and Funding,* RL33053 (Washington, D.C.: CRS, Library of Congress, June 7, 2011), fas.org/sgp/crs/homesec/RL33053.pdf. McCarthy explains, "Congress appropriates money to the Disaster Relief Fund (DRF) to ensure that… federal assistance…is available to help individuals and communities stricken by severe disasters. Funds appropriated to the DRF remain available until expended. Such accounts are referred to as 'no-year' accounts. Appropriations to the DRF generally evoke little controversy. Supplemental appropriations measures are generally required each fiscal year to meet the urgent needs of particularly catastrophic disasters" (18).

11 Aaron Schroeder and Gary Wamsley, "The Evolution of Emergency Management in America: From a Painful Past to a Promising but Uncertain Future," in *Handbook of Crisis and Emergency Management,* ed. Ali Farazmand (New York: Marcel Dekker, 2002).

12 Dianne Rahm, *United States Public Policy: A Budgetary Approach* (Belmont, Calif.: Wadsworth, 2004), 97–113.

13 See David K. Twigg, *The Politics of Disaster: Tracking the Political Effects of Hurricane Andrew* (Gainesville, Fla.: University of Florida Press, 2012).

14 Kevin Arceneaux and Robert M. Stein, "Who Is Held Responsible When Disaster Strikes? The Attribution of Responsibility for a Natural Disaster in an Urban Election," *Journal of Urban Affairs* 28 (January 2006): 43.

15 Ann M. Beauchesne, *A Governor's Guide to Emergency Management* (Washington, D.C.: National Governors Association, 1998); National Research Council (NRC), Committee on Assessing the

Costs of Natural Disasters, *The Impacts of Natural Disasters: A Framework for Loss Estimation* (Washington, D.C.: National Academies Press, 1999).

16   FEMA Internet news release, March 23, 1995.

17   Ibid.

18   Susan L. Cutter, ed. *American Hazardscapes: The Regionalization of Hazards and Disasters* (Washington, D.C.: Joseph Henry Press, 2001); Dennis S. Mileti, *Disasters by Design: A Reassessment of Natural Hazards in the United States* (Washington, D.C.: Joseph Henry Press, 1999).

19   Roy S. Popkin, "The History and Politics of Disaster Management in the United States" in *Nothing to Fear: Risks and Hazards in American Society,* ed. Andrew Kirby (Tucson: University of Arizona Press, 1990).

20   Claire B. Rubin, Irmak Renda-Tanali, and William Cumming, *Disaster Time Line: Major Focusing Events and Their Outcomes (1979–2005)* (Arlington, Va.: Claire B. Rubin & Associates, 2006), disaster-timeline.com.

21   SARA Title III in Superfund Revitalization Act of 1986; Title III in the Emergency Planning and Community Right-to-Know Act.

22   United Nations Scientific Committee on the Effects of Atomic Radiation (UNSCEAR), *The Chernobyl Accident: UNSCEAR's Assessments of the Radiation Effects* (August 3, 2011), unscear.org/unscear/en/chernobyl.html.

23   U.S. General Accounting Office (GAO), *Nuclear Safety Reactor Design and Preparedness at Fort St. Vrain,* RCED-88-8 (Washington, D.C.: U.S. Government Printing Office, November 1987), archive.gao.gov/d29t5/134670.pdf.

24   Ted Steinberg, *Acts of God: The Unnatural History of Natural Disaster in America* (New York: Oxford University Press, 2000), 181.

25   This action by the federal government was a precursor of modern antipandemic or bioterrorism preparedness initiatives.

26   James David Barber, "Presidential Character," in *American Government: Readings and Cases,* ed. Karen O'Connor (Boston: Allyn and Bacon, 1995), 204.

27   Naim Kapucu et al., "U.S. Presidents and Their Roles in Emergency Management and Disaster Policy 1950–2009," *Risk, Hazards, and Crisis in Public Policy* 2, no. 3 (2011).

28   GAO, *Disaster Assistance: Improvement Needed in Disaster Declaration Criteria and Eligibility Assurance Procedures,* Report to the Subcommittee on VA, HUD, and Independent Agencies, Committee on Appropriations, U.S. Senate (Washington, D.C.: U.S. Government Printing Office, August 2001), 1.

29   Ibid, 2.

30   Personal communication with Francis X. McCarthy of the CRS, November, 2011.

31   See Public Entity Risk Institute (PERI), "All about Presidential Disaster Declarations," peripresdecusa.org (last accessed January 14, 2012).

32   David R. Godschalk, David J. Brower, and Timothy Beatley, *Catastrophic Coastal Storms: Hazard Mitigation and Development Management* (Durham, N.C.: Duke University Press, 1989).

33   Rubin, Renda-Tanali, and Cumming, *Disaster Time Line.*

34   Frances L. Edwards, "Homeland Security from the Local Perspective," in *Homeland Security Law and Policy,* ed. William C. Nicholson (Springfield, Ill.: Charles C. Thomas, 2005), 114.

35   Rutherford H. Platt and Claire B. Rubin, "Stemming the Losses: The Quest for Hazard Mitigation," in *Disasters and Democracy: The Politics of Extreme Natural Events,* ed. Rutherford B. Platt (Washington, D.C.: Island Press, 1999); Mileti, *Disasters by Design.*

36   Mileti, *Disasters by Design*; Cutter, *American Hazardscapes.*

37   John C. Pine, *Technology in Emergency Management* (Hoboken, N.J.: John Wiley & Sons, 2007).

38   NRC, Committee on Disaster Research in the Social Sciences, *Facing Hazards and Disasters: Understanding Human Dimensions* (Washington, D.C.: National Academies Press, 2006).

39   "HAZUS," fema.gov/plan/prevent/hazus/index.shtm.

40   NRC, *Facing Hazards and Disasters.*

41   Robert Bolin and Lois Stanford, *The Northridge Earthquake: Vulnerability and Disaster* (London: Routledge, 1998).

42   William L. Waugh Jr., *Living with Hazards, Dealing with Disasters* (Armonk, N.Y.: M. E. Sharpe, 2000).

43   Kathleen Tierney, Michael K. Lindell, and Ronald W. Perry, *Facing the Unexpected: Disaster Preparedness and Response in the United States* (Washington, D.C.: Joseph Henry Press, 2001), 146.

44   Disaster Relief Act of 1950, Pub. L. No. 81-875, 64 Stat. 1109 (1950).

45   Ibid.

46   Rutherford H. Platt, "Federalizing Disasters: From Compassion to Entitlement," in *Disasters and Democracy: The Politics of Extreme Natural Events,* ed. Rutherford B. Platt (Washington, D.C.: Island Press, 1999), 23–26.

47   Keith Bea, *Federal Stafford Act Disaster Assistance: Presidential Declarations, Eligible Activities, and Funding,* CRS Report to Congress (Washington, D.C.: CRS, Library of Congress, April 28, 2006), 30–32.

48   Disaster Relief Act of 1974, Pub. L. No. 93-288, 88 Stat. 143 (1974).

49   Richard T. Sylves, "President Bush and Hurricane Katrina: A Presidential Leadership Study," in *Shelter from the Storm: Repairing the National Emergency Management System after Hurricane Katrina,* ed. William L. Waugh Jr., *The Annals of the American Academy of Political and Social Science* 604 (March 2006): 26–56.

50   PERI, "All about Presidential Disaster Declarations."

51   Allen K. Settle, "Disaster Assistance: Securing Presidential Declarations," in *Cities and Disaster: North American Studies in Emergency Management*, ed. Richard T. Sylves and William L. Waugh Jr., 33–56 (Springfield, Ill.: Charles C. Thomas, 1990), 50.

52   Albert Gore, *Creating a Government That Works Better and Costs Less: The Report of the National Performance Review* (Washington, D.C.: U.S. Government Printing Office, September 7, 1993), 46.

53   Waugh, *Living with Hazards*, 12.

54   Haddow, Bullock, and Coppola, *Introduction to Emergency Management*, 88.

55   Gary L. Wamsley et al., *Coping with Catastrophe: Building and Emergency Management System to Meet People's Needs in Natural and Manmade Disasters* (Washington, D.C.: National Academy of Public Administration, 1993), ix.

56   The Volkmer Amendment to the Hazard Mitigation and Relocation Assistance Act of 1993 (P.L. 103-181) amended the 1988 Stafford Act.

57   House Subcommittee on Water Resources and the Environment of the Committee on Public Works and Transportation, *Midwest Floods of 1993: Flood Control and Floodplain Policy and Proposals* (103-57), Statement of the Honorable Harold L. Volkmer, 103rd Cong., 1st sess., October 27, 1993, 241.

58   Platt and Rubin, "Stemming the Losses," 78.

59   Michael K. Lindell, Carla Prater, and Ronald W. Perry, *Introduction to Emergency Management* (Hoboken, N.J.: John Wiley & Sons, 2007), 361–362.

60   Sylves, *Disaster Policy and Politics*, 69.

61   William J. Petak and Arthur A. Atkisson, *Natural Hazard Risk Assessment and Public Policy* (New York: Springer-Verlag, 1982), 76–79.

62   Haddow, Bullock, and Coppola, *Introduction to Emergency Management*, 91–92.

63   Platt and Rubin, "Stemming the Losses," 84.

64   Waugh, *Living with Hazards*, 61.

65   See Allen K. Settle, "The Coalinga Earthquake," in *Crisis Management: A Casebook,* ed. Michael T. Charles and John Choon K. Kim (Springfield, Ill.: Charles C. Thomas, 1988). Settle documents how Coalinga's mayor skillfully used the media and political influence to secure substantial disaster relief aid from the federal and state governments, which he then used to refashion and rebuild the downtown into a seismically safe shopping plaza.

66   Platt, "Federalizing Disasters," 251–252.

67   James F. Miskel, *Disaster Response and Homeland Security* (Westport, Conn.: Praeger Security International, 2006), 78; Richard J. Roth Jr., "Earthquake Insurance Protection in California," in *Paying the Price: The Status and Role of Insurance against Natural Disasters in the United States,* ed. Howard Kunreuther (Washington, D.C.: Joseph Henry Press, 1998).

68   PERI, "All about Presidential Disaster Declarations."

69   Bea, *Federal Stafford Act Disaster Assistance*.

70   Robert Klebs and Richard T. Sylves, "The Northridge Earthquake: Memoirs of a FEMA Building Inspector," in *Disaster Management in the U.S. and Canada,* ed. Richard T. Sylves and William L. Waugh Jr. (Springfield, Ill.: Charles C. Thomas, 1996).

71   Keith Bea, *FEMA and Disaster Relief,* 97-159 GOV (Washington, D.C.: CRS, Library of Congress, updated March 6, 1998), hsdl.org/?view&did=15130. Bea states, "For most disasters, a threshold of $64 per capita (statewide) has been used to determine when a waiver may be granted. That is, if the damages from a declared disaster in a state exceed $64 multiplied by the entire state population, a waiver has been considered. Once that threshold has been reached, FEMA has adjusted the cost-share requirements" (15). He also notes, "The President may waive, and has waived, some or all of the cost-sharing required for public assistance after particularly destructive catastrophes. The match requirement for human services (which the Stafford Act sets at 25% of eligible costs) cannot be waived, except for insular areas" (14).

72   The bill for repairing and/or replacing the four hospitals that had been damaged totaled more than $947 million, paid for by FEMA, the state of California, and local contributors.

73   FEMA, Office of Emergency Information and Public Affairs, "FEMA to Provide Nearly $1 Billion for Earthquake-Damaged Hospitals," March 12, 1996, press release.

74   Thomas A. Birkland, "Federal Disaster Policy: Learning, Priorities, and Prospects for Resilience," in *Designing Resilience: Preparing for Extreme Events,* ed. Louise K. Comfort, Arjen Boin, and Chris C. Demchak (Pittsburgh, Pa.: University of Pittsburgh Press, 2010), 122–123.

75   William L. Waugh Jr., "Hurricanes," in *Handbook of Emergency Management: Policies and Programs for Dealing with Major Hazards and Disasters,* ed. William L. Waugh Jr. and Ronald J. Hy (Westport, Conn.: Greenwood Press, 1990), 61–80.

76   Pine, *Technology in Emergency Management*; Jack Williams and Bob Sheets, *Hurricane Watch: Forecasting the Deadliest Storms on Earth* (New York: Vintage Books, 2001).

77   David R. Godschalk, *Catastrophic Coastal Storms: Hazard Mitigation and Development Management* (Durham, N.C.: Duke University Press, 1989), 100.

78   "Storms of the Century: 1989 Hurricane Hugo," weather.com/newscenter/specialreports/sotc/honorable/1989.html. The devastation of Hurricane Hugo was exceeded by that caused by Hurricane Andrew in 1992 and by several other storms since then, but Hugo remains one of the costliest hurricanes in U.S. history.

79   Saundra K. Schneider, *Flirting with Disaster: Public Management in Crisis Situations* (Armonk, N.Y.: M. E. Sharpe, 1995).

80   National Oceanic and Atmospheric Administration (NOAA), "Hurricane Andrew," noaa.gov/hurricaneandrew.html.

81   Stephen P. Leatherman, "Hurricanes Make Public Policy" (unpublished draft paper for the International Hurricane Research Center, Florida International University, Miami, Florida, 2005), 3.

82   Schneider, *Flirting with Disaster*, 95.

83   Ibid.

84   Ibid. FEMA has recently embarked on a $1 billion Map Modernization Program to develop new maps for coastal and riverine floodplains.

85   Haddow, Bullock, and Coppola, *Introduction to Emergency Management*, 214–215.

86   Sylves, *Disaster Policy and Politics*, 122.

87   Rich Tobin, *A Chronology of Major Events Affecting the National Flood Insurance Program* (Washington, D.C.: American Institutes for Research, December 2005), 50, fema.gov/pdf/nfip/chronology.pdf.

88   House Committee on Homeland Security, *Redirecting FEMA toward Success,* February 2006, 16, hsdl.org/?view&did=461850.

89   Stanley A. Changnon, *The Great Flood of 1993: Causes, Impacts, and Responses* (Boulder, Colo.: Westview Press, 1996).

90   House Committee on Homeland Security, *Redirecting FEMA toward Success,* 16.

91   *Sharing the Challenge: Floodplain Management into the 21st Century,* Report of the Interagency Floodplain Management Review Committee to the Administration Floodplain Management Task Force (Washington, D.C., June 1994), floods.org/PDF/Sharing_the_Challenge.pdf.

92   Personal communication with Larry Larson, executive director of the Association of State Floodplain Managers, November, 2011.

93   Louise K. Comfort, ed., *Managing Disaster: Strategies and Policy Perspectives* (Durham, N.C.: Duke University Press, 1988).

94   Sylves and Waugh, *Disaster Management,* 1996.

95   GAO, *Disaster Assistance,* 2–3.

96   Platt, "Federalizing Disasters," 16–17.

97   Daniels and Clark-Daniels, *Transforming Government,* 12.

98   Ibid., 8.

99   Platt, "Federalizing Disasters"; Miskel, *Disaster Response and Homeland Security.*

100 See Ute J. Dymon and Rutherford H. Platt, "U.S. Federal Disaster Declarations: A Geographical Analysis," in *Disasters and Democracy: The Politics of Extreme Natural Events,* ed. Rutherford B. Platt (Washington, D.C.: Island Press, 1999), 47–66.

101 Stanley A. Changnon, "Factors Affecting Temporal Fluctuations in Damaging Storm Activity in the United States Based on Insurance Loss Data," *Journal of Applied Meteorology* 6 (1999): 1–10; Changnon, *The Great Flood of 1993;* Stanley A. Changnon and David Changnon, "Record-High Losses for Weather Disasters in the United States during the 1990s: How Excessive and Why?" *Natural Hazards* 18 (1999): 287–300.

102 Roger Pielke and Christopher W. Landsea, "Normalized Hurricane Damages in the United States: 1925–1995," *Weather and Forecasting* 13 (January 1998): 621–631, aoml.noaa.gov/hrd/Landsea/USdmg.

103 Sylves, *Disaster Policy and Politics,* 108–128.

104 Wamsley et al., *Coping with Catastrophe.*

105 Sylves, *Disaster Policy and Politics,* 61.

106 Jason McNamara, presentation to the students of the graduate course "Crisis and Emergency Management" at The George Washington University, December 5, 2011.

Chapter 6

Emergency Management Restructured: Intended and Unintended Outcomes of Actions Taken since 9/11

John R. Harrald

The national emergency management team that responded to the terrorist attacks of September 11, 2001, was not the product of unilateral federal action; rather, it evolved from the bottom up, demonstrating that emergency management is primarily a local responsibility. As discussed in the previous chapter, the federal legislation that created the organizations and systems in place on 9/11 recognized that the federal government was responsible for supporting state and local governments in a coordinated, effective manner in order to minimize human suffering and economic loss and enhance sustainable recovery.

The evolution of the functions and profession of emergency management in the United States is described in detail in textbooks.[1] It is also demonstrated graphically in the *Disaster Time Line* and *Terrorism Time Line* products developed by Claire B. Rubin & Associates.[2] Major milestones in this evolution include

- The development of a comprehensive emergency management taxonomy in the late 1970s, based on an all-hazards approach and the four phases of disaster (mitigation, preparedness, response, and recovery)

- The establishment of the Federal Emergency Management Agency (FEMA) in 1979, consolidating federal mitigation, preparedness, response, and recovery activities into one agency reporting directly to the president

- The National Wildfire Coordinating Group's acceptance in 1982 of the revised FIRESCOPE incident command system (ICS) as the organizing protocol of the National Interagency Incident Management System (NIIMS), which formed the basis for the National Incident Management System (NIMS) created in response to the 9/11 attacks (see discussion below)

- The development of the Certified Emergency Management Program by the International Association of Emergency Managers (IAEM) in 1993, offering certification for emergency managers

- The formation of the National Emergency Management Association (NEMA) as the professional association of state emergency management directors in 1974 and its formal affiliation with the Council of State Governments in 1990

- The publication of the Federal Response Plan (FRP) in 1992, which provided a mechanism for organizing and coordinating the resources of twenty-three (later twenty-seven) federal agencies and departments and the American Red Cross

- The development in 1995/1996 of NFPA 1600, Standard on Disaster/ Emergency Management and Business Continuity Programs, by the National Fire Protection Association Standards Committee (with assistance from the Disaster Recovery Institute International and the Business Continuity Institute), which was significantly revised in 2004 and endorsed by FEMA, IAEM, and NEMA

- The creation of the state-to-state mutual aid program in 1996 in the Emergency Management Assistance Compact (EMAC), which was adopted by NEMA and ratified by Congress in 1996

- NEMA's creation in 1997 of the Emergency Management Accreditation Program, a voluntary assessment and accreditation process for state/territorial, tribal, and local government emergency management programs

- The amendment of the FRP in 1999 by the inclusion of a terrorism annex to coordinate emergency management (or "consequence management") and law enforcement (or "crisis management") during a terrorist attack. Also, a Federal Bureau of Investigation (FBI)/FEMA Concept of Operations Plan (CONPLAN) was adopted in 2001

- The Association of State Flood Plain Managers (ASFPM) created the Certified Flood Plain Manager Program in 1999.

These steps provided a uniform organization and doctrine for responding to and recovering from all types of disasters. The resulting all-hazards approach continued to be a guiding principle for FEMA's efforts to fulfill its legislative responsibilities throughout the 1990s. However, the overall federal approach to emergency management vested responsibility for individual hazards or classes of hazards among several federal agencies and plans (see Table 6–1). Depending on the type of threat, each of these plans specified a different federal lead agency and different relationship among federal, state, and local governments. Under the FRP, the federal government played a support role, through FEMA, for state and local responders. Under the National Oil and Hazardous Substances Pollution Contingency Plan (NCP), the federal and state governments responded to oil spills and hazardous material releases with equal authority, with the federal response coordinated by the U.S. Environmental Protection Agency (EPA) or the U.S. Coast Guard. In the case of a radiological incident, the Federal Radiological Emergency Response Plan (FRERP) specified federal leadership coordinated by the U.S. Nuclear Regulatory Commission and FEMA.

NIIMS, which was created by the National Wildfire Coordinating Group, standardized the doctrine for state and federal agency use of the ICS, unified

Type of Event	Federal Plan	Lead Agencies	Government Roles
Presidentially declared disaster (natural disaster, terrorist attack)	Federal Response Plan (FRP)	Federal Emergency Management Agency (FEMA), Federal Bureau of Investigation (FBI)	State has lead role, supported by federal government resources
Environmental disaster (release of oil, toxic substances)	National Contingency Plan (NCP)	Environmental Protection Agency, Coast Guard	Parallel federal government and state government roles
Nuclear/radiological release	Federal Radiological Emergency Response Plan (FRERP)	Department of Energy, FEMA	State and local support of federal response
Wildfire	National Interagency Incident Management System (NIIMS)	U.S. Department of Agriculture; National Wildfire Coordinating Group	Federal government leads on federal lands; states lead on state lands
Biohazard epidemic	Health and Medical Services Support Plan; National Disaster Medical System	Department of Health and Human Services; Centers for Disease Control and Prevention	Federal government support of state and local medical and public health response
Terrorist attack	Interagency Domestic Terrorism Concept of Operations Plan (CONPLAN)	Department of Justice/FBI; FEMA	Federal government leads; state and local governments request federal assistance

Table 6–1. U.S. Disaster Plans in 2001.

Source: John Harrald, "Agility and Discipline: Critical Success Factors for Disaster Response," *Annals of the American Academy of Political and Social Sciences* 604 (Spring 2006): 256–272.

command, and multiagency coordination system (MACS) in fighting wildfires. It was assumed that during a wildfire the state or federal agency responsible for the affected geographic area would take the lead.

In general, since the 1970s the system has changed in an evolutionary manner, with issues over authority and responsibility being settled on an incident-by-incident basis. For example, the Coast Guard, EPA, and FEMA had worked out a protocol to link the FRP and NCP authorities when oil spill response efforts occurred within the context of a presidential disaster declaration; however, FEMA quickly ceded all responsibility for the 1989 *Exxon Valdez* spill to the Coast Guard when a presidential declaration was not forthcoming.[3] In another case, FEMA and the FBI, through the establishment of the Terrorism Incident Annex to the FRP and CONPLAN, tried to integrate law enforcement and response activities by ensuring that the FBI had the lead for crisis management activities while FEMA retained the status as lead agency for the consequence management phase. This artificial division had little meaning in the field, but through this superficial attempt at integration, the U.S. Department of Justice and FEMA appeared to be collaborating while ceding no authority to each other.

The Response to 9/11

The federal government responded to the 9/11 attacks on the World Trade Center and the Pentagon under the framework described above. In New York City and Arlington County, Virginia, incident management commands were led by the city and county fire departments, respectively, and organized under the ICS. The ICS has long served as the basic protocol for many firefighting organizations, and the establishment of an ICS-based organization was standard operating procedure for the New York City Fire Department and the Arlington County Fire Department (ACFD). The assets of the federal government were coordinated in both locations, using the protocols of the FRP. Some organizational problems occurred, and in both cases, the coordination of federal, state, and local governments required extensive improvisation and creativity.

The integration of the Department of Defense, local law enforcement, and emergency management forces into a locally directed, high-performing ICS-based organization during the response to the attack on the Pentagon was accomplished without organizational conflict.[4] The findings from the after-action report funded by the National Science Foundation and conducted by the George Washington University summarize the reasons for the effective response effort at the Pentagon:

- The response system designed for natural disasters was effective for managing the consequences of a terrorist attack. The ability of the ACFD to establish an ICS-based organizational structure and the acceptance of this organization by federal responders (including the Defense Department) was the key to success.

- Unified command worked well for coordinating multiple disparate assets.

- Federal assets and teams were obtained through the FRP structure and used effectively.

- An effective on-scene response organization was rapidly created, and goals were defined and met.

- The organization that evolved was based upon ICS, but creativity and coordination resulted in a flexible, effective organization. "Management" rather than "command" approaches may have contributed to the successful coordination of multiple disparate organizations.

- Organizations with diverse organizational cultures (fire, search and rescue, military, medical, and law enforcement) were effectively coordinated. Preestablished personal relationships greatly eased potential organizational problems.

- Information management and media relations were critical to actual and perceived success.[5]

The initial response to the attack on the World Trade Center in New York City was made by the city's fire and police departments, emergency medical system, Office of Emergency Management, and Department of Design and Construction, as well as by the New York/New Jersey Port Authority police. The response was complicated by the loss of the New York State and New York City emergency operations center (EOC) in Building 7 of the World Trade Center, a state-of-the-art facility when it was constructed in 1999, and of all communications at FEMA Region II office at 26 Federal Plaza. Following the collapse of the towers, the deaths of 343 New York City firefighters, 37 Port Authority police, and 23 New York City police put an enormous strain on the multiagency response.[6] But the city quickly reestablished its EOC and initiated a unique on-scene coincident command coordinated by the fire department and the Department of Design and Construction. The Office of Emergency Management was able to fully participate in a unified command with the federal and state governments.

Although on-scene incident management remained under the control of New York City, the federal government was immediately involved in response operations, using the procedures of the FRP. The response was massive. FEMA urban search and rescue teams were requested within fifteen minutes after the first plane struck.[7] Although the Region II office was disabled by the communications outage, FEMA Region II maintained communications and control of the federal response by using the capabilities of the Region I operations center. However, federal, state, and local coordination was impeded by the inability of different agencies to communicate with one another during the immediate response—a result of the loss of high-level antennas and of incompatible radio equipment and frequencies.[8] The improvisation and creativity required to restore intergovernmental coordination during the relocation of the EOC, first to the New York City Police Academy and then to Pier 92, is described in detail in Tricia Wachtendorf's doctoral dissertation, *Improvising 9/11,* and in a 2002 working paper by Wachtendorf and James Kendra.[9]

Faced with the most devastating attacks on U.S. soil in modern history, the existing federal emergency management structure performed adequately at the World Trade Center. The FRP's problematic differentiation of responsibilities for crisis management (FBI law enforcement) and consequence management (FEMA disaster response) was not a major issue. The attacks occurred without warning, the perpetrators died in the attack, and rescue and recovery operations took precedence over preservation of the crime scene.

The federal emergency management structure performed well at the Pentagon. The ACFD proved exceedingly capable in coordinating a highly complex, interorganizational response using an ICS structure and the principles of unified command. The state and local governments were not overwhelmed; their preparation, professionalism, and competence were exceptional. New York City was also able to quickly reestablish its EOC, establish a unique on-scene co-incident command coordinated by the fire department and the Department of Design and

The debris from the collapsed World Trade Center dwarfs rescue workers. Photo courtesy of the Federal Emergency Management Agency.

Construction, and fully participate in a unified command with the federal and state governments.

Overall, local infrastructure did not fail. Communication, transportation, power, and water systems, located just a few blocks away from ground zero in New York and from the Pentagon, remained intact. In addition, the high fatality rate among those who were unable to evacuate resulted in relatively few survivable injuries at both locations, and the immediate needs of survivors were relatively minimal; as a result, the medical systems in both New York City and Northern Virginia had the capacity to manage the injuries. It was primarily the response and recovery workers, not disaster victims, who needed water, food, and shelter.

The Federal Government Reaction to 9/11

As part of its reaction to the 9/11 attacks, the U.S. government reexamined its structure for preparing for and responding to extreme events. The examination identified a need for a fuller integration of law enforcement and emergency management during the response to a terrorist attack, and for the creation of a true national response system that can integrate the efforts of local, state, and federal civilian and military response forces.

As shown in Table 6–2, which lists key milestones in the development of the National Response System following 9/11, President George W. Bush established the White House Office of Homeland Security and the Homeland Security Council in October 2001. The national strategy for homeland security, issued by the Office of Homeland Security in July 2002, identified the following vision for a national response system:

> We will strive to create a fully integrated national emergency response system that is adaptable enough to deal with any terrorist attack, no matter how unlikely or catastrophic, as well as all manner of natural disasters.[10]

The national strategy called for the government to

- Integrate separate federal response plans into a single all-discipline incident management plan

- Create a national incident management system

- Improve tactical counterterrorist capabilities

- Enable seamless communication among all responders

- Prepare health care providers for catastrophic terrorism

- Augment America's pharmaceutical and vaccine stockpiles

- Prepare for chemical, biological, radiological, and nuclear contamination

- Plan for military support to civil authorities

- Build the Citizen Corps

- Implement the First Responder Initiative of the FY 2003 budget

- Build a national training and evaluation system.[11]

These were the first steps in a series of actions that produced the National Response System first tested during the late summer of 2005 by Hurricane Katrina. The remainder of this chapter describes how these actions produced the system, discusses the system's strengths and weaknesses, and identifies some of the major policy choices that were made.

July 2002	National Strategy for Homeland Security
October 2002	Department of Defense Northern Command (NORTHCOM) operational
November 2002	Homeland Security Act of 2002
March 2003	Department of Homeland Security operational
February 2003	Homeland Security Presidential Directive 5 (HSPD-5), "Management of Domestic Incidents"
May 2003	Initial National Response Plan (NRP)
July 2003	National Incident Management System (NIMS) initial system
December 2003	HSPD-7, "Critical Infrastructure Identification, Prioritization, and Protection" HSPD-8, "National Preparedness"
February 2004	Final draft of NIMS Draft of NRP
March 2004	Final NIMS
January 2005	Final NRP
January 2005	Final Draft: Catastrophic Incident Supplement to the NRP
March 2005	Interim National Preparedness Goal
November 2005	Draft National Infrastructure Protection Plan (NIPP)

Table 6–2. Post-9/11 National Response System Critical Dates.

The formation of the U.S. Department of Homeland Security (DHS) occurred concurrently with the development of the integrated National Response System that replaced the fragmented responsibilities of the plans described in Table 6–1. The new department incorporated many existing agencies and agency functions. For some agencies, this transition went relatively smoothly. The Secret Service was moved with form and function intact. The Coast Guard moved from the U.S. Department of Transportation to DHS without losing its unique status as an independent entity, and it gained a direct reporting relationship to the secretary of homeland security. With this reorganization, DHS became a cabinet-level agency responsible for reacting to a wide range of disasters.

FEMA, however, lost much of its bureaucratic and operational strength. Although it kept its name, it lost its independent agency status, becoming instead the core agency in DHS's Emergency Preparedness and Response Directorate, where it joined with unfunded elements from the Departments of Justice (National Domestic Preparedness Office), Health and Human Services (Office of Emergency Preparedness and Strategic National Stockpile), and other departments and agencies.[12] The Office of Domestic Preparedness moved from the Department of Justice to DHS as part of the State and Local Government Coordination and Preparedness Office in a different directorate, becoming a competitor with FEMA for mitigation and recovery funding.

Richard Sylves and William Cumming point out that when FEMA had previously occupied the role taken over by DHS, it had become a president-serving and president-dependent agency.[13] However, President Bush's Homeland Security Presidential Directive 5 (HSPD-5) formally transferred this role from FEMA to DHS by designating the secretary of homeland security as the "principal Federal official for domestic incident management...responsible for coordinating Federal operations within the United States to prepare for, respond to, and recover from terrorist attacks, major disasters, and other emergencies."[14] HSPD-5 also directed the secretary to "establish a single, comprehensive approach to domestic incident management...[that] treats crisis management and consequence management as a single, integrated function, rather than as two separate functions."[15] Following on the congressional mandate in the Homeland Security Act of 2002, HSPD-5 specifically directed DHS to develop a national incident management system based on a core set of principles "covering the incident command system; multi-agency coordination systems; [and] unified command" and to develop an "all-discipline, all-hazards" national response plan.[16]

Within this organizational context, DHS created a process that would establish a unified and integrated national response system and embarked on implementation efforts. It convened an interagency working group to create a national incident management system and contracted with the RAND Corporation, a nonprofit think tank, to facilitate the development of a draft national response

The 9/11 terrorist attacks on the World Trade Center changed the focus and conduct of U.S. disaster management more than any other single event in the history of the nation. Photo courtesy of the Federal Emergency Management Agency.

plan. Parallel to these efforts, the interagency national response team conducted a review and reconciliation of existing federal response plans.[17]

Table 6-3 shows the key elements of the HSPD-5 work plan, as well as the target dates for completing the work and the dates when each milestone was actually met. Unfortunately, the unrealistic deadlines set out in the directive resulted in a process that limited state and local participation in policy formulation, limited time for review and comment, and relied on contractors to draft key documents. As a result, the initial draft required significant revisions.

Product Required	HSPD-5 Target Date	Date Achieved
Initial version of NRP	4/1/03	5/14/03
Draft NIMS standards, guidelines, and protocols	6/1/03	7/1/03
Identification of legislative changes necessary to implement draft NRP	9/1/03	2/25/04
Final draft NIMS		2/10/04
Final NIMS		3/04
Final NRP		12/04
All departments to be NIMS compliant	8/1/03	10/1/05
All recipients of federal grants and contracts to be NIMS compliant	10/1/04	10/1/06

Table 6-3. National Response Plan (NRP) and National Incident Management System (NIMS) Implementation Time Line.

The National Incident Management System

NIMS, the national incident management system that emerged from this process, established a national standard for the uniform adoption of the ICS, which had been developed in the 1970s to coordinate the mobilization of resources to fight wildfires. In 1982, the National Wildfire Coordinating Group adopted the ICS as the National Interagency Incident Management System (NIIMS). The National Fire Academy and the National Fire Protection Association both recommended the ICS as a firefighting standard; the ICS was also adopted by the U.S. Coast Guard for oil spill response and by FEMA's national urban search and rescue teams. It became the standard incident management system for local firefighters and other first responders.[18]

Prior to the establishment of NIMS in 1994, the ICS had not been used as an organizing system for natural disasters at the federal level. Many social scientists saw it as a "command-and-control" system that was ill suited to the complex, unexpected issues encountered in large disaster response operations.[19] But the national adoption of NIMS temporarily ended the debate on how to organize for response, and established a standard set of ICS structures and protocols to be followed by all response organizations throughout the country.

NIMS goes beyond ICS, unified command, and the multiagency coordination system (MACS). NIMS specifies principles of preparedness consistent with the National Preparedness Goal. (The Interim National Preparedness Goal was first issued by DHS on April 1, 2005. In 2011, DHS issued a final National Preparedness Goal, which may be found at fema.gov/pdf/prepared/npg.pdf.) Currently, NIMS compliance is required as a prerequisite for federal grant and contract funding. A NIMS implementation center within DHS provides doctrine, guidance, and training to response organizations nationwide.[20]

The creation of the NRP in 2004 proved to be a more difficult task than adopting NIMS and ICS. The initial draft NRP created by the RAND Corporation departed significantly from the philosophy and structure of the FRP. In particular, the plan rejected the all-hazards approach for an agent-specific incident response doctrine. In addition, it did not incorporate the emergency support function (ESF) structure used in the FRP to assign federal responsibilities and identify potential federal resources. Since most states used an all-hazards approach and had spent the prior decade organizing their emergency management systems to reflect the federal ESF structure, the proposed elimination of this structure was met with strenuous opposition from state, local, and tribal authorities. States also questioned the need for a principal federal official (PFO) as an on-scene representative of the president, viewing that role as redundant to that of the federal coordinating officer (FCO, the lead federal official specified by the FRP and continued by the NRP) and the on-scene coordinator (the lead federal official for oil and hazardous spill response specified by the NCP).

Once revised, the NRP retained many of the features of the FRP (including the ESF structure), while also adopting the goals of integrating crisis and consequence management and response to terrorist threats. Additionally, the plan was broadened to include the full incident management spectrum of prevention, protection and mitigation, preparedness, response, and recovery. This was done through fifteen ESF annexes that assign functional and operational responsibilities, nine support annexes that describe general incident management support requirements, and seven incident support annexes that describe issues unique to each incident type (see Table 6–4). Despite opposition from the states, the final plan contained the PFO concept.

In April 2005, the NRP received final approval from twenty-eight federal agencies, the chief executive officer (CEO) of the American Red Cross, the postmaster general, the CEO of the Corporation for National and Community Services, and the president of the National Voluntary Organizations Active in Disaster.

Implementation of the NRP and NIMS provided for the first time both the structure and the doctrine to effectively and consistently apply federal capability and resources to prepare for, respond to, and recover from incidents of national significance (see Figure 6–1). The NRP policy integrated federal resources, knowledge, and ability; NIMS provided the doctrine to enable command and control, align structures, define terminology, and specify operational protocols.

The publication and implementation of the NRP and NIMS were part of a larger DHS strategy for establishing a common approach to national incident management. The national infrastructure protection plan (required by HSPD-7) and the national preparedness goals, planning tools, and guidelines (required by HSPD-8) were other key components of the national strategy (see Figure 6–2).

In concordance with these measures, the federal government began disbursing preparedness funds directly to state and local governments through a variety of grant mechanisms, including State Homeland Security grants, Urban Area Security Initiative grants, Port Security grants, Emergency Management Performance grants, Assistance to Firefighter grants, Metropolitan Medical Response System grants, Law Enforcement grants, and, of course, congressional earmarks. The

Emergency Support Function Annexes	
ESF 1: Transportation	ESF 9: Urban Search and Rescue
ESF 2: Communications	ESF 10: Oil and Hazardous Materials Response
ESF 3: Public Works and Engineering	ESF 11: Agricultural and Natural Resources
ESF 4: Firefighting	ESF 12: Energy
ESF 5: Emergency Management	ESF 13: Public Safety and Security
ESF 6: Mass Care, Housing, and Human Services	ESF 14: Long-term Community Recovery and Mitigation
ESF 7: Resource Support	ESF 15: External Affairs
ESF 8: Public Health and Medical Services	
Support Annexes	
Financial Management	Science and Technology
International Coordination	Tribal Relations
Logistics Management	Volunteer and Donations Management
Private Sector Coordination	Worker Safety and Health
Public Affairs	
Incident Annexes	
Biological Incident	Nuclear/Radiological Incident
Catastrophic Incident	Oil and Hazardous Materials Incident
Cyber Incident	Terrorism Incident Law Enforcement and Investigation
Food and Agriculture Incident	

Table 6–4. Functional, Support, and Incident Annexes of the National Response Plan.

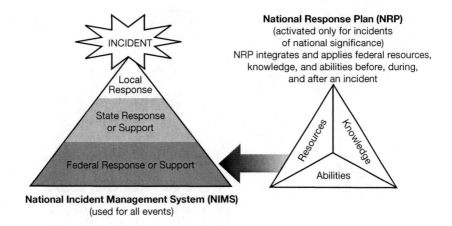

Figure 6–1. Relationship between NIMS and NRP.

Note: NIMS aligns command, control, organizational structure, terminology, communication protocols, resources, and resource–typing to synchronize all levels of response.

Source: DHS.

federal government also funded ICS, weapons of mass destruction (WMD) training, and other training for police, fire, emergency medical services, and other first responders. The implicit assumption was that development of strategy and doctrine at the higher levels of government in Washington, combined with local funding and training, would result in improved preparedness and response capability.

The Stafford Act Amendments

Although approved by Congress on October 10, 2000, essential provisions of the Disaster Mitigation Act of 2000 (P.L. 106-390) did not become fully effective until 2002 and were therefore part of the post-9/11 evolution of emergency management. The legislation amended the Stafford Act and promoted pre-disaster planning and mitigation and required state and tribal governments to have FEMA-approved mitigation plans in place by 2004 to receive federal disaster assistance. Other provisions of the Stafford Act were meant to control federal costs for response and recovery operations and enhance the role of voluntary agencies. However, the act had significant impacts on the federal government's ability to provide individual assistance to disaster victims as it restricted the types of assistance provided, capped housing assistance, and restricted eligibility for assistance.[21] These concerns were addressed in the Post-Katrina Emergency Management Reform Act of 2006, which became fully effective March 31, 2007. This later act and other initiatives substantially recombined preparedness planning and grants and response under an independent and strengthened FEMA within DHS.

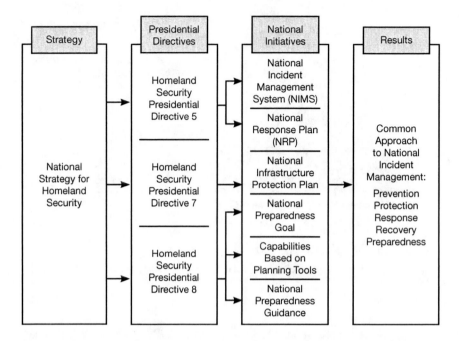

Figure 6–2. National Strategy for Homeland Security: Directives, Initiatives, and Results.

Source: *Interim National Preparedness Goal: Homeland Security Presidential Directive 8; National Preparedness* (Washington, D.C.: DHS, March 31, 2005), 2, ojp.usdoj.gov/odp/docs/InterimNationalPreparednessGoal_03-31-05_1.pdf.

The System in Transition: The Hurricanes of 2004

As the nation entered the 2004 hurricane season, its response system was in transition. Housed within DHS, FEMA maintained its Stafford Act responsibilities, including the obligation to appoint an FCO for each state included in a presidential disaster declaration. NIMS had become a national standard in 2004, but its implementation throughout the federal government was not yet complete (see Table 6–3). The final NRP was in draft form; the governing policy document essentially continued the policies and practices of the FRP with changes made to acknowledge the location of FEMA within DHS. The secretary of DHS was designated as the PFO for all incidents of national significance, but no changes were made to FEMA's leadership role or to the functional structure of the FRP.

The 2004 hurricane season was among the most devastating in the history of Florida (see Figure 6–3). In August and September, five major storms struck the coast of Florida in just forty-eight days: Tropical Storm Bonnie (August 12), Category 4 Hurricane Charley (August 13), Category 2 Hurricane Frances (September 5), Category 3 Hurricane Ivan (September 16), and Category 3 Hurricane Jeanne (September 26).[22] These storms cumulatively caused more dam-

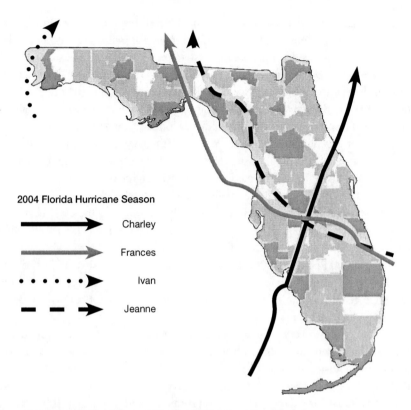

2004 Florida Hurricane Season

➡ Charley

➡ Frances

• • • • • ► Ivan

– – – ➡ Jeanne

Figure 6–3. Graphic Depiction of Florida's 2004 Hurricane Season.

age than Hurricane Andrew, resulting in 117 fatalities and $23 million in insurance claims in Florida alone.[23]

Since the hurricanes were declared presidential disasters, the federal response was coordinated completely within FEMA. The agency's organizational location within DHS helped it to obtain and coordinate other DHS resources, such as the U.S. Coast Guard, but in general, the disaster response was managed using pre-DHS procedures and protocols. The scale of the response was immense. FEMA established a disaster field office and assigned an FCO for each affected state (Florida sustained the greatest impact, but Alabama and Georgia were also affected). FEMA successfully established a unified command with the state coordinating officer in each state and established twenty-three logistics staging areas.[24]

The state of Florida had an experienced and capable emergency management system and was able to coordinate closely with FEMA. The 2004 hurricanes also became the first major test of the interstate Emergency Management Assistance Compact (EMAC), which had been established by 1996 federal legislation (P.L. 104-321).[25] During the response to the Florida hurricanes, assistance through

EMAC was closely coordinated with the federal response effort through the Florida director of field operations; reimbursement for mutual aid through EMAC was coordinated outside of the federal system on a state-to-state basis.

In general, government agencies, operating under the transitional FRP, responded reasonably well to the 2004 hurricane onslaught. There was relatively little political or personal conflict between the national and state political leaders, which facilitated coordinated response operations. In addition, Florida's emergency management system had been much improved and tested since Hurricane Andrew in 1992. Sufficient infrastructure existed within the state to support the FCO's actions and disaster field office operations within the affected area. Because neighboring states did not sustain heavy damages, they were able to provide assistance through EMAC.

As with almost any response operation, the response to the 2004 hurricanes had to overcome unanticipated obstacles. Almost 10 million people were evacuated, and at times, the scale of the disaster exceeded the Red Cross's ability to provide shelter and FEMA's ability to distribute water and food. Most of the problems resulted from strained capacity and capability and, to some degree, a bureaucratic federal decision-making structure. But these problems did not overwhelm or disable response operations.

Long-term recovery was less successful, however. The system for funding the transition from immediate response to long-term recovery was inadequate, despite its inclusion in the FRP as an emergency support function. At the start of the 2005 hurricane season, thousands of Floridians displaced by the 2004 hurricanes were still in "temporary" housing trailers, and thousands of homes still had temporary roofs (commonly referred to as FEMA blue tarps). The failure to coordinate permanent housing and repair programs indicated that the nation was still inadequately prepared to meet long-term recovery needs.[26]

The Revised National Response System

The response to the hurricanes of 2004 was the last major effort conducted under the framework of the FRP (as institutionalized by the interim plan). On April 11, 2005, the final NRP was given final signoff, directing federal agencies to become NIMS compliant. This represented a significant change in the way the nation prepared for and responded to extreme events. The new system would be severely tested in 2005.

In 2004, in an "invited comment" in the *Natural Hazards Observer,* Charles Hess and John Harrald raised several questions about both the need for and the future effectiveness of the new National Response System:

- Will a centralized, highly structured, closed system entrusted solely to trained professionals work effectively for managing complex events?

- Was such a sweeping change necessary to achieve immediate policy goals?

- What will be the unintended consequences of this policy initiative?[27]

According to Harrald, the system defined by the NRP and NIMS was potentially much more of a closed system than the system it replaced. NIMS has important features that enhance its ability to be scaled to hazard- and response-driven requirements. As shown in Figure 6–4, however, the NRP creates an artificial barrier between formal and informal response systems, potentially excluding critical groups. Specifically, it restricts formal access to those trained and certified in NIMS, potentially excluding local volunteers and emergent groups that have historically played an important role in disaster response.[28]

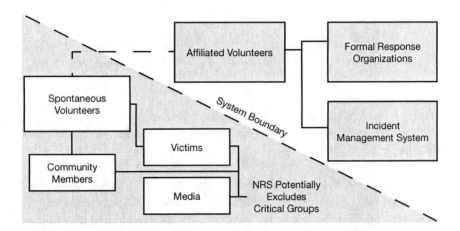

Figure 6–4. The National Response System.

Source: Lauren Fernandez, "Volunteer Management System Design and Analysis for Disaster Response and Recovery" (PhD diss., The George Washington University, 2007), 58.

Factors in the Development of the National Response System

The development of emergency management policy and structure following 9/11 was the extension of a thirty-year trend. Since the 1970s, the U.S. emergency management community—consisting of federal signatories to the FRP, state emergency management offices, and Voluntary Organizations Active in Disaster—had increased its ability to structure and manage a large response through improved plans and adoption of the ICS. The result of this evolution is the National Response System.

Over the past several decades, social scientists and other disaster researchers have documented and described the nonstructural factors, such as improvisation, adaptability, and creativity, that are critical to successful coordination, collaboration, communication, and problem solving in response operations. These two streams of thought represent two dimensions—discipline and agility—that are necessary in effective emergency response. Nevertheless, the post-9/11 evolution of the U.S. National Response System has focused almost exclusively on building discipline in a closed organizational system. This more structured and less creative process tends to produce a bureaucratic and procedural response (Figure 6–5).

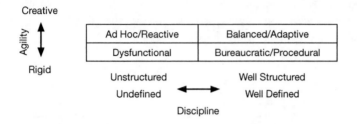

Figure 6–5. Agility and Discipline as Dimensions of Effective Organizational Response.
Source: John Harrald, "Agility and Discipline: Critical Success Factors for Disaster Response," *Annals of the American Academy of Political and Social Sciences* (Spring 2006): 268.

The ability of the national system to scale to a truly catastrophic incident was also questioned. Actions taken following 9/11 had significantly strengthened the capabilities of police, fire, and other first responders and had provided funding to state homeland security and emergency management agencies, but they had not added significant capacity or capability to FEMA. The nature and challenge of a potential catastrophic incident was captured by DHS in the draft of the Catastrophic Incident Supplement to the NRP (see accompanying sidebar).

Prior to the publication of this annex, E. L. Quarantelli identified the political and social implications of a catastrophic disaster:

- Most or all of the built environment is heavily affected.

- Local officials are unable to undertake their usual roles and responsibilities (this often extends into the recovery period); outsiders to the community might have to assume leadership roles as a result.

- Help from nearby communities cannot be provided.

- Most, if not all, of the everyday community functions are sharply and concurrently interrupted.

- The mass media system constructs catastrophes even more than it does disasters; the public perception of a catastrophic event is determined by what and how the media reports an event.

- The political arena becomes even more important. National government and top officials become involved.[29]

National Response Plan, Catastrophic Incident Supplement

The following excerpt from the NRP's Catastrophic Incident Supplement gives insight into the complexity of planning for a catastrophic event.

- The response capabilities and resources of the local jurisdiction (to include mutual aid from surrounding jurisdictions and response support from the state) may be insufficient and quickly overwhelmed. Local emergency personnel who normally respond to incidents may be among those affected and unable to perform their duties.

- A catastrophic incident may cause significant disruption of the area's critical infrastructure, such as energy, transportation, telecommunications, and public health and medical systems.

- A detailed and credible common operating picture may not be achievable for 24 to 48 hours (or longer). As a result, response activities must begin without the benefit of a detailed or complete situation and critical needs assessment.

- Federal support must be provided in a timely manner to save lives, prevent human suffering, and mitigate severe damage. This may require mobilizing and deploying assets before they are requested via normal NRP protocols.

- Large numbers of people may be left temporarily or permanently homeless and may require prolonged temporary housing.

- A catastrophic incident may produce environmental impacts...that severely challenge the ability and capacity of governments and communities to achieve a timely recovery.

- A catastrophic incident has unique dimensions/characteristics requiring that response plans/strategies be flexible enough to effectively address emerging needs and requirements.

- A catastrophic incident results in a large number of casualties and/or displaced persons, possibly in the tens of thousands.

- A catastrophic incident may occur with little or no warning. Some incidents, such as rapid disease outbreaks, may be well under way before detection.

- Large-scale evacuations, organized or self-directed, may occur. The health-related implications of an incident aggravate attempts to implement a coordinated evacuation management strategy.

Source: Catastrophic Incident Supplement to the National Response Plan, Appendix I, "Basic Planning Assumptions" (Washington, D.C.: DHS, April 2005), A1-A3, cees.tamiv.edu/covertheborder/tools/NRP_CIS.pdf.

Challenges to the System: 2005

By the end of 2004, the federal government had identified the challenges posed by potential catastrophic terrorist attacks as well as by natural and technological disasters. It had gone through a major reorganization and developed extensive policies and guidelines designed to improve the country's ability to prevent, mitigate, prepare for, respond to, and recover from such events. The nation had invested billions to improve first-responder capacity and capability. However, most of this funding and doctrine development focused on preventing and preparing for another terrorist attack, while earlier planning efforts for catastrophic natural and technological disasters were put aside. Minimal efforts were made to ensure that the nation had the capacity and capability to respond to a catastrophic natural disaster.

The restructuring of the National Response System had produced both intended and unintended outcomes, all of which would become apparent during the response to Hurricane Katrina in 2005. One structure and doctrine was provided for all organizations, but some federal agencies and key state and local organizations had not yet implemented the structure when Katrina struck. The federal government had created new positions of authority and coordination mechanisms: the DHS secretary became responsible for all incident management, the PFO became the lead presence on the ground, and the Homeland Security Operations Center became the primary information coordination center for the federal government. However, the authority of the PFO was not clearly specified by the NRP and was not understood by state officials. The process of obtaining Department of Defense resources was modified, and Northern Command (NORTHCOM) became the key coordinating command for military assistance. System discipline had been increased through training and credentialing, but the insistence upon NIMS compliance and proper credentials created problems for volunteer organizations. In addition, while some states had progressed in developing their response capabilities, capacity, and competencies, others had not.

The restructuring of the National Response System also had unintended consequences that would prove to be critical during the response to Hurricane Katrina. First, the specification of detailed doctrine, structure, and process reduced system agility, creativity, and flexibility and increased the tendency toward bureaucratic solutions. The scalability and expandability attributes of NIMS would have to be used to counter this tendency. In addition, the NIMS structure implied, but did not define, an information flow that would ensure a common situational awareness at all levels of the distributed decision network (including the Joint Field Office, National Response Coordination Center, Homeland Security Operations Center, and the White House).

The new structure caused by the creation of DHS and defined in the NRP inadvertently increased the layers between operational and political leaders. Whereas FEMA was once a cabinet-level organization with direct access to the president, the FEMA director was now three levels down in a very complex departmental structure. The FCO in the Joint Field Office had to communicate through the PFO, the National Response Coordination Center, the Homeland Security Operations Center, and the DHS secretary to pass time-sensitive information to the White House.

The intent of the NRP was that the PFO would be a coordinating official while decision making continued to reside with the FCO. As the president's representative, however, the PFO is perceived as the leader of operations, not a coordinator, and would thus be seen by state and local officials as the key on-scene decision maker. This diminished the role of the state FCOs, created yet another bureaucratic layer in the response system, and added to the confusion about who is authorized to make decisions.

DHS and the Defense Department had created parallel planning and preparedness efforts, but the boundary between homeland security and domestic defense was not clearly drawn. The procedures for engaging NORTHCOM and using Defense Department assets under DHS control also were not clearly defined.

The nation entered the hurricane season of 2005 with a revised and expanded, but basically untested, national response system that made emergency management an integral part of homeland security. The system was to be the responsibility of DHS and directed by it, but there had been little effort to identify the skills, knowledge, responsibilities, and experience that, by implication, would be required of senior DHS managers. By focusing on doctrine and process, DHS left unresolved major policy questions that would become crucial political issues before the close of 2005. These questions include the following:

- What actions should the federal government be prepared to take and what services should it provide following a catastrophic incident?

- How are federal responsibilities best coordinated with states?

- Does comprehensive emergency management and the all-hazards approach make sense when terrorism is included?

- Should we separate organizational responsibilities for mitigation, preparedness, response, and recovery?

- Can a response and recovery directorate within DHS operate as effectively as an independent FEMA with direct access to the president?

- What is the appropriate role for the Department of Defense, particularly NORTHCOM, during response to an extreme event?

- What level of preparedness should we expect from state and local governments, and how do we achieve it?

The National Response System was severely tested when Hurricane Katrina struck Alabama, Mississippi, and Louisiana on August 29, 2005. The organizational confusion created by the overlapping roles of the PFO and FCOs became painfully obvious when President Bush assigned FEMA director Michael Brown as the PFO for Katrina, and Brown became the de facto coordinator of the federal response. Other ad hoc organizational steps occurred when then Vice Admiral Thad Allen was assigned in rapid succession as PFO for New Orleans (September 5), as PFO for Louisiana (September 9, replacing Michael Brown who then resigned), and as PFO and FCO for Louisiana, Mississippi, and Alabama (September 21).

The inability of the federal, state, and local governments to relieve the immediate suffering of Hurricane Katrina victims, to effectively coordinate humanitarian assistance, and to initiate effective recovery actions became the source of media criticism, congressional hearings, and internal reviews. In response, DHS initiated a complete review of the NRP in 2007, which resulted in the issuance of a revised National Response Framework in January 2008. The change in the title from *Plan* to *Framework* was a tacit admission that the federal government had created a coordinating structure but did not yet have viable incident response and recovery plans. The NRF provides some substantive changes from the NRP, notably in the creation of partner annexes that further define the roles of state, local, private sector, and nongovernment partners. DHS and FEMA also initiated a comprehensive catastrophic disaster preparedness project, using catastrophic event scenarios as the basis for planning and exercising.

As shown by the initial response to the *Deepwater Horizon* blowout and oil spill in 2010 (see Chapter 8), however, the goal of creating a national response system capable of dealing with a catastrophic natural disaster, technological event, or terrorist attack remains elusive.

Endnotes

1   See, for example, Richard T. Sylves, *Disaster Policy and Politics: Emergency Management and Homeland Security* (Washington, D.C.: CQ Press, 2008); William W. Waugh Jr., *Living with Hazards, Dealing with Disasters: An Introduction to Emergency Management* (Armonk, N.Y.: M.E. Sharpe, 2000); and George Haddow and Jane Bullock, *Introduction to Emergency Management* (Burlington, Mass.: Elsevier Butterworth-Heinemann, 2003).

2   Claire B. Rubin, Irmak Renda-Tanali, and William Cumming, *Disaster Time Line: Major Focusing Events and U.S. Outcomes (1979–2005),* and *Terrorism Time Line: Major Focusing Events and U.S. Outcomes (2001–2005)* (Arlington, Va.: Claire B. Rubin & Associates, 2006), disaster-timeline.com.

3   John R. Harrald, Henry S. Marcus, and William A. Wallace, "The EXXON Valdez: An Assessment of Crisis Prevention and Management Systems," *Interfaces* 20 (September 1990): 14–20.

4   Arlington County, Virginia, "Arlington County After-Action Report on the Response to the September 11 Terrorist Attack on the Pentagon" (Arlington County, 2002), arlingtonva.us/departments/Fire/Documents/after_report.pdf.

5   John R. Harrald et al., *Observing and Documenting the Inter-Organizational Response to the September 11 Attack on the Pentagon* (Washington, D.C.: Institute for Crisis, Disaster and Risk Management, The George Washington University, July 15, 2002), gwu.edu/~icdrm/publications/PDF/NSF911_finalJuly8-1.pdf.

6   National Commission on Terrorist Attacks upon the United States, *The 9/11 Commission Report* (New York: Norton and Co., 2004), 278–311, 9-11commission.gov/report/911Report.pdf.

7   Ibid., 293.

8   Ibid., 397.

9   Tricia Wachtendorf, *Improvising 9/11: Organizational Improvisation Following the World Trade Center Disaster* (PhD diss., University of Delaware, 2004); James Kendra and Tricia Wachtendorf, *Creativity in Emergency Response after the World Trade Center Attack,* working paper (Newark: Disaster Research Center, University of Delaware, 2002).

10   U.S. Department of Homeland Security (DHS), *National Strategy for Homeland Security* (Washington, D.C.: DHS, 2002), 42, dhs.gov/xlibrary/assets/nat_strat_hls.pdf.

11   Ibid., 42–45.

12   Keith Bea, *Organization and Mission of the Emergency Preparedness and Response Directorate: Issues and Options for the 109th Congress,* CRS Report RL 33064 (Washington, D.C.: Congressional Research Service, Library of Congress, 2005), digital.library.unt.edu/ark:/67531/metacrs7803/m1/1/high_res_d/RL33064_2005Sep07.pdf; Richard Sylves and William R. Cumming, "FEMA's Path to Homeland Security: 1979–2003," *Journal of Homeland Security and Emergency Management* 1 (January 2004).

13   Sylves and Cumming, "FEMA's Path to Homeland Security."

14   "Homeland Security Presidential Directive/HSPD-5," whitehouse.gov/news/releases/2003/02/20030228-9.html.

15   Ibid.

16   Ibid.

17   U.S. National Response Team, "Reconciling Federal Emergency Response Plans–NRT Homeland Security Recommendations: A Reconciliation Analysis of the Federal Response Plan, National Oil and Hazardous Substances Pollution Contingency Plan, U.S. Government Interagency Domestic Terrorism Concept of Operations Plan, and the Federal Radiological Emergency Response Plan" (Washington, D.C.: U.S. National Response Team, July 31, 2003).

18   For details of the system, see nimsonline.com.

19   Russell R. Dynes, "Community Emergency Planning: False Assumptions and Inappropriate Analogies," *International Journal of Mass Emergencies and Disasters* 12 (August 1994): 141–158.

20   *National Incident Management System* (Washington, D.C.: DHS, March 2004), 59, fema.gov/pdf/emergency/nims/NIMS_core.pdf.

21   New York City Voluntary Organizations Active in Disaster (VOAD), "Amendments to the Stafford Act, The Disaster Mitigation Act of 2000: What the Changes Mean for Families and Their Homes."

22   National Weather Service, National Hurricane Center, "2004 Atlantic Hurricane Season," nhc.noaa.gov/2004atlan.shtml.

23   Emergency Management Assistance Compact (EMAC), *2004 Hurricanes After-Action Report*, 2.

24   Ibid., C-3.

25   As discussed in the previous chapter, EMAC, coordinated by the National Emergency Management Association (NEMA), is a mechanism for states to request assistance directly from other states without the intervention of the federal government.

26   Bea, *Organization and Mission,* 16.

27   Charles Hess and John Harrald, "The National Response Plan: Process, Prospects, and Participants," *Natural Hazards Observer* 28 (July 2004): 1–2.

28   John Harrald, "Agility and Discipline: Critical Success Factors for Disaster Response," *Annals of the American Academy of Political and Social Sciences* (Spring 2006): 256–272.

29   E. L. Quarantelli, "Emergencies, Disaster and Catastrophes Are Different Phenomena," Preliminary Paper 304 (Newark: Disaster Research Center, University of Delaware, 2000) 2–3, dspace.udel.edu:8080/dspace/bitstream/handle/19716/674/PP304.pdf?sequence=1.

Chapter 7

2005 Events and Outcomes: Hurricane Katrina and Beyond

Melanie Gall and Susan L. Cutter

The year 2005 was a record year for hazards and disasters in the United States. Most of the losses were associated with Hurricane Katrina, which caused damage in excess of $100 billion[1] and cost more than 1,800 lives. The drought that plagued the Midwest from early to mid-2005 caused crop damages of at least $1 billion[2]—a figure that in any other year would have been staggering but was dwarfed by the devastation of that summer's hurricanes.

The year's stunning losses were a spike in a gradual upward trend of total losses due to hazards over the past half-century (see Figure 7–1). Why have these losses continued to increase? Putting aside theories about global warming and a rise in extreme climate events, losses have escalated because there is simply more at stake than ever before, particularly along U.S. coastlines. A wealth of economic activity, such as tourism, energy exploration, and mineral production, encourages migration into hazardous locations. From an emergency management perspective, vulnerability is exacerbated not only by the sheer influx of new residents—in 2009, almost 160 million people, or roughly 52 percent of the U.S. population, lived in 675 coastal counties[3]—but also by increased urbanization along the coast.

The movement of people into high-risk areas—along the coast, into floodplains, and in the midst of seismically active areas—poses major challenges for emergency management at all levels. Efforts to reduce vulnerability compete with the desire of people to live where they choose, which is often in scenic, high-risk areas. Those who call for mitigation are often in opposition to housing and commercial developers as well as to residents who have not experienced local hazards. With potentially more severe weather in the near future and continued population growth, these challenges could become even more profound. What steps can emergency managers take to reduce the vulnerability of communities in these hazard-prone areas?

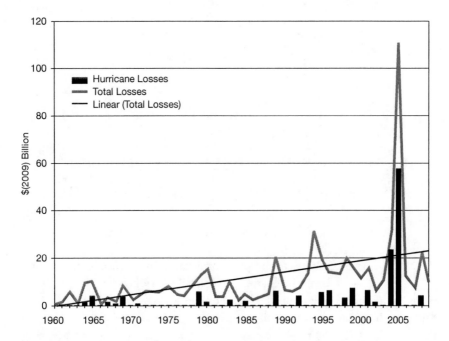

Figure 7-1. Hazard Losses in the United States, 1960–2009.

Source: Based on the Spatial Hazard Events and Losses Database for the United States (SHELDUS™ 8.0).

Note: The figures have been adjusted for inflation; the base year for inflation adjustments was 2009.

To address these questions, this chapter examines 2005's major disaster events and reviews some of the lessons that have been learned since then regarding effective mitigation, sustainable recovery, and vulnerability awareness. It also highlights some of the weaknesses of the existing mitigation and recovery strategies, including the diminished local preparedness, response, and recovery capacities in a post-9/11 environment.

Billion-Dollar Events in 2005

As shown in Figure 7–2, weather-related events account for almost three-quarters of the total hazard losses—in excess of $570 billion—between 1960 and 2009, with hurricanes, tropical storms, and floods as the leading causes. Hurricane Katrina alone cost more than $125 billion in both direct and indirect losses.

The 2005 hurricane season was the most active period of hurricanes in the Atlantic since systematic records began in 1851. It produced twenty-seven named storms, topping the all-time record of twenty-one storms in 1933. Of these twenty-seven storms, fifteen hurricanes developed, and an unprecedented number of Category 5 hurricanes—Katrina, Rita, and Wilma—destroyed lives, property, and

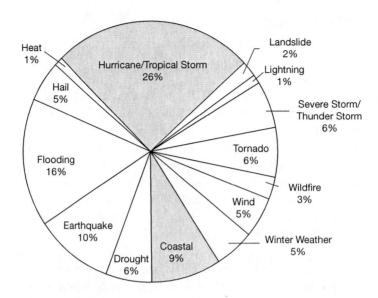

Figure 7-2. Causes of Hazard Losses, 1960–2009.

Source: Spatial Hazard Events and Losses Database for the United States (SHELDUS™ 8.0).

Notes: Hurricane-related events are highlighted in gray. The category of coastal hazards includes storm surge and rip currents, as well as event descriptions with an explicit "coastal" designation, such as coastal flooding, coastal erosion, and so forth.

trust in the national emergency response system.[4] Hurricane Dennis was "only" a Category 3 storm, but it ushered in the hurricane season with a vengeance, wreaking more than $2 billion in destruction. The paths of the 2005 hurricanes are shown in Figure 7–3.

Hurricane Dennis

On July 10, 2005, Hurricane Dennis made landfall as a Category 3 storm near Pensacola, in the western Florida panhandle. Before reaching the U.S. mainland, Dennis ravaged Cuba and Haiti; it killed sixteen people in Cuba, making it that island nation's deadliest hurricane since Hurricane Flora in 1963.[5] In the United States, losses topped $2.23 billion in insured and uninsured damages, with three direct and twelve indirect deaths attributed to the storm.[6]

Because the hurricane affected the area that Hurricane Ivan had hit just ten months earlier, many residents were in the midst of reconstruction, and about fifty thousand homes still had FEMA blue tarps. Some residents who had registered with FEMA for disaster assistance after Ivan reregistered after Dennis. The hurricane had delivered an emotional and psychological blow to a region that was trying to recover from the previous assault.

Hurricane Katrina

If Hurricane Dennis profoundly affected the psychology of the residents of the Florida panhandle, Hurricane Katrina had a profound effect on the nation. Katrina developed as a tropical depression on August 23, 2005, in the southeastern Bahamas. It first made landfall as a Category 1 storm near Hollywood in South Florida and continued westward across the state into the Gulf of Mexico; there, conducive weather conditions, warm sea-surface temperatures, and an upper-level anticyclone allowed it to develop into a major Category 5 hurricane. By the time it made landfall at the Mississippi-Louisiana border on August 29, the huge storm system had a 25- to 30-nautical-mile radius. Although it had diminished to a strong Category 3 storm, it crashed into the shore with sustained winds of about 125 miles per hour.[7] Just six hours later, Hurricane Katrina weakened to a tropical storm northwest of Meridian, Mississippi.[8]

By the time it died out, Katrina had set damage records. With direct losses estimated at more than $81 billion, it became the costliest hurricane in U.S. history. Although there is no comprehensive inventory of the rebuilding costs, it is probably fair to assume that Hurricane Katrina also ranks as the costliest event in terms of reconstruction costs, which have been tallied up to $157 billion as of August 2010.[9] Roughly ninety thousand square miles in parts of Alabama, Louisiana, and Mississippi—an area slightly larger than that of Great Britain—were devastated. The storm also became the third deadliest hurricane since the Galveston Hurricane in 1900 and the Lake Okeechobee Hurricane in 1928, with a final death toll standing at 1,867 deaths (1,464 deceased and 135 missing—and presumed dead—in Louisiana, 230 in Mississippi, 14 in Florida, and 24 in Alabama).[10] More than 1.7 million homes in the Gulf Coast and more than 1.3 million homes in southeastern Florida lost electricity, and more than a million people were displaced.[11]

Hurricane Katrina was a strong system, with a catastrophic combination of high winds, extreme storm surge, and flooding from floodwall collapses and levee breaches. In terms of storm surge, the areas hardest hit were Hancock and Harrison Counties in Mississippi, which experienced surge heights of 24–28 feet; the surge flattened block after block in the cities of Waveland, Bay St. Louis, Pass Christian, and Long Beach. The rest of Mississippi's coast saw surge heights of 17–22 feet. Extending six miles inland and up to twelve miles along bays and rivers, the surge left behind nothing but a few concrete slabs and pilings.[12]

The disaster in New Orleans was initiated by a different series of events from those in Mississippi. There, a combination of strong Category 1 winds, a storm surge that funneled up the Mississippi River Gulf Outlet (which the U.S. Army Corps of Engineers [USACE] finally closed in 2009), heavy rainfall, and human error caused the floodwalls to fail on August 29—one day after the storm had

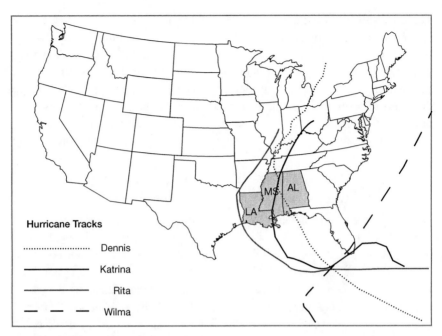

Figure 7–3. The Paths of the Four Major Hurricanes of 2005.
Source: NOAA Coastal Services Center.

passed east of the city. Water from the lakes and canals surrounding New Orleans poured in, flooding at least 80 percent of the city at depths of up to twenty feet. Efforts to drain New Orleans were then stymied by Hurricane Rita, which hit the Gulf Coast on September 23 and reflooded the city. Given the cascading nature of events, it took USACE forty-three days to drain New Orleans of its floodwaters.[13] A year after Katrina, USACE repaired and restored 220 miles of floodwalls and levees,[14] but a review panel has questioned whether the level of protection now is what it had been before Katrina hit.[15]

The overwhelming extent of disruption and destruction at all levels of emergency management, and particularly during the preparedness and response phases, made Hurricane Katrina a human catastrophe as well as a natural disaster. Almost instantly, informal, prosocial behavior emerged among the storm's survivors to organize rescue operations, retrieve survivors, and provide relief. Likewise, first responders improvised to find and evacuate as many people as possible, as well as to provide emergency health care to those in need.[16] But in communities all along the Gulf Coast, and particularly in New Orleans, organizational breakdowns added to the desperate plight of residents. Roads leading out of the area were clogged with traffic and later made impassable by rising floodwaters. Search-and-rescue operations were understaffed and ill prepared. Elderly and sick residents were stranded in hospitals and nursing homes, and living conditions in the Superdome and in shelters of last resort were deplorable. For days, the entire disaster area was without food, potable water, power, medication, sanitation, adequate sheltering, and any form of organizational help. By documenting these problems in detail (while also misrepresenting occurrences of looting), the media not only touched the hearts of people throughout the United States and beyond but also raised the public's concerns about both the political will of local, state, and federal leaders and the capability of the emergency management system to prepare for and respond to disasters.

Hurricane Rita

Following on the heels of Katrina, Hurricane Rita dealt another devastating blow to the state of Louisiana. Three days after drenching the Keys and the southern tip of Florida, the Category 3 storm made landfall near the Texas-Louisiana border on September 23, 2005, causing $16 billion in damage and seven direct fatalities.[17] Rita's storm surge of up to fifteen feet devastated communities along the southwestern Louisiana coast and spawned rain and tornadoes as far east as Alabama. The hurricane leveled Cameron Parish, Louisiana's largest parish; almost no structure was left standing. Rita also sent an eight-foot storm surge to New Orleans, which passed over the provisionally repaired levees in the city and prolonged the drainage of the floodwaters in the area.[18]

In anticipation of Rita, officials in Texas and Louisiana called for the voluntary evacuation of more than three million people—the largest evacuation in U.S. history—including many residents who had fled Katrina. The highways leading away from the coast became bottlenecks. The evacuation caused at least fifty-five fatalities from carbon monoxide poisoning, accidents, and heat exhaustion.[19]

Hurricane Rita aggravated and prolonged the recovery from Hurricane Katrina, a situation that was then exacerbated five years later when the BP *Deepwater Horizon* rig exploded and sank, precipitating the largest oil spill in U.S. history. Although this triple strike left Louisiana eligible for disaster assistance, organizing a coherent recovery process overwhelmed the administrative structures at the local, state, and federal levels, slowing ongoing post-disaster recovery.

Hurricane Wilma

Until Hurricane Wilma struck on October 24, the state of Florida had been spared most of the 2005 hurricane season. As it moved slowly toward the coast, Wilma was a Category 5 storm with sustained winds of more than 170 miles per hour—one of the strongest storms ever recorded. After battering the Yucatan Peninsula and Cuba, Wilma made landfall near Everglades City, Florida, where it caused five deaths and $12 billion in losses. About six million Florida residents lost power, including the entire stretch of the Florida Keys, marking the most widespread power outage in Florida's history.[20]

Wilma was a relatively quick-moving storm, and Florida was spared the torrential rainfall that Cuba and Mexico had withstood. Storm surges accounted for most of the damages; Collier County recorded surges of up to eight feet—a number that some experts say is too low.[21]

Reinventing U.S. Emergency Management

Despite extensive training and funding for terrorism preparedness since 2001, the U.S. Department of Homeland Security (DHS) and FEMA were ill prepared to respond to an event of the magnitude of Hurricane Katrina. As discussed in the previous chapter, procedural and organizational changes within DHS had compromised FEMA's response capabilities, contributing to a cascade of failures. FEMA was unfamiliar with the roles and responsibilities detailed in the new National Response Plan (NRP)[22] and the National Incident Management System (NIMS).[23] The emergency support functions found in the outdated federal response plan[24] had not been realigned to fit the new NIMS management structure.[25] Discrepancies in awareness and knowledge of the incident command system (ICS), a key component of NIMS, adversely affected the response. While firefighters generally had knowledge of and experience with the ICS, local law enforcement, health care providers, and rural emergency management officials had not yet received adequate training.[26] Breakdowns in communication, problems with interoperability, and ineffective execution of command and control further hampered response operations.

Overall, FEMA failed to fulfill its responsibilities as the lead coordinating emergency management institution. It failed to coordinate military and international assistance, compounding the grossly inadequate and chaotic provision of commodities, emergency sheltering, and temporary housing.[27] Many people in the disaster community saw a recurring pattern and were reminded of FEMA's poor responses to Hurricanes Hugo (1989) and Andrew (1992).[28]

Assessing Existing Shortcomings

In the aftermath of Hurricane Katrina, a vigorous debate arose regarding how to improve FEMA's response capability. Numerous personnel and procedural adjustments were made at the lower and intermediate managerial levels. FEMA director Michael Brown became a political casualty: on September 9, 2005, the embattled official was stripped of his duties overseeing the relief efforts. Brown resigned amid growing criticism and was replaced by R. David Paulison, a federal official with three decades of firefighting experience and a background in emergency management; Paulison had led the U.S. Fire Administration since 2001.

In February 2006, DHS secretary Michael Chertoff announced several measures to strengthen FEMA's core functions, including logistics, customer service, communication, and coordination. DHS proposed to upgrade the emergency

Department of Homeland Security Centers of Excellence

In January 2005, the Department of Homeland Security's Science and Technology Directorate began the process of establishing a network of university-based centers to conduct multidisciplinary programs and develop innovative educational programs related to the study of high-consequence event preparedness and response.

According to the DHS website, there are currently twelve Centers of Excellence across the country:

- **Center for Risk and Economic Analysis of Terrorism Events (CREATE).** Led by the University of Southern California, CREATE "develops advanced tools to evaluate the risks, costs and consequences of terrorism."

- **Center for Advancing Microbial Risk Assessment (CAMRA).** Led by Michigan State University and Drexel University established jointly with the U.S. Environmental Protection Agency, CAMRA "fills critical gaps in risk assessments for mitigating microbial hazards."

- **Center of Excellence for Zoonotic and Animal Disease Defense (ZADD).** Led by Texas A&M University and Kansas State University, ZADD "protects the nation's agricultural and public health sectors against high-consequence foreign animal, emerging and zoonotic disease threats."

- **National Center for Food Protection and Defense (NCFPD).** Led by the University of Minnesota, NCFPD "defends the safety and security of the food system by conducting research to protect vulnerabilities in the nation's food supply chain."

- **National Consortium for the Study of Terrorism and Responses to Terrorism (START).** Led by the University of Maryland, START "informs decisions on how to disrupt terrorists and terrorist groups through empirically grounded findings on the human element of the terrorist threat."

- **National Center for the Study of Preparedness and Catastrophic Event Response (PACER).** Led by Johns Hopkins University, PACER "optimizes our nation's preparedness in the event of a high-consequence natural or man-made disaster."

- **Center of Excellence for Awareness & Location of Explosives-Related Threats (ALERT).** Led by Northeastern University and the University of Rhode Island, ALERT "will develop new means and methods to protect the nation from explosives-related threats."

- **National Center for Border Security and Immigration (NCBSI).** Led by the University of Arizona in Tucson (research co-lead) and the University of Texas at El Paso (education co-lead), NCBSI is "developing technologies, tools, and advanced methods to balance immigration and commerce with effective border security."

alert system,[29] establish a more sophisticated tracking and logistics management system, increase procurement staff, and upgrade infrastructure and information technology systems.[30] By August 2006, FEMA had hired senior experts, had pre-designated federal incident commanders, and had added to joint field offices the position of civil rights/civil liberties liaison (expert for highly vulnerable groups).

- **Center for Maritime, Island and Remotes and Extreme Environment Security (MIREES).** Led by the University of Hawaii and Stevens Institute of Technology, MIREES "focuses on developing robust research and education programs addressing maritime domain awareness to safeguard populations and properties in geographical areas that present significant security challenges."

- **Coastal Hazards Center of Excellence (CHC).** Led by the University of North Carolina at Chapel Hill and Jackson State University in Jackson, Mississippi, CHC "performs research and develops education programs to enhance the nation's ability to safeguard populations, properties, and economies from catastrophic natural disaster."

- **National Transportation Security Center of Excellence (NTSCOE).** Established in April 2007 in accordance with HR1, Implementing the Recommendations of the 9/11 Commission Act of 2007, NTSCOE "will develop new technologies, tools and advanced methods to defend, protect and increase the resilience of the nation's multimodal transportation." It comprises seven institutions:

  - Connecticut Transportation Institute at the University of Connecticut
  - Tougaloo College
  - Texas Southern University
  - National Transit Institute at Rutgers, the State University of New Jersey
  - Homeland Security Management Institute at Long Island University
  - Mack Blackwell National Rural Transportation Study Center at the University of Arkansas
  - Mineta Transportation Institute at San José State University.

- **Center of Excellence in Command, Control and Interoperability (C2I).** Led by Purdue University (visualization sciences co-lead) and Rutgers University (data sciences co-lead), C2I "will create the scientific basis and enduring technologies needed to analyze massive amounts of information to detect security threats."

Mandate

From the Homeland Security Act of 2002:

"The Secretary, acting through the Under Secretary for Science and Technology, shall designate a university-based center or several university-based centers for homeland security. The purpose of the center or these centers shall be to establish a coordinated, university-based system to enhance the nation's homeland security."

Source: Department of Homeland Security, "Homeland Security Centers of Excellence," dhs.gov/files/programs/editorial_0498.shtm.

The agency also increased its cache of relief supplies to be able to sustain an estimated one million people for seven days. Outreach capacities were enhanced through an updated ready campaign[31] and a revamped website.

In summer 2006, however, after having completed a thorough review of state and urban area emergency plans, FEMA alarmingly concluded that the United States was still unprepared for extreme events, including terrorist attacks and Category 5 hurricanes. According to the review, evacuation, command structure, resource management, and attention to special-needs populations were areas still in particular need of improvement.[32]

The New FEMA

In the political arena, debates about FEMA—its organizational structure and administrative location within DHS—continued long after Katrina's floodwaters receded. Members of Congress introduced a number of bills to amend the Stafford Disaster Relief and Emergency Act and/or the Homeland Security Act; some of these bills would have elevated FEMA again to cabinet-level status. On October 4, 2006, Congress passed the Post-Katrina Emergency Management Reform Act of 2006 (P.L 109-295), which kept FEMA under the authority of DHS but increased the agency's organizational autonomy.

The Post-Katrina Reform Act instituted a multitude of organizational, functional, and administrative changes for FEMA, DHS, and affiliated emergency management organizations at all levels. Most notable was the restoration of the core elements of comprehensive emergency management (preparedness, response, recovery, and mitigation, plus an added component of prevention), which had been moved to DHS by the Homeland Security Act of 2002. Overall, FEMA reestablished its leadership and resources to manage all hazards, including catastrophic incidents.[33] The agency also gained additional responsibilities for first-responder effectiveness, emergency management training and education, administration and implementation of the NRP, continuity of government and operations, and disaster housing.

To improve FEMA's presence and effectiveness at the local levels, the Post-Katrina Reform Act called for the establishment of a national advisory council, regional advisory councils, regional emergency communications coordination working groups, ten regional offices, and regional office strike teams coordinated by a national integration center. It also addressed recruitment, training, and retention of FEMA personnel; procurement and accountability practices; and other administrative issues. In recognition of the inadequate response to Hurricane Katrina, FEMA gained new positions, including a disability coordinator and a small-state and rural advocate.[34]

The reintegration of functions of the Preparedness Directorate was only partial, however. FEMA does not include the functions of the Office of Infrastructure
Protection, the Office of the Chief Medical Officer, or the National Communications
System (NCS). The exclusion of the NCS is particularly worrisome because communications and interoperability problems were identified as root causes of the
response problems following Hurricane Andrew in 1992 and again in the aftermath of the 2001 terrorist attacks on the World Trade Center.[35] In a 2006 survey,
80 percent of the 183 U.S. cities surveyed had yet to receive sufficient resources to
ensure full communications interoperability between the communication systems
of first responders and emergency response officials; furthermore, 72 percent of
those cities had not been notified by FEMA about a preassigned principal federal
official.[36] These examples, along with the questionable effectiveness of the Urban
Area Security Initiative,[37] illustrate the difficulties of implementing top-down
solutions from the federal level that go beyond conceptualization to equip local
emergency agencies with the resources, capacities, and knowledge to proactively
manage and respond to emergencies. FEMA's top-heavy bureaucracy may be part
of the problem; some policy analysts argue for the decentralization of emergency
functions and the strengthening of local capabilities.[38]

The Implementation Gap

Although perhaps justified, the post-Katrina criticism of FEMA and DHS tended
to blur cause and effect. FEMA and DHS failed terribly in their response to the
impact of Hurricane Katrina. The creation of DHS, the degradation of FEMA
from an independent agency with cabinet-level status to a directorate within DHS,
the subsequent institutional brain drain, and the implementation of the new NRP
and the ICS clearly contributed to FEMA's meltdown. Combined with the total
failure of a structural protection system, these administrative and organizational
changes contributed to making a disaster into a catastrophe.[39]

Considerable speculation on the absence of leadership fueled comparisons
between the FEMA of 2005 and the agency under previous administrations, especially under the leadership of James Lee Witt.[40] Critics have argued that under Witt's
direction, FEMA would have planned more realistically for Hurricane Katrina and
responded more effectively, lessening the catastrophic impact. There are at least
three reasons often cited for FEMA's earlier strength: its cabinet-equivalent status
in which its director reported directly to the president, its all-hazards approach, and
its strong focus on natural hazards mitigation.

Current (as of time of writing) FEMA administrator Craig Fugate, with
his extensive, hands-on experience as head of the state emergency management
office in Florida, appears to be reinvigorating the all-hazards approach as well
as introducing new initiatives, such as the increased use of social media and the

involvement of citizens and the private sector. Under his leadership, the administration of President Barack Obama has ushered in a new focus on socially vulnerable populations, meaning that FEMA now actively engages in emergency planning for the functional needs of children and adults with disabilities.[41]

Two key factors that contributed to the losses from Hurricane Katrina have been relatively ignored. First, the losses were a direct result of local governments' ineffective and/or nonexistent efforts toward hurricane mitigation (e.g., their inadequate maintenance and/or upgrades of flood control structures, which resulted in the collapse of the floodwalls in New Orleans; their failure to evacuate populations with functional needs; and so on). Second, the slow pace of relief and continued suffering of victims exposed the federal government's lack of a long-term vulnerability reduction and recovery strategy for the nation.

The Black Hole of Mitigation

In 2004, the near hit of New Orleans by Hurricane Ivan again gave rise to speculation about how the city would fare in a major storm.[42] Recognizing the vulnerability of New Orleans, FEMA and local authorities in Louisiana hired consultants in 2005 to assist in developing action plans should a major hurricane hit the coast and cause major flooding. A five-day tabletop exercise simulated a slow-moving Category 3 storm that, in retrospect, possessed an eerie resemblance to Hurricane Katrina.[43] The yearlong study of the emergency management system in New Orleans exposed serious shortcomings, including the failure of the local government and agencies to build adequate emergency management capacity internally, instead relying on external contractors. The consultants also predicted that the implementation of well-intended plans would overwhelm the capacities and capabilities of many local emergency managers.

Mitigation, a crucial but underdeveloped part of the emergency management cycle, is often a daunting task for local communities. Mitigation activities cover a large suite of measures: structural solutions, such as dams, levees, and stream channel modifications; economic efforts, such as insurance or financial incentives; and educational approaches, such as training and public awareness campaigns. The most common mitigation tools are hazard identification and mapping, building codes and enforcement, land use planning, insurance, and structural controls.[44] While FEMA and its regional offices provide technical guidance in "how-to" publications, many local governments request assistance from other localities, consultants, or academia to accomplish what needs to be done.

A 2005 study by the Multihazard Mitigation Council suggests that preimpact mitigation provides, on average, long-term savings from disasters in a ratio of four to one. In other words, for every $1 spent on mitigation, there is $4 in savings.[45] However, decisions to invest in mitigation usually take place in a public and political environment that does not routinely face an imminent hazard threat, so they compete with seemingly more urgent calls for investment, such as those contributing to economic growth and prosperity. Hurricane Katrina, for example, disclosed a dichotomy between the need for mitigation and the desire for increased revenue, especially in economically depressed areas. Prior to the hurricane, the quest for new development to increase local tax revenues assumed a higher priority than hurricane mitigation. Thus, instead of leaving wetlands and swamps (the natural buffers for flood-prone areas) undisturbed, local authorities converted them for residential and commercial uses and ensured protection through participation in the National Flood Insurance Program (NFIP). Providing federally backed flood insurance removed the financial risk from homeowners for their poor choice of housing location, further

stimulating the development of hazard-prone areas. In New Orleans, the elaborate flood protection system exempted residents from the need to participate in the NFIP. In fact, the flood insurance rate maps considered the areas behind levees to be free from the risk of flooding.

At the same time, local authorities ignored mitigation measures, including the enforcement of building codes, land use planning, and private and public insurance. Public risk management expert Raymond Burby found that, compared with other coastal states, Alabama, Louisiana, and Mississippi generated excessive NFIP-insured flood losses, which he attributes to the absence of comprehensive plans and local building codes in all

Residents of New Orleans, Louisiana, push boats through floodwaters following Hurricane Katrina. Katrina severely tested post-9/11 federal disaster response and policy. Photo courtesy of the Federal Emergency Management Agency/Jocelyn Augustino.

three states. Although the NFIP mandates local building codes on new construction in flood zones, the program lacks two important components: (1) the willingness to enforce codes at the local level by exercising probation and suspension procedures and (2) incentives for communities and/or homeowners to reduce repetitive flood losses.[46]

Shortly after Katrina, FEMA began redefining structural standards for hurricane- and flood-proofing; it also began surveying the affected areas to determine base flood elevations. These lengthy undertakings introduced lots of uncertainty into the reconstruction process. Today, more than six years after Katrina, new base flood elevations and building codes are in effect for most of the affected counties, but some Louisiana parishes are appealing even preliminary maps while others are being remapped because of disputes and/or new benchmarks. As a result, reconstruction guidelines—and hence the insurability of new construction—have been relying heavily on prestorm or advisory flood insurance rate maps. As floodplains change, so too do flood insurance rate maps, building codes, and base flood elevations. What does not change is the engineered level of protection: the 100-year, or 1 percent, annual chance of flooding. Despite all the flood losses outside the 100-year floodplain as well as the inadequate 100-year protective system in New Orleans, there has been no discussion about increasing design standards. A 100-year level of protection will not be enough in a region plagued by subsidence and rising sea levels. There will always be another Katrina. The National Research Council has concluded candidly: "The risk of inundation and flooding can never be fully eliminated by protective structures no matter how large or sturdy those structures may be."[47] Thus, flood mitigation needs to shift from structural to nonstructural measures, and while it includes multiple lines of defense, mitigation remains under the purview of homeowners, who may or may not choose to be proactive in their own behalf, with or without guidance from local authorities and FEMA.

Ultimately, disasters are local phenomena, and mitigation must begin with the local level of government. In terms of funding, personnel, knowledge, infrastructure, and political will, however, the local level remains the least equipped and sometimes the most negligent of all levels of government to mitigate hazards.

Emergency Management for Whom?

Even more disturbing than the lack of mitigation measures is the lack of resources needed at all levels of government to identify and protect the most highly vulnerable groups. This is particularly true after the economic recession that began in 2008 resulted in severe budget cuts for localities and states. Poverty, unemployment, low educational attainment, single-parent or female-headed households, disabilities, health problems, and many other conditions can reduce the ability of some segments of society to cope, especially in catastrophic situations.[48]

Prior to Hurricane Katrina, Mississippi and Louisiana were among the poorest states in the United States, with poverty rates well above the national average;[49] this is still the case today. In urban areas, conditions are aggravated by segregation, neighborhood decline, socioeconomic deprivation, health inequalities, and marginalization of the poor. According to the U.S. Census Bureau, more than one-quarter of New Orleans's citizens (27.9 percent) lived below the poverty level in the early 2000s.[50]

Although Hurricane Katrina affected people of all backgrounds, fatalities were concentrated in Louisiana. Clearly, the high death toll could have been avoided with better disaster mitigation and preparedness. Understanding the circumstances and conditions in which people live, the spatial distribution of various segments of the population, and the factors underlying social vulnerability are prerequisites for advancing disaster policies and practices at a societal level.[51]

Just as New Orleans's political elite failed to recognize the fragility of the city's flood/hurricane protection system,[52] it also failed to appreciate the needs of inner-city residents. Yet New Orleans (Orleans Parish) has a long-standing history of extreme social vulnerability.[53] Despite national improvements in socioeconomic indicators since 1960, Orleans Parish has shown virtually no change in its level of social vulnerability. For the past four decades, it has ranked consistently in the ninety-seventh percentile of the socially most vulnerable counties in the United States.[54] Compared with other Katrina-affected counties, Orleans is still the most socially vulnerable parish.

The damage pattern of Hurricane Katrina reflected New Orleans's preexisting societal conditions, as did the recovery process. Following a major catastrophe, the more affluent and insured homeowners usually are able to rebuild their homes and resume their lives (maybe even bigger and better) relatively quickly, while more vulnerable groups—the poor, the elderly, the uninsured—often find it almost impossible to recover. Vulnerable residents suffer more acutely from unemployment, defaulted loans, ruined credit, foreclosure, crowded living conditions, deterioration in physical and/or mental health, and much more.

In the case of Louisiana, the U.S. Census Bureau found that the people who were most affected by Hurricane Katrina were the slowest to return.[55] Initially, Orleans Parish lost about two-thirds of its population, and St. Bernard Parish lost almost 95 percent. A year after the hurricane, only 50 percent of New Orleans's former population had returned; two-thirds of the city's local public schools, more than half of its hospitals, and roughly half of its food retailers remained closed. Only 50 percent of the city's transportation infrastructure was operational back then, and Charity Hospital—a key health provider for the uninsured and indigent population—closed permanently.[56]

According to 2010 census data, the New Orleans metropolitan area (consisting of seven parishes) has regained almost 90 percent of its prestorm (2000) population—a percentage that includes many new residents since not everyone who left returned to the city.[57] The urban core, however, has suffered a significant loss of almost 30 percent, as reflected by the tens of thousands of vacant homes and lots. Hurricane Katrina did not just accelerate a persistent population loss but, in fact, shaped it: many of those who left were poor, nonwhite, and families with children.[58]

Hurricane Katrina did not forge these demographic shifts alone. The nature and rate of recovery directly influenced those who were able to return and rebuild and the public policies that supported them.[59] Gradually, the New Orleans area morphed into a whiter, older, and slightly wealthier community than it was before Katrina, and these changes appear to be long lasting. Some even claim that this outcome was deliberately engineered through the hampered reconstruction of low-income housing and an unequal pace of reopening and restoring affected areas.[60] Rebekah Green and colleagues found that neighborhood recovery depended much less on the degree of damage than on such factors as residents' resources (e.g., availability and location of temporary housing and transportation); public support and services (e.g., water, gas); access to recovery grants and insurance claims; reconstruction of flood protection systems; and rebuilding of local infrastructure, such as sewage systems, schools, fire departments, and grocery stores—all of which were lacking or painstakingly slow in the Lower Ninth Ward.[61] The effects of other long-term developments, such as the citywide experiment of converting the majority of public schools into charter schools as well as large-scale redevelopment projects that drove the city's poor into suburbia, remain to be seen.[62]

The Long Road Home

Some researchers estimated that the recovery of the Gulf Coast region would take from eight to eleven years.[63] In the initial recovery phases, the region and its people relied on ad hoc recovery plans and developed individual solutions to common problems. Comfort and her colleagues counted eighteen plans for the larger New Orleans area, ranging from plans by USACE to redevelopment plans for single neighborhoods.[64] It took the city (and state) almost two years to finally adopt a recovery plan, which many say has failed to spur recovery for all New Orleanians.[65] The fact that recovery was left to state and local communities in a laissez-faire approach opened the floodgates for favoritism in redevelopment, particularly in a state and city known for corruption and mismanagement. Local recovery plans, as released by Mayor Ray Nagin's Bring New Orleans Back Commission, started out by proposing selective development or green space development—in other words, holding back building permits for the most damaged areas. The public ultimately rejected such plans, but they set the stage for the discriminating development exercised across New Orleans.

While the White House issued a *Roadmap for Restoring Ecosystem Resiliency and Sustainability* in 2010,[66] there is still no national recovery plan to regulate comprehensive issues related to individual, corporate, institutional, infrastructure, and environmental recovery (e.g., building codes, taxation, low-interest loans, deferments of credit payments, and debris removal and environmental cleanup). Nor has FEMA had a recovery blueprint, which has contributed to the mismanagement of victim registration, housing assistance, and debit card programs.[67] (FEMA did issue the final version of the National Disaster Recovery Framework in late September of 2011, but it is too early to assess its merits at the time of this writing.)

As of April 2011, FEMA had approved more than one million individual disaster applications, directly distributing at least $6.6 billion to the applicants. Examples of recovery programs and expenditures for Mississippi and Louisiana alone are listed in Table 7–1.

Disaster Assistance	Louisiana	Mississippi
Number of approved applications	738,318*	274,761*
Number of families still living in temporary housing	<800	175
Cost (in $ billions)		
Housing assistance	$3.7	$0.9
Other nonhousing needs assistance	$1.5	$0.4
Total public disaster assistance (obligated)	$10.2	$3.2
Debris removal and emergency protective measures	$3.3	$1.2
Permanent work (e.g., roads, bridges)	$6.8	$1.9
Permanent housing options (e.g., cottages)	$0.008	$0.3
Total individual disaster assistance	$5.3	$1.3

Table 7–1. Coverage and Cost of FEMA Disaster Assistance Programs.

Sources: Federal Emergency Management Agency (FEMA), "Louisiana Hurricane Katrina" (2010), fema.gov/news/event.fema?id=4808; FEMA, "Mississippi Hurricane Katrina" (2010), fema.gov/news/event.fema?id=4807.

*The number of disaster applicants is conflicting. Some FEMA resources claim there were 518,100 disaster applicants for Mississippi (fema.gov/media/2010/rebuilding-lives/mississippi.shtm) while others claim a total 1,498,722 for Louisiana (fema.gov/pdf/hazard/hurricane/2005katrina/la_progress_report_0810.pdf).

Other federal agencies also are involved in the recovery of the Gulf Coast. Out of the $109 billion in federal appropriations approved by Congress during fiscal years 2005 and 2006, $16.7 billion went for Community Development Block Grants (CDBGs) administered by the U.S. Department of Housing and Urban Development (HUD) to help rebuild housing and infrastructure. The U.S. Department of Transportation set aside $2 billion to repair highways, bridges, and air transportation infrastructure. The Small Business Administration has approved more than $10.3 billion in disaster loans.[68]

HUD's involvement in the recovery process underscores the absence of federal recovery plans for large-scale events. The CDBG program is a long-standing program designed to help communities address a wide range of community development needs through block grants. Although it was not intended as a recovery program, it has become the largest housing recovery program in U.S. history.[69] The responsibility of coordinating and allocating these funds for recovery from Katrina was with the Louisiana Recovery Authority, which ended, by sunset provisions, on June 30, 2010, and has now transitioned to Louisiana's Office of Community Development.

Overall, recovery has been slow. Projects were stuck in a bureaucratic quagmire. In March 2009, President Obama established public assistance decision teams composed of federal and state experts to expedite eligibility decisions and start implementing projects. A few months later, a newly established arbitration process involving a neutral third party started resolving the most contentious disputes.[70]

Findings and Observations

The devastation of recent hurricane seasons should have been a wake-up call for governments at all levels to adjust the U.S. emergency management system—to move toward a real emphasis on long-term loss reduction from all possible hazards. Only by addressing the shortcomings of the emergency management system will the nation be able to address the root causes of inequities in disaster response and recovery. Thus far, a comprehensive (or candid) evaluation has been lacking. Despite the requirement by the Post-Katrina Reform Act for an annual federal preparedness report, only a single report was completed; issued in 2009, this report has a generally positive tenor: "As a Nation, we are significantly better prepared for all hazards than we were five years ago."[71] And this might be true in terms of terrorism-related preparedness; however, it certainly is not true in areas such as medical preparedness, information sharing, private sector preparedness, and community recovery.

President Obama partially acknowledged this in March 2011 by issuing a new Presidential Preparedness Directive 8. The new directive, which replaced the Homeland Security Presidential Directive 8 of 2003, continues the original call for the development of a national preparedness goal and a national preparedness system but encourages catastrophic risk planning as well as planning specific to local risks instead of a narrow focus on the national planning scenarios. The directive also strengthens capabilities-based planning, including that for the private sector.

Hurricane Katrina is now imprinted on the nation's conscience as *the* catastrophic event. Thus far, worst-case scenario planning resembles planning for another Katrina instead of surprise events that have not yet happened. Even the complex and cascading devastation caused by the Japanese earthquake, tsunami, and radioactive releases have not triggered a serious look at the nation's state of hazard resiliency or lack thereof. It appears to be business as usual: no major improvements in the nation's critical infrastructure, hazard mitigation, environmental regulation, catastrophic planning, or medical preparedness. It is safe to say that Hurricane Katrina did not trigger the same type of sweeping organizational changes as were seen post-9/11. An objective observer might say that we have wasted a crisis because we are continuing to exacerbate vulnerabilities and risks instead of mitigating them.

Endnotes

1   This figure refers to direct losses in current dollars from Hurricane Katrina according to the National Climate Data Center (NCDC) storm data publications.

2   NCDC, "Billion Dollar U.S. Weather/Climate Disasters" (June 17, 2011), ncdc.noaa.gov/oa/reports/billionz.html. Figure is in current dollars.

3   U.S. Census Bureau, "The 2012 Statistical Abstract: Population in Coastal Counties: 1980 to 2010," census.gov/compendia/statab/2012/tables/12s0025.pdf.

4   NCDC, "Climate of 2005 Atlantic Hurricane Season" (January 18, 2006).

5   NCDC, "Billion Dollar U.S. Weather/Climate Disasters."

6   Jack Beven, *Tropical Cyclone Report Hurricane Dennis* (updated March 17, 2006) (Miami, Fla.: National Hurricane Center), nhc.noaa.gov/2005atlan.shtml.

7   Richard D. Knabb, Jamie R. Rhome, and Daniel P. Brown, *Tropical Cyclone Report: Hurricane Katrina, 23–30 August 2005* (Miami, Fla.: National Hurricane Center, 2005), nhc.noaa.gov/pdf/TCR-AL122005_Katrina.pdf; NCDC, *Hurricane Katrina,* 2005, ncdc.noaa.gov/special-reports/katrina.html.

8   Knabb, Rhome, and Brown, *Tropical Cyclone Report: Hurricane Katrina.*

9   Louise K. Comfort et al., "Retrospectives and Prospectives on Hurricane Katrina: Five Years and Counting," *Public Administration Review* 70, no. 5 (2010): 669–678.

10   Sebastiaan N. Jonkman et al., "Loss of Life Caused by the Flooding of New Orleans after Hurricane Katrina: Analysis of the Relationship between Flood Characteristics and Mortality," *Risk Analysis* 29, no. 5 (2009): 676–698.

11   Ibid.; NCDC, *Hurricane Katrina.*

12   Knabb, Rhome, and Brown, *Tropical Cyclone Report: Hurricane Katrina*; in this report, the authors estimate that New Orleans experienced only Category 1 and Category 2 winds, indicating that New Orleans levees did not adhere to their protective standard of Category 3 winds.

13   Ibid.

14   Office of the Federal Coordinator for Gulf Coast Rebuilding, *Continuing Progress: A 1-Year Update on Hurricane Recovery and Rebuilding* (Washington, D.C.: U.S. Department of Homeland Security [DHS], 2006), dhs.gov/xlibrary/assets/GulfCoast_Katrina1yearFactSheet.pdf.

15   American Society of Civil Engineers (ASCE), Hurricane Katrina External Review Panel, *Hurricane Katrina One Year Later: What Must We Do Next?* (Reston, Va.: ASCE, 2006), cbr.tulane.edu/PDFs/next.pdf. For extensive discussions on the performance and vulnerability of New Orleans's protective systems, see National Research Council, *The New Orleans Hurricane Protection System: Assessing Pre-Katrina Vulnerability and Improving Mitigation and Preparedness* (Washington, D.C.: National Academies Press, 2009), and the nine volumes produced by the Interagency Performance Evaluation Task Force.

16   Havidán Rodríguez, Joseph Trainor, and Enrico L. Quarantelli, "Rising to the Challenges of a Catastrophe: The Emergent and Prosocial Behavior following Hurricane Katrina," in *Shelter from the Storm: Repairing the National Emergency Management System after Hurricane Katrina,* ed.

William L. Waugh Jr., *Annals of the American Academy of Political and Social Science* (March 2006): 82–101.

17 NCDC, "Billion Dollar U.S. Weather/Climate Disasters."

18 Richard D. Knabb, Daniel P. Brown, and Jamie R. Rhome, *Tropical Cyclone Report: Hurricane Rita, 18–26 September 2005* (Miami, Fla.: National Hurricane Center, 2006), nhc.noaa.gov/pdf/TCR-AL182005_Rita.pdf.

19 Ibid.

20 Richard J. Pasch et al., *Tropical Cyclone Report: Hurricane Wilma, 15–25 October 2006* (Miami, Fla.: National Hurricane Center, 2006), nhc.noaa.gov/pdf/TCR-AL252005_Wilma.pdf.

21 Pasch et al., for example, believe that the storm surge reached even higher levels, but there are no official high-water marks because the landfall occurred in Florida's uninhabited Everglades; see *Tropical Cyclone Report: Hurricane Wilma.*

22 DHS, *National Response Plan* (Washington, D.C., December 2004), iir.com/Information_Sharing/global/resources/fusioncenter/NRPbaseplan.pdf.

23 DHS, *National Incident Management System* (Washington, D.C., December 2008), fema.gov/pdf/emergency/nims/NIMS_core.pdf.

24 Federal Emergency Management Agency (FEMA), *Federal Response Plan,* 9230.1-PL (Washington, D.C., 1999), biotech.law.lsu.edu/blaw/FEMA/frpfull.pdf.

25 White House, *The Federal Response to Hurricane Katrina: Lessons Learned* (Washington, D.C.: U.S. Government Printing Office, February 23, 2006), library.stmarytx.edu/acadlib/edocs/katrinawh.pdf.

26 Keith Bea, *The National Preparedness System: Issues in the 109th Congress,* CRS Report RL32803 (Washington, D.C.: Congressional Research Service [CRS], Library of Congress, March 10, 2005), au.af.mil/au/awc/awcgate/crs/rl32803.pdf. Louisiana emergency officials and National Guardsman were trained in basic NRP and ICS procedures two days after Katrina.

27 U.S. House of Representatives, *A Failure of Initiative: Final Report of the Select Bipartisan Committee to Investigate the Preparation for and Response to Hurricane Katrina* (Washington D.C.: U.S. House of Representatives, February 15, 2006), gpoaccess.gov/katrinareport/fullreport.pdf.

28 Naim Kapucu, "Examining the National Response Plan in Response to a Catastrophic Disaster: Hurricane Katrina in 2005," *International Journal of Mass Emergencies and Disasters* 24 (August 2006): 271–299; U.S. House of Representatives, *Failure of Initiative*; and David M. Walker, *Statement by the Comptroller General David M. Walker on GAO's Preliminary Observations Regarding Preparedness and Response to Hurricanes Katrina and Rita,* Preliminary Report, GAO-06-365R (Washington, D.C.: U.S. Government Accounting Office, February 1, 2006).

29 The Emergency Alert System is jointly administered by FEMA and the Federal Communications Commission and operates in cooperation with the National Weather Service; see Linda K. Moore, *Emergency Communications: The Emergency Alert System (EAS) and All-Hazard Warnings,* CRS Report RL32527, updated September 13, 2006 (Washington, D.C.: CRS, Library of Congress, 2006), fas.org/sgp/crs/homesec/RL32527.pdf.

30 DHS, "Strengthening FEMA to Maximize Mission Performance" (February 13, 2006), gov/dhspublic/display?content=5413 (site no longer available).

31 See ready.gov.

32 DHS, "Hurricane Season Preparations" (August 24, 2006), dhs.gov/xprepresp/editorial_0846.shtm (site no longer available); DHS, "Remarks by Secretary of Homeland Security Michael Chertoff at the Emergency Management and Disability and Aging Populations" (June 30, 2006), dhs.gov/xnews/speeches/speech_0286.shtm; and DHS, in cooperation with the U.S. Department of Transportation (DOT), *Nationwide Plan Review,* Phase 2 Report (Washington, D.C.: DHS and DOT, June 16, 2006), dhs.gov/xlibrary/assets/Prep_NationwidePlanReview.pdf.

33 Keith Bea et al., *Federal Emergency Management Policy Changes after Hurricane Katrina: A Summary of Statutory Provisions,* CRS Report RL33729 (Washington, D.C.: CRS, Library of Congress, November 15, 2006), policyarchive.org/handle/10207/bitstreams/3018.pdf.

34 Ibid.

35 Walker, *Statement by the Comptroller General David M. Walker.*

36 U.S. Conference of Mayors, Homeland Security Monitoring Center, *Five Years Post 9/11, One Year Post Katrina: The State of America's Readiness* (Washington, D.C.: U.S. Conference of Mayors, July 26, 2006), usmayors.org/pressreleases/documents/disasterpreparedness_072606.pdf.

37 Erica Chenoweth and Susan E. Clarke, "All Terrorism Is Local: Resources, Nested Institutions, and Governance for Urban Homeland Security in the American Federal System," *Political Research Quarterly* 63, no. 3 (2010): 495–507.

38 Russell S. Sobel and Peter T. Leeson, *Flirting with Disaster: The Inherent Problems with FEMA*, Policy Analysis no. 573 (Washington, D.C.: CATO Institute, July 19, 2006), cato.org/pub_cat_display.php?pub_cat=2.

39 Kathleen J. Tierney, "Recent Developments in U.S. Homeland Security Policies and Their Implications for the Management of Extreme Events," in *Handbook of Disaster Research,* ed. Havidán Rodríguez, Enrico L. Quarantelli, and Russell R. Dynes, 405–412 (New York: Springer, 2007).

40 Russell S. Sobel, Christopher J. Coyne, and Peter T. Leeson, "The Political Economy of FEMA: Did Reorganization Matter?" *Journal of Public Finance and Public Choice* 17, nos. 2–3 (2007): 49–65; Russell S. Sobel and Peter T. Leeson, "Government's Response to Hurricane Katrina: A Public Choice Analysis," *Public Choice* 127, nos. 1–2 (2006): 55–73.

41 FEMA, "Rebuilding Lives, Revitalizing Communities—Louisiana Recovery Efforts Five Years after Katrina and Rita" (August 23, 2010), fema.gov/media/2010/rebuilding-lives/louisiana.shtm.

42 Shirley Laska, "What If Hurricane Ivan Had Not Missed New Orleans?" *Natural Hazards Observer* 29 (November 2004): 5–6.

43 Madhu Beriwal, "Hurricanes Pam and Katrina: A Lesson in Disaster Planning," *Natural Hazards Observer* 30 (November 2005): 8–9.

44 George D. Haddow and Jane A. Bullock, *Introduction to Emergency Management* (New York: Elsevier Butterworth-Heinemann, 2003).

45 Multihazard Mitigation Council, *Natural Hazard Mitigation Saves: An Independent Study to Assess the Future Savings from Mitigation Activities,* vol. 1, *Findings, Conclusions, and Recommendations* (Washington, D.C.: National Institute of Building Sciences, 2005), floods.org/PDF/MMC_Volume1_FindingsConclusionsRecommendations.pdf; Philip T. Ganderton et al., "Mitigation Generates Savings of Four to One and Enhances Community Resilience: MMC Releases Study on Savings from Mitigation," *Natural Hazards Observer* 30 (March 2006): 1–3.

46 Raymond J. Burby, "Hurricane Katrina and the Paradoxes of Government Disaster Policy: Bringing about Wise Governmental Decisions for Hazardous Areas," in *Shelter from the Storm*, 171–191 (see note 16). Building codes and elevated construction would not have completely protected communities from Katrina's storm surge; the bayfront properties in Diamondhead, Mississippi, which had improved standards for elevation and housing construction, were completely destroyed in the hurricane.

47 National Research Council, *New Orleans Hurricane Protection System,* 4.

48 Susan L. Cutter, "Vulnerability to Environmental Hazards," *Progress in Human Geography* 20, no. 4 (1996): 529–539; and Susan L. Cutter, Bryan J. Boruff, and W. Lynn Shirley, "Social Vulnerability to Environmental Hazards," *Social Science Quarterly* 84 (January 2003): 242–261.

49 In 2004, the average poverty rate in the United States in 2004 was 12.7 percent; Louisiana had a poverty rate of 17 percent and Mississippi 17.7 percent; see Carmen DeNavas-Walt, Bernadette D. Proctor, and Cheryl Hill Lee, *Income, Poverty, and Health Insurance Coverage in the United States: 2004,* Current Population Reports P60-229 (Washington, D.C.: U.S. Census Bureau, 2005). By 2008, both states ranked first and second, with poverty levels at 21.2 percent in Mississippi and 17.3 percent in Louisiana; see U.S. Census Bureau, "The 2012 Statistical Abstract," census.gov/compendia/statab/rankings.html.

50 U.S. Census Bureau, *State and County Quick Facts,* quickfacts.census.gov/qfd/states/22/2255000.html.

51 Heinz Center for Science, Economics, and the Environment, *Human Links to Coastal Disasters* (Washington, D.C.: Heinz Center, 2002), heinzctr.org/Major_Reports_files/Human%20Links%20to%20Coastal%20Disasters.pdf.

52 ASCE, *Hurricane Katrina One Year Later.*

53 As indicated by social vulnerability index developed by Cutter, Boruff, and Shirley in "Social Vulnerability to Environmental Hazards," this index synthesizes forty-two socioeconomic

and built-environment variables—for example, age, income, race, workforce, education, and housing—to provide a single metric that compares different localities. Among the statistically dominant factors that contribute to social vulnerability are low socioeconomic status, development density or urbanized areas, the age of the population, race, ethnicity, and gender.

54   Susan L. Cutter et al., "The Long Road Home: Race, Class, and Recovery from Hurricane Katrina," *Environment* 48, no. 2 (2006): 8–20.

55   Kim Koerber, *Migration Patterns and Mover Characteristics from the 2005 ACS Gulf Coast Area Special Products* (Washington, D.C.: U.S. Census Bureau, 2006), census.gov/newsroom/emergencies/additional/gulf_migration.html.

56   Amy Liu, Matt Fellowes, and Mia Mabanta, *Special Edition of the Katrina Index: A One-Year Review of Key Indicators of Recovery in Post-Storm New Orleans* (Washington, D.C.: The Brookings Institution, 2006), brookings.edu/reports/2006/08metropolitanpolicy_liu.aspx.

57   U.S. Census Bureau, *2011 Statistical Abstract*, census.gov/compendia/statab/2011/2011edition.html.

58   Allison Plyer, "Population Loss and Vacant Housing in New Orleans Neighborhoods," *Census Fact Brief* (New Orleans: Greater New Orleans Community Data Center, February 5, 2011), gnocdc.org/PopulationLossAndVacantHousing/index.html.

59   Christina Finch, Christopher T. Emrich, and Susan L. Cutter, "Disaster Disparities and Differential Recovery in New Orleans," *Population and Environment* 31, no. 4 (2010): 179–202.

60   Comfort et al., "Retrospectives and Prospectives"; Rebekah Green, Lisa K. Bates, and Andrew Smyth, "Impediments to Recovery in New Orleans's Upper and Lower Ninth Ward: One Year after Hurricane Katrina," *Disasters* 31, no. 4 (2007): 311–335.

61   Green, Bates, and Smyth, "Impediments to Recovery."

62   Amy Liu and Allison Plyer, *The New Orleans Index at Five* (Washington, D.C.: The Brookings Institution, August 2010), brookings.edu/~/media/Files/rc/reports/2010/08neworleansindex/08neworleansindex.pdf.

63   Robert W. Kates et al., "Reconstruction of New Orleans following Hurricane Katrina: A Research Perspective," *Proceedings of the National Academy of Sciences* 103, no. 40 (2006): 14653–14660.

64   Comfort et al., "Retrospectives and Prospectives."

65   Vincanne Adams, Taslim van Hattum, and Diana English, "Chronic Disaster Syndrome: Displacement, Disaster Capitalism, and the Eviction of the Poor from New Orleans," *American Ethnologist* 36, no. 4 (2009): 615–636; Dominique Duval-Diop, Testimony before the U.S. House of Representatives Committee on Financial Services, Subcommittee on Housing and Community Opportunity, Field Hearing on the "Implementation of the Road Home Program Four Years after Hurricane Katrina" (August 20, 2009), gpo.gov/fdsys/pkg/CHRG-111hhrg53250/html/CHRG-111 hhrg53250.htm; Shirley Laska, "The 'Mother of All Rorschachs': Katrina Recovery in New Orleans," *Sociological Inquiry* 78, no. 4 (2008): 580–591; Robert B. Olshansky and Laurie A. Johnson, *Clear as Mud: Planning for the Rebuilding of New Orleans* (Chicago: APA Press, 2010).

66   Louisiana-Mississippi Gulf Coast Ecosystem Restoration Working Group, *Roadmap for Restoring Ecosystem Resiliency and Sustainability* (Washington, D.C.: The White House, March 2010), whitehouse.gov/administration/eop/ceq/initiatives/gulfcoast/roadmap.

67   Gregory D. Kutz and John J. Ryan, *Hurricanes Katrina and Rita Disaster Relief,* GAO-06-844T (Washington, D.C.: U.S. General Accounting Office, June 14, 2006), gao.gov/new.items/d06844t.pdf.

68   Office of the Federal Coordinator for Gulf Coast Rebuilding, *Continuing Progress;* Matt Fellowes and Amy Liu, *Federal Allocations in Response to Katrina, Rita, and Wilma* (Washington, D.C.: The Brookings Institution, August 21, 2006), brookings.edu/~/media/Files/rc/reports/2006/08metropolitanpolicy_fellowes/20060712_Katrinafactsheet.pdf.

69   Office of the Federal Coordinator for Gulf Coast Rebuilding, *Continuing Progress*.

70   FEMA, "Louisiana Katrina/Rita Recovery" (August 20, 2010). fema.gov/pdf/hazard/hurricane/2005katrina/la_progress_report_0810.pdf.

71   DHS, *The Federal Preparedness Report* (Washington, D.C.: DHS, January 13, 2009), iii, iaem.com/committees/governmentaffairs/documents/FPR-Jan2009.pdf.

Chapter 8

The System Is Tested: Response to the BP *Deepwater Horizon* Oil Spill

John R. Harrald

As described in the previous chapter, the U.S. emergency response system was tested severely in the first decade of the twenty-first century. However, lessons were learned from September 11, Hurricane Katrina, the Haiti earthquake, and other events during that decade, and positive steps were taken to incorporate those lessons into the system: the Department of Homeland Security (DHS) revised its emergency response doctrine with the publication of the National Response Plan (NRP) and then the National Response Framework (NRF); the Federal Emergency Management Agency (FEMA) and the U.S. Coast Guard (USCG) coordinated and held national-level exercises; and the Obama administration filled critical leadership positions within DHS and FEMA with experienced emergency management professionals, starting with the appointment of Craig Fugate, the former director of the Florida Division of Emergency Management, as administrator of FEMA.

Then, on the morning of April 20, 2010, the newly strengthened system that was designed to provide strong DHS leadership in the response to all incidents met its first major test, and it was one that few expected: the blowout of the BP (formerly, British Petroleum) Macondo 252 oil well in the Gulf of Mexico. It was the first crude oil blowout into the Gulf in over thirty years and the first blowout ever in water over 4,000 feet deep. The crisis was precipitated by a series of events occurring nearly a mile below the surface at the Macondo Prospect oil field, about forty miles from shore. By the end of the day, the drilling rig *Deepwater Horizon* was engulfed in flames; although 115 of its 126-person crew had escaped the inferno and were rescued, 11 were dead. Far below the surface, the crude oil spewed unchecked into the Gulf for eighty-seven days, the result of a failed attempt to cap and abandon the Macondo well.[1]

The *Deepwater Horizon* rig sank on April 22, damaging the well riser and eliminating any possibility of activating the blowout preventer that had not

Fire boat response crews battle the blazing remnants of the offshore oil rig *Deepwater Horizon*, April 21, 2010. Photo courtesy of the United States Coast Guard.

self-activated as designed. For the next three months, media, political, and public attention was focused on the struggle to stop the flow and contain the oil that threatened the ecological and economic health of the region. By the time the well was finally capped on July 15, 2010, almost 5 million barrels (over 200 million gallons) of crude oil had escaped into the Gulf of Mexico—a volume nearly twenty times that of the 1989 *Exxon Valdez* oil spill.[2] Over 2,500 square miles of ocean were contaminated by oil, and nearly 90,000 square miles of the Gulf were closed to fishing.[3] The spill directly threatened the resources and economies of five coastal states, fifty-three counties/parishes, and two federal regions.

The scale of the event was matched by the scale of the response, which ultimately involved over 48,000 people from hundreds of organizations as well as impressive sea and air assets, including 60 USCG vessels and 22 aircraft, 345 response vessels, 3,200 vessels of opportunity (VOOs),[4] and 127 surveillance aircraft.[5] If the more than 2,500 miles of containment boom (the floating barriers "used to collect and hold oil on the surface of the water for recovery by skimmers or similar collection devices")[6] deployed during the response were laid end to end, the boom would have stretched from Washington, D.C., to Los Angeles, California.

The *Deepwater Horizon*/Macondo oil disaster raised a number of important risk, safety, regulatory, corporate culture, and government policy issues.

Those issues are addressed in *Deep Water: The Gulf Oil Disaster and the Future of Offshore Drilling,* the final report of the National Commission on the BP Deepwater Horizon Oil Spill and Offshore Drilling,[7] as well as in numerous books, papers, and reports.[8] The technical issues that led to the failure of the blow-out preventers and other safeguards, and the engineering and operational creativity required to cap the well, are discussed in detail in three reports in addition to *Deep Water:* the National Commission staff working paper *Stopping the Spill: The Five-Month Effort to Kill the Macondo Well,*[9] the USCG's *Incident Specific Performance Review (ISPR) Deepwater Horizon Oil Spill,*[10] and the final investigative reports of the USCG and Bureau of Ocean Energy Management, Regulation and Enforcement.[11] Therefore, none of those issues will be addressed here. Rather, the objective of this chapter is to examine the emergency management issues created by the spill and discuss the ability of the national response system to adjust and adapt to the challenges it presented.

Complications in the Response to the BP *Deepwater Horizon* Oil Spill

The response to the BP *Deepwater Horizon* spill was complicated by several factors. The first was the uniqueness of the initiating event itself. There had never before been an uncontrolled blowout from a deepwater well. The last comparable experience in the United States was in 1969 with the Santa Barbara Union Oil platform A-21 blowout and oil spill six miles offshore in the Santa Barbara channel.[12] Ten years later, the United States provided extensive assistance to the Mexican government during the Ixtoc I oil spill,[13] but the only pollution that the United States sustained from that disaster was restricted to South Texas beaches.

A related complicating factor during the BP *Deepwater Horizon* response was the difficulty in estimating the rate of oil flow from the Macondo well. Early projections from BP and the National Oceanic and Atmospheric Administration (NOAA) of 1,000–5,000 barrels a day proved to be grossly underestimated, resulting in both operational and credibility problems.[14]

Response leaders also had to deal with unprecedented issues of scale. The response was spread out over a five-state region and thousands of square miles of the Gulf. At times the area of oil on the surface that responders were trying to skim, burn, or disperse was about the size of the state of Delaware. The most heavily oiled surface on May 6, for example, was in a five- to fifteen-mile-wide plume that stretched forty-five miles from the Macondo well site.[15] Response leaders were faced with both the daunting technological task of stopping the spill and minimizing its impact, and the managerial challenge of creating and leading the largest oil spill response in history. Like many extreme events, the BP *Deepwater Horizon* oil spill had crossed the threshold of awareness that leads to intense media scrutiny and high levels of involvement by elected and appointed officials, putting response leaders into a constant crisis management mode.

Finally, one of the least reported and understood complicating factors was that the spill revealed the doctrinal conflicts and inconsistencies between a "top-down" federally directed oil spill response, which was conducted under the authority of the Oil Pollution Act of 1990 (OPA 90) and the National Oil and Hazardous Substances Pollution Contingency Plan, also known as the National Contingency Plan (NCP), and the more familiar "bottom-up" natural disaster response, which was coordinated by FEMA under its Stafford Act authority and NRF doctrine.

Response to the BP *Deepwater Horizon* spill started with a by-the-book NCP approach. Within twenty-four hours, Rear Admiral Mary Landry, commander of the Eighth Coast Guard District in New Orleans, assumed the role of federal on-scene coordinator (FOSC), relieving Capt. Joseph Paradis, commanding officer of the USCG Marine Safety Office in Morgan City, which had responded to the platform explosion and fire. BP activated its contracts with two predesignated private oil spill response organizations (OSROs): Marine Spill Response Corporation and the National Response Corporation. Incident command posts were established by the USCG in Houma, Louisiana, and by BP in Houma and Houston, Texas. Within forty-eight hours, a Unified Command (USCG, BP, and the State of Louisiana) was established at Robert, Louisiana; the National Response Team, a leadership group consisting of the heads of the federal agencies signatory to the NCP, had been activated; and the USCG and BP were mobilizing all available response resources. President Barack Obama was briefed on the spill for the first time on April 23 by DHS secretary Janet Napolitano,[16] who became the principal federal official (PFO) for the response.

A catastrophic disaster, by its very nature, threatens the socioeconomic well-being of a society and makes precarious the future viability of every elected or appointed official and corporate executive connected to the response. As reported in earlier chapters, very real political consequences followed George H. W. Bush's slow reaction to Hurricane Andrew and George W. Bush's perceived lack of personal involvement in the Hurricane Katrina response. As the *Deepwater Horizon* disaster played out, remotely operated vehicles relayed pictures of oil gushing from three different points in the wreckage: the drill pipe, the end of the riser, and a kink in the riser created when the rig sank. Within a week, the spill was the lead story in the twenty-four-hour news cycle, with the dominant story line being the inability of the response team to stop the spill or to contain or control the massive amounts of oil flowing into the Gulf. It was evident that there would be political consequences.

On April 29, Louisiana governor Bobby Jindell declared a state of emergency in Louisiana. That same day, the USCG designated the disaster a spill of national significance (SONS), a designation under the NCP that, among other things, allowed the president to appoint a national incident commander (NIC).[17] The level of this response became clear on April 30, when President Obama dispatched DHS secretary Napolitano, Interior secretary Ken Salazar, Energy advisor Carol Browner, Environmental Protection Agency (EPA) administrator Lisa Jackson, and NOAA administrator Jane Lubchenco to the Gulf to report on progress.[18] He told senior federal officials to make the spill their highest priority; unfortunately, few of these officials had any understanding of the NCP and its assignment of roles and responsibilities.[19]

The White House perceived a need to create coordination mechanisms that were beyond those provided by the NCP and the National Incident Command structure. On April 30, National Security adviser John Brennan convened a White House principals group; involving the same agencies represented in the National Response Team, this group continued to function throughout the spill response, diminishing the role of the National Response Team. The White House also established a daily governors' briefing with affected states.[20] The involvement of multiple agencies resulted in a significant demand for information that, coupled with media demands, strained the response organization's capabilities. Despite these actions, however, the administration had to defend the handling of the spill and prove that it was "in charge" of the response. President Obama appointed USCG commandant Thad Allen as his NIC, and on May 1, Admiral Allen took charge to lead an "all-of-government response."

Obama reacted to the growing public perception that too little was being done and directed the USCG to triple the size of its response, a directive that the Coast Guard found to be both difficult to implement and of questionable benefit. The USCG was critical of the directive:

> Merely adding more people to the response effort may have a negative effect or unintended outcome. The White House's mandate to triple personnel resources did not appear to improve the effectiveness of the response because many of the people assigned were not trained in NIMS/ICS [National Incident Management System/Incident Command System] doctrine.[21]

The public and political pressure continued to build. A *Washington Post* article on May 28, 2010, titled "Obama Struggling to Show He's in Control of Oil Spill," stated that "public confidence in Washington's handling of the spill has dropped sharply" and quoted Sen. Mary Landrieu (D-La.) as charging that "'the president has not been as visible as he should have been on this, and he's going to pay a political price for it, unfortunately.'"[22]

In May, as the oil started to come ashore, the extent of political involvement adversely affected the response in a number of ways not anticipated in existing doctrine and training. The political and media channels available to state and local officials—key stakeholders—enabled those officials to influence the federal decision process, in several instances changing strategic and operational directions (the most significant example being Governor Jindell's insistence upon creating protective berms along the Louisiana shoreline).[23] But the state representatives in Unified Command were the senior state oil spill response officials, and they did not speak for the governors in ways that emergency management directors can during a Stafford Act response. Moreover, the response organization had no component or protocols to accommodate state and local interests except for the Unified Command structure. Since these interests were not initially involved in response planning, Unified Command had no way to take advantage of local stakeholders' ability to identify local issues. The resultant public perception of failure was predictable.

Two examples of the politicization of the response were the allocation of containment boom and the management of the Vessels of Opportunity (VOO) program. The USCG, in its after-action review, was highly critical of how it was pressured to allocate containment and removal assets. According to the *ISPR Deepwater Oil Spill,*

> Public and political pressure to show response activity during the Deepwater Horizon incident caused undue and inappropriate emphasis on boom and skimmer resources. Local officials measured success by the amount of boom in their jurisdiction, despite the fact that it may be the incorrect or inappropriate response resource for the operating environment.[24]

The review notes that "even with examples of failed booming operations carried out to meet local demands, there was intense pressure to appease local officials. The Department of Homeland Security and the NIC gave direction to the Unified Area Command to 'do whatever it takes to make the Parishes happy.'"[25] This directive placed tremendous pressure on Unified Command to reexamine its operational objectives in order to more effectively address the demands of the governors and parishes. Admiral Allen, in his personal report to Secretary Napolitano, stated that the USCG experienced the "political rejection of the multiple Area Contingency Plans (ACPs) that outlined response strategies" and that the state and local governments "employed response strategies that I believe... will prove to be ineffective and may have long term ecological consequences."[26]

VOOs had been used successfully in Prince William Sound for the *Exxon Valdez* spill response, but they were not part of the Coast Guard Area Contingency Plans or the industry oil spill response plans in the Gulf. The VOO program was started in the Gulf only after local governments strongly objected to contracted OSRO resources arriving from out of state and demanded that the USCG and BP use local vessels that had been idled by the spill. As documented in the USCG's *ISPR,*

> In the early stages of the response, there was no direct connection between the number of VOOs recruited and the number needed, and there was more

Members of a certified shoreline boom retrieval team operate on a vessel off the north shore of Trinity Island, La., September 11, 2010. Photo courtesy of the United States Coast Guard/Nate Littlejohn.

> interest in the VOO Program than the oil spill response organization could handle. There was widespread frustration and some abuse on the part of some members of the VOO Program.[27]

The USCG concluded its review, however, by noting that VOOs are not only invaluable but will be used—a recognition that the USCG and the response community must resolve the inherent conflict between OSROs and VOOs. OSROs are required to preidentify their subcontract resources to be certified. VOOs are, by definition, local resources that make themselves available at the time of the spill. Finding a way to incorporate VOOs into the response objectives identified in preincident contingency plans while still maintaining a credible contract response force will be difficult.[28]

Conflicting Doctrines and Procedures

Closely related to the politicization of the response to the *Deepwater Horizon* oil spill was the failure to reconcile NCP doctrine and procedures with state and local government expectations—namely, that the federal response would entail the Stafford Act–type of activities they were familiar with during their frequent hurricane and flooding experiences. As noted by the National Commission, "State and local officials in the Gulf are accustomed to setting up emergency-response structures pursuant to the Stafford Act, under which the federal government provides

U.S. Coast Guard commandant Admiral Thad Allen meets with Rear Admiral Mary Landry. Photo courtesy of the United States Coast Guard/Michael De Nyse.

funding and assists the state and local governments during a major disaster. In contrast, the National Contingency Plan, which governs oil spills [as well as hazardous materials incidents], gives the Federal On-Scene Coordinator the power to direct all response actions" and, in the case of an SONS, requires an NIC to ensure coordinated federal leadership. "Thus, while the Stafford Act envisions a state-directed (though in large part federally funded) response, the National Contingency Plan puts federal officials in charge."[29] The USCG after-action review, the *ISPR,* concluded that during the BP-*Deepwater Horizon* response, "there was extensive confusion between doctrines set forth in the NRF and the NCP. The 'emergency management' community comprising State and local emergency management officials, was unfamiliar with the NCP and the 'oil spill response' community did not see the applicability of the NRF to an oil spill." The ISPR also observes that the "NRF does not contemplate an oil spill as an initiating event under the NRF."[30]

The potential conflict between a Stafford Act response and an NCP response has been long recognized.[31] The first NCP was written in 1968 in response to the Torrey Canyon oil spill in the United Kingdom in 1967. The plan recognized the federal government's responsibility to "remove or arrange for the removal" of oil or hazardous substance spills, and it created a unique response structure in which predesignated FOSCs from either the USCG (coastal areas) or EPA (inland areas) would direct the federal response; in 1980 this plan became a regulation (40 CFR 300) required by the Comprehensive Environmental Response, Compensation, and Liability Act.[32] The NCP was revised in 1994 following passage of OPA 90. The revisions both strengthened the role of the federal government by increasing the FOSC's authority to direct response actions by the responsible party and encouraged close collaboration with the states. According to the NCP, "the basic framework for the response management structure is a system (e.g., a unified command system) that brings together the functions of the federal government, the state government, and the responsible party to achieve an effective and efficient response."[33]

Under the NRP and the NRF, the underlying concept of federal response is the bottom-up approach of local and then state response bolstered by federal support. This is a continuation of the response philosophy adopted by the first Federal Response Plan in 1992, and it has remained the organizing concept for the federal government.

In 2003, in preparation for the development of the first NRP after the formation of DHS, the National Response Team conducted an analysis to address gaps between that plan and the plans it would incorporate into the NCP as an operational supplement to Emergency Support Function 10 (ESF 10). The NRP would then supersede the Federal Response Plan, the Federal Radiological Emergency Response Plan, and the Concept of Operations Plan. The NRP was intended to end any confusion over who would be "in charge" in any incident.[34] Unfortunately, this analysis did not address the conflicting interpretations of the federal-state relationship during a response—that is, the top-down, federally controlled NCP process versus the bottom-up, state-led, federally supported response envisioned by the Federal Response Plan. In a 1992 review of the *Exxon Valdez* spill and the OPA 90 response philosophy, John Harrald and William Wallace point out that the evolving oil spill response doctrine had to reconcile the roles of and relationships among three entities likely to be involved in any SONS: OSROs (such as the Marine Spill Response Corporation), states, and FEMA (for a concurrent Stafford Act response).[35] As noted later by Claire Rubin and John Harrald, the NRP avoided clarifying these relationships by making oil and hazardous substance response an emergency support function (ESF 10) without defining the relationship between the federal coordinating officer and the FOSC or between the PFO and the NIC.[36] The latter relationship was clarified somewhat by the NRF's designation of the DHS secretary as PFO for all domestic incidents. For the *Deepwater Horizon* incident, Secretary Napolitano was assigned as PFO and Admiral Allen as NIC. This relationship appears to have worked reasonably well, as Secretary Napolitano defined the role of the PFO as focusing on information sharing in Washington through meetings of the principals and deputies, and on issues broader than those addressed in the NCP, such as economic impacts and claims procedures.[37]

The federal government's relationship with the states was hindered by (1) the expectation of a Stafford Act response, (2) the weak involvement of local governments in Unified Command, and (3) the limited ability to compensate economic losses through NCP financial mechanisms. The USCG's *ISPR* is openly critical

Response workers clean up tar balls that washed up along the beach in Response District seven, September 30, 2010. Work continues in cleanup operations for marshes and beaches throughout Plaqueminse Parish. Photo courtesy of the United States Coast Guard/Timothy Tamargo.

of Unified Command's ability to manage what the authors term the "intersection of the National Response Framework and the National Contingency Plan."[38] The National Commission observed that "during this spill,…the Governors and other state political officials participated in the response in unprecedented ways, taking decisions out of the hands of career oil-spill responders," and that "state and local officials largely rejected the pre-spill plans and began to create their own response structures" that made decisions and took actions outside of Unified Command. Also, "Louisiana declined to empower the officials that it sent to work with federal responders within Unified Command, instead requiring most decisions to go through the Governor's office," which significantly diminished the coordinating ability of the Unified Command.[39] As a result, the state representative in Unified Command could not represent state and local interests or make commitments for the state. As Raffi Khatchadourian wrote in the *New Yorker*, "The Governor had sidelined the state agency responsible for oil spills and begun to manage Louisiana's response with his closest staffers."[40]

The lack of understanding of the NCP and the resulting unwillingness to follow the lead of Unified Command were even greater issues at the local level. In his *National Incident Commander's Report*, Admiral Allen notes that "many local officials rejected federal primacy in oil spill response operations. They often and publicly expressed their displeasure with the Unified Command's response efforts and at times worked independently of the Unified Command."[41] Plaquemines Parish president Billy Nungesser led an effort to obtain local power over response decisions, telling the press and President Obama that "Thad Allen is…not doing his job."[42] States aided this local independence by making agreements with BP and by distributing $25 million provided by BP to Alabama, Florida, Louisiana, and Mississippi to implement local contingency plans. In Louisiana, parish presidents "wanted to assert [the] same control" over cleanup operations that they did over other emergencies, "and many used money distributed by BP to purchase their own equipment and establish their own operating centers outside of Unified Command."[43] The decisions and actions taken by state and local political leaders resulted in "what Admiral Allen would later call 'the social and political nullification' of the National Contingency Plan."[44]

The fault for poor state-federal coordination did not lie solely with the state and local governments. The NCP/NIMS organization does not provide the coordinating mechanisms that the Stafford Act provides, such as federal staff in state operations centers. The NCP also does not consider state-to-state aid that could be provided under the Emergency Management Assistance Compact (EMAC). USCG officials were unfamiliar with EMAC, and USCG response resource databases did not include state personnel. As a result, EMAC use was marginal even though many states did respond to EMAC requests for "trained oil spill response personnel and oil spill clean-up equipment."[45] The USCG tried to resolve conflicts and coordinate with the states as best it could, assigning liaison officers to parish operations centers to ensure communications at the operational level; the weekly administration governor's call by National Security Adviser Brennan, Secretary Napolitano, and Admiral Allen that enhanced understanding and acceptance of strategic decisions; and extensive interaction between Admiral Allen and his NIC staff and state and local officials to detect and react to problems and issues as they occurred. As Admiral Allen concludes, however,

> attempting to reconcile the NRF [National Response Framework] and the NCP during a major disaster is not a good business practice, and will likely lead to a less than optimal response. The conflict between the NCP and the NRF must be reconciled in law, policy, and doctrine to avoid similar situations in the future.[46]

The Responsible Party

The federal government–responsible party relationship defined by OPA-90 and the NCP was also problematic. The "responsible party" is the party deemed responsible for the event, and with the advantages gained from hindsight, the media are always quick to identify the errors in judgment, bad decisions, corporate greed, and negligence that caused the oil spill. Because of this public scrutiny and blame, the role of the responsible party during a response to an oil spill of national significance can become a major source of conflict. After the *Exxon Valdez* spill, the State of Alaska Oil Spill Commission, recognizing the responsible party's vested interest in the response efforts, recommended that the responsible party partici-pate in but not lead the response.[47] The Clean Water Act, OPA 90, and the NCP, however, recognized that the responsible party should pay for the standby person-nel, equipment resources, and cleanup operations and that the companies that spill oil have the technological capabilities required to fight a spill. Acknowledging the problems with the federal government–responsible party relationship but not willing to remove the spiller from the response, OPA 90 strengthened the federal role during response, allowing for the federal deployment of resources without facing an all-or-nothing choice of removing the responsible party from leadership by "federalizing" the spill response. It also established the Oil Spill Liability Trust Fund, funded by the oil industry, to pay for federal and state removal costs, natural resource damage and restoration, individual claims for removal costs and damage, and research and development; and it set a $75 million limit of liability for the responsible party, which was waived by BP.[48]

During the *Deepwater Horizon* spill, BP was the focus of media and public anger, and the USCG quickly realized that it was toxic to be perceived as being too close to the corporation. As observed by the National Commission staff, the USCG experience and Unified Command doctrine viewed BP

> as a co-combatant in the fight against the oil. This was not a view shared by…the public or by high-ranking officials in other government agencies, who viewed the relationship as a far more adversarial one. On April 29, 2010, at a press conference involving senior Administration officials…, Coast Guard Rear Admiral Sally Brice O'Hara referred to BP as "our part-ner," prompting Secretary Napolitano to quickly correct the record, saying, "they are not our partner!"[49]

Referring to BP, Secretary of the Interior Ken Salazar was quoted as promis-ing that the government would "'keep our boot on their neck.'"[50] Admiral Allen, when appointed NIC, took note of the push to disavow association with BP, and on June 1 he terminated the joint press conferences previously held by the FOSC and BP. On July 4, the federal government distanced itself further from BP by disengaging from the joint BP/government website and establishing a federally managed response website, restoretheGulf.com.

The relationship between the NIC/FOSC and the responsible party BP was not made any easier by a series of dysfunctional media statements made by senior BP executives, which undermined public trust in the Unified Command concept. Admiral Allen stated, "We could never get past the perception—not the law, the perception—that somehow BP was making decisions independently, and that those decisions weren't in the best interest of the response."[51] Typical of the coverage of BP chief executive officer (CEO) Tony Hayward was the *New York Times* article titled "Another Torrent BP Works to Stem: Its CEO," in which Hayward is quoted as saying that the Gulf "'is a very big ocean' and 'the environmental impact of this disaster is likely to have been very, very, modest,'" and, on a U.S. tour imply-ing that this was about him, "'You know, I'd like my life back.'"[52] Admiral Allen concludes in his Incident Commander's report that

> the public's fundamental concern was a lack of trust in the RP [Responsible Party]. They did not believe the RP would place public and environmen-tal interests above the interests of the company and its shareholders. This general uneasiness with the role of the RP contributed to the political and social nullification of the NCP, a rejection of the role of the RP mandated by law.[53]

The distrust of BP was further exacerbated by flow-rate estimates that proved to be much too low. The BP Oil Spill Response Plan, dated June 30, 2009, and approved by the Minerals Management Service (MMS), estimated a worst-case discharge scenario from the uncapped well at 250,000 barrels per day, and the BP exploration plan for the Macondo well anticipated a maximum release of 162,000 barrels a day that could result from an uncontrolled release.[54] (The accepted esti-mate of the maximum release rate during the event was 60,000 barrels a day).[55] Since the penalties assessed under the Clean Water Act and OPA 90 are linked in part to spill volume, BP had a vested interest in minimizing the spill size esti-mate.[56] The USCG's acceptance of these estimates may have slowed the SONS declaration, the appointment of an NIC, and the mobilization of resources.

The evolution of the response activities and the concurrent organizational and leadership status are summarized in Table 8–1, which divides the response into three phases: Phase 1, the emergency phase from the time of the event until the declaration of an SONS; Phase II, the National Response phase, starting with the SONS declaration and concluding with the capping of the well; and Phase III, which ended with the effective testing of the relief well and the disestablishment of the National Incident Command.

Phase/ Date	Event Status and Activities	Organizational/Leadership Status
Phase I: April 20–April 28	April 20: *Deepwater Horizon* rig explodes at about 9:56 p.m., burns, and sinks; 11 crewmen killed, 115 evacuate Macondo well. Initial estimate is 13,000 gallons/hour spilling from rig, no undersea release. April 22: *Deepwater Horizon* sinks at 10:21 a.m., and the fire is extinguished. Oil is discharged from three different seafloor locations: the drill pipe, the end of the riser, and a kink in the riser. Evidence exists of blowout preventer failure. April 24: National Oceanic and Atmospheric Administration overflights estimate an oil release of 5,000–10,000 barrels/day.	BP activates contracts with two oil spill response organizations (Marine Spill Response Corporation and National Response Corporation). Rear Admiral Mary Landry, commander, Coast Guard Division 8 (CCGD8) assumes the position of federal on-scene coordinator (FOSC). An incident command post is established in Houma, Louisiana. The Regional Response Team is activated. BP establishes a command post at corporate headquarters in Houston with Doug Suttles, operating officer for Exploration and Production. The National Response Team is activated. The U.S. Coast Guard (USCG) establishes incident command posts in the BP facility in Houma and at BP headquarters in Houston, Texas, and Mobile, Alabama. The USCG establishes Unified Command post at Robert, Louisiana (later moved to New Orleans).
Phase II: April 28–October 1	Oil is reported ashore at Venice, Louisiana. BP starts drilling a primary relief well from *Development Driller III*. BP ceases attempts to close the blowout preventer. Cofferdam attempt fails. Environmental Protection Agency authorizes the use of subsea dispersants. BP starts drilling a backup relief well. Top-Kill Operation starts up and then fails after three attempts over three days. National Marine Fisheries Service closes 37 percent of the federal Gulf fishing zone. July 12: A three-bore capping stack is installed on the Macondo well. July 15: The choke valve is closed, oil stops flowing, and BP successfully secures the wellhead.	April 29: *Deepwater Horizon* oil spill is declared to be a spill of national significance. Gov. Bobby Jindell declares a state of emergency in Louisiana. Admiral Thad Allen is appointed national incident commander (NIC) by DHS secretary Janet Napolitano. National Incident Command Organization is established. The NIC asks the Interagency Solutions Group (ISG) to provide scientifically based information on discharge rate; the ISG forms Flow Rate Technical Group (FRTG). President Obama creates the National Commission on the BP Deepwater Horizon Oil Spill and Offshore Drilling. Dr. Marcia McNutt, director of U.S. Geological Survey, is assigned as lead for FRTG. President Obama announces a drilling moratorium in the Gulf. The NIC approves the construction of an offshore berm requested by Governor Jindell and to be funded by BP. June 15: Louisiana FRTG revises its estimate to 35,000–60,000 barrels/day. President Obama appoints Kenneth Feinberg to run a $20 billion claims fund funded by BP.

Phase/ Date	Event Status and Activities	Organizational/Leadership Status
Phase III: September 3– October 1	September 3: A blowout preventer is installed. September 17: BP successfully completes the relief well. September 19: The relief well is successfully tested and sealed.	October 1: The National Incident Command is disestablished and responsibility is transferred to the FOSC.

Table 8–1. Chronology of Event Status and Activities and of Organizational/Leadership Status.

Sources: National Commission on the BP Deepwater Horizon Oil Spill and Offshore Drilling, *Deep Water: The Gulf Oil Disaster and the Future of Offshore Drilling* (Washington, D.C.: U.S. Government Printing Office, January 2011), gpoaccess.gov/deepwater/deepwater.pdf; USCG, *Incident Specific Preparedness Review (ISPR) Deepwater Horizon Oil Spill* (Washington, D.C., March 18, 2011), uscg.mil/foia/docs/DWH/BPDWH.pdf; and the appendix to the USCG, *On Scene Coordinator Report* Deepwater Horizon *Oil Spill* (Washington, D.C.: U.S. Coast Guard, September 2011), uscg.mil/foia/docs/DWH/FOSC_DWH_Report.pdf.

Crisis Management during the BP *Deepwater Horizon* Response

Crisis management in response to extreme events is unique because the scale and scope of these events involves leaders in all levels of government and in the private sector who are not exposed to the crisis conditions they are suddenly expected to manage. Arjen Boin and Paul 't Hart note that major disasters are "extended periods of high threat, high uncertainty, and high politics that disrupt a wide range of social, political, and organizational processes" and that these events are essentially unmanageable through traditional closed organizational systems.[57] Given the potential of an uncontrolled spill causing extreme environmental, economic, and social impacts, the *Deepwater Horizon* disaster presented a number of crisis conditions. As discussed in detail in the USCG *ISPR,* the scale, scope, and duration of the response effort in these crisis conditions affected crisis management in a number of ways:

- The potential social and economic impacts of the spill and the attention it provoked created high political stakes and a highly charged media environment. The public demanded visible action, and national, state, and local politicians had to respond.

- The true size of the potential disaster was uncertain. In particular, flow-rate estimates were critical to decision making, but inaccurate estimates of initial flow rates contributed to a nine-day delay before the spill was designated an SONS and an NIC was assigned, and they may have delayed resource mobilization.

- The size of the response organization exceeded the inventory of people with the necessary skills and knowledge, leading to an organizational knowledge and skill deficit.

- The organizational structure required to manage the response was complex and large. The final federal structure contained a National Incident Command Center, a Unified Command Center, incident command posts in four states, seventeen branch incident command posts, thirty-two staging areas, and one aviation coordination center.[58] State and local operations centers and agency operations centers in Washington, D.C., and various Department of Defense operations centers also participated in the response.

- Individuals and organizations not anticipated by the NCP (e.g., the Interagency Solutions Group, the Source Control Group, and the Flow Rate Technical Group [FRTG]) were included in the decision-making process.

- Agency heads and department secretaries were directly involved in decision making. USCG commandant Admiral Thad Allen was NIC, EPA administrator Lisa Jackson personally made dispersant application decisions, U.S. Geological Survey administrator Marcia McNutt was chair of the FRTG, NOAA administrator Jane Lubchenko was involved in spill size estimates, DHS secretary Napolitano was PFO, Department of Energy secretary Steven Chu chaired the Source Control Group, and Interior secretary Salazar and MMS director Lars Herbst were directing source control operations.

- Although in charge of the spill response, the USCG had to rely on the MMS (later, the Bureau of Ocean Energy Management) and BP for subsurface and source control technology and expertise.

- The technology to control and kill the well was improvised after the blowout and untested.[59]

- BP's crisis management was sabotaged by its preincident management failures. According to the Oil Spill Commission's General Counsel's report, these failures included "(1) ineffective leadership at critical times; (2) ineffective communication and siloing of information; (3) failure to provide timely procedures; (4) poor training and supervision of employees; (5) ineffective management and oversight of contractors; (6) inadequate use of technology; and (7) failure to appropriately analyze and appreciate risk."[60]

- The creation of senior decision and technical support groups (e.g., the FTRG, the Interagency Solutions Group) and the direct involvement of cabinet secretaries and agency heads made the roles of the National Response Team and Regional Response Teams redundant, changing the information

sharing and reporting protocols established by the NCP and reinforced by
USCG training and exercising.

• The desire for information that senior levels within the government
imposed on the NIC and Unified Command overwhelmed and distracted the
response.[61]

These factors forced a shift from the technocratic management style typical
of the highly effective USCG leadership culture to an active, collaborative leadership style that can function in the open, participatory system needed to deal with
extreme events; as a result, leaders had to improvise since much of what they were
facing was beyond their experience. Karl Weick and Kathleen Sutcliffe describe
this situation, in which leaders must draw on what is familiar while recognizing
what is different from all other situations they have faced, as "maintaining ambiva-
lence."[62] It has also been described as a need for agility when working in the complex, dynamic crisis environment, where adaptability, creativity, and improvisation
are as valuable as discipline and structure.[63]

In this case, the discipline and structure provided by the NCP and NIMS
proved to be inadequate, testing the crisis management skills of the NIC and the
FOSCs. The USCG's *ISPR* concludes, "The National Incident Commander concept worked very well in this incident, and provides a model for pre-identifying
individuals with the necessary crisis management skills to lead response efforts
and effectively manage future national incidents."[64]

However, the duration of the spill challenged the ability of the USCG and
BP to staff senior leadership positions for an extended period. Three senior officers—Rear Admirals Mary Landry, James Watson, and Paul Zukunft—rotated
through the FOSC position, but Admiral Allen remained NIC for the duration.
Doug Suttles, BP's director of Exploration and Production and senior on-scene
manager, led the BP technical response, also for the duration. The USCG's *ISPR*
identified the lack of crisis management "bench strength" in government and
industry as an issue:

> The Deepwater Horizon incident placed people in crisis management
> roles; however, not all were able to demonstrate leadership in crisis as a
> core competency. The performance of crisis leaders during this incident
> was uneven at best. In some cases, perceived ineffective leadership led to
> loss of public confidence in the ability of Government and industry to man-
> age the response to the spill."[65]

In the *ISPR*'s chapter on the characteristics and qualifications of an effective
crisis leader, "lessons learned" include that "superb crisis leadership is essential
for effective response to a major national domestic incident" and that "leaders
who are expected to perform as crisis managers need to be trained and experienced in crisis management, and should not be placed into such positions without

Organization	Position and Name
BP	Carl-Henric Svanbert, chairman
	Tony Hayward, chief executive officer
	Robert Dudley, managing director
	Doug Suttles, on-scene manager
	Richard Lynch, vice president–source control
U.S. Coast Guard (USCG)	Admiral Thad Allen, commandant and incident commander
	Vice Admiral Sally Brice O'Hara, vice commandant
	Rear Admiral Mary Landry, commander, USCG Division 8 and federal on-scene coordinator (FOSC)
	Rear Admiral James Watson, FOSC
	Rear Admiral Paul Zukunft, FOSC
Department of Homeland Security	Janet Napolitano, secretary
Department of the Interior	Ken Salazar, secretary
	Marcia McNutt, director, USGS (lead of Flow Rate Technical Group)
Department of Energy	Steven Chu, secretary and Sources Control Group lead
National Oceanic and Atmospheric Administration	Jane Lubchenko, administrator
State of Louisiana	Bobby Jindell, governor
	Charlotte Randolph, president, Lafourche Parish
	Billy Nungesser, president, Plaquemines Parish

Table 8–2. Key Leaders during the BP Deepwater Horizon Response.

applicable training."[66] Table 8–2 provides an overview of the key leadership positions during the BP Deepwater spill response.

The crisis management environment was complex technically, organizationally, and politically. Admiral Allen's successful navigation through this leadership labyrinth preserved the response organization's ability to stay focused and eventually succeed. He demonstrated the crisis management quality that Weick and Sutcliffe define as "mindfulness":

> the combination of ongoing scrutiny of existing expectations, continuous refinement and differentiation of expectations based on newer experiences, willingness and capability to invent new expectations that make sense of unprecedented events, a more nuanced appreciation of context and ways to deal with it, and identification of new dimensions of context that improve foresight and current functioning.[67]

His success as NIC was also due, in part, to his ability to accomplish each of the six critical factors for crisis managers identified by Harrald:[68]

1. *Achieve awareness.* Leaders and decision makers must have a reasonably accurate situational awareness of the reality they are facing and of what should be done.

2. *Demonstrate competence.* Effective leadership is impossible if leaders cannot demonstrate that they understand what can and should be done about the crisis they are facing, that they understand the plans and procedures in place to deal with the crisis, and that they know and trust the people tasked with assisting those affected.

3. *Be honest.* As stated by Peggy Noonan, "Political leadership in times of crisis is a delicate thing. You have to be frank about the fix you're in without being demoralizing. You have to seem confident without seeming out of touch with reality."[69] The public can quickly separate political spin from honest messages.

4. *Be empathic.* You have to be human without indulging all your very human emotions. "Rudy Giuliani set the modern standard on 9/11."[70] As reported by CNN, when asked the inevitable "how many died" question, Guiliani replied, "more than any of us can bear ultimately."[71]

5. *Communicate clearly and frequently.* The National Governors Association identifies the key role of the governor as the chief communicator during a crisis, noting that "during a major disaster or catastrophe the media, the public and the political leadership will rely on the governor as the primary source of information on the nature of the event, needed public response and the status of relief and recovery efforts."[72]

6. *Be able to deal with failure.* Most political, appointed, and corporate leaders achieved their positions because they were always associated with success. In the early days of a catastrophic event, failure is more common than success. Understanding and dealing with the failures are critical, but a common political and personal reaction is denial and deflection.

Conclusions

The environmental, ecological, and social impacts of the BP *Deepwater Horizon* oil spill will not be known for years. A clear sign that the media and public consider response to the spill a success was the complete absence of press coverage on July 15, 2011, the one-year anniversary of the capping and sealing of the Macondo 252 well. Although regional environmental and economic impacts remained, the spill of the century was clearly last year's problem. BP, with a new CEO, has resumed its profitability, and permits have been issued for offshore exploration and drilling in the Gulf. The Obama administration, while trying to avert a historic default of the U.S. government, could claim the spill response as one of its achievements. Four critical factors contributed to this perceived success:

1. BP eventually controlled the source, stopping the spill by capping the well and drilling a relief well.

2. The oil that reached the shore was much less than predicted, resulting in far fewer images of dying birds, turtles, and mammals and of oiled beaches than needed to create lasting public outrage.

3. President Obama was able to persuade BP to fund the $20 billion oil spill claims fund, providing a path for relatively rapid compensation for losses. Although an imperfect solution, it prevented a protracted and adversarial settlement process that would have received extensive media coverage.

4. Admiral Allen, as NIC, managed complex political and media agendas and relationships as well as ensuring that the essential USCG-BP partnership continued to function and that the response effort's strategic direction was maintained.

However, perceptions of success are difficult to correlate with actual response performance measures. Response to the BP *Deepwater Horizon* event was the largest oil spill response in history, and the activity output was truly impressive. According to the USCG's *ISPR,* the output included

- 3.8 million feet of hard boom deployed

- 9.7 million feet of soft boom deployed

- 2,557 miles of boom deployed

- 1.8 million gallons of dispersant applied

- 411 in situ burns ignited.[73]

The oil spill recovery outcomes due to these activities are less impressive. The total oil spilled from Macondo well was estimated to be 4,928,100 barrels +/–10 percent, 19.175 times the *Exxon Valdez* spill and 3.36 times the *Exxon Valdez* cargo capacity,[74] but as shown below, the entire USCG-managed response effort was able to skim, burn, or disperse only 16 percent of the oil. The estimates of the oil outflow outcomes as reported by the commission are

- Recovered from wellhead: 17 percent

- Oil burned: 5 percent

- Oil skimmed: 3 percent

- Oil chemically dispersed: 8 percent

- Oil naturally dispersed: 16 percent

- Oil evaporated or dissolved: 25 percent

- Residual oil: 26 percent.[75]

The most effective technique was to recover oil directly from the wellhead, a method that was constrained by the capacity of surface vessels to load the recovered oil. As in all spills, the natural ability of the ocean to disperse and dissolve the pollutants dwarfed the ability of our technological systems to clean up the ocean's failures. It should also be noted that over one-quarter of the oil spilled was not accounted for and is assumed to be on the ocean floor or suspended in the water column.

The BP *Deepwater Horizon* spill is another reminder not only that low probability/high consequence events will occur but also that the uniqueness and unpredictability of these events will continue to confound our ability to plan and prepare. When they do occur, these events may have high political consequences; and when the political stakes are high, involvement by senior political, appointed, and corporate leaders must be expected and accounted for in planning, preparing, and exercising. Admiral Allen states in his Incident Commander's report that "in the aftermath of events like September 11th and Hurricane Katrina, the public expects (and demands) a robust well-coordinated, whole-of-government response to major domestic incidents."[76] Our response to extreme events in federal government systems requires a strongly led and adequately resourced national response, but it must also respect the needs and prerogatives of state and local governments. Current national doctrine is inconsistent and conflicting on how these simultaneous goals are to be achieved. The BP *Deepwater Horizon* response provides a well-documented case history for those tasked with revising national preparedness and response doctrine.

Endnotes

1   U.S. Coast Guard (USCG), *Report of Investigation into the Circumstances Surrounding the Explosion, Fire, Sinking and Loss of Eleven Crew Members Aboard the Mobile Offshore Drilling Unit Deepwater Horizon in the Gulf of Mexico April 20–22, 2010*, vol. 1 (Washington, D.C.: U.S. Coast Guard, 2011), iii, hsdl.org/?view&did=6700.

2   USCG, *Incident Specific Preparedness Review (ISPR) Deepwater Horizon Oil Spill* (Washington, D.C., March 18, 2011), 34, 156, uscg.mil/foia/docs/DWH/BPDWH.pdf.

3   Peter Lehner, *In Deep Water: The Anatomy of a Disaster, the Fate of the Gulf, and How to End Our Oil Addiction* (New York: OR Books LLC [The Experiment], 2010), 31.

4   As defined in 33 CFR 15, 1020, a vessel of opportunity is "a vessel engaged in spill response activities that is normally and substantially involved in activities other than spill response and not a vessel carrying oil as a primary cargo," 391, edocket.access.gpo.gov/cfr_2001/julqtr/pdf/33cfr155.1020.pdf.

5   USCG, *ISPR,* 156.

6   Ibid., 137.

7   National Commission on the BP Deepwater Horizon Oil Spill and Offshore Drilling (hereafter, National Commission), *Deep Water: The Gulf Oil Disaster and the Future of Offshore Drilling* (Washington, D.C.: U.S. Government Printing Office, January 2011), gpoaccess.gov/deepwater/deepwater.pdf.

8   See, for example, Lehner, *In Deep Water;* Loren C. Steffy, *Drowning in Oil: BP and the Reckless Pursuit of Profit* (New York: McGraw Hill, 2011); and Bob Kavner, *Disaster on the Horizon: High Stakes, High Risks, and the Story behind the Deepwater Well Blowout* (White River Junction, Vt.: Chelsea Green Publishing, 2010).

9   National Commission, *Stopping the Spill: The Five Month Effort to Kill the Macondo Well,* Staff Working Paper 6 (Washington, D.C.: January 2011), oilspillcommission.gov/sites/default/files/documents/Updated%20Containment%20Working%20Paper.pdf.

10   See note 2.

11   USCG, *Report of Investigation;* Bureau of Ocean Energy Management, Regulation and Enforcement, *Report Regarding the Causes of the April 20, 2010 Macondo Well Blowout* (Washington, D.C.: U.S. Department of the Interior, September 14, 2011), boemre.gov/pdfs/maps/dwhfinal.pdf.

12   National Commission, *Deep Water,* 29.

13   Steffy, *Drowning in Oil,* 180.

14   USCG, *ISPR,* 29.

15   USCG, *On Scene Coordinator Report* Deepwater Horizon *Oil Spill* (Washington, D.C.: USCG, September 2011), 28, uscg.mil/foia/docs/DWH/FOSC_DWH_Report.pdf.

16   USCG, *ISPR,* 85.

17   USCG, *On Scene Coordinator Report,* 1.

18   White House, "Statement by the President on the Economy and the Oil Spill in the Gulf of Mexico," April 30, 2010, whitehouse.gov/the-press-office/statement-president-economy-and-oil-spill-gulf-mexico.

19   USCG, *ISPR,* 75.

20   Ibid., 76.

21   Ibid., 91.

22   Karen Tumulty, "Obama Struggling to Show He's in Control of Oil Spill," *Washington Post,* May 28, 2010, washingtonpost.com/wp-dyn/content/article/2010/05/27/AR2010052701172.html (accessed November 11, 2011).

23   USCG, *ISPR,* 75.

24   Ibid., 118.

25   Ibid., 76.

26   Thad Allen, *National Incident Commander's Report: MC252 Deepwater Horizon* (October 1, 2010), 20, nrt.org/production/NRT/NRTWeb.nsf/AllAttachmentsByTitle/SA-1065NICReport/$File/Binder1.pdf?OpenElement.

27   USCG, *ISPR,* 121.

28   Ibid., 124.

29   National Commission, *Deep Water,* 138.

30   USCG, *ISPR,* 71.

31   John R. Harrald and William A. Wallace, "We Were Always Reorganizing…Some Crisis Management Implications of the *Exxon Valdez* Spill," *Industrial and Environmental Crisis Quarterly* 6, no. 3 (1992): 197–217; Ann Hayward Walker et al., *Implementing an Effective Response Management System,* white paper for 1995 International Oil Spill Conference, Technical Report IOSC-0001 (Washington, D.C.: American Petroleum Institute, 1995).

32   National Response Team, *Interim Final Reconciliation Analysis of the Federal Response Plan, National Oil and Hazardous Substances Pollution Contingency Plan, U.S. Government Interagency Domestic Terrorism Concept of Operations Plan and the Federal Radiological Emergency Response Plan* (Washington, D.C., July 31, 2003), 14.

33   40 CFR 300.135, gpo.gov/fdsys/pkg/CFR-2009-title40-vol27/pdf/CFR-2009-title40-vol27-sec300-135.pdf.

34   National Response Team, *Interim Final Reconciliation Analysis.*

35   Harrald and Wallace, "We Were Always Reorganizing."

36   Claire B. Rubin and John R. Harrald, "The National Response Plan, the National Incident Management System, and the Federal Response Plan," in *The McGraw Hill Homeland Security Handbook,* ed. David G. Kamien, 677–688 (New York: McGraw-Hill, 2006).

37   USCG, *ISPR,* 61, 63.

38   Ibid., 71.

39   National Commission, *Deep Water,* 138–139.

40   Raffi Khatchadourian, "The Gulf War: Were There Any Heroes in the BP Disaster?" *New Yorker,* March 14, 2011.

41   Allen, *National Incident Commander's Report,* 17.

42   Khatchadourian, "Gulf War," 49.

43   National Commission, *Deep Water,* 139.

44   Ibid., 139.

45   USCG, *ISPR,* 105.

46   Allen, *National Incident Commander's Report,* 9.

47   Alaska Oil Spill Commission, *Spill: The Wreck of the Exxon Valdez* (State of Alaska, 1990).

48   National Commission, *Staff Working Paper 14 Unlawful Discharges of Oil: Legal Authorities for Civil and Criminal Enforcement and Damage Recovery* (Washington, D.C., January 2011), 7–8.

49   National Commission, *Decision-Making within the Unified Command,* Staff Working Paper 2 (originally released October 6, 2010; updated January 11, 2011), 13, oilspillcommission.gov/sites/default/files/documents/Updated%20Unified%20Command%20Working%20Paper.pdf, citing Tim Dickinson, "The Spill, the Scandal, and the President," *Rolling Stone,* June 24, 2010.

50   Matthew Bigg, "U.S. Keeps 'Boot on Neck' of BP over Spill," Reuters (May 24, 2010), reuters.com/article/2010/05/24/us-oil-rig-leak-idUSTRE6430AR20100524 (accessed November 11, 2011).

51   Khatchadourian, "Gulf War," 40.

52   Jad Mouawad and Clifford Krauss, "Another Torrent BP Works to Stem: Its CEO," *New York Times,* June 3, 2010, nytimes.com/2010/06/04/us/04image.html (accessed November 11, 2011).

53   Allen, *National Incident Commander's Report,* 12.

54   USCG, *ISPR,* 28.

55   Ibid., 146–147.

56   Steffy, *Drowning in Oil,* 186.

57   Arjen Boin and Paul 't Hart, "Public Leadership in Times of Crisis: Mission Impossible?" *Public Administration Review* 63, no. 5 (2003): 545, gfoa.org/downloads/LeadershipToolkitPAECrisis.pdf.

58   USCG, *ISPR,* 156.

59   Ibid., 110.

60   National Commission, Chief Counsel's Report, *Macondo: The Gulf Oil Disaster* (Washington, D.C., 2011), 225, oilspillcommission.gov/sites/default/files/documents/C21462-407_CCR_for_print_0.pdf.

61   USCG, *ISPR,* 96.

62   Karl E. Weick and Kathleen M. Sutcliffe, *Managing the Unexpected: Assuring High Performance in an Age of Complexity* (San Francisco: Jossey-Bass, 2001), 168.

63   John R. Harrald, "Agility and Discipline: Critical Success Factors for Disaster Response," *Annals of the American Academy of Political and Social Sciences* 604, no. 1 (March 2006): 256–272.

64   USCG, *ISPR,* 57.

65   Ibid.

66   Ibid, 60.

67   Weick and Sutcliffe, *Managing the Unexpected,* 42.

68   John R. Harrald, "Hurricane Katrina: Crisis Leadership That Failed a Country," in *Mega-crises: Understanding the Prospects, Nature, Characteristics and Effects of Cataclysmic Events,* ed. Ira Helsloot et al. (Springfield, Ill.: Charles C. Thomas, 2012), 48.

69   Peggy Noonen, "After the Storm," *Wall Street Journal,* September 1, 2005, online.wsj.com/article/SB122487570244867421.html (accessed August 13, 2011).

70   Ibid.

71 CNN.com Transcripts, "New York's Governor and Mayor of New York City Address Concerns of the Damage," September 11, 2001, transcripts.cnn.com/TRANSCRIPTS/0109/11/bn.42.html (accessed August 13, 2011).

72 NGA, Office of Management Consulting and Training, "Lessons Learned," 4.

73 USCG, *ISPR*, 156.

74 Ibid., 34.

75 Ibid., 156.

76 Allen, *National Incident Commander's Report*, 5.

Chapter 9

From a Painful Past
to an Uncertain Future

Patrick Roberts, Robert Ward,* and Gary Wamsley

In their discussions of the evolution of U.S. emergency management over the past century, the preceding authors addressed three critical areas: (1) the historical legacy that frames many current views of emergency management and particularly the role of the federal government; (2) the underlying processes affecting these views and the increasing expectations of government's responsibilities; and (3) the heightened and intensified debate that took place at all levels of government in the aftermath of the devastation wrought by Hurricanes Katrina, Rita, and Wilma in 2005 and the *Deepwater Horizon* explosion and oil spill in 2010. The authors sought to answer a critical, overriding question: What should be the role and functions of the federal government for major and catastrophic disasters in the United States?

The Role of the Federal Government in Emergency Management until 1950

In Chapters 2 and 3, David Butler shows that the federal government has had a long and checkered history in emergency management. Federal assistance to communities affected by natural disasters can be traced back to the early 1800s, but the federal government usually intervened only well after the event, and its involvement was limited to relieving the suffering of the affected communities and restoring critical infrastructure. In the immediate aftermath of a disaster, victims sought assistance from neighbors, religious groups, and the civic community, but not necessarily from government. Natural disasters were viewed as acts of God—unavoidable events that exceeded a government's power both to prevent and to redress their consequences.

---

* Sadly, Robert Ward, one of the chapter's original authors, died on February 3, 2011.

The federal government's limited, ad hoc approach to natural disasters began to change at the beginning of the twentieth century. Butler shows that this shift in attitude was affected by three critical factors in the late 1800s. First, the sheer magnitude of several events, including the Great Chicago Fire of 1871 and the Johnstown Flood of 1889, raised awareness of the potential devastation to communities. Second, the emergence of a scientific understanding of hazard risk contributed to programs to mitigate risk; such programs would bear fruit in the twentieth century in legislation such as California's 1933 Field Act, which mandated earthquake protection in the construction of schools. Finally, the American Red Cross demonstrated that a new type of entity, a humanitarian organization, could develop a credible capacity for organizing relief efforts for the affected communities. Although the federal government remained at a distance from disaster response operations, it chartered the American Red Cross as the official disaster response agency. These were the first tentative steps toward ongoing federal involvement in emergency management.

During the first half of the twentieth century, major catastrophes focused government and public attention on the need to develop more structured and permanent systems to respond to catastrophic events. The Galveston Hurricane of 1900 and the San Francisco Earthquake of 1906 demonstrated the vulnerability and frailty of communities located in disaster-prone areas. The scale of these two disasters required the mobilization of unprecedented response and recovery efforts, which included government resources. Yet despite the severity of these events, government officials at all levels continued to deny that government could or should play a role in minimizing the effects of a disaster. The role of the federal government therefore remained limited to post-disaster assistance.

Continued experiences with disasters during the 1920s and 1930s gradually changed perceptions of government's role in relation to major events and influenced the degree to which the federal and state governments engaged in disaster and emergency management. Following the Great Mississippi Flood of 1927, President Calvin Coolidge appointed the first "flood czar" (Herbert Hoover) to coordinate relief efforts. The federal government's role began to expand with the development of flood control systems to mitigate the potential harm from nature. Similarly, after the earthquake that struck Long Beach in 1933, the state of California began taking a series of steps to acknowledge and deal with its earthquake hazards and risks, including the effort to create and codify building standards for at-risk areas.

The drought that became known as the Dust Bowl in the 1930s brought on further involvement by federal and state governments in land management for both land preservation and pre-disaster mitigation. Yet governments at all levels neglected to develop formal systems to deal with pre-disaster mitigation and post-disaster recovery.

Civil Defense and the Dual-Use Approach to Emergency Management: 1950–2001

By the second half of the twentieth century, the role of government at all levels—and of the federal government in particular—began to shift. As discussed in Chapters 4 and 5, the shift resulted, in part, from changes in the definition of a disaster and from an expanded view of the factors that pose threats to people and the communities in which they live. Prior to World War II, Americans viewed disasters as the effects of powerful earthquakes, hurricanes, and other weather systems. But with the war, the definition gradually expanded to include the effects of man-made catastrophes: those that resulted from unintentional consequences of complex industrial systems within communities and the subsequent failures of people to adequately manage and/or control such systems. It further expanded to include the effects of attacks from abroad. The possibility of air raids and bombings, the shelling of an oil company's maintenance facility by a submarine off the coast of California, and the landing of saboteurs on the East Coast all indicated the need for dealing with intentionally harmful actions.

The expansion of the definition of disaster to include the effects of intentional acts led to the development of civil defense systems designed to both prevent and deal with those consequences. The Cold War and the successful acquisition of nuclear weapons by the Soviet Union (and later other countries) broadened the scope of such threats and placed new demands on emergency management systems.

As Keith Bea discusses in Chapter 4, the federal government initially viewed the need to develop effective civil defense systems as an opportunity to formalize its response to both natural disasters and intentional acts of harm. While reaction to a form of dual-use policy was positive at first, the concept was eventually rejected in favor of the development of two interlocking systems for dealing with disasters: one focused on natural and unintentional human-caused events and the other on intentional human acts to cause harm.

In 1950, the Federal Disaster Assistance Act (P.L. 81-875) spelled out the federal government's response to natural disaster. Once the president issued a disaster declaration, federal equipment, supplies, and people could be brought into the affected areas. The president would then delegate administrative control of relief efforts to the Housing and Home Finance Administration. But while the legislation enshrined a federal role in disaster relief in law, it also reinforced the idea that the primary responsibility for natural and unintentional human-caused disasters lay with local and state governments and that the federal role in such events was supplemental.

Congress also passed the Civil Defense Act in 1950, paving the way for the Federal Civil Defense Administration (FCDA), an independent federal agency that reported directly to the president. The FCDA had authority to coordinate civil defense efforts by federal, state, and local governments, but state and local governments assumed primary responsibility for planning and response. Most of the early civil defense funding flowed through interstate compacts and state and local coffers.[1]

During the 1950s and 1960s, escalating tension between the United States and the Soviet Union, especially as it related to the nuclear arms race, reinforced the civil defense side of emergency management. Funding for disaster relief increased, but preparation for attack was the federal government's first priority. The linkage between civil defense efforts and the U.S. Department of Defense was thus strengthened, but the inclusion of natural hazards and disaster planning with civil defense approaches proved problematic.[2]

In the years that followed, the search for balance between an effective natural disaster system and an effective civil defense system led to a series of reorganizations and reassignments of authority. Attempts to decentralize natural disaster response and separate it from civil defense resulted in a confusing set of loosely coordinated response systems. In addition, several major natural disasters—the Alaska earthquake of 1964, the San Fernando earthquake on 1971, and hurricanes on the Gulf Coast—exposed weaknesses in the emergency management system that was in place. Once again, public and political pressure mounted for the federal government to redesign the nation's approach to disaster response.

After pressure from state governments seeking a single national-level disaster organization rather than an alphabet soup of agencies, President Jimmy Carter created the Federal Emergency Management Agency (FEMA) by executive order in 1979. This marked a resurgence of the concept of a dual-use policy capable of handling both natural and man-made disasters. As originally conceived, FEMA was to focus primarily on natural disaster response and secondarily on civil defense, but subsequent administrations changed these priorities. As part of a broad strategy to defeat the Soviet "evil empire" during the Cold War, Ronald Reagan's administration gave FEMA the responsibility to develop and oversee its "continuity of government program." Supported by a seven-year, $4.2 billion budget, the program was to ensure that the government could continue to operate in the event of a nuclear attack and to provide for the survival of at least some of the population. This placed FEMA at the center of developing the facilities and equipment needed to sustain government operations in the event of a nuclear war, as well as of overseeing a crisis evacuation plan intended to save 70–80 percent of the population.[3]

FEMA's new civil defense focus drew attention and resources away from the natural disaster response system. In the 1980s and 1990s, the agency was widely criticized for the federal government's slow response to earthquakes in California, hurricanes in Puerto Rico and South Carolina, and Hurricane Andrew, which hit the Florida coast just weeks before the 1992 presidential election that pitted incumbent George H. W. Bush against Arkansas governor Bill Clinton. The political lessons learned from these disasters were not lost on President Clinton or on James Lee Witt, whom Clinton appointed FEMA director in 1993. Following recommendations posed in emergency management studies conducted by the National Academy of Public Administration (NAPA), the Government Accountability Office, the Congressional Research Service, and FEMA's inspector general, Clinton and Witt swiftly reduced FEMA's civil defense function and made the natural disaster response system a priority. The dual-use policy was again scrapped in favor of a new, all-hazards approach to emergency preparedness and response.

As Richard Sylves's examination of presidential emergency declarations makes clear (Chapter 5), both disaster relief funding and the types of disasters considered eligible for relief increased at the end of the twentieth century. Together, growth in political support for relief efforts and increased professionalism in emergency management created an environment where the federal government's role expanded and the political and public perceptions of a professionally run, competent federal system began to emerge. As in previous periods, focusing events served as the primary driver for the expanding role of the federal government.

Emergency Management in the Age of Terrorism

So what should the role of the federal government be in minor, major, and catastrophic disasters in the United States? What form should federal involvement take?

In Chapter 6, John R. Harrald outlines the answer in his description of the changes that have occurred in FEMA and emergency management since September 11, 2001. The emergency management response to the attacks on the World Trade Center and the Pentagon revealed that an all-hazards system could be effective in responding to terrorist attacks. The after-action analysis, however, advanced the proposition that the United States needed to better integrate intelligence, law enforcement, and emergency management. As a result, as directed by President George W. Bush, a major reorganization of the federal government was undertaken in 2002, in which dispersed functions were folded into the newly created U.S. Department of Homeland Security (DHS). The Bush administration further mandated a single national plan for response, and the official National Response Plan (NRP) was finalized in December 2004.

The National Incident Management System (NIMS) served as the operational basis for the NRP. As discussed in Chapter 7, NIMS formalizes processes across incident types and professional fields. It incorporates the Incident Command System (ICS), which the Department of Agriculture's Forest Service has used effectively as a standardized coordinating system for fighting forest fires and brushfires. However, some experts argue that it is not sufficiently flexible to deal with diverse disasters or the variety of unexpected issues that typically arise during a disaster response operation.[4]

The NRP and NIMS were intended to create a centralized coordinating system under the control of the federal government. In order to receive DHS funds, state and local governments were required to comply with the newly established centralized system. The NRP modified the all-hazards approach used in the emergency management systems of most state and local governments, however, substituting agent-specific systems and annexes (chemical, biological, etc.). This caused significant complications at the state and local levels. *The Federal Response to Hurricane Katrina: Lessons Learned* takes the NRP to task and notes that emergency plans "came up short."[5]

While the new system indeed created a centralized coordinating structure, it also established an artificial barrier between formal response systems and the informal networks that had historically formed at the local level to respond to disasters. In essence, it stripped local response systems of their flexibility and adaptability in favor of a closed, highly structured, and rigid system.

When Hurricane Katrina made landfall on the Gulf Coast in August 2005, the NRP (having been finalized only eight months earlier) had not yet been fully integrated at the state and local government levels, which negated any potential benefits of the new approach. The situation demanded clarity and flexibility, but the NRP provided the rigidity of hierarchy with all the confusion that comes with a new system. Many responders at all levels of government, including the highest level of the federal government, had little understanding of who was responsible for what or what the new lines of authority were. In addition, a high wall of security was built into the newly established system, making it nearly impossible to take advantage of volunteer assistance and thus limiting the system's response capacity. The media tracked the ineffective, confused response in real time before national and international audiences, and commentators lay much of the blame with FEMA. The failure of the response efforts reopened discussion about the emergency management system and focused debate on the federal government's role in disaster response.

Blaming the federal government for disaster losses is a common but ultimately misleading narrative. State and local governments, the business community, and the public have all contributed to the failure of the emergency management response system. Even the Red Cross has experienced major problems and failures. As Melanie Gall and Susan L. Cutter discuss in Chapter 7, by allowing an influx of residents into flood zones, along the coastlines, and into other high-risk areas; by ignoring the need to preserve natural areas that would buffer development from the wrath of a storm; by failing to enact and enforce strict building codes; and by neglecting to adequately plan for evacuation, citizens and state and local governments have all contributed to the increased vulnerability of communities to disasters.

For many years, the federal government—primarily through FEMA—has encouraged local communities to plan for disasters and to engage in mitigation measures to reduce whatever impact disasters might have. By and large, however, communities have resisted such measures, viewing mitigation as an economic brake that would slow growth and undermine prosperity. Many localities have instead relied on the National Flood Insurance Program and other approaches that transfer the risk rather than reducing it. Attempts by the federal government to limit the number of claims for losses in these localities have been met with stiff resistance and have failed to deter expansion into areas of great potential harm. Nevertheless, while citizens expect the federal government to come to their rescue when disaster strikes, it is the capacity of the local community that determines how well a community survives and how quickly life is restored to normal.

This aerial view of the damaged Mississippi Gulf Coast shows the destruction and debris carried inland by the storm surge. Photo courtesy of the Federal Emergency Management Agency/ Marty Bahamonde.

A New Kind of Test

The first major test of the post-Katrina emergency response system was one of the least expected. When the *Deepwater Horizon* rig exploded on April 20, 2010, and sank two days later, oil gushed into the Gulf of Mexico, and by the time the well was capped on July 15, five million barrels of crude oil had escaped, a volume nearly twenty times larger than that of the 1989 *Exxon Valdez* oil spill. As Jack Harrald explains in Chapter 8, the unusual nature of the disaster exposed fissures in the response system. The oil spill occurred in U.S. waters, so the response was conducted according to the Oil Pollution Act of 1990 and the National Contingency Plan (last revised in 1994). However, few senior government officials understood how the National Contingency Plan assigned roles and responsibilities. At the same time, FEMA conducted its response according to guidance provided by the familiar Stafford Act authority and National Response Framework doctrine of 2008.

The severity of the event and the around-the-clock media coverage put pressure on President Barack Obama to take action. Among other things, the president directed the Coast Guard to triple the size of the response, an order that was difficult to implement and may have actually slowed progress because many of the new personnel on the scene were not trained in NIMS or ICS. But despite some confusion, the administration's staff and appointed agency leaders managed to reconcile interagency processes to coordinate an effective response. While the federal government distanced itself publicly from BP, which was then a target of outrage, the White House and federal agencies worked with BP behind the scenes as an important partner in the response and recovery.

In the end, the oil spill response exposed the difficulties in preparing for the unexpected. For example, BP had only a boilerplate advance safety plan. The 583-page document, titled *Regional Oil Spill Response Plan—Gulf of Mexico,*[6] offers suggestions for how to handle the news media in the event of a crisis but says little about how to respond to gushing oil from a deepwater well.[7] The government's disaster plans were also of little help: they were relatively clear about how to respond to earthquakes or hurricanes within the United States, but oil spill response had not received much attention since the *Exxon Valdez* spill two decades earlier in Alaska. Following that event, the federal government passed the Oil Pollution Act of 1990, which, among other things, provided for a phasing in of a double-hull ship design.

The *Deepwater Horizon* incident, however, was a very different kind of accident, occurring at a well in the Gulf of Mexico, not a ship in Alaskan waters. Government agencies competed with private companies and with each other for leadership in the response, and eventually the White House made capping the Macondo 252 well and cleaning the waters a priority under intense media pressure. The oil dispersed through natural and human efforts, and the one-year anniversary of the capping and sealing of the well received almost no coverage. In disaster politics, sometimes no news is good news.

The *Deepwater Horizon* response faded into memory, and history may count it as a mixed success. Nevertheless, the overlapping authorities and delayed responses raise the question of how the government will prepare for the disasters of the future. New diseases and industrial accidents will test existing plans, and earthquakes and hurricanes will occur in unexpected places, outside the reach of most people's lifetime memories. Understanding how the federal government's role in disaster management has grown requires turning from a litany of the disasters themselves to an analysis of the policy process and the unusually fragmented structure of the U.S. government.

Endnotes

1   Andrew Grossman, *Neither Dead nor Red: Civil Defense and American Political Development during the Early Cold War* (New York: Taylor & Francis, 2001), 70; Wilbur J. Cohen and Evelyn F. Boyer, "Federal Civil Defense Act of 1950: Summary and Legislative History," *Social Security Bulletin* (April 1951): 11–16.

2   Dee Garrison, *Bracing for Armageddon: Why Civil Defense Never Worked* (New York: Oxford University Press, 2006); James M. Landis, "The Central Problem of Civilian Defense: An Appraisal," *State Government* 23, no. 11 (November 1950).

3   Gary L. Wamsley et al., *Coping with Catastrophe: Building an Emergency Management System to Meet People's Needs in Natural and Manmade Disasters*. (Washington, D.C.: National Academy of Public Administration, 1993).

4   See, for example, Russell R. Dynes, "Social Capital: Dealing with Community Emergencies," *Homeland Security Affairs* 2 (July 2006): 1–26, hsaj.org/pages/volume2/issue2/pdfs/2.2.5.pdf.

5   Frances F. Townsend, *The Federal Response to Hurricane Katrina: Lessons Learned* (Washington, D.C.: The White House, February 2006), 1.

6   BP, *Regional Oil Spill Response Plan—Gulf of Mexico* (June 2009), publicintelligence.net/bp-gulf-of-mexico-regional-oil-spill-response-plan.

7   Patrick S. Roberts, "Our Responder in Chief," *National Affairs* (Fall 2010): 75–102.

Chapter 10

The Evolving Federal Role in Emergency Management: Policies and Processes

Patrick Roberts, Robert Ward, and Gary Wamsley

As demonstrated throughout this book, the U.S. emergency management system has developed in reaction to events, rather than proactively according to comprehensive and well-conceived plans. It is natural for the public to expect such plans and the effective implementation of them. But emergency management in the United States, with the exception of a few instances and notable interludes, has gained a reputation for its ad hoc character. Policy makers and administrators often seem to craft plans and procedures in response to the last disaster, and the government appears to get caught by surprise when the next event occurs.

While the public's expectations are understandable, they may be somewhat unreasonable given the complex nature of the government our Founders created. We incorrectly think and speak of our government as one based on the "separation of powers," but while the institutions and levels of our complex, democratized republic are "separate" in that they are institutionally distinct from one another, in actuality the Constitution makes their powers shared or overlapped. This makes meeting the demands of planning for and responding to emergencies and disasters profoundly difficult for emergency management agencies in the United States. It requires of emergency managers a quality of nonpartisan, political, and interorganizational administrative and management skills that is hard to find and even harder to cultivate and practice.

Still another reason for the criticism heaped upon emergency management lies in the character or nature of disasters. Disasters are rare, attention-grabbing, tragic, and even catastrophic events, and so, by nature, they catch people by surprise even when there is a history, statistically predictable pattern, and likelihood of their occurrence. It is hard to raise revenues and commit millions of dollars for events that may be foreseeable but for which timing is not easily predictable.

Some of the difficulty of the field and profession lies in the fact that long-range planning for emergencies is not as politically popular nor as newsworthy as covering the damage and suffering that follows the unpredictable but inevitable emergency or disaster. And in the mid- to late twentieth century, the media played an increasingly important role in defining what counts as a problem, and that usually means a focus on the immediate, the here and now, and not on some possible future event even if it is inevitable. News and politics is of the here and now; emergency management is of the inevitable but unpredictable future. The reputation of emergency management inevitably faces formidable challenges in America.

To understand how emergency management has evolved in the United States and how it is influenced by the government's organizational structure as well as by outside forces, one must delve into the policy and organizational processes that have framed that evolution.

The "Streams" of Policy Making

The "policy streams" model, introduced by John Kingdon in 1984, offers an avenue for better understanding the development of the U.S. emergency management system.[1] Kingdon views policy making as the merging of three distinctive streams, or stages: problem recognition, policy ideas, and politics and policy adoption. These streams form independently of each other and not necessarily in any given sequence; eventually, however, they join and form an opportunity called a policy window. When a policy window opens, it allows laws to develop and public policy to emerge.

Problem Recognition

During the problem recognition stream, the policy-making community must recognize that a problem exists that government should be engaged in solving. Standing in the rubble of their demolished homes, disaster victims might wonder with incredulity at the lack of attention given to their plight by elected officials. From the distant perspective of the state or national capital, however, policy makers may view the disaster as beyond the government's capacities or charge.

Even when some policy makers recognize the need for government attention to the problem, no action is usually taken unless a sufficiently large and powerful group within the policy-making process agrees. The failure to admit that a problem exists may linger for years, and the resulting inaction only compounds the problem. When the problem reaches critical mass, either through sudden events that command attention or through a slow accumulation of evidence, the problem definition stream makes way for a policy window, but the window will not open unless the other two streams—policy ideas and politics and policy adoption—converge.

Robert Ward criticizes the Kingdon model's premise that mass mobilization is required to engage the policy-making community.[2] He points out that policy is made in a number of ways: by changes in departmental regulations or interpretation, by published presidential statements accompanying bill signings, by court decisions, by Office of Management and Budget reviews of proposed regulations, or by budgetary decisions at all levels of government. The Department of Homeland Security (DHS), for example, was created after public pressure demanded that the government do something in the wake of the September 11, 2001, terrorist attacks; DHS itself then reorganized the components of the all-hazards approach and at least initially deemphasized its independent intelligence analysis function, both policies outside the mandate of the Homeland Security Act.[3] Yet regardless of how conditions develop into items to be included on decision makers' agendas, another stream must converge in order to bring about policy change: policy makers must reach consensus on the nature of the problem and on a viable and appropriate solution drawn from ideas about proposed policies.

Policy Ideas

During the problem definition stream, policy makers examine and debate possible solutions. If the problem is of sufficient importance, the search for a solution may be played out in the media and thus in full view of the public. The congressional hearings on the response to Hurricane Katrina, for example, received broad public exposure. Federal agency directors, governors, mayors, directors of emergency response organizations, researchers, and academics all presented their opinions about the critical problems to be addressed and the possible solutions.

As Kingdon points out, unless a consensus is reached on the nature of the problem and the solution to it, this debate might end without any action being taken. A review of U.S. emergency management shows that failure to reach consensus on the nature of a problem often leads to a denial that the problem even exists. After the San Francisco earthquake in 1906, for instance, policy makers failed to recognize—and therefore to address—the risk posed by earthquakes, and thus they continued to build in disaster-prone areas. Whether policy makers actually fit a problem to a solution depends on whether the third stream converges with the other two.

Politics and Policy Adoption

In Kingdon's model, the third stream—politics and policy adoption—is driven by the public mood and electoral politics. This is not the only way in which policy is made, but it is the way most likely to involve open debate. At this point, consensus has been reached regarding the nature of the problem and the potential solution. Now consensus on the proposed solution must be achieved within that part of the policy-making community that can implement the solution, either by passing legislation or by other means.

New opposition can surface during the political phase. The public might have a negative reaction to the proposal, or lawmakers might try to attach unrelated matters to it (as when riders are attached to legislation that is thought to have the necessary consensus to pass). Compromise and negotiation are integral to fitting the problem to policy solutions in a way that is consistent with the public mood and electoral politics.

When the three streams converge temporarily to form a policy window, a new policy emerges. In disaster policy, the result might be a law restructuring budgets, authorities, and organizations. For example, in chartering the American Red Cross to provide disaster assistance and in creating the Federal Emergency Management Agency (FEMA), policy makers attempted to meet public needs by "commissioning" or chartering a nongovernmental organization to play an important role in emergency management and disaster relief. And through reorganization and with congressional approval, President Jimmy Carter created in FEMA a new government organization that took over many of the roles and functions previously scattered throughout several different federal agencies.

The "Punctuated Equilibrium" Theory and Emergency Management

The development of emergency management in the United States illustrates Kingdon's theory in action. The streams of problem recognition, problem definition (or policy ideas), and politics and policy adoption converged repeatedly for well over one hundred years, yet many of the solutions crafted to address the problems of emergency management seemed to fall short of producing the desired or expected results, eventually leading to systemic shortcomings, failures, and another round of policy, programs, and management changes.

For example, when DHS was formed, FEMA had achieved an all too rare status of being well regarded, owing to the skillful management of James Lee Witt, its director during the Clinton administration. Policy makers therefore included FEMA within DHS in order to enhance the new department's reputation. Soon after, however, the merger into DHS, with its focus on security threats, along with the appointment of a FEMA director with no significant knowledge or experience in emergency management (unless one considers having been President George W. Bush's campaign manager to be a qualification) led to problems for both the agency and the department. Although some agency subunits managed to resist DHS's new focus on terrorism and security, FEMA's overall effectiveness was significantly weakened. Its weakness triggered disruptions and policy volatility across DHS,[4] thus undermining that department's credibility and leading to still further reorganizational efforts. This cycle of reform, failure, and reorganization was still one more instance of a historical and ongoing pattern for emergency management in the United States.

The "punctuated equilibrium" theory posed by Frank Baumgartner and Bryan Jones in 1993 sheds some light on this ongoing cycle.[5] This theory posits that policy making is an inherently unstable process; no matter what problem solution is codified into law (or other forms of policy implementation), there remain critics who oppose it and will work to alter it. In time, these critics, abetted by external events, erode confidence in the solution, allowing those in opposition to undermine or overturn it and replace it with an option they prefer. How long the solution has remained in effect as public policy is irrelevant; external forces eventually open the problem definition stream and debate begins anew over the nature of the problem. Once this occurs, the existing equilibrium within the policy arena becomes unsettled (or punctuated), and what was once a reasonably stable policy environment now becomes fraught with instability or disequilibrium.

Considering (1) the overlapping of powers among the three branches of government at all levels; (2) the intersecting and overlapping of federal, state, and local governmental functions; and (3) the myriad ways that policy and administrative proposals can be advanced and advocated by interest groups, professional organizations, voluntary associations, and individual politicians, it is virtually impossible to resolve policy issues and disputes permanently. Even the most widely popular policy proposals and solutions may eventually come under attack, and ideas that were once ignored or scorned may at some point be promoted.

In the United States, emergency management appears to be among the policy arenas in which punctuated equilibrium is most evident. The field contains a wide variety of people and organizations with vastly diverse backgrounds and perspectives. First-responder organizations, volunteer and relief agencies, nonprofit organizations, private businesses, appointed and elected officials at all levels of government, and military and paramilitary organizations are all involved in the system, each bringing to it specific policy interests and priorities. In light of this diversity, it is not surprising that different problem definitions and a wealth of often-contradictory solutions abound. And in the unstable environment of disaster response, in which unprecedented and unanticipated events can exceed the capacity of any given solution, change may be the only constant.

The Organizational Context

Organizational theory provides another lens through which to understand emergency management. In *Rediscovering Institutions: The Organizational Basis of Politics,* James March and Johan Olsen discuss problems associated with attempts to reform government organizations that exist in highly unstable environments.[6] As the authors illustrate, all governments place a priority on achieving both efficiency and stability within their organizations and bureaucracies. In the United States, this has been especially true since the late 1800s, when the Progressive movement emphasized the professionalization of public administration. At that time, the increasing demands for government regulation of business resulted in a growing effort to justify service delivery procedures and internal operations. To this end, the public sector began to apply to their practices the principles and findings from various fields of academic research.

The effort to explain administrative processes from a rational perspective so as to distinguish them from being politically motivated is what public administration scholars refer to as the political/administrative dichotomy. This division reflects the conventional perception that all politics resides within the legislative and political executive arenas, whereas the resultant policies are implemented by the government bureaucracy (i.e., the administrative branch) using methods derived from science.

But research in public administration, policy analysis, and political science confirms what wise practitioners like James Lee Witt know intuitively and acknowledge: that the distinction between politics and administration is a false dichotomy. Politics is an integral part of policy making and implementation whether we acknowledge it or not. Nonetheless, this false dichotomy continues to shape perceptions and behavior within both the political and administrative systems. The result is that government decision makers often pursue political agendas in accordance with the assumption that government agencies can and will be able to use rational methods of management, thereby maximizing efficiency and economy in implementing policies. But they cannot always do so, and "blame games" inevitably ensue among the participants.

Fulfilling the aims of political agendas while maintaining the stability and efficiency that rational methods require is inherently problematic. March and Olsen describe the weaknesses of this approach:

> An equilibrium may not exist, or it may not be unique, or it may not be achievable. Even if there is an equilibrium that is, in principle, achievable, historical processes can easily be slow enough relative to the rate of change in the environment that the equilibrium of the process is unlikely to be achieved before the environment, and thus the equilibrium, changes. Unless an environment is perfectly stable, or an institution instantaneously adaptive, of course, there will always be some delay in the adaptive process,

> thus some degree of mismatch between an environment and the institutions existing within it. But where an environment changes quickly relative to the rate at which an institution adapts, an adaptive process can easily and persistently fail to reach an equilibrium.[7]

The events of September 11 may have brought about the kind of rapid changes in the environment of FEMA and of emergency management in general that March and Olsen have in mind. The federal government's role in emergency management reveals a historical pattern of seeking to achieve the organizational equilibrium and stability assumed essential for rational methods of management. But sudden changes in the environment, such as the events of 9/11 and the perceived necessities that ensued, have continually outstripped the available abilities and capacities of emergency management systems and denied them the time needed to achieve stability and professional maturity.

The root of the problem is therefore political, not scientific. In a complex system in which there is such an overlapping of political authorities, the failure to achieve an effective response to a disaster leads to a political blame game. This process is fueled by the ever-present myth of "can do" rationality in administration in general and emergency management in particular. In emergency management, rising expectations of politicians and citizens—as evidenced by the expanded definitions of a disaster and the concomitant increase in the number of presidential disaster declarations—exacerbate the problem. As public expectations rise, the likelihood of a failure to live up to them increases as well. Thus, when a disaster leaves victims and the public at large demanding an explanation for the loss of their loved ones and their property, it should come as no surprise that no one is willing to accept blame.

Citizen exasperation with perceived failure following a disaster—exasperation that may or may not be based on realistic expectations—increases concerns among elected officials. They know that voters often vent their frustration at the polls, as occurred in Florida after Hurricane Andrew in 1992, so they are quick to shirk responsibility and shift blame. While this may be an effective electoral strategy, it complicates objective, in-depth analyses of the emergency management processes and systems.[8] Clear, unbiased analysis is required to understand the complexity and confusion that surrounds a response to disasters, especially when the disaster response system has failed. The difficulty of objectively analyzing complex and changing systems in a political environment contributes to the seeming inability of the United States to develop a stable system of response.

The Downside of the "Can Do" Myth

To analyze failures within any complex system is almost impossible. Citizens tend to view efficiency and effectiveness in government through a national narrative.

From this perspective, the United States is the nation that won World War II, rebuilt Europe through the Marshall Plan, sent men to the moon, and defeated the Soviet Union in the Cold War. This view solidifies in the national consciousness the belief that ours is a nation of "doers"—efficient, effective, and organized. Further magnifying or amplifying the myth is the enduring belief that government can and should be "run like a business" (a belief that ignores the fact that government in general, and emergency management in particular, is far more complicated than business).

It is precisely this national consciousness—this myth—that enables us to maintain a profound faith in the application of rational governance in pursuit of organizational efficiency and thus allows the blame game to be so effective. In our rush to find out who or what is responsible for failure, we ignore the complexity of the system and the role that this complexity has played. Rejecting excuses for failure, we substitute simplistic and convenient answers that are grounded on faulty analysis. By identifying the wrong problem—or an incomplete one at best—we formulate a misguided solution. This inevitably results in future system and organizational failures.

Complexity and Confusion

As the authors of previous chapters have demonstrated, expanding the federal role in emergency management has increased the complexity of the emergency management system. The growing number of governments, agencies, and sectors infused into the system has meant a concomitant growth in the levels of coordination and the complexity of interactions. While this has resulted in greater capabilities and many successes, it has also produced heightened expectations of successful outcomes. Perhaps more important, the increased complexity has made it difficult to determine how the system functions and, when it fails, how to identify who or what within it has failed and to what degree. The government's response to the *Deepwater Horizon* accident in 2010 is a notable example of confusion over who is responsible for what.[9]

The after-disaster reports following the 2005 Gulf Coast hurricanes exposed the absence of a common framework in practice for guiding response to catastrophic disasters. The U.S. House of Representatives Select Bipartisan Committee to Investigate the Preparation for and Response to Hurricane Katrina, for instance, concluded that the National Response Plan (NRP), as designed, was inadequate to support state and local first responders:

> The failure of local, state, and federal governments to respond more effectively to Katrina—which had been predicted in theory for many years, and forecast with startling accuracy for five days—demonstrates that whatever improvements had been made to our capacity to respond to natural

or man-made disasters, four and half years after September 11, we were still not fully prepared. Local first responders were largely overwhelmed and unable to perform their duties, and the National Response Plan did not adequately provide a way for federal assets to quickly supplement or, if necessary, supplant first responders.[10]

The U.S. Senate Committee on Homeland Security and Governmental Affairs, on the other hand, placed blame more generally on leaders at all levels of government:

Among the many factors that contributed to these failures, the Committee found that there were four overarching ones: (1) long-term warnings went unheeded and government officials neglected their duties to prepare for a forewarned catastrophe; (2) government officials took insufficient actions or made poor decisions in the days immediately before and after landfall; (3) systems on which officials relied...to support their response efforts failed; and (4) government officials at all levels failed to provide effective leadership.[11]

The White House took a slightly different view of the issue, stating that failure occurred at all levels of government planning and coordination.

Emergency plans at all levels of government, from small town plans to the 600-page National Response Plan—the Federal government's plan to coordinate all its departments and agencies and integrate them with state, local, and private sector partners—were put to the ultimate test, and came up short.[12]

A Chronically Failing System

As John Harrald discusses in Chapter 6, the present federal emergency management system still suffers from defects stemming from the creation of DHS. In particular, DHS incorporated emergency management procedures too hastily into its terrorism missions. In addition, it developed a national response system (the NRP) that underestimated the need for cooperative interaction among federal, state, and local governments during a truly catastrophic event. (The NRP was structured to prepare for more routine natural disasters, not catastrophic ones that overwhelm state and local governments.) Both problems stemmed in part from political pressure for a timely solution that failed to allow sufficient time for problem identification and the consideration of alternative solutions. During the creation of the NRP, feedback from all participants in the system was curtailed and insufficient time was provided for making adjustments. The NRP was adopted before it had been completely vetted, and as a result, it was part of the reason that the response system failed at a critical point during Hurricane Katrina.

Historically, part of the problem in developing an effective emergency management system has also been the process used to examine failures. When focusing events give rise to questions about the current system's effectiveness, the process of governmental reform begins again. Invariably, a group of people comes together to take testimony, gather facts, and make recommendations (e.g., in research studies, formal congressional hearings, or fact-finding presidential commissions).

As Claire B. Rubin and her associates show in their popular *Disaster Time Line* charts, a focusing disaster event usually leads to a series of studies that then may lead to legislative, administrative, policy, and/or organizational or programmatic changes. Sometimes entirely new agencies or organizations are created. The 1971 San Fernando earthquake contributed to the enactment of the National Earthquake Hazards Reduction Program in 1977. A series of natural and man-made disasters in the 1960s and 1970s resulted in the formation of FEMA in 1978. The September 11 terrorist attacks resulted in the formation of DHS and the reorganization of several federal agencies. All these responses flowed to some degree from recommendations of various commissions and research groups seeking to deal with the public outcry following one or more disasters.

While these efforts to identify needed reforms are laudable, they cannot prevent another disaster. Nor can they influence other external events that will capture the attention of citizens and, hence, government officials. Eventually, a new crisis occurs, media coverage shifts, and attention to reform wanes. As the attention of the public diminishes, so too does the political will to take action, leaving reformers with recommendations that are only partially implemented or reports that are completely ignored. This also leaves the door open for individual experts, interest groups, and participating organizations to enter the process with a dizzying array of recommendations, many of which contradict one another.

The process produces what some theorists refer to as a garbage can of solutions in search of the problem. From these solutions, decision makers select those that are politically desirable and feasible or potentially expedient rather than those that will ultimately resolve the problem.[13] The result is marginal or offsetting reforms that satisfy some within the emergency management community but leave others dissatisfied, looking for future opportunities to change the system. Ultimately, emergency management reform becomes a history of problems that are only partially identified and never fully resolved.

Breaking the Cycle of Preparing for the Last Disaster

Locating the point at which the equilibrium of the emergency management system has been punctuated is a logical place to begin to break this cycle of ad hoc reform focused on preparing for the last disaster. Elected officials, researchers, and emergency managers should be involved in examining the system, identifying and defining the problems, and seeking rational solutions and methods for reorganizing efforts. This requires people to recognize that the system is enmeshed in partisan politics; shaped by our constitutional structure; and mislead by myths about science, efficient management, and the possibility of rational decision making in government. As former FEMA director James Lee Witt has said, "disasters are very political events."[14] Any effective reform must begin with a solid understanding of the scientific, organizational, and political factors that influence the system.

Disasters as Political and Media Events

There was a time in American history when most citizens accepted the notion that disaster response was not a responsibility of the federal government and that the causes of disaster losses were outside of government control. Today, most citizens view this perspective as a lapse in leadership abilities and an admission of failure. When a crisis arises, elected officials and other leaders at all levels of government must convey a sense of effective action. Leaders who claim that disaster losses are beyond their control are perceived as frozen in fear or incompetent to act, as reflected in the media portrayals of FEMA director Michael Brown, Louisiana governor Kathleen Blanco, and New Orleans mayor Ray Nagin during and immediately following Hurricane Katrina. Failure on the part of leaders is seen as the unwillingness to make an attempt. In the national psyche, failure is unacceptable. President Obama appeared to have learned this lesson when he mobilized officials across government to make response to the *Deepwater Horizon* oil spill their first priority. In effect, Obama had become the nation's "responder in chief."[15]

Since CNN was launched in 1980, twenty-four-hour cable news has provided detailed coverage of disasters by reporters on the scene. Although many newscasters lack an understanding of the appropriate role of various disaster response organizations—including government—and cannot accurately report on events, camera crews linked to satellites can often penetrate disaster areas and project scenes of which emergency responders and officials have little or no knowledge. As the camera sends images of devastation and despair into the homes of viewers, selected information about the event filters out to attentive publics through the media.[16] The media's tendency to personalize the suffering of victims—or to become advocates for victims against a seemingly indifferent government bureaucracy—casts governments and their leaders in a negative light.

The consequences of a media narrative can be significant. Negative media coverage often undermines the efforts of those who are charged with disaster response and recovery. During Hurricane Katrina, as the cameras interviewed the stranded residents of New Orleans taking shelter in the Superdome and the Moriel Convention Center, the political pressure to locate buses for evacuation led to confusion on the part of both the state and FEMA staff. Contradictory orders were issued for buses, which not only contributed to further hardship on the part of the stranded citizens but also escalated finger-pointing by the government officials.[17] Furthermore, media frames overemphasize lawlessness and looting, while most people actually abide by the law and do not panic during disaster.[18]

Overzealous media attention can also have a negative impact on efforts to bring the most important aid or relief to an affected area. The media tends to emphasize the breakdown of law and order by emphasizing dramatic scenes of looting and general disorder. The House committee report cited earlier on the response to Hurricane Katrina discussed the media's impact on the perceptions of public officials:

> Public officials lacked access to the facts to address media reports. Throughout the early days of the response, media reports from New Orleans featured rampant looting, gunfire, crime, and lawlessness, including murders and alleged sexual assaults at the Superdome and Convention Center. Few of these reports were substantiated, and those that were—such as the gunfire—were later understood to be actually coming from individuals trapped and trying to attract the attention of rescuers in helicopters.[19]

Many residents of New Orleans who could not evacuate the city sought shelter in the Superdome, which proved to be massively inadequate for the large number of evacuees. Media coverage of events inside the Superdome brought national attention to the plight of victims and the inadequate planning by officials. Photo courtesy of the Federal Emergency Management Agency.

Within the NRP are fifteen emergency support functions, the last of which is external affairs. The purpose of this function is "to provide accurate, coordinated, and timely information to affected audiences, including governments, media, the private sector, and the local populace."[20] Following hearings on Hurricane Katrina, however, the House concluded, "At the strategic level, public officials did not have a strategy to get ahead of the 'information curve' to use the media to the public's advantage and quell rumors."[21]

The failure of government agencies to deal effectively with the media during Hurricane Katrina is only the latest example in a long history of such failures during disasters. It is not unusual for the media to exaggerate the looting and lawlessness after a disaster or to overstate the plight of victims. Their doing so reinforces the disaster myth that anarchy and lawlessness will occur in a disaster situation, and it often results in the failure of responders to prioritize needs appropriately—sending in police officers or military troops to maintain order, for example, instead of evacuating the sick or repairing the infrastructure. As discussed, public perception of events based on media coverage often defines the credibility of the overall response system; media reports may produce public outrage over the steps that were or were not taken by responders. As this can contribute to the failure of politicians to correctly identify problems in response operations, so too can it help determine the political futures of elected officials.

There is no single solution to the problem of overzealous or inaccurate media coverage. Reporters are suspicious of government and always seem to be looking for disingenuous statements or even outright lies by government leaders. For emergency managers and public officials, communication skills are critical. Only by embracing the media as a tool for informing the public can leaders minimize the negative effect of inaccurate or incomplete reporting. Giving the public bad news may not be a pleasant task, but speaking honestly about disaster events and their consequences is becoming an increasingly critical aspect of effective emergency management.[22]

The Political Use of Science

The perception developed by the media during a disaster lingers after the event has passed. A negative impression of response operations requires political leaders to take action to reestablish public confidence in government and its leaders. The most useful political tool for conveying this impression is science.

Political leaders use science as a means of legitimatizing their actions. Science can show that decisions are made according to rational and objective data, not politics. Stated intentions to use scientific research as the basis for taking action may be more important than the actions themselves. Political leaders often use science to imply that humans have control over an unstable environment and to offer hope in the face of a random, indifferent natural order. Scientific evidence that questions such underlying beliefs must be rejected.

The reorganization of governmental functions further reinforces cultural, social, and political beliefs in the power of science and reaffirms that mastery over nature is possible. In so doing, it offers another opportunity to create a symbol of a legitimate government at work and reinforce confidence in political leadership. However, reorganization and reform efforts are actually classic examples of "satisficing behavior" in that groups make decisions not according to what is the optimal solution, but rather on the basis of what meets the immediate preferences or needs of the majority.[23] The result is decisions that meet a minimum standard of comfort, undermining the possibility of effective reform or reorganization.

Effective change in emergency management will require all those engaged in the process to understand the political nature of the reform process. Reformers must seek to work within the political context, no matter how difficult that might be, in order to bring about a better future for emergency management and for all citizens.

The Role of the President in the Emergency Management Process

The political impact of emergencies, their potential for escalation, and the president's powers of response as commander-in-chief of the armed forces make emergency management too important to remain outside the realm of presidential involvement. Yet the episodic nature of most emergencies (in contrast to other urgent and unrelenting political matters) means that presidential concern and interest in emergency management tends to be short-lived.

President Bill Clinton was unusual in this regard. Aware that much of his victory was owing to the failure of George H. W. Bush's administration to pay sufficient attention to emergency management, Clinton appointed James Lee Witt to be the director of FEMA. Not only did Clinton believe Witt to be politically trustworthy, but Witt also had knowledge of and experience in emergency management, both as a state emergency management agency director and as a local elected official.[24]

By the time George W. Bush had succeeded Clinton as president, emergencies had lapsed into "normalcy" and politicians had succumbed to a "not likely on my watch" syndrome, a mindset in which they conclude that it is unlikely that a serious emergency or disaster will occur during their time in office.[25] From this perspective, spending time or money on something that has not happened or is unlikely to happen makes no sense, particularly when there are many more urgent matters that need attention. Presidents caught up in this mentality tend to make relevant personnel decisions on the basis of partisanship rather than professional skills. Bush, for instance, selected his campaign manager, Joe Allbaugh, to direct FEMA despite the fact that Allbaugh had no emergency management experience or related credentials.[26]

The serious problem of presidential lack of attention goes beyond the selection of political appointees. The less attention the president pays to emergency management, the more influence Congress will have. Congress can affect FEMA in many ways—for example, by controlling appropriations, refusing to confirm appointees, changing or amending legislative authority, or continuing oversight by select committees. During the senior Bush's administration, Wallace Stickney became FEMA director only after nine of the ten agency political appointees who required Senate confirmation had been through the confirmation process. These appointees had developed strong relations with committee members and staffers that sometimes seemed more important than any they had with Stickney. The end result was that budget allocations and program development were often directed by the preferences of the various committees of Congress rather than by the priorities established inside FEMA. This phenomenon is an ever-present threat for presidents who fail to exert influence on behalf of FEMA's leadership.

Each president has fought to maintain authority over some if not all facets of emergency management, but retaining presidential authority has meant that any recommendations for change must keep the president at the apex of the hierarchical system. This is at odds with what we have come to learn about emergency management: while emergency management may require presidential attention, nonhierarchical and networklike cooperation across federal, state, and local governments, as well as across public, nonprofit, and private sectors, is critical to its effectiveness.

Presidents' opposition to the reduction of their authority over emergency management, coupled with indifferent stewardship, drives reorganization efforts toward centralization and a highly structured hierarchy. This trend is reinforced by the assumption that having a hierarchy simplifies the development of a command-and-control system that can coordinate activities across the multiple and complex levels of government. Organizational theorist Paul Adler writes:

> Hierarchy uses authority (legitimate power) to create and coordinate a horizontal and vertical division of labor. Under hierarchy, knowledge is treated as a scarce resource and is therefore concentrated, along with the corresponding decision rights, in specialized functional units and at higher levels of the organization.[27]

It is difficult to argue against hierarchy in large organizations with clear missions, such as to deliver the mail to all households and businesses in the United States or to send checks to millions of social security recipients on time. The operations may be incredibly complex and involve large groups of people and machinery, but the tasks are repetitive and routine, and there is clear accountability for decisions and operations. Hierarchy embodies the presumption not only that others will comply with lawful orders, but also that established rules and procedures will be followed. "Hierarchy can provide institutional support for the current bundle of routines, information systems, values, and other key elements that influence production," explain researchers Laurence O'Toole Jr. and Kenneth Meier, "offering a crystallization of stable, cooperative effort, [and] the operational status quo."[28]

But while hierarchy may have its place in the institutional or organizational components of response, the great difficulties in any large-scale response to an emergency involve working across organizations, levels of government, and sectors under crisis conditions, in which circumstances are often highly dynamic, established procedures and rules lose their meaning, and matters are anything but routine.[29] With more than thirty federal agencies and several nongovernmental agencies identified within the NRP, the scale of agency coordination in disaster response is overwhelming. These agencies have to interact effectively not only with one another but also with state and local government agencies and private and nonprofit organizations. In a crisis with unforeseeable issues that need to be addressed, hierarchical decision making and strict adherence to rules can impede effective response. Charles Wise writes that the notion of hierarchy

> rests on the notions that the organizations to be coordinated have been identified or can be readily identified by the headquarters coordinators; that the relationships of these organizations to each other are well understood; that agreement has been reached about what objectives will be accomplished by altering certain of these inter-organizational relationships; and that the authority and means to effectuate desired goals exist to alter the relationships in the desired direction. It assumes the hierarchy will facilitate the implementation.[30]

Investigations into response failures during the 2005 hurricane season reveal that the centralized, hierarchical system of response failed when it interacted with agencies and groups outside the federal government. The system failed to communicate effectively with state and local systems because it held little understanding of the local systems in the affected areas. As the consequences of the disasters unfolded, responding organizations were faced with unprecedented problems that they had not considered in their response scenarios. The hierarchy of FEMA and DHS was suddenly called on to reprogram its coordination, think and act outside the prescribed lines of authority and control, and seek creative solutions to the problems that emerged. When this happens, the strength of a hierarchy becomes a weakness.

The Network Context

It is impossible to design an emergency management system involving the federal government without recognizing the ultimate role of presidential authority, but this need not preclude the possibility of developing an effective response system that is not based on a centralized, hierarchical system.

In 1978, President Carter took a tentative step toward developing a decentralized system of emergency management while retaining presidential authority. His administration's initial concept for FEMA emphasized pulling together the scattered elements of federal emergency response into a "one-stop shop." This approach assumed a collaborative system across all levels of government and emphasized natural disaster response. The Clinton presidency expanded on this approach, recognizing presidential authority and basing the emergency management system on the existing capacities of federal, state, and local governments. The result was an emergency management system that was effective and professional.

Developing an effective system of emergency management requires understanding how networks function. O'Toole defines networks as "structures of interdependence involving multiple organizations or parts thereof, where one unit is not merely the formal subordinate of the others in some larger hierarchical arrangement."[31] In government, management networks are composed of independent agencies but share a common focus across agency and jurisdictional lines. These networks also include nongovernmental organizations, such as the American Red Cross, that work with governments at all levels to accomplish complex tasks. Public management networks are "led or managed by government representatives as they employ multi-organizational arrangements for solving problems that cannot be achieved, or achieved easily, by single organizations."[32]

Since governmental and nongovernmental organizations have legal and constitutional independence, they cannot be required to cooperate. To cooperate, they must find some mutual advantage. This advantage might be couched in terms of their mission (to serve the public good), values (such as loyalty, patriotism, or humanitarianism), budget, or reputation and legitimacy. In constructing cooperative systems, then, it is critical that all members negotiate their roles and relationships with one another before the systems become operational. This requires a willingness to compromise in order to achieve a common desired outcome.

Pooling capacities within a single, well-coordinated network can create a synergy that allows for not just an incremental increase but often a doubling or tripling of capacity. Networks are particularly effective where there is uncertainty and where quick, effective decision making is required. The loose coupling of various organizations allows for flexibility and adaptability across the network. Thus, networks are particularly well suited for disaster response.

Networks do have weaknesses, however. As discussed, they require cooperation, which in turn requires trust in other members of the network and a common purpose. In resilient networks, trust and collaborative skills are key ingredients for success.[33] Yet in cases of organizational failure, it is often difficult or impossible to assess the performance of any given unit within a network. As a result, accountability is undermined. Thus, if a network fails in its response to a disaster, it is often difficult to determine where the failure lies.

Analysis of FEMA and the federal government's role in disaster management shows that a network approach offers the best opportunity for effectiveness. President Clinton's system, for instance, did not reject centralized decision-making authority or reduce the president's role in emergency management. But with Witt at the helm of FEMA, Clinton replaced the command-and-control philosophy of the prior Bush administration with an approach that viewed the authority vested in the federal government as the catalyst for action among a wide variety of independent organizations and agencies. In their analysis of the evolution of emergency management, Aaron Schroeder, Gary Wamsley, and Robert Ward write, "In this model, while the central agency is no longer envisioned as holding a superior, hegemonic position, it is nonetheless viewed as being on at least an equal footing with other interested entities and having special responsibilities for catalyzing, convening, synthesizing, and in general exerting leadership in the public interest."[34]

The changes that took place in the emergency management system in the 1990s positioned the system neither at one centralized point within the federal government nor with state and local governments. Rather, the system resided in some middle ground between these levels of government. After the concerns of all the entities involved in the disaster response system were considered, the resulting perspective reflected a "multiactor" environment that was based on an understanding of the capacities of the various entities and the context in which each of the principal response organizations operated.

The key to the success of this network approach was communication between a central lead agency—FEMA—and the many other members that made up the network. Ultimately, the office of the president was charged with developing an effective emergency management system to serve the national public interest, but state and local governments and private entities were considered equal partners with specific constraints that needed to be addressed realistically and pragmatically. FEMA's role in the 1990s was to uncover potential barriers to collective action and collaboration and to develop incentives to overcome them. To accomplish this, the agency sponsored tabletop and field exercises, and relied extensively on personal relationships and discussions with governmental and nongovernmental organizations throughout the United States. The goal was to establish solid relationships among all potential responders prior to an actual disaster.

Plans for disaster response were flexible. FEMA established goals and targets, but the actual response systems were developed within local capacities through direct negotiations between federal representatives and local officials. To foster cooperation, FEMA provided financial incentives, including a payroll subsidy for key state and local emergency management directors. Finally, the agency encouraged further professionalization of emergency management by establishing training institutes and encouraging the development of emergency management educational programs at institutions of higher learning. The training programs provide an opportunity for emergency management professionals to meet one another, fostering relationships among different levels of government and building a collective framework for analyzing emergency management problems and solutions.[35]

Strengths and Weaknesses of the Network Approach

Under the network approach developed while Witt was director, FEMA took the role of central actor. The agency assumed responsibility for ensuring that an effective emergency management system, based on nationally set priorities, was developed, and it served as a catalyst for discovering and removing impasses among network partners. This approach led to a flexible organizational structure that could adapt when responding to the uncertainties of a disaster. Open lines of communication among key players contributed to improved response systems and a genuine feeling of partnership in the overall system. A professional emergency management culture emerged, with a common mission and a focus on the public interest. In addition, the trust that was built among the members of the network aided in the process of removing and overcoming any obstacles to working together.[36]

Given time, the network that was developed in the 1990s probably would have evolved into a system that stabilized the emergency management arena. The reorganization and recurring issues regarding presidential authority that regularly punctuated the system's equilibrium would have been resolved. But emergency management was once again influenced by external events—this time by the attacks of September 11—and the network faded from existence. The intergovernmental and interorganizational cooperation that resulted from the trust forged during 1990s became the exception rather than the rule.

The Suboptimization of FEMA after September 11

The September 11 terrorist attacks delivered a powerful shock to the national psyche. The nation's leaders struggled to determine how and why such events occurred and what could be done to ensure that they would not happen again. In hindsight, given the Hurricane Katrina fiasco, many emergency management experts believe that 9/11 caused political leaders to overreact. By focusing too much attention on the risk of terrorism, they again centralized authority, undermining the effectiveness of emergency management, which by its nature must span many levels of government, involve both governmental and nongovernmental entities and, at times, both military and nonmilitary organizations, and more often than not require improvisation in decisions and actions.

In systems analysis, the term *suboptimization* is used to describe the process whereby efforts to improve the performance of a system are focused on one aspect of the system—one subsystem—while the effect of that subsystem on the work of the other subsystems is ignored. But improvements in one element of an overall system often have a negative impact on the performance of other elements, ultimately impairing the performance of the entire system. Suboptimization occurs when an analyst fails to fully understand the complexity of the system and the interconnectivity of the various units. The inclusion of FEMA in DHS exemplifies this problem.

In theory, FEMA could have been as effective within DHS as it had been as an independent agency. This would have required those responsible for DHS to appreciate the complexity of the emergency management system and to accept the collaborative nature of the agency. In the post-9/11 atmosphere, however, collaboration fell by the wayside. In addition to emergency management, law enforcement, intelligence, and defense were involved in the massive reorganization of the federal government. In each area, the new organization emphasized centralized command and control and reasserted presidential authority.[37]

While this approach might have been effective in improving the performance of federal agencies under the control of the executive branch, it failed to recognize the limited control that federal agencies have over independent agencies, autonomous units of government (including state and local governments), and the private sector. The new approach undermined the trust, communication, and flexibility that had formed the basis of the emergency management system. Combined with renewed emphasis on defense against terrorist attacks, which relegated emergency management to a secondary concern, failure was perhaps inevitable.

Unresolved Issues

Reconstituting the FEMA of the 1990s and the collaborative network that characterized it is unlikely to fix the nation's disaster response problems, but returning to this approach might be a good start in solving these problems. While historically the network approach has been successful in emergency management, a number of critical issues that have always plagued emergency management in the United States have not yet been resolved.

Moral Hazard and Pre-Disaster Mitigation

At its most basic level, a moral hazard emerges when people with some form of insurance for or shelter from risk decide to take greater risks than they otherwise would. With the costs or burdens of their actions shifted elsewhere—to an insurance provider or a relief organization, for instance—people may behave in a manner that is neither wise nor prudent. In many ways, the relationship that has developed between the federal government with its disaster relief programs and governments in states where there is a risk of disaster represents a moral hazard or, as some call it, a "charity hazard," because localities expect that the federal government and private charities will compensate them for their losses.[38]

As discussed, rapid population growth and unchecked development in vulnerable areas have increased the impact of natural and human-induced disasters. In most instances, it is the local government that has the greatest control over development, but local governments can transfer at least some of the risk to others—insurers or state governments, for example—and thereby create a moral hazard. Allowing substandard building or development in areas at risk of flooding, hurricanes, or earthquakes has increased the devastation that such disasters wreak. Rather than situate development away from danger, communities have chosen to build dams, levees, and other structures to protect them from natural forces. The lack of strong safety requirements in hazardous waste transportation systems and facilities also increases the risk to humans.

The need for effective pre-disaster mitigation, which Witt called "the ultimate form of emergency management," has historically been the weakest link in the emergency management system.[39] Growth pressures in communities have resulted in the failure of governments to enact stricter building and disaster prevention standards that would reduce the need for and the cost of disaster response and recovery.

This moral hazard is on a large scale. Although the National Flood Insurance Program (NFIP) and other programs seek to reduce risk for people in disaster-prone areas by transferring that risk away from residents and local communities, such programs inadvertently encourage risk taking. Some localities have failed to establish land use plans that prevent development in areas vulnerable to flooding. After floodwaters recede, they apply for federal flood insurance and rebuild the community in the same spot. But as Witt has pointed out more than once, it is often cheaper to buy an entire town and move it to a new location than to rebuild it again and again.[40]

Our nation's responses to hurricane risks offer a vivid example. The extension of the levee system along the Mississippi River opened up the area to shipping, which enabled economic growth in southern Louisiana. The resulting population growth extended the built environment into coastal areas. The levee system also increased the speed of water flow, and the wetlands and other natural areas that had once served as a buffer zone from hurricanes were washed away. Without this buffer zone, hurricanes have a more profound impact, not only on coastal communities but also on those communities a few miles inland. The NFIP, which allows for communities to be rebuilt following a hurricane's devastation, also transfers the risk from these communities to the national taxpayers, thereby encouraging further growth in the process.[41]

All along the Atlantic Coast, similar patterns of development have occurred. On the barrier islands in North Carolina, for instance, large luxury homes crowd beaches where until recently there was little or no development. Many of these houses are used as vacation homes or rental properties, and losses from a hurricane or flooding would be absorbed by the federal government. This is moral hazard in action.

To some people, the solution is to refuse to transfer risk. Private insurance companies have withdrawn from several markets, including the high-risk, hurricane-prone areas of Florida. Congress, which has historically funded community rebuilding efforts, is now showing increased reluctance to do so. But this raises several important questions: At what point does federal responsibility for disaster prevention and preparation cease? If private insurers refuse to assume risk, does this become the responsibility of state and local governments? What are the responsibilities of private citizens and businesses?

In recent history, state and local governments have seemed to feel entitled to federal funds for disaster relief and prevention measures. The federal government cannot continue to provide funding without strings attached, however. The system must require state and local governments to consider the consequences of building in disaster-prone areas and engage in proper mitigation.

Citizens also play a role in moral hazards. Research has shown that only when a disaster is imminent do citizens take the necessary steps to prepare for it and protect their families. People who choose to live in an area vulnerable to disaster must understand the nature of the risk and take responsibility for planning accordingly. This includes understanding and heeding the government's warning signals, knowing evacuation and shelter procedures, and following the directions of government officials in a disaster situation.

Political Accountability vs. Professionalism

Professionalism within emergency management is critical to its success. Using political patronage to fill positions within the federal government dates back to the founding of our country, but in areas such as emergency management, making decisions on the basis of politics rather than skill can cost the lives of citizens.[42] Many researchers agree that the lack of emergency management experience and training on the part of FEMA directors Joe Allbaugh and Michael Brown contributed to the problems encountered during and after Hurricane Katrina.[43]

Within FEMA, the issue of professional competency versus political appointments goes much deeper than just the position of director. Beginning in 2001, FEMA suffered a "brain drain" as experienced emergency management professionals left to work in the private sector or in state and local governments.[44] Many left because FEMA was incorporated into DHS, and with the ensuing struggles over that integration and the attendant difficulties of adjustment, many others who were eligible to retire chose to do so. By the fall of 2005, when Hurricane Katrina hit, seven or eight well-qualified persons had turned down offers to assume some of the top positions in FEMA, most of which were subsequently filled by people with virtually no experience in emergency management or disaster response. This lack of professionalism undermined confidence in FEMA and contributed to morale problems within the agency. Following Brown's resignation after Katrina, FEMA's reputation was so bad that few professional emergency managers applied to be the agency's new director.

Is it possible to assure citizens and partners in the emergency management network that competent and experienced professionals will direct federal emergency management activities?

One option is for FEMA (or any other agency charged with emergency management) to follow the precedent of the Federal Reserve System and the Government Accountability Office (GAO), in which presidential and congressional oversight balance partisanship and expertise. Like other agency directors, the chair of the Federal Reserve Board is appointed by the president and confirmed by the Senate, but the term of the office means that the chair's tenure will coincide with that of neither the president nor legislators. The term of the comptroller general, who heads the GAO, is similar. Moreover, the professional qualifications for both of these positions are always impeccable; Congress would refuse to confirm any candidate who did not have extensive experience in fiscal management, because the role of these organizations is considered critical to the welfare of the nation. Is this not equally true—if not more true—of federal emergency management? Leaving the critical field of emergency management in the hands of unqualified individuals is a risky proposition. Some presidents have made the calculation that having a qualified emergency manager lead the agency was in their interests; surprisingly, however, some did not. The Post-Katrina Emergency Management Reform Act of 2006 put limits on who the president can nominate as FEMA administrator, specifying that the administrator come "from among individuals who have...a demonstrated ability in and knowledge of emergency management and homeland security" and at least five years of experience.[45] Unfortunately, the act may have been somewhat blunted if not made ineffective by Bush's attachment of a signing statement to the law because he claimed that the act limits the president's appointment authority.

Civilian vs. Military Control

Although the events occurred over a decade apart, the responses to Hurricane Andrew and Hurricane Katrina share many features. One of the most obvious similarities is the central role that the National Guard and the Department of Defense played. In the aftermath of both hurricanes, military personnel and equipment were incorporated into civilian rescue and relief efforts, primarily to assist with logistics and communications but also to maintain order.

Perhaps the most critical issue to be decided in a unified response system is who should be in control. Some leaders feel that active-duty military units have the necessary training and resources to respond to a catastrophic disaster; others believe that giving the military this authority would be tantamount to changing the constitutional regime of the United States.[46] Following Hurricane Andrew, the National Academy of Public Administration (NAPA) recommended that civilian and military linkages be carefully defined and limited.[47] The Clinton administration subsequently put emergency management under civilian control with liaison channels to the Defense Department for information, advice, and military support.

The issue of military involvement has taken on even greater significance since 9/11. The decision to link disaster response with terrorism prevention has led to the reestablishment of links between civilian and military authorities in domestic emergency management. Historical evidence seems to confirm that linking civilian and military systems into a single system de-prioritizes natural disaster response while strengthening response to intentionally caused disasters. It may also weaken incentives for state, local, and nongovernmental organizations to improve their capabilities. Today's linkages must deal not only with the consequences of disasters, regardless of cause, but also with the intelligence, military, and law enforcement efforts aimed at preventing intentionally caused disasters.

The National Guard, the arm of the military most likely to play a role in disaster response, is under the control of state governors unless ordered into federal service under the Department of Defense. With the stroke of a pen, the Guard can be transformed from a quasi-state agency in "reserve" status into a mobilized military unit. This transfer of authority has been undertaken many times in U.S. history, most recently to secure manpower for the war in Iraq.

However, U.S. legislation passed more than a century ago continues to restrict the military's role in disaster response and law enforcement. The 1878 Posse Comitatus Act, which was passed to placate southerners after the Civil War, specifically bars active-duty military from acting as a domestic police force.[48] This legacy from the Reconstruction Era has strong advocates among state governments who fear that overturning its provisions will weaken state authority.

In a nutshell, posse comitatus bans the Army, Navy, Air Force, and Marines from participating in arrests, searches, seizure of evidence, and other police-type activity on U.S. soil. The Coast Guard and National Guard troops under the control of state governors are excluded from this ban, however, and subsequent acts of Congress and jurisprudence have allowed for a growing number of exceptions to the initial legislation's strict interpretation.[49] In particular, differentiation has been made between the passive role of providing advice and support and the active role of enforcing laws.

After Hurricane Katrina hit, National Guard troops responded from states that had interstate compacts with Louisiana, but Louisiana governor Blanco refused to allow the troops to be "federalized"—that is, brought under direction of the Department of Defense and the president as commander in chief. In light of posse comitatus, the problems associated with involvement of the National Guard (and of other military units) raise important questions that need to be addressed: What are the rules of engagement? If National Guard personnel are on patrol to maintain order, what are they to do if they encounter criminal behavior? How should they respond if fired upon?

In a 1997 study of the National Guard's role in emergency management, NAPA concluded that the emergency management system must coordinate with the

Department of Defense planners who dictate the Guard's location, equipment, and training if the Guard is to be effective in disaster response.[50] The current planning involves a combination of tradition and mobilization for national purposes, with little regard for the needs of different states for emergency management.[51] The National Guard Bureau has worked to bring to bear the necessary resources to address emergencies, and states have worked out a web of interstate compacts to make it possible to send guard troops from one state into another, but this has been effective only for smaller-scale emergencies.[52] The National Guard was hard-pressed to provide significant help in the wake of Katrina, for instance, in part because many units were in Iraq while others had returned but without their equipment.

Ultimately, those responsible for emergency management must determine the proper balance between civilian and military control over emergency management. At what point should civilian authorities ask for help from the military? What training and resources do National Guard units need in order to be effective in emergency management? Determining the time and the conditions under which such action should be taken requires a deeper analysis of the laws, missions, and capacities of participating organizations than has been conducted to date.

Disaster Research

In *Coping with Catastrophe,* NAPA criticized the lack of funding available for disaster-related research, especially research grounded in the social sciences.[53] In the years following that report, FEMA continued to offer only limited funding for research. In fact, the majority of funds for research in natural hazards, disasters, and emergency management have come from the National Science Foundation.

Despite the relative lack of support, a small but viable disaster research structure has emerged. For more than forty-five years, social science–related disaster research has been undertaken by the Disaster Research Center at the University of Delaware under the direction of such eminent scholars as sociologists Henry Quarantelli and Russell Dynes.[54] The Natural Hazards Center at the University of Colorado at Boulder, which was established by renowned geographer Gilbert White,[55] continues to provide important scientific findings related to disasters, especially for areas and communities with disaster risks. Since 1977, the National Earthquake Hazards Reduction Program, funded by the National Science Foundation, has provided research support in such disciplines as geography, sociology, political science, psychology, economics, decision science, regional science and planning, public health, and anthropology—all targeted at improving society's response to hazards and disasters. This research has resulted in a growing body of knowledge about disasters and disaster response. Many important findings have remained in the purview of the academic community, however, and have had little or no influence over emergency management policies, procedures, or practice. In essence, policy makers and emergency management planners remain woefully unaware of some critical information that would be useful in planning and implementing effective disaster operations.[56]

Another weakness of disaster research is its emphasis on disaster response and recovery, with little attention to risks or the vulnerability of populations. A 2006 report from the National Research Council concludes:

> Disaster research, which has focused historically on emergency response and recovery, is incomplete without the simultaneous study of the societal hazards and risks associated with disasters, which includes data on the vulnerability of people living in hazard-prone areas. Historically, hazards and disaster research have evolved in parallel, with the former focusing primarily on hazards vulnerability and mitigation, the latter primarily on disaster response and recovery, and the two veins intersecting most directly with common concerns about disaster preparedness. It is vital…that future social science research treats hazards and disaster research interchange-ably…within a single overarching framework.[57]

Following the 2005 hurricane season, Congress engaged in a series of hear-ings and studies to learn about what happened. While these reports provided ample information about the events that occurred, they did not include any sys-tematic analysis of the information or identify common factors across events. More systematic analysis, however, is critical for designing effective systems: it could provide agency heads and planners with a deeper understanding of the dif-ferences between types of disasters as well as of the different types of assets and organizational arrangements needed for effective response. It also could inform policy makers in their efforts to improve security and restore communities after devastating events. But this type of analysis requires thorough, in-depth, and can-did after-action research, and unless additional funding is targeted to this type of research, emergency management systems will continue to be based on incom-plete information and ill-conceived models, planting the seeds of future failures.

While social science research is critical for improving emergency man-agement, it must also be concerned with and relate to broader questions about improving governance in general. Public administration and policy studies, while they are more narrowly and specifically focused, nonetheless are also concerned with questions about improving governance in general; thus, as William Waugh writes, there are difficulties in "sorting out the contributions of public adminis-tration (to emergency management) from those of other fields…largely because public administration is an interdisciplinary field."[58] Traditionally, public admin-istration research has not focused on the emergency management system, but in recent years a number of scholars have turned their attention to questions about how to improve disaster governance and relationships among organizations within the emergency management systems.[59]

Conclusion

Public safety has been a core responsibility of the U.S. government since its beginning, but disaster management emerged as part of the government's safety and security mission only during the twentieth century. The government initially kept citizens safe from foreign invaders, leaving preparation for and response to most natural disasters (as well as policing matters) in the hands of localities or citizens. As our systems of coping with disasters expanded, societal expectations of governments' responsibility for public safety also grew, along with societal views of legitimate versus illegitimate government action. The organizations and programs used in preparation for attack were sometimes conflated with preparation for weather-related disasters, whether during the civil defense or the homeland security eras. The public came to expect the government to prepare for many kinds of safety threats, and politicians took credit for these efforts. However, flawed responses to a threat to public safety—in the form of a natural disaster or terrorist attack—can seriously erode public confidence in government. When disaster responses go awry, politicians issue blame, often toward administrative agencies.

Today, after several major disasters, the United States has a unique opportunity to redesign the emergency management system and reestablish public confidence. Will this renewed focus on emergency management better prepare communities for a disaster, or will it lead to an increasing dependence on federal government responses at the expense of community preparation and mitigation efforts? Can we resolve the critical flaws in the emergency management system that hinder the system's ability to protect citizens? A decade from now, what answer will emergency management researchers give to the question, "What went wrong?" Perhaps, if politicians and the emergency management profession learn from past efforts to prepare for disaster, future scholars may be fortunate enough to also ask what went right.

Endnotes

1   John Kingdon, *Agendas, Alternatives, and Public Policy Politics* (New York: HarperCollins, 1984). Several experts in policy and political science note how the development of emergency management policy closely tracks Kingdon's theory; see Thomas A. Birkland, *After Disasters: Agenda Setting, Public Policy, and Focusing Events* (Washington, D.C.: Georgetown University Press, 1997); and William J. Petak and Daniel J. Alesch, "Organizational Decision Making with Respect to External Events: Healthcare Organizations Response to California's SB1952," *Research Progress and Accomplishments in 2003–2004* (Buffalo, N.Y.: Multidisciplinary Center for Earthquake Engineering Research, University of Buffalo, 2004).

2   Robert C. Ward, "The Chaos of Convergence: A Study of the Process of Decay, Change, and Transformation within the Telecommunications Policy Subsystem of the United States" (PhD diss., Center for Public Administration and Policy, Virginia Polytechnic Institute, 1997), scholar.lib.vt.edu/theses/available/etd-0698-91234/unrestricted/etd.pdf.

3   An example of the ongoing law-making process can be found in the creation of the U.S. Department of Homeland Security (DHS) and the inclusion of FEMA within it. FEMA's all-hazards approach included preparation, mitigation, response, and recovery, but after FEMA became part of DHS, control over state and local government grants administration was transferred to

a separate division. This administrative decision effectively separated the four components of the all-hazards approach and was done outside the original intentions of the Homeland Security Act. As this example shows, the ongoing process of lawmaking does not end once a law enters Kingdon's policy window but continues on in a different venue with different strategies.

4   Peter J. May, Joshua Sapotichne, and Samuel Workman, "Widespread Policy Disruption: Terrorism, Public Risks, and Homeland Security," *Policy Studies Journal* 37, no. 2 (2009): 171–194.

5   Frank R. Baumgartner and Bryan D. Jones, *Agendas and Instability in American Politics* (Chicago: University of Chicago Press, 1993).

6   James G. March and Johan P. Olsen, *Rediscovering Institutions: The Organizational Basis of Politics* (New York: Free Press, 1989).

7   Ibid., 55.

8   The perceived failures to effectively respond to Hurricane Katrina may also have played a role in the 2006 elections, in which control of both Houses of Congress passed from the Republican to the Democratic party.

9   Thomas A. Birkland and Sarah E. DeYoung, "Emergency Response, Doctrinal Confusion, and Federalism in the Deepwater Horizon Oil Spill," *Publius: The Journal of Federalism* 41 (Summer 2011): 471–493; Patrick S. Roberts, "Our Responder in Chief," *National Affairs* 5 (Fall 2010): 75–102.

10 U.S. House of Representatives, *A Failure of Initiative: Final Report of the Select Bipartisan Committee to Investigate the Preparation for and Response to Hurricane Katrina* (Washington, D.C.: U.S. Government Printing Office, February 16, 2006), 1, gpoaccess.gov/katrinareport/fullreport.pdf.

11 U.S. Senate, Committee on Homeland Security and Governmental Affairs, "Executive Summary," *Hurricane Katrina: A Nation Still Unprepared* (Washington, D.C.: U.S. Government Printing Office, 2006), 2, gpoaccess.gov/serialset/creports/pdf/sr109-322/execsummary.pdf.

12 White House, *The Federal Response to Hurricane Katrina: Lessons Learned* (Washington, D.C.: Office of the President, 2006), 1, library.stmarytx.edu/acadlib/edocs/katrinawh.pdf.

13 The "garbage can" decision-making model was originally developed in 1972 in a paper by Michael D. Cohen, James G. March, and Johan P. Olsen. In its original form, the model assumes that "problems, solutions, decision makers, and choice opportunities are independent, exogenous streams flowing through a system"; see March and Olsen, *Rediscovering Institutions*, 12.

14 James Lee Witt, "Statement before the VA-HUD and Independent Agencies Subcommittee on Appropriations" (Washington, D.C.: U.S. House of Representatives, 1996).

15 Roberts, "Our Responder in Chief."

16 Saundra K. Schneider, "Government Response to Disasters: The Conflict between Bureaucratic Procedures and Emergent Norms," *Public Administration Review* 52 (March/April 1992): 135–145; Benign Aquirre and E. L. Quarantelli, "Methodological, Ideological, and Conceptual—Theoretical Criticisms of the Field of Collective Behavior: A Critical Evaluation and Implications for Future Study," *Sociological Focus* 16 (1983): 195–216.

17 Kathleen Tierney, Christine Bevc, and Erica Kuligowski, "Metaphors Matter: Disaster Myths, Media Frames, and Their Consequences in Hurricane Katrina," *Annals of the American Academy of Political and Social Science* 604, no. 1 (2006): 57–81.

18 Aaron Schroeder, Gary Wamsley, and Robert Ward, "The Evolution of Emergency Management: From a Painful Past to a Promising but Uncertain Future," in *Handbook of Crisis and Emergency Management,* ed. Ali Farazmand (New York: Marcel Dekker, 2001).

19 U.S. House of Representatives, *A Failure of Initiative,* 169.

20 Ibid., 35.

21 Ibid., 248.

22 James Lee Witt successfully changed FEMA's public image through a variety of means, including hiring one of Washington's most capable publicists for FEMA's public affairs office.

23 The concept of "satisficing behavior" was developed in 1958 by organizational theorists James G. March and Herbert A. Simon; see March and Simon, *Organizations* (New York: John Wiley & Sons, 1958).

24 Patrick S. Roberts, "FEMA and the Prospects for Reputation-Based Autonomy," *Studies in American Political Development* 20 (Spring 2006): 57–87.

25   Gary L. Wamsley et al., *Coping with Catastrophe: Building an Emergency Management System to Meet the People's Needs in Natural and Manmade Disasters* (Washington, D.C.: National Academy of Public Administration, 1993).

26   David E. Lewis, *The Politics of Presidential Appointments, Political Control and Bureaucratic Performance* (Princeton, N.J.: Princeton University Press, 2008): 141–171.

27   Paul S. Adler, "Market, Hierarchy, and Trust: The Knowledge Economy and the Future of Capitalism," *Organization Science* 12 (March/April 2001): 216, www-bcf.usc.edu/~padler/research/MHT-2.pdf.

28   Laurence O'Toole Jr. and Kenneth Meier, "Modeling the Impact of Public Management: Implications of Structural Context," *Journal of Public Administration Research and Theory* 9 (October 1999): 507.

29   Louise Comfort and Anthony G. Cahill, "Increasing Problem-Solving Capacity between Organizations: The Role of Information in Managing the May 31, 1985, Tornado Disaster in Western Pennsylvania," in *Managing Disaster: Strategies and Policy Perspectives*, ed. Louise K. Comfort (Durham, N.C.: Duke University Press, 1988), 180–198; Richard Daft, *Essential Organizational Theory and Design* (Cincinnati, Ohio: South-Western College Publishing, 1998); and Henry Mintzberg, *The Nature of Managerial Work* (Englewood Cliffs, N.J.: Prentice Hall, 1980).

30   Charles R. Wise, "Organizing for Homeland Security," *Public Administration Review* 62 (March/April 2002): 141, glennschool.osu.edu/news/Organizing%20for%20Homeland%20Security%20after%20Katrina.pdf.

31   Laurence J. O'Toole Jr., "Treating Networks Seriously: Practical and Research-Based Agendas in Public Administration," *Public Administration Review* 57 (January 1997): 45, doc.utwente.nl/1662/1/O'Toole97treating.pdf.

32   Robert Agranoff and Michael McGuire, "Big Questions for Public Network Management Research," *Journal of Public Administration Research and Theory* 11 (July 2001): 295.

33   Louise K. Comfort, Arjen Boin, and Chris C. Demchak, eds., *Designing Resilience: Preparing for Extreme Events* (Pittsburgh, Pa.: University of Pittsburgh Press, 2010); Anne M. Khademian and Edward Weber, "Wicked Problems, Knowledge Challenges, and Collaborative Capacity Builders in Network Settings," *Public Administration Review* 68 (2008): 334–349.

34   Schroeder, Wamsley, and Ward, "Evolution of Emergency Management," 387.

35   Roberts, "FEMA and the Prospects for Reputation-Based Autonomy," 65–67.

36   Schroeder, Wamsley, and Ward, "Evolution of Emergency Management," 387.

37   Patrick S. Roberts, "Dispersed Federalism as a New Regional Governance for Homeland Security," *Publius* 38, no. 3 (Summer 2008): 416–443; Paul N. Stockton and Patrick S. Roberts, "Findings from the Forum on *Homeland Security after the Bush Administration: Next Steps in Building Unity of Effort*" (with Paul Stockton), *Homeland Security Affairs* 4 (June 2008), hsaj.org/?article=4.2.4.

38   Mark J. Browne and Martin Halek, "Managing Flood Risk: A Discussion of the National Flood Insurance Program and Alternatives," in *Public Insurance and Private Markets*, ed. Jeffrey R. Brown (Washington, D.C.: AEI Press, 2010), 148–149.

39   Witt, "Statement before the VA-HUD;" Patrick S. Roberts, "A Capacity for Mitigation as the Next Frontier in Homeland Security," *Political Science Quarterly* 124 (Spring 2009): 127–142.

40   Witt, "Statement before the VA-HUD."

41   As part of the restoration program for New Orleans, the levees have been rebuilt. The State of Louisiana is currently engaged in an expensive wetlands restoration program to rebuild the buffer zone.

42   Paul Light, *Thickening Government: Federal Hierarchy and the Diffusion of Accountability* (Washington, D.C.: The Brookings Institution, 1995); Gary L. Wamsley and Aaron D. Schroeder, "Escalating in a Quagmire: The Changing Dynamics of the Emergency Management Policy Subsystem," *Public Administration Review* 56 (May/June 1996): 235–244.

43   David E. Lewis, *The Politics of Presidential Appointments, Political Control and Bureaucratic Performance* (Princeton, N.J.: Princeton University Press, 2008): 141–171.

44   When Hurricane Katrina hit, 20 percent of the agency's allocated work positions were vacant because of resignations and retirements.

45 P.L. 109-295, § 611(11), new HSA Sec. 503(c)(2); Keith Bea et al., "Federal Emergency Management Policy Changes after Hurricane Katrina: A Summary of Statutory Provisions," *CRS Report for Congress*, November 15 (Washington, D.C.: Congressional Research Service, 2006).

46 Kathleen Tierney and Christine Bevc, "Disasters as War: Militarism and the Social Construction of Disaster in New Orleans," in *The Sociology of Katrina: Perspectives on a Modern Catastrophe*, 2nd ed., ed. David L. Brunsma, David Overfelt, and J. Steven Picou (Lanham, Md.: Rowman & Littlefield, 2010).

47 National Academy of Public Administration (NAPA), *The Role of the National Guard in Emergency Preparedness and Response* (Washington, D.C.: NAPA, 1997).

48 *Posse comitatus* means "the power of the county," reflecting the inherent power of sheriffs in the Old West to call upon a posse of able-bodied men to supplement professional law enforcement to maintain the peace.

49 Craig T. Trebilcock, "The Myth of Posse Comitatus," *Journal of Homeland Security* (October 2000), homelandsecurity.org/journal/articles/Trebilcock.htm; Matthew Carlton Hammond, "The Posse Comitatus Act: A Principle in Need of Renewal," *Washington University Law Quarterly* 75 (Summer 1997), law.wustl.edu/WULQ/75-2/752-10.html.

50 NAPA, *Role of the National Guard*.

51 Ibid.

52 Ibid., 135.

53 Wamsley et al., *Coping with Catastrophe*, 97–98.

54 Successors to Quarantelli and Dynes are Havidán Rodríguez, Joanne Niggs, Sue McNeil, and James Kendra.

55 Successors to White are Dennis Mileti, William Travis, and Kathleen Tierney.

56 National Research Council, *Facing Hazards and Disasters: Understanding Human Dimensions* (Washington, D.C.: National Academies Press, 2006).

57 Ibid., 2.

58 William L. Waugh Jr., "Public Administration, Emergency Management, and Disaster Policy," in *Disciplines, Disasters and Emergency Management: The Convergence and Divergence of Concepts, Issues and Trends from the Research Literature,* ed. David A. McEntire (Washington, D.C.: Emergency Management Institute, Federal Emergency Management Agency, 2006), 167.

59 Journals in the field now devote special issues to emergency and disaster management. For example, see *Public Administration Review*'s special issue, "Administrative Failure in the Wake of Katrina," vol. 67, December 2007.

Suggested Readings

Alesch, Daniel J., Lucy A. Arendt, and James N. Holly. *Managing for Long-Term Community Recovery in the Aftermath of Disaster.* Fairfax, Va.: Public Entity Risk Institute, 2009.

Barry, John Barry. *Rising Tide: The Great Mississippi Flood of 1927 and How It Changed America.* New York: Simon and Schuster, 1997.

Beatley, Timothy. *Planning for Coastal Resilience: Best Practices for Calamitous Times.* Washington, D.C.: Island Press, 2009.

Berke, Philip R., and Thomas J. Campanella. "Planning for Postdisaster Resiliency." *ANNALS of the American Academy of Political and Social Science* 604, no. 1 (2006): 192–207.

Berke, Philip R., David R. Godschalk, and Edward J. Kaiser, with Daniel A. Rodriguez. *Urban Land Use Planning.* 5th ed. Urbana: Illinois University Press, 2006.

Berke, Philip, and Gavin Smith. "Hazard Mitigation, Planning, and Disaster Resiliency: Challenges and Strategic Choices for the 21st Century." In *Building Safer Communities: Risk Governance, Spatial Planning and Responses to Natural Hazards,* edited by Urbano Fra Paleo, 1–20. Amsterdam: IOS Press, 2009.

Bicknell, Jane, David Dodman, and David Satterthwaite. *Adapting Cities to Climate Change: Understanding and Addressing the Development Challenges.* London: Earthscan, 2009.

Birch, Eugénie L., and Susan M. Wachter, eds. *Rebuilding Urban Places after Disaster: Lessons from Hurricane Katrina.* Philadelphia: University of Pennsylvania Press, 2006.

Birkland, Thomas A. *After Disaster, Agenda Setting, Public Policy, and Focusing Events.* Washington, D.C.: Georgetown University Press, 1997.

———. *Lessons of Disaster: Policy Change after Catastrophic Events.* Washington, D.C.: Georgetown University Press, 2006.

Brinkley, Douglas. *The Great Deluge: Hurricane Katrina, New Orleans, and the Mississippi Gulf Coast.* New York: Harper Collins, 2006.

Burby, Raymond. "Making Plans That Matter: Citizen Involvement and Government Action." *Journal of the American Planning Association* 69, no. 1 (2003): 33–39.

Burns, Peter, and Matthew O. Thomas. "The Failure of the Nonregime: How Katrina Exposed New Orleans as a Regimeless City." *Urban Affairs Review* 41, no. 4 (2006): 517–527.

Campanella, Thomas J. "Urban Resilience and the Recovery of New Orleans." *Journal of the American Planning Association* 72, no. 2 (2006): 141–146.

Chang, Stephanie E., and Scott B. Miles. "Resilient Community Recovery: Improving Recovery through Comprehensive Modeling, MCEER Research Progress and Accomplishments: 2001–2003." *MCEER-03-SP01* (May 2003): 139–148. mceer.buffalo.edu/publications/resaccom/03-sp01/10chang.pdf.

Citizen Corps. *Citizen Corps: A Guide for Local Officials.* Washington, D.C.: The White House, 2002. pimahealth.org/cc/guide_local_officials.pdf.

Citizens for Responsibility and Ethics in Washington (CREW). *The Best Laid Plans: The Story of How the Government Ignored Its Own Gulf Coast Hurricane Plan.* Washington, D.C.: CREW, 2007. citizensforethics.org/files/Katrina%20 DHS%20Report.pdf.

Cutter, Susan, ed. *American Hazardscapes: The Regionalization of Natural Hazards and Disasters.* Washington, D.C.: Joseph Henry Press, 2001.

Davis, Mike. *Ecology of Fear: Los Angeles and the Imagination of Disaster.* New York: Vintage Books, 1998.

Derthick, Martha. "The Transformation That Fell Short: Bush, Federalism, and Emergency Management." Paper sponsored by the Nelson A Rockefeller Institute of Government, Albany, N.Y.; August 2009. rockinst.org/pdf/disaster_ recovery/gulfgov/gulfgov_reports/2009-08-Transformation_That_Fell.pdf.

Drabek, Thomas E., and David E. McEntire. "Emergent Phenomena and the Sociology of Disaster: Lessons, Trends and Opportunities from the Research Literature." *Disaster Prevention and Management* 12, no. 2 (2003): 97–112.

Duncan, James B."Financing Public Infrastructure." In *Local Planning: Contemporary Principles and Practice,* edited by Gary Hack, Eugénie L. Birch, Paul H. Sedway, and Mitchell J. Silver, 332–335. Washington, D.C.: ICMA Press, 2009.

Farazmand, Ali, ed. *Handbook of Crisis and Emergency Management.* New York: Marcel Dekket, 2001.

Flynn, Stephen. *The Edge of Disaster: Rebuilding a Resilient Nation.* New York: Random House, 2007.

Fothergill, Alice. "Knowledge Transfer between Researchers and Practitioners." *Natural Hazards Review* 1, no. 2 (2000): 91–98.

Freitag, Bob, Susan Bolton, Frank Westerlund, and J. L. S. Clark. *Floodplain Management: A New Approch for a New Era.* Washington, D.C.: Island Press, 2009.

Freudenberg, William R., Robert Gramling, Shirley Laska, and Kai Erikson. *Catastrophe in the Making: The Engineering of Katrina and the Disasters of Tomorrow.* Washington, D.C.: Island Press, 2009.

Geschwind, Carl-Henry. *California Earthquakes: Science, Risk, and the Politics of Hazard Mitigation.* Baltimore: Johns Hopkins University Press, 2001.

Godschalk, David R. "Urban Hazard Mitigation: Creating Resilient Cities." *Natural Hazards Review* 4, no. 3 (2003): 136–142.

Godschalk, David R., Timothy Beatley, Philip Berke, David J. Brower, and Edward J. Kaiser. *Natural Hazard Mitigation: Recasting Disaster Policy and Planning.* Washington, D.C.: Island Press, 1999.

Godschalk, David R., Samuel Brody, and Raymond Burby. "Public Participation in Natural Hazard Mitigation Policy Formulation: Challenges for Comprehensive Planning." *Journal of Environmental Planning and Management* 46, no. 5 (2003): 733–754.

Kates, Robert W., Craig E. Colten, Shirley Laska, and Stephen P. Leatherman. "Reconstruction of New Orleans after Hurricane Katrina: A Research Perspective." *Proceedings of the National Academy of Sciences* 103, no. 40 (2006): 14653–14660.

Klein, Naomi. *The Shock Doctrine: The Rise of Disaster Capitalism.* New York: Henry Holt and Company, 2007.

Klinenberg, Eric. *Heat Wave: A Social Autopsy of Disaster in Chicago.* Chicago: University of Chicago Press, 2002.

Kunreuther, Howard. "Has the Time Come for Comprehensive Natural Disaster Insurance?" In *On Risk and Disaster: Lessons from Hurricane Katrina,* edited by Ronald J. Daniels, Donald F. Kettl, and Howard Kunreuther, 175–201. Philadelphia: University of Philadelphia Press, 2006.

Larson, Eric. *Isaac's Storm: A Man, a Time, and the Deadliest Hurricane in History.* New York: Vintage Books, 1999.

Larson, Larry A., Michael J. Klitzke, and Diane A. Brown, eds. *No Adverse Impact: A Toolkit for Common Sense Floodplain Management.* Madison, Wis.: Association of State Floodplain Managers, 2003.

Lindell, Michael K., and Ronald W. Perry. *Behavioral Foundations of Community Emergency Management.* Washington, D.C.: Hemisphere Publishing Corporation, 1992.

Lindell, Michael K., Carla Prater, and Ronald W. Perry. *Introduction to Emergency Management.* Hoboken, N.J.: John Wiley & Sons, 2007.

May, Peter. "Disaster Recovery and Reconstruction." In *Managing Disaster: Strategies and Perspectives,* edited by Louise Comfort, 236–254. Durham, N.C.: Duke University Press, 1989.

———. *Recovering from Catastrophes: Federal Disaster Relief Policy and Politics.* Westport, Conn.: Greenwood Press, 1985.

May, Peter J., Raymond J. Burby, Neil J. Ericksen, John W. Handmer, Jennifer E. Dixon, Sarah Michaels, and D. Ingle Smith. *Environmental Management and Governance: Intergovernmental Approaches to Hazards and Sustainability.* London: Routledge, 1996.

May, Peter, and Walter Williams. *Disaster Policy Implementation: Managing Programs under Shared Governance.* New York: Plenum Press, 1986.

Mileti, Dennis. *Disasters by Design: A Reassessment of Natural Hazards in the United States.* Washington, D.C.: Joseph Henry Press, 1999.

Multihazard Mitigation Council. *Natural Hazard Mitigation Saves: An Independent Study to Assess the Future Savings from Mitigation Activities.* Washington, D.C.: National Institute of Building Sciences, 2005.

National Academy of Public Administration (NAPA). *Coping with Catastrophe: Building an Emergency Management System to Meet People's Needs in Natural and Manmade Disasters.* Washington, D.C.: NAPA, 1993.

National Research Council. *Facing Hazards and Disasters: Understanding Human Dimensions.* Washington, D.C.: National Academies Press, 2006.

————. *Private-Public Sector Collaboration to Enhance Community Disaster Resilience: A Workshop Report.* Washington, D.C.: National Academies Press, 2010.

Nelson, Marla, Renia Ehrenfeucht, and Shirley Laska. "Planning, Plans, and People: Professional Expertise, Local Knowledge, and Governmental Action in Post-Hurricane Katrina New Orleans." *Cityscape: A Journal of Policy Development and Research* 9, no. 3 (2007): 23–52.

Olasky, Marvin. *The Politics of Disaster: Katrina, Big Government, and a New Strategy for Future Crisis.* Nashville, Tenn.: Thomas Nelson, 2006.

Oliver-Smith, Anthony, and Susanna M. Hoffman, eds. *The Angry Earth: Disaster in Anthropological Perspective.* New York: Routledge, 1999.

Olshansky, Robert B., and Stephanie Chang. "Planning for Disaster Recovery: Emerging Research Needs and Challenges." *Progress in Planning* 72, no. 4 (special issue, 2009): 200–209.

Olshansky, Robert B., and Laurie A. Johnson. *Clear as Mud: Planning for the Rebuilding of New Orleans.* Chicago: American Planning Association, 2010.

Patton, Ann, and Arrietta Chakos. "Tulsa's Story," in chap. 4, "Community-Based Hazard-Mitigation Case Studies." In *Global Warming, Natural Hazards, and Emergency Management,* edited by Jane A. Bullock, George D. Haddow and Kim S. Haddow. Boca Raton, Fla.: CRC Press, 2009.

Pine, John C. *Natural Hazards Analysis: Reducing the Impact of Disasters.* Washington, D.C.: Taylor & Francis, 2009.

Platt, Rutherford. *Disasters and Democracy: The Politics of Extreme Natural Events.* Washington, D.C.: Island Press, 1999.

Prater, Carla S., and Michael K. Lindell. "The Politics of Hazard Mitigation." *Natural Hazards Review* 1, no. 2 (2000): 73–82.

Quarantelli, E. L., ed. *What Is a Disaster? Perspectives on the Question.* London: Routledge, 1998.

Richard, Anne C. "Katrina Aid: When the World Wanted to Help America." *New York Times,* August 30, 2006.

Rodríguez, Havidán, Enrico L. Quarantelli, and Russell Dynes, eds. *Handbook of Disaster Research.* New York: Springer, 2006.

Rubin, Claire B., and Daniel G. Barbee. "Disaster Recovery and Hazard Mitigation: Bridging the Intergovernmental Gap." *Public Administration Review* 45 (special issue, 1985): 57–63.

Rubin, Claire B., Irmak Renda-Tanali, and William Cumming. *Disaster Timeline.* Arlington, Va.: Claire Rubin & Associates, 2008. disaster-timeline.com.

Schwab, James C., ed. *Hazard Mitigation: Integrating Best Practices into Planning.* Planning Advisory Service (PAS) Report 560. Chicago: American Planning Association, 2010.

Schwab, Jim, with contributions from Kenneth C. Topping, Charles D. Eadie, Robert E. Deyle, and Richard A. Smith. *Planning for Post-Disaster Recovery and Reconstruction.* Planning Advisory Service (PAS) Report 483/484. Chicago: American Planning Association, 1998.

Smith, Gavin. "Disaster-Resilient Communities: A New Hazards Risk Management Framework." In *Natural Hazards Analysis: Reducing the Impact of Disasters,* edited by John C. Pine, 249–267. Washington, D.C.: Taylor & Francis, 2009.

———. "Lessons from the United States: Planning for Post-Disaster Recovery and Reconstruction." *Australasian Journal of Disaster and Trauma Studies* 2010-1 (2010). massey.ac.nz/~trauma/issues/2010-1/smith.htm.

———. "Planning for Sustainable and Disaster Resilient Communities." In *Natural Hazards Analysis: Reducing the Impact of Disasters,* edited by John C. Pine, 221–247. Washington, D.C.: Taylor & Francis, 2009.

Stallings, Robert A. "Conflict in Natural Disasters: A Codification of Consensus and Conflict Theories." *Social Science Quarterly* 69, no. 3 (1988): 569–586.

Stallings, Robert A., and E. L. Quarantelli. "Emergent Citizen Groups and Emergency Management." *Public Administration Review* 45 (special issue, January 1985): 93–100.

Stehr, Steven D. "The Political Economy of Urban Disaster Assistance." *Urban Affairs Review* 41, no. 4 (2006): 492–500.

Stone, Deborah A. "Causal Stories and the Formation of Policy Agendas." *Political Science Quarterly* 104, no. 2 (1989): 281–300.

Sullivan, Mark. "Integrated Recovery Management: A New Way of Looking at a Delicate Process." *Australian Journal of Emergency Management* 18, no. 2 (2003) 4–27.

Sylves, Richard T. *Disaster Policy and Politics: Emergency Management and Homeland Security.* Washington, D.C.: CQ Press, 2008.

Tierney, Kathleen, Michael K. Lindell, and Ronald W. Perry. *Facing the Unexpected: Disaster Preparedness and Response in the United States.* Washington, D.C.: Joseph Henry Press, 2001.

Topping, Kenneth C. "Toward a National Disaster Recovery Act of 2009." *Natural Hazards Observer* 33, no. 3 (January 2009): 1–9.

Townsend, Frances F. *The Federal Response to Hurricane Katrina: Lessons Learned.* Washington, D.C.: The White House, February 2006. library.stmarytx .edu/acadlib/edocs/katrinawh.pdf

Turoff, Murray, and Starr Roxanne Hiltz. *Information Seeing Behavior and Viewpoints of Emergency Preparedness and Management Professionals Concerned with Health and Medicine.* Report to the National Library of Medicine. 2008. web.njit.edu/~turoff/Papers/FinalReportNLMTuroffHiltzMarch19.pdf.

Turoff, Murray, Starr Roxanne Hiltz, Connie White, Linda Plotnick, Art Hendela, and Xiang Yoa. "The Past as the Future of Emergency Preparedness and Management." *International Journal of Information Systems for Crisis Response and Management* 1 (January–March 2009): 12–28.

Tyler, Martha Blair, Katherine O'Prey, and Karen Kristiansson. *Redevelopment after Earthquakes.* Portola Valley, Calif.: Spangle Associates, 2002.

U.S. Government Accountability Office (GAO). *Disaster Assistance: Improvement Needed in Disaster Declaration Criteria and Eligibility Assurance Procedures.* Report to the Subcommittee on VA, HUD, and Independent Agencies, Committee on Appropriations, U.S. Senate. Washington, D.C., August 2001. gao.gov/new.items/d01837.pdf.

———. *Disaster Recovery: FEMA's Long-term Assistance Was Helpful to State and Local Governments but Had Some Limitations.* GAO-10-404. Washington D.C., March 2010. gao.gov/new.items/d10404.pdf.

————. *Disaster Recovery: Past Experiences Offer Insights for Recovering from Hurricanes Ike and Gustav and Other Recent Natural Disasters.* Report to the Senate Committee on Homeland Security and Governmental Affairs. GAO-08-1120. Washington, D.C., September 2008. gao.gov/new.items/d081120.pdf.

————. *National Disaster Response: FEMA Should Take Action to Improve Capacity and Coordination between Government and Voluntary Sectors.* GAO-08-369. Washington, D.C., February 2008. gao.gov/new.items/d08369.pdf.

U.S. Senate. Committee on Homeland Security and Governmental Affairs. Ad Hoc Subcommittee on State, Local, and Private Sector Preparedness and Integration. *The Next Big Disaster: Is the Private Sector Prepared?*, 111th Cong., 2nd sess., testimony of Stephen Flynn, "Building a More Resilient Nation by Strengthening Private-Public Partnerships," March, 4, 2010. centerfornationalpolicy.org/ht/display/ContentDetails/i/17679.

Vale, Lawrence J., and Thomas J. Campanella. *The Resilient City: How Modern Cities Recover from Disasters.* New York: Oxford University Press, 2005.

Waugh, William L., Jr. "Mechanisms for Collaboration: EMAC and Katrina." *The Public Manager* 35, no. 4 (Winter 2006–2007): 12–15.

Waugh, William L., Jr., and Richard T. Sylves. "The Intergovernmental Relations of Emergency Management." In *Disaster Management in the U.S. and Canada: The Politics, Policymaking, Administration and Analysis of Emergency Management.* 2nd ed., edited by Richard T. Sylves and William L. Waugh Jr., 46–48. Springfield, Ill.: Charles C. Thomas, 1996.

Webb, Gary R. *Individual and Organizational Response to Natural Disasters and Other Crisis Events: The Continuing Value of the DRC Typology.* Preliminary Paper #277. Newark: Disaster Research Center, University of Delaware, 1999.

Wenger, Dennis E. *Emergent and Volunteer Behavior during Disaster: Research Findings and Planning Implications.* HHRC publication 27P. College Station: Hazard Reduction and Recovery Center, Texas A&M University, 1992.

Wenger, Dennis E., Charles E. Faupel, and Thomas F. James. *Disaster Beliefs and Emergency Planning.* Newark: Disaster Research Center, University of Delaware, 1980.

About the Authors

Claire B. Rubin (Editor, Chapter 1) is president of Claire B. Rubin & Associates, LLC (clairerubin.com), a small business specializing in disaster research and consulting, located in Arlington, Virginia, and CEO of the Disaster Bookstore (disasterbookstore.com). She has been affiliated with the Institute for Crisis, Disaster and Risk Management at The George Washington University in Washington, D.C., since 1998. She was the cofounder of the *Journal of Homeland Security and Emergency Management* and served as managing editor for six years. With thirty-four years of experience as a researcher, practitioner, and academic in the field of emergency management, she has authored more than eighty publications and delivered numerous lectures and presentations on emergency management and homeland security topics. Ms Rubin holds a BS from Simmons College and an MA from Boston University.

Keith Bea (Chapter 4) retired in 2011 from his duties as a specialist in American national government in the Government and Finance Division of the Congressional Research Service (CRS), having spent almost four decades in federal service. In addition to his research duties, Bea coordinated the work of other CRS analysts as team leader and section manager for homeland security emergency preparedness and response policy matters. He is founder and director of Logistics/Emergency Assistance for Families (LEAF), which serves the local community with shelter aid, food pantry operations, and emergency management consultation. Bea received a BA in history from Ohio University and an MPA from American University.

David Butler (Chapters 2 and 3) served as senior editor at the Natural Hazards Center, University of Colorado, from 1984 to 2002. There he wrote and edited books, papers, and periodicals regarding disaster mitigation and hazards management. In the 1980s and 90s he was a pioneer in the use of Internet technology to disseminate hazard information. Since leaving the center in 2002, he has continued his work in hazards/disaster information and communications as a consultant to numerous disaster organizations around the world. His latest projects include the editing of a biography, the creation of a website, and the construction of a flood-level marker and monument on Boulder Creek in honor of his mentor and friend, hazards scholar Gilbert F. White (see colorado.edu/hazards/gfw).

Susan L. Cutter (Chapter 7) is a Carolina Distinguished Professor of Geography at the University of South Carolina and the director of the Hazards and Vulnerability Research Institute. Having worked in the risk and hazards fields for thirty years, she is a nationally and internationally recognized scholar. Her primary research interests are in the area of vulnerability and resilience science, with a particular focus on how vulnerability and disaster resilience are measured, monitored, and assessed. Cutter is a fellow of the American Association for the Advancement of Science (AAAS) and a former president of the Association of American Geographers and the Consortium of Social Science Associations (COSSA), and she serves on many national advisory boards and committees, including those of the AAAS, the National Research Council, National Institute of Standards and Technology, and the National Science Foundation. She is also a MunichRe Foundation chair on Social Vulnerability through the United Nations University in Bonn, Germany. She received her BA from California State University–Hayward and her MA and PhD from the University of Chicago.

Melanie Gall (Chapter 7) is a research assistant professor in the Department of Geography and Anthropology at Louisiana State University. She is a hazards geographer with expertise in geospatial technologies, risk assessments, and hazard mitigation planning. Her work and publications have focused on flood modeling, issues of social vulnerability, hazard losses, and emergency sheltering. She received a BS from the University of Heidelberg in 1998, an MS from the University of Salzburg in 2002, and a PhD from the University of South Carolina in 2007.

John R. Harrald (Chapters 6 and 8) is a research professor at Virginia Tech and professor emeritus of engineering management and systems engineering in the George Washington University School of Engineering and Applied Science. He co-founded and directed the GWU Institute for Crisis, Disaster, and Risk Management and has chaired the National Research Council Disasters Roundtable Steering Committee. As a researcher in his academic career and a practitioner during his career as a U.S. Coast Guard officer, Harrald has been actively engaged in the fields of emergency and crisis management and maritime safety and port security. He received his BS in engineering from the U.S. Coast Guard Academy; an MA in liberal studies from Wesleyan University; an MS from the Massachusetts Institute of Technology, where he was an Alfred P. Sloan Fellow; and an MBA and PhD from Rensselaer Polytechnic Institute.

Patrick S. Roberts (Chapters 9 and 10) is an assistant professor at the Center for Public Administration and Policy in the School of Public and International Affairs at Virginia Tech in Alexandria, Virginia. He spent 2010–2011 as the Ghaemian Junior Scholar-in-Residence at the University of Heidelberg Center for American Studies in Germany. He has published in a variety of scholarly and popular journals, including *Studies in American Political Development, Political Science Quarterly, Publius, Presidential Studies Quarterly, Administration & Society, Public Organization Review, National Affairs, Policy Review,* and *USA Today.* His research has been funded by the National Science Foundation, the United States Naval Research Laboratory, the Federal Emergency Management Agency, and the Social Science Research Council. Roberts holds a PhD in government from the University of Virginia, and he has been a postdoctoral fellow at Stanford University's Center for International Security and Cooperation and at Harvard University's Program on Constitutional Government.

Richard T. Sylves (Chapter 5) is a professor and senior research scientist at the Institute for Crisis, Disaster, and Risk Management of the George Washington University. He is also an emeritus professor of political science and international relations, and former Senior Policy Fellow at the Center for Energy at the University of Delaware. He has written four books on disaster management, the latest being *Disaster Policy and Politics* (Congressional Quarterly Press, 2008). From 2002 to 2005 he served on the executive committee of the National Academy of Science Disaster Roundtable. He established and maintains the Public Entity Risk Institute website "All about Presidential Disaster Declarations" (peripresdecusa.org). He received a PhD in political science from the University of Illinois at Urbana-Champaign in 1978.

Gary Wamsley (Chapters 9 and 10) is a professor emeritus of the School of Public and International Affairs at Virginia Tech University. His fields of interest include public administration theory, budgeting, national security policy, and emergency management. He is best known academically for his part in developing the "Refounding" school of thought in public administration theory. He participated in studies of military manpower policy for President Carter's Presidential Reorganization Project. He also directed the National Academy of Public Administration's 1993 study of emergency management and its 1997 study of the role of the National Guard in emergency preparedness and response. He was elected to the National Academy of Public Administration in 1998 and has been the editor of *Administration & Society* for over thirty years. He received his bachelor's degree and master's degree from the University of California, Los Angeles, and his PhD from the University of Pittsburgh.

Robert Ward (Chapters 9 and 10) passed away on February 3, 2011. At the time of his death he was a professor, teaching and engaged in research at Louisiana State University in Baton Rouge. Prior to his career in academia, he spent more than thirty years working for federal, state, and local governments. His research interests were in organizational theory and public policy theory, especially in areas related to information technology and decision making. Ward held a PhD in public administration and public affairs from Virginia Polytechnic Institute.

Index

Note: Page numbers with *f* indicate a figure; those with *t*, a table; an "n" following a page number indicates an endnote.